THEODORE ROOSEVELT IN THE FIELD

THEODORE ROOSEVELT
IN THE FIELD

✶ MICHAEL R. CANFIELD ✶

The University of Chicago Press

CHICAGO AND LONDON

MICHAEL R. CANFIELD is the editor of *Field Notes on Science and Nature*, as well as the dean at Eliot House and a lecturer on organismic and evolutionary biology, both at Harvard University. He lives in Cambridge, Massachusetts.

The University of Chicago Press, Chicago 60637
The University of Chicago Press, Ltd., London
© 2015 by The University of Chicago
All rights reserved. Published 2015.
Printed in China

Frontispiece: John Singer Sargent, *Theodore Roosevelt*. 1903. Oil on canvas. White House Historical Association (White House collection).

24 23 22 21 20 19 18 17 16 15   1 2 3 4 5

ISBN-13: 978-0-226-29837-5 (cloth)
ISBN-13: 978-0-226-29840-5 (e-book)
DOI: 10.7208/chicago/9780226298405.001.0001

Library of Congress Cataloging-in-Publication Data
Canfield, Michael R., author.
Theodore Roosevelt in the field : / Michael R. Canfield.
    pages ; cm
Includes bibliographical references and index.
ISBN 978-0-226-29837-5 (cloth : alk. paper) —
ISBN 978-0-226-29840-5 (ebook) 1. Roosevelt, Theodore, 1858–1919—Knowledge—Natural history. 2. Roosevelt, Theodore, 1858–1919—Travel. 3. Natural history—Field-work—United States. 4. Presidents—United States—Biography. 5. Naturalists—United States—Biography. I. Title.
E757.C26 2015
973.91'1092—dc23
[B]   2015014452

This paper meets the requirements of ANSI/NISO Z39.48-1992 (Permanence of Paper).

TO MY SONS,

Mitchell and Riley

Contents

3

RETURN *to the* FIELD

Introduction

Cold rain beat down on the White House grounds, glancing off of the new electric lights on its terraces, glazing the buds of the southern magnolias on the South Lawn—trees that Andrew Jackson had planted some seventy years before—and soaking into the soil that would soon be home to the first lady's favored geraniums and nasturtiums. This foul weather did nothing, however, to dampen the welcoming rhythms of the house itself, a home that pulsed with childhood energy and was the domain of a man who had always been gregarious. The president loved to talk, and would talk with anyone. It was February 11, 1903, a Wednesday, and the house was abuzz, as it regularly was, with the methodical work of ushers, maids, butlers, cooks, janitors, cleaning staff, and secret service officers, ensuring that it was in perfect shape, in this case for a much-anticipated visit from the painter John Singer Sargent.

Inbound from Boston, Sargent was traveling to a house that had earned a welcoming reputation. On New Year's Day that year it hosted almost seven thousand people.[1] On that day a cross-section of the population—doctors, tradesmen, laborers, diplomats, aristocrats, children, infants, ladies—quickly shook the president's hand and filed through the East Room.

Some of these guests perhaps had visited in September of 1901, when William McKinley's body had lain in repose in the East Room after an assassin's bullet had brought Theodore Roosevelt to the White House. But walking in the glow of three crystal chandeliers and a new Steinway, more positive associations dominated. This was the room where the Roosevelts welcomed people from all parts of their lives. It had not been long since, in that room, the president and his wife had entertained the US Supreme Court justices, had welcomed guests at a formal state dinner, and had hosted a debutant ball for Roosevelt's oldest daughter, Alice. It would not be long until in that room the president gave a mundane speech to the Allied German Societies, until he received two hundred sailors from the USS *Mayflower* and USS *Sylph*, until his first daughter was married, and until he staged a wrestling match to determine the relative dominance of the American and jujitsu styles.[2] Much later, this would be the room over which Roosevelt's presidential portrait would preside. Even more than gazing at the newly renovated features, visitors to the East Room had just shaken the hand of a president who thrived on direct experience and connection. But first-of-the-year guests and attendees at formal events had only a brief glimpse of White House life. Overnight guests saw more.

It was not uncommon for house guests to brush past senators, princes, famous musicians, diplomats, and dignitaries: the very building had been constructed a century before to provide a place for the American president to live, entertain, and conduct business, now the business of a nation that was growing as a world power, one with a leader who had strong notions of empire. But the sum of the activities within its walls reflected how this president embraced a much wider than average arc of the human experience. And here it was wise to expect the unexpected.

Children whizzed by on roller skates and on bicycles.[3] Mysterious rustlings coming from the ceiling spooked the uninitiated, at least until an usher explained that the younger of the president's children found ways to squirm into the spaces between the floors and ceilings to explore, like mole rats. At times the number of children in the house was so great that it seemed to Roosevelt as if "their arms and legs would stick out of the windows."[4] The White House residents, the president not excluded, brought the outside in, welcoming all manner of life—badgers, parrots, snakes, even ponies—continuing a practice that the president had started in his own childhood home almost four decades earlier in Manhattan, when he kept a natural history museum in his bedroom. The integrity of fine upholstery and moldings had always been a secondary concern for him.

Even more than a menagerie, the White House was a gallery, its walls lined with the portraits of previous presidents. The rambunctious band of Roosevelts noticed these men looking down on them, but they did not always pay the kind of respect that a guest, especially a portraitist like Sargent, might expect. At one point, a group of children led by the Roosevelt's youngest, Quentin, added a three-dimensional element to the portrait of Andrew Jackson using balls of "masticated newspaper."[5]

The White House inhabitants directed their vigor outwardly, too, toward the natural areas on the grounds, into pens and enclosures that housed their outdoor pets, and afield to the Potomac and Rock Creek Park. Roosevelt often invited his guests on his horseback rides and daily jaunts. Some of these became legendary rambles in which participants were encouraged to swim in the icy Potomac with their leader and return frigid, wet, and exhausted, although onlookers described that none of this would wipe the wide smile from the president's face.[6] With his burgeoning band of progeny—Alice, Theodore, Kermit, Ethel, Archibald, and Quentin—he was always entertaining thoughts of larger adventures, too: to their retreat at Oyster Bay, to the western United States, to Africa.[7]

The Maine guide who had schooled Roosevelt in hunting, Bill Sewall, had just paid a four-day visit. Sewall had embraced Roosevelt long before, when he showed up at Sewall's remote home in Island Falls, Maine, in 1878 as an awkward college student. Sewall had quickly recognized the strength of Roosevelt's will despite his comparative naivete in the outdoors. So strong a bond developed on Roosevelt's visits with Sewall, as the men tramped along the Mattawamkeag River, took shots at foxes and ducks, and snowshoed over hills and bogs, that when Roosevelt later bought a ranch in the Badlands he asked Sewall and his partner, Wilmot Dow, to oversee its operations. Now, visiting the White House, Sewall brought his own children and Dow's widow and family along. Sewall and Roosevelt again exchanged stories of their time in the West, and compared their own hunting and shooting skills to those of their children. They even looked forward to having their boys hunt together in Maine.[8] When Roosevelt asked Sewall how he liked the White House, Sewall replied, "It looks to me as how you've got a pretty good camp."[9] Despite their rural character, the Sewalls and Dows "showed to great advantage," and there were no hitches in entertaining them. Roosevelt embraced their roots and was known to tell some of his Badlands companions that if the White House staff didn't allow them admittance, they should simply shoot their way in.[10]

On this Wednesday there were few shenanigans. The president had been ill, fighting off a cold. Uncharacteristically, at least given his outward image of strength and power, he had been staying inside in hopes of avoiding bronchitis.[11] He was a man who had suffered his share of physical adversity. Asthma had plagued him as a child, so much so that he had sometimes coughed up blood, and his parents had offered him any possible remedy, even an occasional cigar. Graduating from college he had learned in his final physical exam that he had a heart irregularity, one that left him with doctor's orders, promptly ignored, to lead a relatively inactive life.[12] As a soldier in the Spanish-American War, Roosevelt had contracted malaria, and this permanent companion, which he called his "Cuban fever," periodically resurfaced and laid him out for several days at a time with severe symptoms. But he was a man who raged against adversity and did not accept the shackles of any condition. His ailments rarely kept him from action for more than a few days.

Roosevelt stood a modest five feet, nine inches, but it was not hard to overestimate his stature. His barrel chest was intimidating, especially to children—a prominent feature he had earned from his youthful days fighting against his infirmity, doing push-ups, rowing the Charles River, swimming Oyster Bay, and boxing. Now, in the White House, he still prioritized physical exertion, exchanging beatings with his old Rough Rider companion, Leonard Wood, in their frequent games of singlestick. There were wrestling matches, and regular pillow fights with children.

These efforts to stay active did not keep him as svelte as he had been as a child rambling in the Catskills, as a student chasing New England's birds, or as a Badlands rancher. In future adventures he would lose the inches that had come with the presidency, but for now his waistline was expanding.

His face no longer displayed the slim lines of youth, but its now more rounded features did not define it. His eyes locked in on things: he was a fierce observer. He wore pince-nez spectacles, both a necessary implement and a symbol of his wide-ranging intellect. His teeth emerged in a wide grin, which he frequently employed, and which endeared him to millions in America and millions more throughout the world. He now wore a walrus mustache—gone were the lamb chops he had worn at Harvard—that framed his most powerful feature, his mouth.

Roosevelt used his words to impressive effect. He paired them with his smile, enhancing his rare talent for making wide swaths of the public feel that he had a personal connection with them. He regularly used his words in jest with children, bonding with them almost as a peer. He also used them more seriously, communicating the vision and priorities he had established in his first two years as president. His words weren't always well received, of course; some thought of him as a bear, others as a protective monarch.[13] On any given day he used his words to conjure love, fear, anger, ideas, and despair. He used them for effective management, to wheedle and cajole, to convince, and to badger. He directed his words at staff, congressmen, heads of state, the press, his wife, his children, and of course the team of stenographers and typewriters who tried to keep up with his torrent of writing in letters, speeches, articles, and even books. Sometimes he spoke so forcefully his face turned bright red.[14]

While in Washington, Roosevelt dressed in the general fashion of the day; he was not overly fancy. But a diverse wardrobe hung at attention in his closets, ready to outfit the adventurous life that defined him. Riding boots and jackets stood alongside suits. The dull colors of the clothes he wore on his rambles offset the crisp lines of his tuxedos. His favorite buckskin hunting jacket waited for him. His campaign hat and cavalry gloves were always ready for action.

Given that he was still recovering from his cold and was facing another long day, Roosevelt likely snapped to attention that morning. In a nearby guest room a bed stood ready, as Sargent would soon arrive for a nine-day visit with the hope of capturing something of Roosevelt's complex identity in an official presidential portrait.

In the shadow of the two towering smoke stacks of the RMS *Lucania*, Sargent had disembarked and received a warm reception in New York from his friend and colleague Carroll Beckwith on January 18.[15] Almost three decades previous, Sargent and Beckwith had worked on the murals together at the Luxemburg Palace in Paris. Despite the personal warmth of his reception in New York, Sargent only spent two days there before heading north to install the second section of his mural cycle in the Boston Public Library. But, at least in the eyes of *The New York Times*, these "decorations" were simply a diversion from his true work as the foremost of living portraitists.[16] As Sargent made for Washington after several weeks in Boston, he could expect a unique kind of warmth at the Roosevelt White House.

Roosevelt had personally written Sargent the previous May and asked him to come; after all, he felt that Sargent was "the one artist who should paint the portrait of an American President."[17] Little of this fawning tone lingered, however, as the men began to consider the appropriate setting for the portrait. As in most areas of his life, Roosevelt held strong opinions about his image, and another artist's attempt at his portrait had not been a success.

When the French painter Théobold Chartran had painted Edith Kermit Roosevelt—the first lady, Roosevelt's childhood friend and second wife—he had received praise in the White House and in the salons of Paris, but when he had rendered the president during the weeks before Sargent arrived, the resulting canvas was relegated to a back hallway.[18] The eye that had captured the first lady sitting on a bench in a frilly and stylish dress, combining feminine strength and dignity, failed to grasp the essence of the president. When Chartran's portrait of Roosevelt was sent out of the White House to be burned only six years later, even Edith agreed that Chartran had captured nothing of who Roosevelt actually was, and that his coy rendering looked more like a mewing cat than the powerful president.[19] Surely, a feminine angle was not appropriate for Theodore Roosevelt.

Luckily, Sargent was no stranger to the challenges of painting prominent, powerful, and aristocratic people. In the past several years he had offered sittings to a baron, a landscape painter, a railroad magnate, a coal company leader, and even the sculptor Auguste Rodin.[20] He and the president began their stroll, considering an appropriate place for the portrait sitting.

Although Sargent understood the merits of painting subjects en plein air, as he had done in his portraits of the impressionist painter Claude Monet and the Boston landscape architect Fredrick Law Olmsted, he and the president remained indoors. Part of what Chartran had missed, despite depicting Roosevelt in an outdoor setting, was the president's rugged strength; he presented him as a dandy rather than an outdoorsman. Roosevelt's time in the woods, on the hunting field, and on the battlefield had had a profound effect on his identity, on how he worked with people, on how he conceptualized the world, and on how he made decisions. But given the formality of the presidential portrait, Sargent now needed to find a subtle way to encapsulate Roosevelt's naturalistic roots and forceful nature.

Even inside the White House, Sargent could find elements that evoked the outdoors. Planters with tropical foliage lined the halls; a moose head hung over the mantle in the state dining room. There were fresh walls comprising a palette of colors with natural associations: vivid blues, greens, reds, and yellows, which a painter like Sargent could sample to harness the vastness of the sky, the power of the oceans, the vitality of foliage, the savageness of blood, the sheer energy of the sun. But Sargent passed on each of these aspects of the decor.

In some of his portraits, Sargent had used objects to help tell his subject's story. He staged Olmsted holding a cane in one hand and grasping a handful of flowers with the other. Captain John Spicer held a hat and coach whip; and William Cazalet, an English businessman, posed with a horse. The landscape painter William Chase held a brush and palette. Walking through the rooms of the White House, Sargent was amidst portraits that represented precedents for including a symbolic object even in the portrait of a president. In their renderings, George Washington and Zachary Taylor held swords. Others like John Quincy Adams grasped, leaned on, or touched sheaves of important-looking papers. Roosevelt's life offered so many possibilities: field glasses, revolvers and rifles, a characteristic hat, a bearskin rug. His identity, however, was not easily captured in a single object; it was synthetic. What made him unique was how he brought diverse facets together.

Finally, at least in the version of the story recounted by the usher Isaac Hoover, Roosevelt and Sargent found themselves on a staircase, in a state of mutual frustration. [21] Roosevelt put his hand firmly at rest on the globe atop a newel post, ready to launch into a diatribe on Sargent's fickleness. But Sargent stopped him there, recognizing that Roosevelt's commanding posture and grasping hand provided symbol enough. And he began to paint.

Thursday was another of Roosevelt's characteristically long workdays. He was making a habit of spending twelve hours on his feet, working straight through lunch and dinner.[22] It didn't take long for Sargent to understand that he would only get a small fraction of Roosevelt's time. One White House usher, who had met hundreds of influential politicians since his early days as a bodyguard for Abraham Lincoln, set Roosevelt apart, describing that his work proceeded at a "pace that surprised the world."[23]

Roosevelt displayed an uncommon level of commitment to this profession of politics, a tack he had been on since college. When he had arrived at Harvard he had hoped to be a scientist, but that undertaking was different from what he had envisioned. Gone were the days where men like his heroes Elliott Coues, John James Audubon, and Charles Darwin dominated natural science. Roosevelt had watched as the discipline had become more professionalized, men of the field replaced by microscope devotees and section cutters, and he pivoted toward a political profession.

Roosevelt underwent his own changes during college, too, as the importance of a settled and comfortable domestic life became more important than his dreams of a professional life involving outdoor study, especially once he became engaged to his first wife, Alice Lee. After graduation he took on the roles as assemblyman, police commissioner, and governor in New York, and as vice president of the United States, with vigor, but not to the exclusion of what had attracted him to a life in the field. Yes, the age of the gentleman naturalist was over, and he was not going to become a career naturalist. Many of his peers were content to understand by reading and talking with others. Roosevelt was certainly a voracious reader and talker as well, but for him these were only the first steps in a cycle of adventure, a pattern of experiencing and learning about the world by which people envisioned expeditions, enacted them, and then returned home to render them in words, images, lectures, and even legends. It was a way of knowing that involved direct connection with the world, of learning by experience. And it was an adventurous mode that involved a departure, a transformation—however minor—and a return, elements of the ancient "hero cycle" that Roosevelt both attempted to achieve in his travels and recounted in his own "hero tales" of Daniel Boone and George Rogers Clark.[24] His early experiences with such an outdoor cycle, however, suggest that he first adopted his own cyclical approach from the traditions of the great explorers and naturalists.[25]

And throughout his life, within and around the commitments of his various political posts, Roosevelt chose to weave this tradition of adventure and exploration into the fibers of his being. Even on busy days, he still made time for adventure.

It was not a surprise to the White House staff when the president and first lady made their way to the stables and mounted up for a short ride up the rain-gorged Potomac to Cabin John Bridge.[26] It was a small escape, but a daily version of a well-worn pattern. Roosevelt was a person who looked forward to getting away: the feeling of the horse, the possible sightings of early spring birds, the view of the foliage passing by. The most noteworthy aspects of this ride were mud and conversation, but after he returned he recorded it, in this case in a letter to his son Kermit, who was studying at the Groton School outside Boston. Even with this modest ride, Roosevelt anticipated, enacted, and rendered—a pattern that had become an old habit for him.

The fresh air and brisk ride did not prevent Edith from coming down with a cold the next day. The dinner party she had arranged for that night would go on, however, and musicians—a baritone, a soprano, and a pianist—could still be counted on to perform.[27] Sargent attended and was counted as one of the notable guests, but beneath the surface his frustration was beginning to build.

It wasn't only the scene on the staircase that bothered Sargent. He could deal with the gawkers, like Congressman James W. Wadsworth, who remarked how the shades and cloths that Sargent had hung above the stairs to perfect the lighting made it look like a laundry, and who fretted that these sometimes billowing sheets would spoil the painting.[28] But it was becoming harder and harder for Sargent to get Roosevelt's time. He painted whenever he could convince Roosevelt to sit, and then he turned to other affairs, such as starting his portrait of Secretary of State John Hay. He also continued to correspond with his close friend Isabella Stuart Gardner in Boston, confiding in her that he wished that he were instead with her in his "delightful quarters at the Palazzo"—in Gardner's museum, which had just opened on New Year's Day—able to continue guiding her in art purchases.[29] He was particularly interested in seeing the new Tintoretto she had bought on his advice. In truth, the president's style and forceful personality were grating on him, and he later admitted that he felt like a "rabbit in the presence of a boa constrictor."[30]

On the weekend, Roosevelt took a Sunday walk with his close friend and adviser Henry Cabot Lodge. Lodge was a steadfast counselor for Roosevelt, providing his frank opinions throughout Roosevelt's political life. At this point the question of the Alaska treaty, a dispute with England over the border between Alaska and Canada, was an immediate concern.[31] Lodge could identify with Roosevelt's sittings with Sargent as well, because in 1890 Sargent had painted him, too.

But Lodge's experience and image were different. For one, it seems certain that he had been an easier subject than Roosevelt; his identity was not bound to a body that gave the impression of perpetual motion, and he was less likely to be compared to a boa constrictor. Sargent had captured him in an introspective pose, pegging him as a man of ideas and a quintessential politician, with his chin slightly lifted and his eyes looking off to the side. He showed Lodge fiddling with his watch fob, as if he were wondering when the painting would be complete and he could get on to legislation. The painting of Roosevelt exposed a different challenge: Sargent needed to find a way to capture the essence of a man who held the highest political post in the land, but who, unlike Lodge, was not defined by his political life. The typical features of a politician did not encompass the aspects of Roosevelt's synthetic identity—naturalist, hunter, rancher, writer, soldier, conservationist, and explorer—that had become integral to his success. As Sargent's image developed, Roosevelt emerged as a somewhat unfocused man of power. The painting did not show fine detail, and Roosevelt's hand wasn't twiddling; Sargent instead made it appear as if it might crush the sphere it was holding.

By Tuesday there were more escapes. Edith went to Philadelphia to see the opera, and Roosevelt, despite the demands of a normal workday and of being tied more domestically in her absence, left the White House for a ride in a blizzard. The snow covered the streets of Washington, and Roosevelt trotted off into Rock Creek Park to enjoy what he saw as a "wonderfully wild piece of scenery."[32] When he returned, he recorded the scene in a letter to Kermit, in the voice of his Badlands writings: "The steep hillsides were covered with snow which lay in strips on the limbs of the trees, and the stream churned noisily between the ice-rimmed banks and among the ice-coated boulders."[33]

That night, Roosevelt reveled in the last phase—the rendering of the field—of his adventurous cycle. He and the children had their requisite playtime—often consisting of a pillow fight and then an enactment of battles between bears, dragons, and heroic youngsters.[34] Once the lights were dimmed, Roosevelt slipped easily into his role as a wilderness sagaman. He began with some Norse stories, but quickly transported his listeners to the Badlands as he dipped into the legends he himself had created.[35]

Roosevelt's well of stories was deep. He had once used his boxing skills to knock out a bullying cowboy in a Western saloon. At another point he had stood his ground with his trusty Winchester rifle as he stared down an advancing party of Native Americans.[36] Maybe his best story grew from the time he and his partners had chased a trio of boat thieves down the ice-clogged Little Missouri River. Like his field companions and readers, the children loved to hear his tales; and this story, like many others, had been honed by repeated retellings. It was only one of a varied trail of stories and writings Roosevelt created, which chart the development of his love of adventure and give a firsthand account of his approach to learning about the world. As the children drifted off to sleep, Roosevelt spun tales that had evolved from his early observations and from his diaries, notebooks, and letters.

By the end of the night Roosevelt was also fighting to stay awake, and he identified with how Edith had been similarly challenged on many such nights.[37] His stamina was no longer what it had been in the Badlands; his days of spending forty hours in the saddle without sleeping were behind him.

When Sargent finished the painting on Thursday, having taken just over a week to complete his work, Roosevelt was pleased with the result. Although the painting has since become an iconic image, it still only provided a singular lens on Roosevelt. It in no way conveyed what was actually twinkling in Roosevelt's eyes as it was being completed. In fact, Roosevelt's thoughts were focused on his upcoming cross-country trip, one that would afford him a brief visit to Yellowstone National Park. He wondered whether he could arrange for a hunt there, given his constraints. He was president now, so finding a way to hunt without rankling those who were critical of his lifelong passion would be especially hard. Could he arrange for a cougar hunt just outside the park? Could he get his old hunting guide, John Goff, to send out some of his colorful pack of dogs? Might he convince John Burroughs, his dear friend and an esteemed naturalist and writer, to come with him? There were many details to attend to for the trip.[38] That night, Sargent was ferried off to a comedy, *The Altar of Friendship*, at the National Theatre.[39] Roosevelt did not attend. His body and mind were elsewhere.

On Friday, Sargent finally left the White House for Philadelphia to receive an honorary degree, after which he would attend to his murals and other portraits. His portrait of Roosevelt went off to Fischer's Gallery to be framed, and then to wait for rights and permissions to be sorted out.[40] There already had been considerable interest in the painting, and Robert Collier, editor of *Collier's Weekly*, had written to Roosevelt well before in an attempt to obtain rights to publish a copy in his magazine.[41] As the portrait sat at Fischer's, there were "keys to turn and grated doors to open" before anyone could get a glimpse of it.[42] Henry Adams, Roosevelt's longtime colleague and critic, was one of the few who were able to gain access to the "sanctum sanctorum," and he did not mince words in his assessment.[43] Adams described the painting as a "good Sargent and not very bad Roosevelt," an image that was "for once less brutal than its subject."[44]

Continuing his commentary, Adams incisively pegged Roosevelt as one who was in many ways painting his own portrait: "It is not Theodore, but a young intellectual idealist with a taste for athletics, which I take to be Theodore's idea of himself."[45] Roosevelt was image-conscious; some descriptions, like that of Adams, suggest that he was functioning as an actor playing the part of Theodore Roosevelt. But we all shape our images and have different modes for different people; we act differently with friends than with colleagues, with peers than with children. Only a decade after Sargent painted his portrait, Roosevelt recounted elements of his own life story in his autobiography.[46] But he left a much fuller portrait of his life's adventures, with its coarse brushstrokes in plain sight, in the stacks of field notebooks, journals, diaries, and letters he left behind.

Roosevelt's notes reveal that his motivations for taking to the field changed throughout his life. As a child, he was drawn in by narratives of adventure and was fascinated by the natural world. He was content to observe, count, collect, skin, and describe nature's splendor. As his love for nature and adventure grew, it was fostered by his aristocratic position. This privileged perch afforded him time to ramble throughout the northeastern United States, Europe, the Middle East, and Africa, and placed him among museum founders—a position that cultivated his dedication to science and collecting. There were the larger forces of his time, too, that urged him to take to the manly exploits of hunting and ranching on the Western frontier, those of a period when a man's role—especially those in the elite world Roosevelt inhabited—was changing as steam shovels replaced muscle, and Darwin's ideas on survival challenged how both nations and men justified their hierarchies and empires. In going to war, Roosevelt's political philosophies and the echoes of his family experience—that his father had paid for a replacement in the Civil War—were factors in his quest to get into the fight in Cuba. The field was a place that allowed for extreme challenge as well as escape, and a place for him to adopt the role of mythmaker and storyteller. Taken together, myriad individual forces fueled Roosevelt's adventurous pattern of taking to the field to learn about and experience the world through action, a mode that he adopted from the traditions of his heroes John James Audubon, Charles Darwin, and Elliott Coues, and from his friends George Bird Grinnell, Robert Peary, and Leonard Wood.

Roosevelt easily could have nurtured his interest in animals by studying them in the laboratory, following the movement afoot at Harvard while he was in college. He could have developed his manliness solely in the backrooms of business or in battle on the floor of a political chamber. He even could have bolstered his reputation as man of war who believed in his nation's expansion without getting bloody on the battlefield. But Roosevelt's pattern of adventure in the field—of leaving home to find an outdoor place where he could directly engage with the larger world—reveals a man who chose to define himself in open spaces, an identity that placed his actions in stark relief against backdrops like the sublime outcroppings of Yosemite, that put him in the midst of the naturalistic struggle for life and death, that highlighted the wonder of the natural world, and that allowed for extreme challenge, escape, and solitude. What Roosevelt found in the field—the timeless value of firsthand experience and observation—has not been lost on those who have followed him, those who have flocked to the large open tracts that he helped conserve.

As Sargent's portrait made its way back to the White House, Roosevelt departed on his fourteen-thousand-mile presidential journey.[47] On this trip a breakneck slate of parades and speeches had been prepared, but he also wedged in a visit to Yellowstone with John Burroughs—in the end, the only animal that died by Roosevelt's hand was a vole—and a wilderness summit on conservation with John Muir in Yosemite. He gave a moving speech at the Grand Canyon. But, even at age forty-four, this was nowhere near his last trip. In his postpresidential years he would travel to places he had long dreamed of visiting. He would hunt lions, elephants, rhinos, and giraffes in British East Africa, moose in Quebec, and giant manta rays off the coast of Florida. In South America he would explore an unknown river, and later visit the field station of his friend, the eminent naturalist William Beebe. These travels describe a pattern, as Roosevelt packed the interstices of his life with outdoor experiences. In and among the major phases of his life as a student, assemblyman, police commissioner, president, and public intellectual and writer, he struck off to encounter his world through a cycle that began with reading and imagination, grew into direct contact through action in the outdoors, and then looped back to his own renderings of those experiences in his stories and writings. These loops outline a story of how Roosevelt's quest for discovery in open spaces shaped his identity and influenced his behavior. It is a story full of entertainment, suspense, tragedy, mishap, exploration, and some even say embellishment. And this story is one that begins and ends in the field.

1

DEVELOPMENT
of an IDENTITY

First Love

Even Broadway has a natural history, and clues of its former life were apparent to a boy who scampered uptown over its cobblestones past the market where he often stopped for groceries. In this habitat, blackpolls and palm warblers flew over what two centuries earlier had been a marshy paradise, and some of these migrants may have still paused in the trees that lined the Manhattan street. Seeds of native plants lay deep in the soil, and beetles and caterpillars could be found on relictual plants, now resigned to the status of weeds in the cracks and crevices among brownstones. But the fingers of white cedar swamp and salt marsh that had wound their way into the land were largely gone, the scents of roundleaf orchid had evaporated, and the song of the marsh wren had fallen silent, all replaced by the sounds and smells of horses. The smoke of coal-fired industry hung over the comparatively barren landscape like the warm haze after a forest fire. Even in the midst of this fundamentally altered landscape, the young Theodore Roosevelt found enough natural kindling to ignite a lifelong passion.

One day when he was about seven, Roosevelt found adventure and inspiration not flitting in the trees or burrowing in the ground, but instead lying lifeless on a slab of wood on the sidewalk.[1] Onlookers and passersby may have wondered why this boy, entranced and oblivious, was circling a dead seal, just one of the many objects pulled out of the harbor and onto the city streets. Despite the fact that New York was, by Roosevelt's own later historical assessment, in the middle of "the worst decade in the city's political annals," it would be many years before he focused his attention on the larger trends of cities and politics.[2] Now, he did not find his own behavior odd, as his attention and observations were on what lay before his eyes. He had just made a discovery, and this massive specimen was just the type of magnificent animal he had previously encountered only in the dusty books of his family's library. This was a turning point, an epiphany.

After an extended consideration of the specimen, Roosevelt eventually returned home. But he was back the following day armed with equipment. It didn't matter that the rigid folding rule he used to measure the specimen was wholly unsuited for the job. Here, in this most unlikely place, a portal to nature had opened to him, and his mind and body were entirely absorbed. Even in this relatively brief encounter, Roosevelt showed passion and aptitude. He serially logged observations on paper and in his prodigious memory; he made quantitative measurements; he found the love of the organism. Many years later, Roosevelt recalled this as the moment where his love for nature had started. Like a gosling permanently locking in on its mother's identity, on this street Roosevelt imprinted on the field.

Even before being smitten by the Broadway seal, Roosevelt had flirted with natural history study. Riding the early wave of wealthy New Yorkers who crossed the Hudson in search of a summer refuge with the natural beauty that Manhattan had long since lost, the Roosevelt family escaped the pollution and population of the metropolis to Madison, New Jersey.[3] Only paces from their rental home, Loantaka (pronounced "Lowonicka") Brook meandered through fields toward the Great Swamp of northern New Jersey. Formed at the end range of the Wisconsin Glacier, this massive wetland was a haven for mink and skunk, red-eared sliders and five-lined skinks, and more than two hundred resident and migratory birds like the hermit thrush and the blue-gray gnatcatcher. Roosevelt did not need to step far from one of the porches of Tower Hill, the estate home they rented on Kitchell Road, to sample this wildlife. The home extended skyward with an observatory tower that dovetailed with its natural setting to provide an inspiring field station for the young Roosevelt.[4]

Roosevelt did not always have the strength of a bull moose—he spent many days at home in poor health as a child—but at Loantaka he adventurously plowed through wetlands and forests. His sister Corinne remembered how, even at five years old, Theodore surged ahead as the leader in their band of explorers, and that this was where "his more accurate interest in natural history began."[5] Corinne placed Theodore's rank among the Roosevelt children—Anna ("Bamie, or "Bye"), Theodore, Elliott ("Nell," or "Ellie"), and Corinne ("Conie" or "Pussie")—by saying "we others—normal and not particularly intelligent little children—joyed in the delights of the country . . . but he was not only a leader of us in everything, but he also led a life apart from us, seriously studying the birds, their habits and their notes."[6] Even then, as a neighbor helped him learn to ride a horse, there were glimmers of the colonel riding off into unexplored plains and hills ahead of his companions. And there was so much to explore even a short trot from Tower Hill.

For a boy who would eventually become a war hero, it is tempting to imagine that his early play would have been dominated by armies and cannon, and his horseback ambles to historic battlefields. The area near Loantaka Brook was infused with history—George Washington's army had spent the long winter of 1779–80 just a few miles away, at the Jockey Hollow encampment—but cannon and musket balls exerted less pull than his magnetic attraction to nature. And, vacationing adjacent to a massive watershed, he found plenty to engage him.

In the woods surrounding Loantaka, elusive black-billed cuckoos flitted through the foliage, pausing to munch on caterpillars and cicadas. The veery's cascade of song echoed around the wetlands, providing a distinctive lesson in birdsong. In the crepuscular hours, masked shrews and starnose moles sauntered through poorly drained fields. The wildlife of this teeming wetland fueled Roosevelt's growing desire to understand and identify all aspects of the natural world. When he returned to New York City after his summers near Loantaka, he was primed for his imprinting experience with the seal on Broadway. His retentive memory held his vivid experiences, and he quickly began to establish a serious center of nature study.

The Roosevelt Museum of Natural History—the museum that Theodore helped found in his own home—opened with little public fanfare. Theodore was part of a skeleton crew of investigators who had only a bedroom at their disposal for the collections from their field adventures. Roosevelt was initially limited to collecting natural curiosities from the areas around his home, but as he matured his scope quickly widened and the museum grew with him. It worked through the politics of a juvenile governing board, and the odor of its specimens, combined with notable escapes from the living collection, caused a rebellion among the domestic staff which "received the approval of the higher authorities" (Roosevelt's parents) and forced the relocation of the museum out of Theodore's room to a less desirable part of the house.[7] In its service, the museum's young curator studied, observed, and collected, formalizing his commitment to field science. No longer was he simply rambling in pursuit of random facts and objects; he now had a purpose. The Roosevelt Museum never matured into an independent institution, but it was an early influence that fanned Roosevelt's passion to take to the field to study nature. It allowed him the benefits of collecting—of learning from direct experience. It was also a springboard for a person who eventually lodged thousands of specimens in other major museums and generated many volumes of published work on natural history and adventure.

Theodore's cousin James West Roosevelt—"West," or "Jimmie"—who participated in the growth of the museum and its natural history society, later described how "at the commencement of the year 1867 Mr. T. Roosevelt Jr. started the Museum with about 12 specimens: at the close of the same year, Mr. J. W. Roosevelt joined him but each one kept his own specimens, these amounting to hardly 100."[8] At first, Roosevelt lodged specimens in his collection that were unlike the birds and mammals he later sent to museums throughout the United States. He had not yet benefited from the tutelage of an eminent taxidermist, nor had he good eyesight or even a gun for collecting. Instead, he used the most basic collecting approach, turning over rocks and logs and using nets to coarsely filter air and water for any and all creatures. But these were days filled with innocent enthusiasm and innate passion, and although some of this fervor may have been generated by the influence of his uncle Robert Barnwell Roosevelt, who lived next door and was always interested in nature, Roosevelt's early love was also spurred along by the solid backing of his parents.

While still only nine, Roosevelt already understood the fact that museum collections grow through the efforts of many. Even the great Linnaeus had a worldwide cast of "apostles" who collected specimens for him to describe.[9] Not yet having attained international standing, however, Theodore pulled other strings to expand his collections. When his parents visited relatives in Roswell, Georgia, he learned that his mother had found a mockingbird, and he appealed to her in a letter to "get some of its feathers if you can."[10] To his father he made an earnest request for pieces of the climbing supplejack vine: "I have a request to ask of you, will you do it? I hope you will, if you will it will figure greatly in my museum."[11] Despite relying on family members for assistance, this developing museum and bestiary was not child's play in Roosevelt's mind; he was serious that these scientific endeavors were part of a greater good. When his mother later dispatched some field mice from his collection, Roosevelt responded, "The loss to Science—the loss to Science!"[12]

The Roosevelt Museum did not arise simply out of a clinical desire to document natural history and taxonomy; Roosevelt interwove scientific objectives with his aim to understand and experience nature. He certainly made the most of his own experiences as he ferreted out every last animal and adventurous moment in the name of his museum, but he also began to imagine more exotic expeditions as he engaged with natural history and adventure stories. For this he needed to go no further than the family nursery, as he had been steeped in wild and fantastical tales of adventure from his earliest days.

In their home on East 20th Street, Roosevelt was weaned on the lore of the field; he had spent hours listening to colorful legends told by his mother and his aunt Anna.[13] Far from tame tales and docile nursery rhymes, these women's stories had grit. Deeply influenced by the lore of the South, the stories introduced Theodore to folk heroes like Davy Crockett. One can imagine the wide-eyed Roosevelt drinking up the tales that circulated about Crockett at the time, such as the often-recounted fable which suggests that Crockett told Congress:

> I am that same David Crockett, fresh from the backwoods, half horse, half alligator, a little touched with the snapping-turtle. I can wade the Mississippi, leap the Ohio, ride upon a streak of lightning, and slip without a scratch down a honey-locust. I can whip my weight in wildcats, and, if any

gentleman pleases, for a ten-dollar bill he can throw in a panther.[14]

The stories his mother and aunt Anna told him were not only the ones circulating on the likes of Crockett; some were specific to his own southern bloodline. One of his Georgian relatives had a plantation in the swamps near Florida, and one of the slaves—"a man of colossal strength, and of fierce and determined temper"— had been attacked and killed in the night by a cougar.[15]

Inspired by those who were "fresh from the backwoods" and manly enough to take on wildcats, Theodore toyed with what would become a lifelong love of storytelling. Corinne described how she and their brother Elliott would listen to Theodore and "drink in these tales of endless variety," which were often part of a "'serial story.'"[16] Theodore's imagination gave "the creatures of forest and field impersonations as vivid as those which Rudyard Kipling has made immortal."[17] Even in the early summers at Loantaka, Theodore made his siblings squeal with stories that explained the nefarious origins of a bloodlike stain on a rock they had found in the forest.[18]

Even before he could read, Roosevelt also tapped into the vast literature of nature and exploration—where real explorers and facts of nature came to life—in his parents' home library. At first it was the images that attracted him: the young Roosevelt dragged descriptive volumes of natural history around the house pointing at pictures and asking for explanations. His father gave him a copy of the Rev. J. G. Wood's recently published *Homes without Hands*, filling his mind with images of menacing spiders lurking behind trap doors, pesky weaverbirds using their sharp beaks to defend their beautifully constructed nests from an aggressive monkey, and the curious burrow of the aardvark.[19] *Missionary Travels and Researches in South Africa* occupied Roosevelt for weeks, portraying the life of ancient Egyptians, a dramatic depiction of a man-eating lion, and a harrowing encounter with an angry hippopotamus. These stories inspired Roosevelt to imagine his own expeditions; he later pointed to the importance of these early stories, and their influence echoed in his writing.[20]

Along with nonfiction, Roosevelt also devoured fictional adventure stories, such as the popular books by novelist Mayne Reid. Although Roosevelt only recorded that he had read "some of Mayne Reid's books," none would seem more attractive to a boy like him than *The Boy Hunters; or, Adventures in Search of a White Buffalo*.[21] Like many boys of his time, Roosevelt encountered in books like this perspectives on race, culture, native peoples, and gender, as well as a code of manhood and of struggle against nature and Native Americans that presented thoughts of empire and imperialism in a romantic context.[22] There was also plenty of hunting, natural history, suspense, intrigue, and daring; and these stories encouraged Roosevelt to envision his own adventures.

Reid brilliantly began *The Boy Hunters* with an invitation to young adventurers: "Go with me to the great river Mississippi." He followed this call by introducing an irresistible band of traveling companions.[23] The three young boys described by Reid had prodigious natural abilities; "they were the best shots of their age, could ride a horse with any, could swim the Mississippi, paddle a canoe, fling a lasso, or spear a catfish, as though they had been full-grown men."[24] Reid pumped up the egos of his adolescent audience by clarifying that these boys were not simply boys, but instead were "*boy men*."[25] And each had his own strengths. Basil was the handsome, dark-haired eldest, a courageous and strong hunter. Lucien, the fair-haired and bookish naturalist, was the intellect of the bunch. Francois rounded out the band with a merry and likeable personality. To complete this clan, brimming with testosterone, there was the father, Mr. Landi, known to the others as "the colonel" because he had fought in Napoleon's army before emigrating to the Mississippi River Valley to assume the life of a naturalist. Unfortunately for the colonel, but essentially for the plot, a tragic fall from a horse had left him with a wooden leg. So when a letter arrived from the old country requesting the pelt of the rare white buffalo, the boys tipped the boy-man balance and lobbied to go in their father's stead.

And what an adventure it was. It is easy to see why narratives like that of *The Boy Hunters* would encourage any young boy to become a serious natural explorer. But for one with Roosevelt's abundant aptitude and drive, the material was inflammatory. The parallels to Reid's story that reach far into the future of Roosevelt's life are impossible to attribute specifically, but they are also too strong to ignore. Just like Colonel Roosevelt's havens in the Badlands and at the Boone and Crockett Club, Colonel Landi's home was appointed with "various implements of the chase, such as rifles, shot guns, pouches, flasks, hunting knives, and, in short, every species of trap, net, or implement, that could be devised for capturing the wild denizens of the earth, air, and water."[26] There were, of course, abundant specimens, with "horns of the stag and elk," bird skins, and insects on pins. "In short, this hall resembled a little museum."[27]

We can even imagine that the loathing that Roosevelt—one who had significant affection for ferocious animals—reserved for crocodiles was influenced by Reid's chapter entitled "The Indian Mother and Caiman."[28] This tragic tale of a mother and child's encounter with a caiman is enough to make even the most hardened sportsman shudder with contempt. And Reid's premise of a journey west to find a white buffalo foreshadows Roosevelt's affinity for this animal which consumed so much of his interest and energy and led to some of his greatest achievements in conservation. It is as if in the fantastic adventures of the boy hunters Lucien, Basil, and Francois, or in other similar stories, Roosevelt had found a home—"the home of a *Hunter Naturalist*."[29]

As the train lumbered northward, carrying summer passengers out of New York toward the Catskills, Roosevelt watched the scenery slowly transition from tightly packed buildings to wide-open countryside. As the train moved up the Hudson, the mountains appeared to rise through the forest floor, and the sights evoked wilderness daydreams of bear, deer, and Indians. Roosevelt had come primed for adventure; in his luggage he had a simple bound notebook for his field notes and observations, a new tool that placed him in the tradition of the great naturalists as he began to render his experiences. Here, he wasn't just imagining; he was experiencing and recording.

On August 10, 1868, Roosevelt began his first journal entry by recounting the suspenseful story he had heard of a growling black bear crashing out of the bushes on top of a rocky hill:

A clear and rather cold day. A gentleman came here to day of whom I do not know the name and he told us that bears of both the brown and black species are still found on the

catskills not ten miles from here. He had an adventure with
one, of which I will relate the main parts.[30]

In content, the story Roosevelt absorbed from this man in the
Catskills pales in comparison to the suspenseful narratives he
later told about staring down grizzlies or dodging buffalo. But in
his notebook the young Roosevelt faithfully records how the man
heard a "growl and rustleng of leaves" and came face-to-face with
a bear.[31] Luckily the unarmed man was spared as the bear absconded through the underbrush. Roosevelt used grammar, spelling, and syntax appropriate to his age, but he recorded the scene
with interest and seriousness, giving glimmers of his devotion to
adventure. By the next week, Roosevelt documented the first field
lore of his own as he and his band went "deep in the woods" and
found an old one-room shack.[32] They promptly laid an entrance
to their camp of small pebbles and soft moss, reminiscent of the
grand approach to Colonel Landi's river lodge in *The Boy Hunters*. In the first pages of his notebook, Roosevelt records details of
how he played, read, wrote, drew, and even "did nothing," all the
time uncovering the beauty of nature: "Today we went down to the
brook. But wonders were in store for us."[33] The glistening waters,
he wrote, were filled with "crayfish, eels, minnows, salamanders,
water spiders, water bugs &c &c."[34] A young hunter, he knocked the
nests of catbirds, swallows, and robins from trees, examining their
contents and sometimes appropriating them for his collection. He
even bravely probed wasp nests. In his first bound field journal,
spanning almost a month, Roosevelt recorded his emerging love
of living organisms, from birds to insects to mammals.

Finding new confidence and independence, and needing transportation as his adventures took him further afield, he started to
take solo rides on his trusted pony Grant. Two days after recording
a six-mile ride, he had another ride of equal length before breakfast, and locked in this accomplishment by determining that "I will
always have a ride of six miles before breakfast now."[35]

Riding over trails and waterways, Roosevelt collected observations that built upon his haphazard examination of the Broadway
seal. He recorded and quantified the attributes of the brook: "in
some places small, in others full of stones," with a swelling along
its route that was about "about 5 feet long, 3 feet wide, and two

feet deep in the middle."[36] Regardless of the forces that caused him to pick up his own pen and refine his work—whether it was a suggestion by a family member or the inspiration of *Missionary Travels*—Roosevelt laid down in ink many of the elements that would consume his outdoor life. In addition to starting a daily journal, Roosevelt also used his time in the Catskills to begin a foray into more formal writing in his notebooks.[37]

Most young children don't take their early fascination with ants much past simple stories of pavement chases or casual observations. But in this case, as in so many others, Theodore Roosevelt was different. Although he recalled late in his life how his animal affections had moved well away from insects—"I do not care for that enormous brand of natural history which deals with invertebrates"—his first written work, largely on insects, contains all the basic elements of natural history descriptions.[38]

Out of a small crack, a black ant ran onto a barren rock. Leaning in close, the young Roosevelt caught a glimpse of several other ants running with small objects he described as "ant loaves."[39] He considered the relative abundance of this type of ant, and aspects of size variation. These careful observations and ideas were recorded in a notebook that, instead of daily journal entries, focused on information on certain species.

Even at nine, Roosevelt filled his notebook with what amounts to a short paper, entitled "About Insects and Fishes," in which he included the who, what, when, and where that give natural history observations and specimens scientific value.[40] In his "Preface" he recorded his identity, "Theodore Roosevelt, Jr.," and locality: "All these insects are native of North America." Unconventionally, but providing a time frame, Roosevelt recorded his age in the postscript as "nine years," a time when he was summering in Barrytown in the Catskills. Even in this basic account, Roosevelt's description points to the identity of this ant as *Formica subsericea*, a species widespread throughout the Northeast, that is regularly found on stones and rock walls carrying pupae, the "ant loaves," from one place to another.[41]

The ubiquitous "brown path ant" and its characteristic nests also merited treatment in Roosevelt's notebook. He observed how on these nests the "entrance is generally at the top" and "the ant hills differ in size and shape very much." Excavating the chambers, "half under ground and half above"—built almost as the chambers of the great pyramids—Roosevelt likely disinterred colonies of *Lasius neoniger*, recording his efforts for posterity in his notebooks in the wide loops of his juvenile script. In another species he noted wide size variation as well as the yellowish abdominal bands of the larger individuals of the "officer" of this "shiny ant."[42] He was paying close attention, as these small bands become apparent when an ant's abdomen expands after it feeds on liquids. Not completely consumed by insects, Roosevelt expanded his studies to include vertebrates as well.

On the banks of rivers and small lakes near Barrytown, fish flopped in and out of Roosevelt's nets, and he did his best to measure and draw them in his notebook. He landed a "gold striped fish [that] is yellowish brown with a stripe on both sides, from head to tail, of gold," which ate "very small insects and crumbs of bread and egg." These notes suggest that he may have pulled out a black-nosed dace and kept it in a bucket for feeding and observation. He also caught several catfish, with "cat's whiskers" that "prick very sharply if brought in contact with the skin."[43]

In this work Roosevelt incorporated another element of his persona: a fierce dedication to accuracy in describing nature. He trumpeted his devotion to real natural history, which eventually led him to join John Burroughs and others in trouncing the "nature fakers" as he described a bluish-green dragonfly, also known then as a "darning needle." With ample confidence, he confronted and dismissed a commonly held myth: "There is a foolish superstition about it sewing up peoples cheeks which I need scarcely add is not true."[44] Another of these early descriptions attempted to correct the record on "the fire fly," which he said was "not nocturnal as is generally thought but gives forth its light in the daytime as well as the night."[45] Here was a young scientist striving to make new and accurate natural history observations; he pursued his passion to experience and describe nature by taking to the field.

But the writings in Roosevelt's early notebooks weren't limited to natural descriptions; he also composed adventure stories. In a composition entitled "My Expeditions and Adventures," he recounted a family adventure in which he, his relatives, and a curious little Scotch terrier named Jack all rowed in a boat to have lunch next to a fifty-foot waterfall.[46] He included an illustrated map to

2

The common black ant
is found in cracks in
the rock and eats the ant loaves.
Pieces of bread, eggs, &c make
these. This ant is a rare one.
Ants are divided into
three sorts for every
species. These kinds
are officer, soilder, and
work. There are about

(ABOVE AND FACING) One of Roosevelt's earliest surviving written documents is a short bound manuscript he titled "About Insects and Fishes," which includes his studies of ants. The "common black ant" he describes is likely to be *Formica subsericea*, which is often seen carrying pupae—Roosevelt's "ant loaves." Roosevelt's "brown path ant" is likely *Lasius neoniger*, a species widespread in the northeastern United States that makes small but conspicuous mounded nests. TRC MS Am 1541 (286).

one officer to ten soilders
and one soilder to two
workers. The office
looks like this.
The officer.
The   The soilder.   The worker.   They are
very strong.

The brown Path ant,
is common. The house
is half under ground
and half above. There
are several rooms in

34

The blackfish.
There are two species
of the blackfish.
One as long as this

resides in the lakes
and one as large as
this ____ resides in rivers
They will eat it al-
-most anything.

"About Insects and Fishes" contains Roosevelt's observations on crayfish and several species of true fish. In his page on "blackfish," Roosevelt identified two possible species, and provided life-size sketches. TRC MS Am 1541 (286).

help the reader visualize the quaint story. In another episode, "Chased by Wild Dogs," he described a frightening occurrence: "Johnny and I were taking a walk in the woods we heard the report of a gun followed by a succession of howls."[47] In a separate three-chapter account entitled "The War of the Woods," Roosevelt encrypted a story in a mysterious code.[48] In this story, Roosevelt's fictional recounting of "the Battle of Stillwater," a "terrible conflict ensued" between Sioux warriors and "whites." In a style that evoked Native American ledger drawings, Roosevelt provided illustrations of battles that illuminated the stories and reflected his western-looking imagination and developing ideology.[49] At this period of his life, the young Roosevelt didn't yet have anything like what he would later send to *Century Magazine* and *Scribner's*, but these short written bursts in his notebooks were the beginning of his hard work of not only documenting natural history but also recounting his own narratives of the Americans' westward expansion.

In early April of 1869, the Roosevelt household was abuzz with talk of natural history. This time, however, it wasn't the younger Theodore who was generating the interest. As a prominent businessman and philanthropist, Theodore Sr. had been approached by an enthusiastic naturalist, Albert S. Bickmore, who had hopes of creating a natural history museum in New York City. Others had turned Bickmore away, but Theodore Sr. had seen the passion that his own son had for nature. And Bickmore embodied the kind of fierce dedication to careful study and adventure narratives to which he saw his son aspiring. Like Roosevelt's own son, Bickmore held close his aspirations for a museum, which literally never left his side while he studied nature: "I carried with me everywhere two things, a Bible and a sketch plan for a museum in New York."[50]

When he called on Theodore Sr., Bickmore had just returned from three years of fieldwork in Asia and had just published *Travels in the East Indian Archipelago*, a volume of the kind of real-life adventure narratives that young Theodore was soaking up in the family library.[51] In one part of the book, Bickmore recounted how his life had flashed before his eyes as he slipped down the steep slope of the Lontar volcano.[52] As he grasped at loose, igneous rocks, Bickmore must have experienced an instantaneous sense of regret and disappointment that he would never see a single brick laid at the foot of his beloved museum—until, that is, "as I

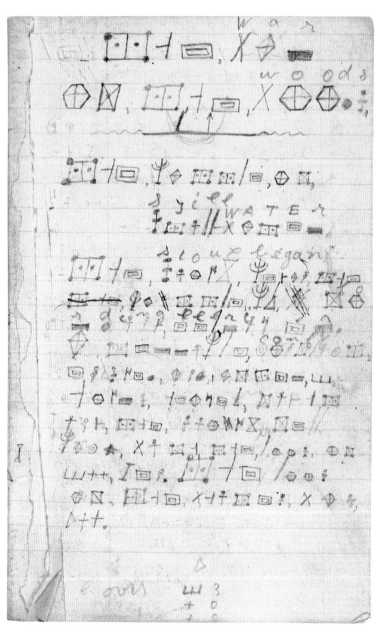

Roosevelt created a three-part story called "The War of the Woods," which he encrypted in a mysterious code. TRC MS Am 1541 (287).

After his story "The War of the Woods," Roosevelt depicted battles in simple figures similar to those in Native American ledger drawings. TRC MS Am 1541 (287).

felt myself going down, I chanced to roll to my right side . . . and, quick as a flash of light, the thought crossed my mind that my only hope was to seize *that fern*."[53]

This fateful brush with mortality was just the kind of field credential that would have made Bickmore a welcome dinner guest at the Roosevelt home on any night of the week. Certainly it would be difficult for Bickmore to top possibly the only fern-saves-man's-life story ever recounted by a naturalist, but his stories of adventure continued with an account of his dramatic search for an escaped python. At the end of his expedition to the East Indian archipelago, Bickmore engaged passage aboard a French ship and reluctantly brought aboard a gigantic python he had received as a parting gift. A bit flummoxed about how to handle the live specimen, he resolved to preserve it the next day, and ordered the box placed for safekeeping in a large boat that was sitting on the deck of the ship. The skittish French crewmen looked unsettled by their new shipmate, and the next morning Bickmore, tired of the trouble the python's presence had already caused, picked up the crate and pitched it over the side of the ship. Just as it was leaving his hands though, he had a terrible realization: the box was far too light. A terrified French sailor screamed in his ear, "*Le serpent n'est pas encore!—pas encore!*" and a frantic search ensued. [54] Bickmore, dressed in a loose Chinese blouse and canvas shoes, finally located the specimen under a board and undertook an epic battle. Wielding handspike and broadax, he fought the serpent, its "red jaws wide open, and his eyes flashing fire like live coals," and eventually collapsed, exhausted, with the beast in several pieces.[55] These were only two of Bickmore's many brushes with death on his trip. His journey had also brought the requisite battle with fever; he remarked how it was so intense that it felt as though someone was "thrusting a handful of red-hot knitting-needles into the top of my head."[56]

In engaging Bickmore's idea for a great museum in New York, Theodore Sr. embraced the interwoven cycle of scientific study and adventure that Bickmore embodied, and sent his son a strong message of support. The junior Theodore did not record whether he had been at home on the evening of April 8, 1869—either with his ear pressed against a door or his eye peering into a keyhole— but his spirit was certainly with the men who gathered in the family's parlor that night.[57] As preparations were ongoing elsewhere in the Roosevelt home for the family's upcoming trip to Europe, the parlor became a historical salon of natural history as those present signed the charter of the American Museum of Natural History (AMNH). This historic moment encapsulates yet another passion—scientific study and collecting—that Roosevelt nurtured in the field throughout his life.

In many ways, the AMNH—Bickmore's brainchild—was a descendent of Louis Agassiz's Museum of Comparative Zoology at Harvard. Bickmore had been one of Agassiz's early students, and he brought into the Roosevelt household the tradition of the great naturalists of the time.[58] Although Agassiz rejected Darwin's notion of evolution by natural selection, his dedication to the rigorous study of nature permeated the natural science of his students. He preached that "the progress of our science is too rapid to allow the use of text-books to any advantage. . . . A student of nature should, therefore, be at once trained in the difficult art of reading for himself in the great book of nature."[59] For Agassiz, the most basic skill of the naturalist was to be able to carefully observe and document actual organisms. It was a mode of direct engagement. The entomologist Samuel Scudder, also one of Agassiz's early students, recounted Agassiz's legendary rite of passage.[60] As soon as they came to the museum, students were given a single fish and asked to observe and document only that specimen. Far from a superficial exercise, Scudder recalls Agassiz returning again and again to ask him what he had found throughout that first long day, and pushing him to transcend basic thoughts and formulate substantial observations and probing questions. Scudder returned the next day only to find his fish waiting for him, and the quiet lesson continued unabated. The classic training in natural history that Agassiz taught to his students—patient observation and thoughtful attention to organisms—was very much present in the values that the founders of the AMNH held. Even as a young boy, Roosevelt absorbed this tradition through his readings and interactions with the likes of Bickmore.

Interwoven with the emphasis that the developing AMNH placed on specimens and direct observation was the importance of rigorous fieldwork; this disciplinary philosophy jibed with the naturalistic struggle Roosevelt had read about in his adventure novels, part of a Victorian struggle for manliness that was instilled in Roosevelt's identity from these early days.[61] And it was a fundamental principle on which even Darwin and Agassiz could agree. These eminent explorer-naturalists understood that the slow march of science was not about flashy discovery, but instead required painstaking and sometimes painful fieldwork. Darwin had famously spent almost five years circumnavigating the globe in the 1830s, famously stopping off in the Galapagos Islands, and laying the groundwork for his momentous books. During that time he frequently had been ill from seasickness and dysentery. Bickmore clearly had had his own brushes with death on his trip, and, although slightly more posh, Agassiz had spent nineteen months collecting in the wilds of Brazil. This reality of fieldwork surely put off many, but Roosevelt was attracted by any opportunity to test his mettle.

Panning forward over the landscape of Roosevelt's life, one sees countless examples of his efforts to overcome hardship as he sought understanding and discovery in the open field. He would experience satisfaction as he reached the summit of frigid mountains, and joy as he captured rare and elusive animals. He would cope with illness and the death of his soldiers in Cuba as he eventually tasted victory in battle. He would seek comfort and healing in the wilds of the Badlands. As he embraced both the rigors and rewards of the field, this tension would become an integral part of his life philosophy. Roosevelt encapsulated these ideas in April of 1899, in a speech given to the Hamilton Club in Chicago that he called "The Strenuous Life":

> I wish to preach, not the doctrine of ignoble ease, but the
> doctrine of the strenuous life, the life of toil and effort,
> of labor and strife; to preach that highest form of success
> which comes, not to the man who desires mere easy peace,
> but to the man who does not shrink from danger, from
> hardship, or from bitter toil, and who out of these wins the
> splendid ultimate triumph.[62]

These were bold proclamations and a rousing sermon that Roosevelt offered as he entered into national politics. But the underlying message—here applied to international conflict and individual

service—was informed by Roosevelt's own ideas on how one—
especially an American man—should confront physical challenges. And some of the power of Roosevelt's words was derived from
the fact that everyone in the audience knew that he was not a
coddled politician. He was a man who had written his own story
as one who had chased down outlaws and shot countless animals.
He not only could articulate the value of the strenuous life; he
embodied it. Roosevelt's listeners knew that his endorsement of
the strenuous life was not a passing fancy but a deeply engrained
value. This drive simply added to the factors—like his growing
love of nature, his scientific collecting, and his drive to celebrate
the Western exploration and white settlement of the American
West—that he played out in the field. And two decades earlier,
these elements had already been percolating when, as a ten-year-
old, he followed in the footsteps of the great naturalists and set
off for a far-flung adventure.

The Craft of the Naturalist

As Theodore Roosevelt Sr., Albert Bickmore, and the other founders of the American Museum of Natural History were wrapping up
their work, the rest of the Roosevelt family was making final preparations for a yearlong tour of Europe that the senior Roosevelt
had planned to facilitate his children's education. Given that his
own living room had just become a historic hub of museums and
natural history, it would be tempting to assume that this trip would
simply be a joyous continuation of the young Roosevelt's naturalistic rambles in Loantaka and the Catskills. However, substantial
"reading in the great book of nature" would need to wait. This was
an adventure that was largely driven by Roosevelt's father in the
tradition of the "grand tours" of the seventeenth and eighteenth
century, in which aristocratic families toured Western Europe in
the interest of family entertainment and education.[1] Theodore Sr.
had been on his own tours of Europe as a child, and he wanted
to pass this tradition down to his own children.[2] The younger
Theodore later recalled his long trip, which became known as
the "Roosevelt Grand Tour," pessimistically. In his *Autobiography*
he recounted how he didn't think he had "gained anything from
this particular trip abroad," and that he had "cordially hated it."[3]

In the notes on this adventure he made at the time, however,
Roosevelt revealed himself as a young explorer who was struggling
to become a naturalist and traveler. Although he was often uncomfortable, his experiences on this trip refined what he wanted his
identity to be and, more important, what he didn't want it to be. He
also wasted no time in adopting a rigorous approach to the most
basic tool of the naturalist. Just as Darwin, Wallace, and Bickmore
had done, Roosevelt recorded both victories and hardships on the
grand tour in his field notes. It was almost as if, before departing,
Roosevelt had read the preface to *Travels in the East Indian Archi-*

pelago, in which Bickmore describes how his field notes were "kept day by day with scrupulous care," and in which "accuracy, even at any sacrifice of elegance," was the aim.[4]

Roosevelt had literally been aboard the *Scotia* only for hours before he started making entries in his diary with a new regularity and seriousness. He sailed for Liverpool on May 12, 1869, and made records that foreshadowed the continuum of experiences, from joy to sadness, that he would find in his life's travels. Roosevelt's journal account for this day records this range of feelings: "We 3 jumped around the deck and played," and "I cried a great deal."[5] This journal account is an edited version of an earlier entry he had made in a diary, and it reveals how Roosevelt developed a habit of returning to his primary field notes, editing them and adding additional material in the tradition of great naturalists like Charles Darwin.[6] In total, Roosevelt's notes from his grand tour peregrinations are contained in four journals and one diary; woven into the entries are the efforts of a young boy beginning to integrate the rigors and rewards of the field.

From May 21, 1869, when the *Scotia* landed in Liverpool, to May 14, 1870, when they departed Europe from that same port, the Roosevelts engaged in what amounted to a long game of Western European hopscotch. Not missing many major cities, they visited London, Edinburgh, Amsterdam, Vienna, Berlin, Brussels, Paris, and Rome. In his sketches and written accounts, Roosevelt revealed the challenges of being hemmed in by carriages and stone walls, a small bit of adventure, and his ever-expanding love of nature.

Given that much of the grand tour was a succession of castles, carriages, and cathedrals, one can see why Roosevelt, a young boy fascinated by nature, was not always pleased by the tour. In recounting a dingy eight-hour ride to York, Theodore described how he "did not like it . . . we were verry dirty when we got there."[7] Although he was always interested in stories, even the narratives he picked up were grim. At Roslin, Scotland, a castle had "the most dreary kind of Dungens" and "one of the pillars of the chapel had been made by a clerk and his master had killed him from jealisy [because he] could not make the others so pretty."[8] In many of his notes, the young Roosevelt recorded tolerance rather than inspiration on the family's historical tours through the grim remnants of the Middle Ages, which provided him with perspectives on civilizations and empires that had failed. Even so, he worked to extract natural history and make quantitative observations from the largely urban sites. While in London, he and his sister Corinne went to "hide park" and "hauled in 70 dead fish about two inches long."[9] In Hastings he "saw two bitterns or herons one of whome drove some young swans of an island."[10]

As he sought out small windows of natural inspiration, Roosevelt also tried to buck his identity as a small and sickly child. In the polluted and urban confines of the grand tour, however, his severe asthma made this particularly hard. At night, he often "did not sleep at all after quarter past two" or "sat up for 4 successive hours."[11] His parents were there with various remedies, some of which were repulsive, as when "Papa made me smoke a cigar" or when "I had some coffy to drink (much to my horror, and good)."[12] Luckily, his parents were tender. When he was extremely sick in the night, his mother would tell him stories and rub his back for hours.[13] Through his honest entries, Roosevelt revealed in his journal the development of a strenuous identity, and how he would not let a debilitating condition keep him from making observations and directly connecting with nature. It seems clear that his time spent approaching the field on this trip, hiking and investigating nature, was part of a remedy for his debilitating symptoms.[14] Directly after a disturbing account of a treatment for asthma—"was rubbed so hard on the chest this morning that the blood came out"—he segued into observations on natural history: "The forrests consist of pine and spotted with other kinds turned yellow now look like the hide of a Leopoerd."[15] On the grand tour, Roosevelt honed a spirit of study and exploration that even the sight of his own blood would not deter.

Approaching his eleventh birthday in the fall of 1869, Roosevelt recorded the ups and downs he encountered while developing as a "boy-man." Amid the bumps and bruises of early adolescence on the road in Europe, Roosevelt juxtaposed his longing and feeling "very doleful and sick and homesick" with his hopeful dreams of more enjoyable trips to come: "Perhaps when I'm 14 I'll go to Minnesota, hip, hip, hurrah'hhh!"[16] It is likely that part of his dislike of the grand tour was that he simply wasn't old enough to enjoy such an extended tour, and the whole premise of a grand tour—a tour organized and directed by the family—made it an adventure that he did not create. Still, his love of nature and innate curiosity about the world drove him to explore, experience, and record. He developed his skills as a rider—a critical talent that would serve him on many hunts and adventures—but even these lessons only sometimes provided enjoyment. He attended "a riding school for big gentlemen," but wrote: "I was sick and went to the same riding school which I hate as much today as I liked it yesterday."[17] In a manner that unknowingly foreshadowed future entries, Roosevelt confronted mortality and grief far away from home. When news arrived that his Uncle Weir had died, he was incredulous: "It is the third relation that has died in my short life. What will come?"[18] He could not have known that he would later record two more devastating losses in his notes.

Roosevelt advanced his goals even in the face of his challenges. Although he did not follow Bickmore's lead in keeping a plan of his museum with him at all times, Roosevelt actively engaged himself as a member of the Roosevelt Museum, and measured the institutions he visited against his own. At the zoological gardens in London he "saw a great maney animals, zebras, lions, camels, Elephants, monkeys, bears, &c &c all comon to other menageries" but "was a little disappointed."[19] He reacted to the British Museum more favorably: "Saw rare and beautiful specimens and [it] interested me a great deal."[20] He bought an ibex horn near Mount Chamonix in Switzerland, and compared the natural history museum in Dresden to his own:

> It has 101 anamils in all of it but has a good collection of reptiles and fish but birds are the chief thing and it has the best collection of nests I have ever seen. I have two of the reptiles and 1 nest and 3 birds in my Museum at home and I have seen severel birds and nests wild at home.[21]

The many museums Roosevelt visited provided a welcome distraction to the drudgery of the trip, and allowed him to accomplish some fieldwork, even under suboptimal conditions.

Along with his museum studies, Roosevelt widened his natural horizons and even dabbled in the green world. The majority of the specimens he had collected up to that point had either fur,

October 19th

We went to the historical
Museum where we saw very
old and interesting armours
and old firearms and King
Mustapha's tent and
Turkish arms. We went
to a museum of casts.
I stayed in.

October 20th

All alone I went to the
Natural History Museum.
It has 10 animals in all of
it but has a good collection
of reptiles and fish but fishes
are the chief thing and it
has the best collection of
nests I have ever seen. I have
two of the reptiles and
I nest and 3 birds in my

(ABOVE AND FACING) In recording the progression of castles and museums he saw on the grand tour, Roosevelt frequently compared them to what he had experienced at home. On October 20, 1869, he compared collections at home to what he observed on a visit to a natural history museum in Saxony. TRC MS Am 1454.55 (4).

Mverin at home and I have
seen several birds, and nests
wild at home. M the
afternoon we went to
Miss Wolf's, where we had
a splendid time. **My journal in Prussia.**

October 21st.
Berlin. The 3 children with
the servants went in advance
(it is 5 hours) and arrived
at 5 and they followed and
arrived at 11. When we
arrived there we explored
the house with less noise
than we ever have before.

October 22d.
We and (the people too) went
to the Dentist. He stopped
their teeth filled **which**

feathers, scales, or six legs. But on the grand tour Roosevelt made a fleeting attempt at botanical study in his small Excelsior diary, where he created a miniature herbarium by pressing within its pages plants that he had encountered. He included no labels, but in these plants Roosevelt preserved a record of his growing curiosity, which ranged across taxa and geography. He was a curious naturalist who was working toward a robust understanding of nature.

The exhausting procession of artworks, castle ruins, dignitaries, and glorious cities that were stops on the grand tour generally failed to impress Theodore; far from distracting his attention from his fundamental goal of becoming a naturalist, it simply put his passion in stark relief. Roosevelt filled his notes with polite passages and moderate praise for buildings, inanimate objects, and mundane travel experiences. On the rare moments when he approached the field, however, he adopted a more lyrical and joyful tone. On what he described as the "happiest Easter I ever spent," Roosevelt searched for eggs among violets in the woods:

> We played . . . in the woods and picked cowslip and heard the cuckoo sing. After dinner we all drove out through the woods to the rocks. . . . We saw a tree 1400 years old and other 300 years old. We saw a stream of pure and cold water. We had such a happy time."[22]

In a description of an after-dinner ramble at Fontainebleau, Roosevelt recounts that they "went to the rocks where we jumped over crevases and ran in them and had such fun and played. In one of our rambles we saw verry fresh traces of a deer."[23] Near Albano, Italy, he found an intriguing bank of caverns, but only had a short time to investigate them. In his words he encapsulated the longing he felt for the field throughout the grand tour, as well as his resolve to not be held back from these experiences in the future: "I think the caverns had never been before explored. . . . I would like to stay here for a good while to explore them thougherly. . . . When I am a man I will explore them all through."[24]

(FACING) After filling the pages of his 1869 Excelsior diary from May 12 to September 14 with daily accounts, Roosevelt began using the book as a miniature herbarium. TRC MS Am 1454.55 (2).

Sunday 7.

Monday 8.

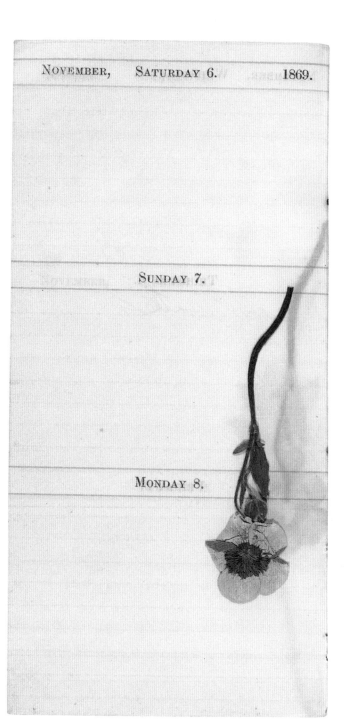

Roosevelt's relief as he and his family boarded the *Russia* bound for New York is evident in his journal, and although it is easy for biographers to agree with Roosevelt's own pessimistic account of this trip, his own field notes stand as evidence that it was critical to the development of his identity as a traveler and naturalist. He worked on his riding. He became a dedicated observer and recorder of his pursuits. Equally important, he learned to endure hardship. For others, this last lesson would have been learned more easily from sleeping on cold ground or from tolerating the urticating insults of life in the woods, but those were things that Roosevelt relished. The grand tour—largely a sightseeing trip full of hotels and cities where his own health was poor—provided Roosevelt with an early example of something he would confront his entire life: his travels in the field, like those of his heroes, would be filled with painful rigors that had to be dealt with and overcome.

On his last day at sea, Roosevelt recounted how "in the afternoon we saw some young whales one of whom came so near the boat that when it spouted some of its water came on me."[25] This return to New York by ship—the first of many for Roosevelt—cleansed him of the strain of long days spent in stale rooms, sometimes with "horrid" playmates who had engaged only in pretend hunts with lead figures.[26] On this day in May of 1870, after eleven years of life, Roosevelt had only cracked open the book of nature. Returning home, he was now prepared to open it wide and tear through its pages.

Roosevelt was likely entranced when he entered John G. Bell's natural history emporium. Bell, an eminent naturalist and taxidermist, kept a shop, not far from Roosevelt's home, that was characteristic of nineteenth-century natural history establishments. Stowed in the mysterious recesses of these stores were boxes of bones, jars of specimens, shiny pins, and gaudy feathers. Although exquisitely mounted specimens patiently waited for their new owners—frozen in mid-flight or with a menacing snarl—commerce was only one facet of a shop such as Bell's. Like tackle shops for anglers or phar-

---

(FACING) In the same expired diary in which Roosevelt pressed plant specimens, he used the pages reserved at the back for "bills receivable" for a tally of the animals he rode on in Europe. TRC MS Am 1454.55 (2).

DATE.	NAME.	AMOUNT.

The animals I rode
on while
in Europe. how
many
times. where
first rode
Southport

Donkey 11

Elephant London
mule were Manchester
Elephant / / / London
Elephant / / London
horse / / / / /
camel / London

pony / London
pony / London

pony / London

pony / London

goat wagon / hastings
here
mule
pony
about write the number of the
elephant /

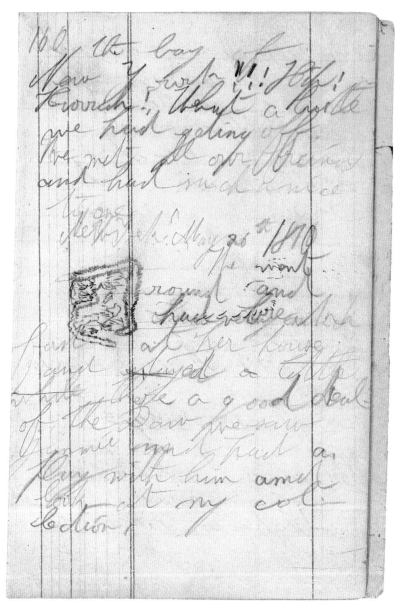

As he returned to New York aboard the *Russia* on May 25, 1870, Roosevelt used five exclamation points to show his relief in being home. By the following day, he was already showing his "collection"—presumably his natural hsitory specimens—around the family. TRC MS Am 1454.55 (6).

macies for early medics, these were gathering places where hunters, scientists, and wealthy amateurs came to share the knowledge and craft of the field. Roosevelt had been captivated by Charles Dickens's description of just such a naturalistic location, kept by Mr. Venus in *Our Mutual Friend*, and in Bell's shop he found a real establishment two miles from his home, where he began to be tutored in the methods of natural history. [27]

Always forward-looking, Theodore Roosevelt Sr. could see that the growing heaps of specimens in his son's collection needed attention, and he "allowed" Roosevelt to look to Bell for guidance.[28] Soon after the Roosevelts had returned from their grand tour, the younger Theodore had taken to his old ways, immediately gathering new observations and specimens as he returned to his old collecting haunts. No organism was safe on earth, in air, or in water as Roosevelt ferreted a Baltimore oriole nest out of a tree, scooped eels from a stream, and flushed "field mouses" from their terrestrial hideaways.[29] He spent much of the following two years in the countryside close to New York City and in the Adirondacks, and, given the rapid growth of his collections and the growing importance of natural history to him, his self-taught preservation of specimens would no longer suffice; he needed training to move his work forward. Unhesitant to use his wide-ranging connections, Roosevelt Sr. likely made arrangements for his son to be tutored in taxidermy by Bell, an old-school naturalist with an impressive pedigree.[30]

When Roosevelt frequented Bell's "Venus-like" shop, John James Audubon loomed large in natural history; Bell had been his right-hand man. The first page of Audubon's journal from his expedition on the Missouri River in 1843 describes "old John G. Bell" as one of his "companions for this campaign."[31] Bell was quick with his rifle, and his collections of diverse specimens, such as shells, toads, and birds' nests, had elicited "delight and utter astonishment" in Audubon.[32] Along their route, Bell had helped collect antelope, elks, bears, squirrels, and wolves, and had even fed Audubon original observations on natural history, such as his "opinion that the Red-collared Ground Finch has its nest in the deserted holes of the Ground Squirrel."[33] The hardships of this expedition had also forged the kinds of bonds soldiers make when they prepare for battle. On a gusty night near the Little Missouri River, the party heard what they thought were the foreboding sounds of gunshots, and they "went to bed all prepared for action in case of an attack; pistols, knives, etc."[34] When Roosevelt began his work with Bell, he was not just coming under the wing of contractor or hired hand; he was getting close to Audubon's trusted inner circle.

Bell's expert skills in taxidermy were valued most by Audubon. After collecting "a very beautiful specimen" of the white-tailed jackrabbit, *Lepus townsendii*, Audubon recorded in his journal that "Bell will make a fine skin of it to-morrow morning."[35] Audubon's breathtaking depictions of birds and mammals depended partly on carefully prepared skins, and no one was better than Bell at preparing his field specimens to serve as models. As Roosevelt mustered the dexterity and concentration to dissect his own specimens in Bell's shop, replacing their soft organs with clean cotton and arsenical soap, he was becoming an apprentice to a master.

In most aspects of his life Roosevelt was more gentleman than tradesman, but in his growing identity as a field naturalist he was not above learning the less-than-glorious aspects of the undertaking. As he learned taxidermy from Bell, he became intimately familiar with organisms as he properly preserved their skins, bones, and feathers, adding substantially to his knowledge of anatomy and adding a new skill to his repertoire. He gained credibility as a natural historian who knew the craft from the inside out.

The type of personal mentoring that Roosevelt received from Bell is how many of the great naturalists learned their craft. Charles Darwin's path into science had been paved at the soirees held by his professor and mentor John Henslow, which brought him into contact with many influential scientists. Over time a more personal relationship grew between Henslow and Darwin, and they began taking lengthy walks during which they discussed all manner of issues in natural history and science. These constitutionals became so fertile and regular that they literally began to define Darwin: people referred to him as "the man who walks with Henslow."[36]

It wasn't simply in-person meetings that influenced Darwin, however. He described how the books of Alexander von Humboldt and John Herschel had "stirred up in me a burning zeal to add even the most humble contribution to the noble structure of Natural Science."[37] These men hadn't simply passed on facts and

Roosevelt looked up to Audubon as a youth, and his natural history studies reflected his devotion to the traditions of the great naturalists. Audubon's image of a belted kingfisher includes detailed insets of its foot and feathers, as well as a note indicating that the picture was made at the "Chute de l'Ohio" on July 15, 1808. Pastel, graphite, and ink on paper. MS Am 21(50), Houghton Library, Harvard University.

ideas through their written works; they had inspired Darwin to become one of their tribe. In turn, the written works of Darwin and others shaped Roosevelt, as he described how in his early studies he had "sat at the feet of Darwin and Huxley; and studied the large volumes in which Marsh's and Leidy's paleontological studies were embalmed."[38] Part of the value of these direct and indirect mentorships was the transmission of skills and knowledge; equally important was the identification with a larger set of values and attributes. In accessing these teachings, Roosevelt consumed theories and facts and also placed himself within a larger genealogy of the field. During his studies of taxidermy, Bell shared stories and anecdotes with him; Roosevelt, in turn, adopted some of the identity of Bell's lineage.[39]

Near the end of his life, Roosevelt recalled that he had long aspired to be a field man like Audubon.[40] In many ways, this would have been a sentiment shared with any naturalist chasing birds throughout the United States in the second half of the nineteenth century. Audubon was a giant in American natural history study, and his works on the birds and mammals of the region were nothing less than stunning. After his work with Bell, however, Roosevelt was no longer an outsider. He now could claim Audubon as somewhat of a naturalistic grandfather. Bell would have been able to provide an account—the kind that only a family member could—of how Audubon had planned his expeditions, undertaken rigorous observation and collecting in the field, and then returned to render nature in *The Birds of America* and other legendary works. This story of intense study and perseverance is an impeccable example of the type of detailed study and documentation of animals that Roosevelt was aspiring to in his own work.

When Audubon had kissed his wife and children goodbye in October of 1820 and began a yearlong trip down the Mississippi, he had commenced his serious study of North American birds.[41] In the pages of his own journal, he spread examples of his keen and perfectionistic work as a naturalist. As Audubon slowly floated south from Cincinnati in November, he "Shot a Beatifull *White headed Eagle*" and then spent four full days drawing it.[42] In mid-December he added natural history to his note on a marsh hawk (northern harrier) he had collected: "I have seen *flocks* of them travelling high and southwesterly—finding them Now plenty on these Shores where great deal of rich food is afforded them by the Numerous quantity of Swamp Sparrows."[43] Fifty years later, Roosevelt ascended Mount Regis in the Adirondacks and captured ornithological observations that followed the template of Audubon: "I also observed several red bellied nuthatches (Sitta canadensis) picking insects from the bark of the dead trees. They appeared to be perfectly indifferent as to whether they were on the upper or the lower side of a branch and I at first thought they were small woodpeckers."[44]

After his trip down the Mississippi, Audubon had used every opportunity to gather material for his project, even though he was regularly short of funds and needed to teach drawing lessons to support it.[45] Once his descriptions and paintings were complete, another herculean effort began. American publishers rejected his project, so he traveled to Europe numerous times to arrange for publication. Finally, the engraver Robert Havell agreed to take on the book, which took twelve years to complete.[46] The original folios contained only the illustrations, however, and Audubon began a separate effort in 1830 to complete his *Ornithological Biography*, which carefully laid out the natural history of each bird. This five-volume set was stuffed with information on each species; the account of the wild turkey alone fills the first seventeen pages of text.[47]

Audubon's extensive cycle of fieldwork had laid the base for his monumental contributions, and Roosevelt's exposure to the culture of hands-on natural history practiced by Audubon and Bell was as important as the technical points he learned as he wielded his scalpel and brush. This wasn't an implied part of the tradition. Audubon specifically addressed this issue for his students:

> But in forming works entirely with a view to distinguish the true from the false, nature *must* be seen first alive, and well studied, before attempts are made at representing it. Take such advantages away from the naturalist, who ought to be artist also, and he fails as completely as Raphael himself must have done, had he not fed his pencil with all belonging to a mind perfectly imbued with a knowledge of real forms, muscles, bones, movements, and, lastly, that spiritual expression of feelings that paintings like his exhibit so beautifully.[48]

Along with the field notes in his daily journal, Roosevelt also began a journal during this period, entitled "Notes on Natural History," that compiled information on his observations and collections.[49] His journal included descriptions and sketches made directly from nature. Over the next several years, Roosevelt branched out from birds and made numerous drawings in the style of Audubon's work on mammals.[50]

After he completed his work on birds, Audubon had turned his attention to the mammals of North America, the project in which he engaged Bell's assistance on the trip up the Missouri River. Again a massive undertaking, this fieldwork and painting resulted in a three-volume set, entitled *The Viviparous Quadrupeds of North America*, which contained 150 lithographs.[51] Roosevelt likely would have squirmed in discomfort if his drawings of moles and shrews were compared to those that appeared in *Quadrupeds*. Notwithstanding the obvious fact that he was not endowed with Audubon's artistic genius, the teenage Roosevelt admirably rendered the shrew *Sorex thompsoni* in a lifelike pose against a natural

(ABOVE) Roosevelt drew a pygmy shrew in its natural setting. (BELOW) Roosevelt's rendering of the mole "Scalops aquaticus" (*Scalopus aquaticus*) included three measured drawings of two paws and the snout. TRC MS Am 1541 (288).

landscape, much like the *Sorex* species Audubon had depicted in *Quadrupeds*.[52] In the drawings from his pre-college years, Roosevelt included the expanded features of organisms that are characteristic of Audubon's early paintings. Roosevelt's page on the common mole, *Scalopus aquaticus*, contains a three-part illustration that includes a magnified sketch of the head and two views of the feet, thus providing a window into the structure of the teeth and claws.[53] In a similar way, Audubon had added a detailed sketch of a feather on his otherwise polished painting of a belted kingfisher.[54] Roosevelt never described how much he directly modeled his own work on that of Audubon as he studied drawing. However, in making the sketches that accompanied his descriptions, he revealed how he followed the larger drawing tradition of which Audubon is an icon. The ability to draw was central to the identity of field naturalists of the time. Well before Audubon, Linnaeus had harped on the importance of this skill to his apostles:

> He should know that he will have done well by himself if he has acquired some skill in the *art of painting*, because a drawing of an object gives a better representation than a description, even though this may be done with the greatest precision.[55]

Those who had not developed their abilities to document the visual aspects of nature recognized their handicap; even Darwin bemoaned how his rudimentary drawing skills limited his ability to publish material from his voyage on the HMS *Beagle*.[56]

Preparing specimens and rendering them in words and drawings are only part of the skills of a naturalist. After lapsing for almost a year, Roosevelt returned to documentation when he was in the Adirondacks in the summer of 1871. Here, he again adopted the teachings of Linnaeus, this time as a student not of art but of linguistics.

At Lake George in August, Roosevelt described seeing a "bald-headed eagle" that was "sailing over the lake."[57] The entry includes the bird's scientific name with a slight misspelling that was characteristic of many of his notes: "*Halietus leucocephalus*." By including a scientific name, Roosevelt modeled another of the fundamental practices of naturalists and aligned his notes with the ones that

Audubon had made on bald eagles in his journal half a century before.[58] Together, both Roosevelt and Audubon followed Linnaeus.

Linnaeus is remembered partly for the names he bestowed on plants and animals. Within the pages of descriptions in his *Systema naturae*, Linnaeus proposed the name *Falco leucocaphalus* for the bald eagle.[59] Although its taxonomic placement later changed to the genus *Haliaeetus*, proper documentation of this animal will always bear his name: *Haliaeetus leucocephalus* (Linnaeus). Providing hundreds of new names for plants and animals, such as the bald eagle, is reason enough for historical reverence. But Linnaeus's accomplishment was far larger: he invented the entire system for naming, putting forth a template in which every species has a unique, two-part name. The first name, the genus, describes the group to which closely related organisms can belong. The second term, the "specific epithet," is a unique moniker for the species. Although these epithets are sometimes Latinized versions of names, as in the case of the ant later described as *Pheidole roosevelti*, many are chosen from Latin or Greek word roots that reflect attributes of the species. In the case of the bald eagle, the Greek root "leuco" refers to the white color, and "cephalus" denotes the head.[60]

It is hard to overestimate the importance of this parlance for an aspiring naturalist like Roosevelt. No longer did the various common names for species, such as Audubon's "white-headed eagle" and Roosevelt's "bald-headed eagle," need to create confusion among ornithologists. Nor did native languages. After Linnaeus, it didn't matter if one's native tongue was Swedish or French or English; all could communicate on equal terms. Although an exacting definition of "species" is elusive, a competent naturalist needs to be able to identify and describe which individuals interbreed— the most basic definition of "species"—in order to understand the variation, distribution, abundance, and behavior of particular organisms. Roosevelt extended this new mode of specificity to virtually all of the organisms he documented during this trip to the Adirondacks: "I also saw a kingfisher (beryle alcyon) dive for a fish and a mink (Putorius vison) swam across the stream while covys of quail (Orytx virgnianus) and grouse (Bonasa umbellus) rose from the banks."[61] As he was adopting the language of Linnaeus, Roosevelt also internalized another major aspect of the professional practice of natural history as he scratched away in his journal.[62]

Linnaeus's influence on the writing tradition of naturalists wasn't just about names. Throughout his copious notes Roosevelt adopted the spirit behind the laws of taxonomic nomenclature. It is almost as if he had read Linnaeus's explicit instructions to his apostles: "He should consider it incumbent upon him to *observe everything*, yet not in the way the simple horde does, but so that nothing escapes his sharp eyesight and rapt attention."[63] Linnaeus goes on to affirm the use of notebooks, and suggests that the collector "must never trust his often failing memory, but must immediately record all his observations in a notebook . . . and, until he has properly edited and written them all down on paper, he should not go to bed and sleep."[64] Never one who was much for sleep, Roosevelt profusely and accurately documented the natural history of the Adirondacks, thus beginning a long series of notebooks infused with Linnaean rigor.

Along with following in the Linnaean tradition of keeping accurate and abundant records, Roosevelt aligned himself with the mode of the great naturalists on another count. He had already experienced the fauna and flora of Europe through zoos, gardens, and a few field experiences, but he largely concentrated on developing a mastery of the nature of his home country. This was also a firm expectation of practicing naturalists: Louis Agassiz had described how "my highest ambition, at the time, was to be able to designate the plants and animals of my native country correctly by a Latin name, and to extend gradually a similar knowledge in its application to the productions of other countries."[65] Not a singular sentiment, the mastery and ownership of a naturalist's local fauna and flora again extended back to Linnaeus:

> A Swede in particular should bear in mind not to leave his own country until equipped with exceedingly solid knowledge of *natural history*, nor until he has observed with a keen eye different parts of his own country so as not to have to cross the river to fetch water and waste money in a foreign country to learn the things he had had the opportunity to learn at home, for free even.[66]

In the Adirondacks, Roosevelt documented his feverish work to learn the names and identities of the creatures of the northeastern

United States, from birds to mammals to amphibians, and he even paid attention to vegetation. He describes how he and West rode up to the falls near Ausable Forks in the back of a wagon and "would, whenever we saw a peculiarly beautiful lichen or moss jump off and get it."[67] In Dobbs Ferry in the summer of 1872, he captured a small frog that "afforded the entire family much amusement, being then let out, and put on the table, by the lamp," where it lunged at insects attracted to the light.[68] His notes and observations on the house sparrow, *Passer domesticus*, reflects seeds of his later dedication to conservation, as even then he could recognize how the wildlife of his home country was changing.[69] In addition to developing a mastery of the names and habits of these animals, Roosevelt began to get serious about understanding how other naturalists had documented their work in the scientific literature.

Throughout his life Roosevelt was a devoted bibliophile; he absorbed countless facts and ideas on natural history through books, in what his tutor Arthur Cutler later described as "his life long habit of omnivorous reading."[70] The sheer number of books that he consulted, at some points dabbling and at others diving in deep for extended nourishment, makes it difficult to pin down particular influences. But when Roosevelt visited Philadelphia in September of 1872, he reveled in the library at the Academy of Natural Sciences, where he "was allowed to have the run of all 38,000 books in its library."[71] Along with the works of Audubon, there are particular books that biographers have traced to his use during this time, such as Spencer Baird's *Mammals* and *Birds*, Nutall's *A Manual of Ornithology of the United States and Canada*, and Godman's *Natural History*.[72] The long and careful process of understanding what others in the community had documented in these and other sources allowed Roosevelt to identify each animal as he held it in his hands, as well as to begin to see what aspects about it were still unknown. In no way irrelevant, these early efforts to methodically study nature and understand the literature later allowed Roosevelt to make his own published contributions.

Roosevelt applied the lessons learned from these luminaries as he ambled in the wilds of New York state, describing treasures of nature like loons and leopard frogs. Equally important to his development as a naturalist, however, was the opportunity to exchange ideas with those of like mind. Roosevelt did have some access to Bell and Bickmore, and his uncles Robert Barnwell Roosevelt and Dr. Hilborne West were there to discuss science, but his peers were his main colleagues during his youth.[73] As the Roosevelt Museum grew, so did the interactions and exchanges among the boys who composed its Natural History Society. At a meeting in November of 1871, members adopted areas of specialty: one a geologist, antiquary, and anatomist; another a conchologist, taxidermist, and entomologist. Roosevelt remained the most general in his duties, and was simply dubbed a "naturalist," an apt title that foreshadowed his wide application of the traditions of natural history.[74] Over the next several years, this group of young naturalists met in the interstices of their individual collecting expeditions and family travels, and they shared their questions and ideas. Theodore gave his own presentations—one called "The Smaller Friends and Foes of Man," and another on migration and hibernation in vertebrates.[75] These meetings were about academic exchange: when "Mr. Eagle inquired do Cetaceans migrate," Roosevelt responded that "he thought that the Right whale did not but that the Sperm whale migrated in herds."[76] Although a youthful natural history society was not particularly unusual at the time, the fervor and professionalism that encircled this particular group was uncommon.[77] Just as natural history museums themselves had moved from cabinets of curiosities to rigorous institutions, so moved Roosevelt's interactions with his childhood peers. He developed a network that reinforced his love for studying nature in the field.

In his developing craft Roosevelt took direction, either in person or through the literature, primarily from those who had a substantial knowledge of natural history. The strong guiding hand of his father, however, gave more general nourishment to his love of nature and adventure. A businessman by trade, Theodore Sr. could not offer his son guidance on taxidermy or taxonomy. Instead, he created opportunities for his son to further his interest in natural history and to get outside. He made the flights from the city happen: to Loantaka, to the Adirondacks, and to Europe. He put his weight behind a museum that would bring natural history to youths, no doubt a nepotistic act. He presented books and materials, like Bailey's *Our Own Birds*, in many naturally inspired gifts he gave young Theodore.[78] Theodore Sr. also put his son in direct contact with professional scientists and naturalists who many adults would have found hard to access. Without specific knowledge to pass on, his father's most important influence may have been simply to help Theodore develop a love for life in the field and the traditions of natural history. John Burroughs, the eminent naturalist and prolific writer who later became close friends with Roosevelt, summed up in characteristic fashion what Theodore Sr. must have already known:

> Love sharpens the eye, the ear, the touch; it quickens the feet, it steadies the hand, it arms against the wet and the cold. What we love to do, that we do well. To know is not all; it is only half. To love is the other half.[79]

In early August, Theodore Sr. took his son deep into the Adirondack bush, and he helped instill this love as they ran their boats over rapids and made arduous portages. In the evenings they pitched their tents by the banks of rivers and cooked fresh trout over open fires. Roosevelt recorded a blissful end to one of these days as he was steeped in one of the most powerful of the American frontier stories: "Father read aloud to us from 'The Last of the Mohicans.' In the middle of the reading I fell asleep."[80] As he was lulled to sleep by the crackle of the fire and his father's voice, he was enveloped by the love and adventure of the field.

One week before he left for his next field expedition to Egypt and the Holy Lands, the thirteen-year old Roosevelt officially placed himself alongside the patrons of natural history. The *Annual Report of the American Museum of Natural History* for 1872 records how P. T. Barnum donated two snakes, one iguana, and a giraffe skull, and Albert Bickmore gave a mounted skeleton of Irish deer. Just after the names of these heavyweights appears a donation from "Mr. Theodore Roosevelt, Jr., New York City. 1 Bat, 12 Mice, 1 Turtle, 1 Skull, Red Squirrel, 4 Birds Eggs."[81] By lodging these specimens Roosevelt began to mark his own territory, as he now had the skills, knowledge, and pedigree to become a respected practitioner of the ancient craft of natural history.

Roosevelt's identity was one of excelling in action and knowledge; he was never a casual huntsman or a weekend birder. Later his

stream while coveys of quail(Ortyx
virginianus) and grouse(Bonasa
umbellus) rose from the banks.
We had to pass through
two small rapids and after
the last of these we pitched
our tents by another and
much larger rapids, down which
only one of our guides attempted
to go and he sprung a leak in
his boat. On the way we had
caught eight trout which we
had for supper. After supper
Father read aloud to us from
"The last of the Mohicans".
In the middle of the
reading I fell asleep. Father
read by the light of the
campfire.

While Roosevelt canoed and camped with his father and family in the late summer of 1871, he
absorbed narratives of adventure as his father read to him aloud from James Fenimore Cooper's
The Last of the Mohicans. TRC MS Am 1454.55 (7).

credibility was sometimes called into question, as when he dressed in a tailored Badlands hunting suit and when he unsheathed a Bowie knife made at Tiffany's.[82] Some grabbed hold of these examples and assumed that Roosevelt couldn't back up his image; they thought he was just pretending. Although he liked field finery, Roosevelt had paid the dues that allowed him to wear it proudly. As a young naturalist learning the traditions of the masters, he had soiled racks of shirts with dirt and blood, and covered piles of pants with arsenic and sweat. Those who went to the field with him knew that he was no poser. When John Burroughs later went birding with Roosevelt, he was astounded when his own knowledge of birds, his specialty, was matched by the president of the United States.[83] Roosevelt's early dedication to his craft allowed him to develop a lifelong identity that rested on intellectual power and a grounded competency in the field.

The word *craft* is often used to describe a narrow set of skills, a manual art or trade. In the larger sense, however, it refers to a branch of learning that requires special skills and knowledge. This broader meaning describes how the young Roosevelt adopted the practices of Bell, Audubon, Agassiz, and Linnaeus. He made collections, argued with his peers, talked science with his uncles, read voraciously, and was lovingly supported by his father as he took to the field to observe and record nature. Through these efforts he began to incorporate into his identity a rigorous and multifaceted woodcraft—literally, Roosevelt's own brand of the craft and practice of the woods—which became the driving force of his teenage field adventures.[84]

A Thousand Thoughts Awakened

The *Russia* landed in Liverpool on October 26, 1872, after a rough passage from New York, and the Roosevelts embarked on another extended family tour. Beginning with short stays in select cities in Western Europe, Theodore Sr. had arranged for his family to then spend four months exploring Egypt and the Holy Lands, after which Theodore, Elliott, and Corinne would stay in Dresden for the summer.

Just after arriving in the Old World, the younger Theodore aroused attention as he wandered through a Liverpool market looking for the ingredients he would need to prepare specimens.[1] Although arsenic was used for a variety of legitimate purposes, including the preservation of scientific specimens, any supplier knew that this substance could also be used as a slow and almost undetectable poison. This bespectacled, thirteen-year-old Yankee did not inspire confidence. To convince a shopkeeper to dispense the full pound of arsenic he requested, Roosevelt had to bring a witness to show that he "was not going to commit murder, suicide or any such dreadfull thing."[2] The seriousness of this substance was not lost on the young Roosevelt, however; he later described his own brush with this occupational hazard on the trip: "On one occasion when a well-meaning maid extracted from my taxidermist's outfit the old tooth-brush with which I put on the skins the arsenical soap . . . [she] partially washed it, and left it with the rest of my wash kit for my own personal use."[3] As he gathered materials and made preparations, Roosevelt—much more so than on his previous trip to Europe—was directing his own adventure.

Two days after he secured the ingredients for his soap, Roosevelt bought some snipe and partridges, his first specimens from Europe, which he skinned "with great success."[4] As they moved on through Brussels, Bonn, and Paris toward Egypt, Roosevelt continued to haunt markets "as usual" and purchased birds and rabbits for his collection.[5] In addition to his notebooks, Roosevelt gathered the appropriate tools for the upcoming adventures. On his birthday he was given "one bag, two pens, two pencils, one inkstand, two penknifes."[6] At fourteen, however, the newly equipped Roosevelt did not have the mindset of a tourist. He was a serious young explorer engaging in his craft. During his family expedition in Europe, Egypt, and the Holy Lands, Roosevelt put the skills and knowledge he had learned from his mentors into practice.

As he coasted toward Alexandria on the steamship *Poonah*, Roosevelt began to apply the mode of study that he had developed over the past two years working in Bell's shop and in the wilds of New York. Some of the importance of this expedition derived from what Roosevelt was doing, as he had started to collect and prepare specimens, using his substantial knowledge of the natural history of the New World to understand that of the Old. Much of the value, however, came from where he was doing it. As travelers learn, standing at the foot of a pyramid is fundamentally different from seeing an image of it or reading a description. Similarly, watching a jackal lounge on the floor of a muddy zoo does not equal seeing one scrambling over rocks in its natural environment. Meaning and inspiration derive from pungent smells and gritty textures. As Roosevelt arrived in Egypt, he recorded in his journal how he was moved by his direct connection with this land:

> At eight oclock we arrived in sight of Alexandria. How I
> gazed on it! It was Egypt, the land of my dreams; Egypt
> the most ancient of all countries! A land that was old when
> Rome was bright, was old when Babylon was in its glory, was
> old when Troy was Taken! It was a sight to awaken a thou-
> sand thoughts, and it did.[7]

Rarely did Roosevelt put so much exclamation in his notebooks; the sensation of being in the place where exotic animals lived and things of significance actually happened exhilarated him. At Pompey's pillar that afternoon, he was literally left speechless:

"On seeing this stately remain of former glory, I <u>felt</u> a great deal but I <u>said</u> nothing. You can not express yourself on such an occasion."[8] At least a portion of these "thousand thoughts" related to the impressions of a young boy seeing firsthand the remnants of failed civilizations, too—a subject that would preoccupy him as he later considered the fate of the country he himself would lead.

The Roosevelts left Cairo on the morning of December 3 for the two-hour trek to see the pyramids at Giza. After arriving, they visited the "Sphynx" and then climbed the Great Pyramid.[9] One can imagine Roosevelt marveling at how an ancient people could have possibly stacked and placed the massive blocks—ones that he struggled even to climb. And the view over the Nile River valley and the Sahara Desert was astounding. From the top, Theodore beheld the "perfectly magnificent" sight of the green Nile River valley on one side and the uneven Sahara on the other, describing in his journal that the sight "gives one some what the same feeling as to look over the ocean or over one of the North American Prairies."[10] Standing on such ancient sites, Roosevelt experienced how being in the field and looking back can put one's own position and experience in stark relief. And his perch wasn't just a beautiful one; he was about to learn that he was sitting atop the site of a major recent discovery.

Three hundred feet below the pyramid's apex and encased by its more than two million granite blocks sits what is still known as the "Queen's Chamber," a room initially believed to be the burial site of King Khufu's bride. Just a few months before Roosevelt's visit, a group of men had methodically chipped away on the chamber's south side. They inserted a long wire into the crack just above the second block from the floor, and found an open space on the other side.[11] Once they had opened a significant hole in the five-inch-thick wall, the pyramid inhaled in a way it had not in more than four thousand years. Clutching a candle, one man wedged his hand and head inside the opening and reported that the passage extended horizontally for about seven feet and then began to ascend upward. This discovery was one of the most important in the pyramid in decades.

Because they knew of twin shafts that similarly rose skyward from the King's Chamber well above them in the pyramid, the

We then (with Corrinne, and Anna)
entered the pyramid.
We first went up
the side for some
distance and then dived
into a low passage
which slanted abr down
very much and was excessively
smooth and slippery, being
only broken here and
there by an indentation
in the rock Down this
we went slipping and
sliding and finally
reached the bottom
where an enormous stone
block stopped the
ongoing passage and
one had been cut
around. The atmosphere
was now perfectly stifling.
and try now to had to
the horrors began to ascend,
and as I had no
guide It could not keep

up with the rest as I was continually stopp falling from the floor being so smooth, or so great an incline, and the section from being forced to bend double. At last they stopped by in a small chamber and he caught up with them. We now came to the well which was situated somewhat like this. 1, passage, 2, well, 3 chamber, 4 elevated ridge, 5,5,5,5, walls. To pass this well we had to go on the little ridge which was not two feet wide, without railing or rope, on a great incline, perfectly smooth and with only some notches in the stone to at intervals of about thirty inches to put your heels in, men moved to the same position on the north wall of the Queen's Chamber and excavated a hole that revealed a second shaft, similar in design to the one they had just discovered. They fired pistols into both openings and determined that the passages were not open to the sky at their other ends, and they puzzled about the reason for their existence. Their colleague in Britain, Charles Piazzi Smyth, had assumed that these structures in the King's Chamber allowed air to flow into the pyramid—the reason why they are still referred to as "air shafts"—but this team, led by Waynman Dixon, showed that these passages were not open to the outside.[12] After the dust settled from the initial opening of the shafts, Dixon and his men continued to explore these spaces and found several intriguing objects in the south passage.

The three significant objects that Dixon found in the rubble could all fit into a cigar box; yet despite their small size, they were another major clue in piecing together the history of the pyramid and its people. One was a gray granite ball, in the form of "an orange squeezed somewhat out of its natural shape," that was likely used by King Khufu's engineers as a measuring device.[13] Close to this ball Dixon found a piece of a cedar rod five inches long, a fragment from a measuring rule or hand tool. Finally, there was a bronze hook that resembled a modern grappling hook, which seemed to have been a ceremonial implement.[14] Dixon sent these artifacts off to Smyth in the fall of 1872, and the findings were published in the highly esteemed journal *Nature*.[15]

The excitement of these discoveries spurred Dixon on; he continued to work to uncover the secrets of the pyramids in the following months. Although this was not his sole occupation, he made a home in a tomb on the west field of the pyramid complex.[16] Like his successors, he found that the cool temperatures and convenient location of one of these empty tombs provided a relatively comfortable existence. Just steps outside his door he could gaze on the magnificent prospect of the pyramid complex. If he had done so on December 3, just three weeks before his discoveries were published, he would have seen a family with a teenage son making their way down the four-foot steps from the Great Pyramid's apex.

The Roosevelts climbed down the Great Pyramid—which Theodore referred to by its Greek name "Cheops"—and took a restful lunch as they prepared to be challenged by the mysteries that were buried inside. After eating, the family walked into the west field of tombs next to the pyramid, and in his journal Roosevelt casually described how he "visited an English gentleman who has made a home (and a most comfortable one) in a tomb, for the purpose of scientific investigation of the Pyramids. He has already discovered two small passages which he thinks will lead to something more."[17] Roosevelt's field notes suggest that after only hours at the pyramids, he engaged with the chief explorer on the site, Dixon.[18] It may well have been Theodore Sr.'s standing as a prominent businessman that allowed the Roosevelts to obtain an individual meeting with Dixon, and, given his recent discoveries, they were certainly treated to a firsthand account of their importance to Egyptological studies. Once again, Theodore Sr. had, as with Bickmore and Bell, placed his son in the company of great explorers.

His interest piqued by Dixon, Roosevelt set out to investigate the internal mysteries of the pyramid. Using the maps of the pyramid that Dixon made that year and Roosevelt's own account in his journal, one can follow Roosevelt's path. He and his family first went slipping and sliding down the main passage into the pyramid, and then made an arduous ascent toward the well. Roosevelt had difficulty keeping up with the others, as he "was continually falling from the floor being so smooth on so great an incline, and from being forced to bend double."[19] He then struggled up the Grand Gallery—a massive passageway with high ceilings— to the King's Chamber on his "hands and knees," with "the way being so excessively slippery."[20] It was rough going, and although Roosevelt was taxed by grasping for foot- and handholds with only the light of candles held by his guides, he still made careful observations. Squadrons of bats dipped and dived close to his head; their "sharp cries seemed literally to pierce the ear."[21] In a later notebook, Roosevelt described these annoying denizens as *Taphozous perforatus*, a species that "frequents the Pyramids and ruined temples and is often a great nuisance flying into your face and clinging to your hair."[22] Once they reached the King's Chamber, they beheld the massive sarcophagus of red sandstone in which King Khufu's mummy had been laid to rest. The room was virtually empty, though, since the pyramid had been looted repeatedly over a thousand years. Despite its lack of gold and jewels, the King's

Chamber still was a treasure, and Roosevelt noted what he would have learned in his meeting with Dixon: a small hole in the wall was a shaft "pointing to the north star," which had a function similar to that of the passages Dixon had just discovered in the Queen's Chamber.[23] Roosevelt applied his skills of observation and note taking in this ancient Egyptian ruin, and was driven by a desire to experience and understand. He left the Great Pyramid completely exhausted, but, unlike in his explorations of the caves near Albano, Italy, two years before, he had not been rushed and he did not leave unsatisfied.

In Egypt Roosevelt came to a new understanding of history and time. Even before he went to the pyramids, he had already begun to recalibrate his concept of age and size. He was not particularly impressed with the almost seventy-foot tall Cleopatra's Needle, because it "was not very large" and "not very old—for Egypt. Only about two thousand years."[24] Later in the trip, he was struck by the "ancient belish at Ohn or Heliopilis" as "it is hard to think of a block of stone, which is 6000 (or at anyrate 4000) years old, and which perhaps Abraham has seen!"[25] Instead of just reading about Biblical figures, Roosevelt was now connecting with them through actual objects and places. In a mosque in Jerusalem, he viewed what was believed to be one of the actual footprints of Jesus Christ.[26] Ever critical, Roosevelt's expanding worldview developed in parallel with his dedication to rigorous interpretation, and when someone pointed out a tree under which Mary and Joseph had rested, Roosevelt recorded an incredulous "but I doubt this" in his journal.[27]

Entwined with his expanding appreciation of history was the experience of retracing the epic discoveries made in the ground over which he walked. Roosevelt the polymath would have relished the fact that as he descended into Belzoni's tomb at Thebes, he was following in the footsteps of a former strongman and performer.[28] Despite his quirky credentials, Giovanni Belzoni had had both a fervent interest in ancient Egypt and a knack for finding tombs. So when he gazed at a curious hillside in Thebes fifty years before Roosevelt's visit, he directed a skeptical group of workers to begin digging. Once they were eighteen feet below ground, Belzoni's hunch was confirmed, and the door of an incredible tomb stood before him.[29] He entered a long corridor filled with stunning hieroglyphics, and there Belzoni found the burial chamber of Seti I, complete with a translucent alabaster sarcophagus. As Roosevelt followed these same steps, he described the magnificent display: "Paintings were in Italio and represented sowing, planting, battles, amusements &c &c."[30] Although he visited other tombs, he saw "none so important."[31] As he left Belzoni's tomb with the spread wings of the vulture goddess Nekhbet looking over him, Roosevelt continued to absorb the power of place.

Ten days after his exploration of the Great Pyramid, Roosevelt's father took him out shooting near Cairo, and on this day the identity of the young hunter-naturalist ratcheted forward one huge notch. In a "walk of a hundred yards" he "procured two small warblers and blew a chat to pieces"; one of these birds was the first he ever shot.[32] No longer was he limited to swooping clumsily with nets, bumbling with sticks to knock nests from high limbs, or simply purchasing specimens. On this morning Roosevelt began to engage in the practice of shooting birds, so important to his heroes like Audubon and Bell, and he was "proportionately delighted."[33] The experience added a whole new facet to his field persona, one that has created no end of perplexity for those who have attempted to comprehend him. In his journal account of that day, Roosevelt himself laid out this tension.

After he shot his first bird that morning, Roosevelt took a break to watch a performance of the howling dervishes. Far from delighted with their performance, Theodore found that all of the "staggering about, shrieking and foaming at the mouth" was the "most barbarous sight [he had] ever seen."[34] Afterwards, he grabbed a gun, went out, and shot a yellow wagtail. This boy of fourteen was genuinely delighted by the experience of shooting an animal. It is possible that the howling dervishes themselves—in chorus with Mark Twain and so many other later critics—would have suggested that Roosevelt was, in fact, the one who was barbaric for shooting such a beautiful little bird. This judgment, however, obscures understanding.

Roosevelt's accounts of collecting as a young boy in Egypt provide a window on his field persona before it was complicated by the politics of conservation and hunting. Many have endeavored

Roosevelt made a series of drawings and watercolors in the 1870s, some of which related to his collections from his trip to Egypt and the Holy Lands. Here he illustrated an adult male bird he placed in the genus *Fringilla*—what was then known as the willow sparrow. It is now known as the Spanish sparrow (*Passer hispaniolensis*, with synonyms including *Fringilla salicicola* and *Passer salicarius*). TRC MS Am 1541 (288).

to understand why humans are driven to hunt, considering factors such as sustenance, sport, a drive for manliness, an innate biological desire, collection for scientific purposes, a desire to connect with and observe animals directly, conservation, or even, as John Muir suggested, a juvenile immaturity on the part of the hunter.[35] Certainly, several different forces can motivate a person to hunt at any one time, and the relative importance of these forces changes between trips and over a lifetime. Roosevelt hunted extensively throughout his life, and in his field notes and published writings we can find evidence for various forces—some that seem in conflict— that drove him to the hunting field.

In his days near the Nile, Roosevelt reported that he—as have so many others throughout history—enjoyed the challenge and experience of shooting animals, and his keen descriptions and dedication to keeping these specimens for his own collection suggest that at this time, natural science was a major driver of these early hunting adventures. Roosevelt wasn't simply out for blood;

This puts me in mind of a tailor's pair of pantaloons. Ground colour black, 1, dark blue, 2, light blue. 3, brown, 4 reddish, 5, 5, 5, 5, 5, 5, 5, 5, small tears and patches.

Now that I am on the subject of dress I may as well mention that the dress of the inhabitants up to ten years of age is — nothing. After that they put on a shirt made descended from some remote ancestor — and never take it off till the day of their death.

Mother is recovering from an attack of indigestion, but the rest are all well and send love to you and our friends, in which I join sincerely, and remain

Your Most Affectionate Nephew

T Roosevelt

a (5)

As he collected throughout Egypt, Roosevelt also related his adventures to relatives in the United States. In a letter to his Aunt Anna from Kom Ombos in January of 1873, he described his collecting and its effects: "The sporting is injurious to my trousers." TRC MS Am 1454.48 (5).

he was entranced both by his specimens and by his observations: he stopped to watch a rare white-tailed plover without firing a shot. And in page after page of his field notes he left evidence that much of what drove him to hunt birds was his desire to understand their morphology, evolution, and behavior. December hunts near Cairo were only the beginning; at Christmas his father gave him a "beautiful" double-barreled shotgun that he put to immediate use as they sailed up the Nile.[36]

Overlooking the sand and granite of the Ramesseum in Thebes and carrying his new shotgun, Roosevelt could not have been inconspicuous even if he had tried. He raised his shotgun to his shoulder, and fired at a small bird. Any of the other tourists visiting the site who turned their heads at the shot would have noticed a small red and brown bird plummeting to the ground. As he approached, Roosevelt noticed that it was a species he hadn't seen before in Egypt, the red-tailed chat.

In his journal and notebooks Roosevelt recorded the scene and the contours of the animal: an "indistinct white line extends from the bill to the eye" and the "rump and tail coverts are rufus brown."[37] At the end of the description, however, he made a casual note that illuminates how his collecting was embedded within his larger explorations of the ancient sites of Egypt. Roosevelt describes that this bird was "perched on a column of the Rameseum at Thebes."[38] And this wasn't the only specimen he shot while there. In the following days he "procured a vinous grosbeak, a sand-lark, four chats, a crested lark, a ringed plover and a dove."[39] Today this would be unthinkable, but the attitude toward the sites of antiquities was much different in the 1870s. This monument to the great Pharaoh Ramesses II, like most of the treasures of antiquity, had already suffered incredible insults. For example, Belzoni himself had been in the Ramesseum in 1817 to undertake the significant challenge of carting off a seven-ton bust of Ramesses II to the British Museum. Putting aside any concerns regarding methods of appropriation, Belzoni didn't think twice about destroying ancient stonework. To remove the massive artifact they needed to "break the bases of two columns."[40] Like Belzoni, Roosevelt went about his work in the context of the day's approach to Egyptian historical sites, and the primary aspect for him was collecting and understanding birds.

The collection of birds went hand in hand with studying their habits, and Roosevelt didn't rely on his observations alone. Just a few weeks after he plucked the chat from the column in the Ramesseum, he collected a bird that was at the time called the spur-winged plover, "*Charadrius spinosus*"—Roosevelt's "zic-zac"—and entered into an ancient debate on its natural history.[41]

Given that it touches on birds, fierce predators, and hunting, the lore of the bird known to the ancient Greeks as the "trochilus" was just the kind of natural history that Roosevelt loved.[42] In the fifth century BCE, the Greek historian Herodotus described how the trochilus was a sort of feathered dentist that cleaned the leech-infested maws of crocodiles. Herodotus explained that it was a peaceful association between bird and reptile, and when the lazy crocodile "leaves the water and comes out upon the land . . . at such times the trochilus goes into his mouth and devours the leeches."[43] Herodotus's interpretation persisted for centuries, at least until a passionate young student named Gardner Wilkinson arrived in Egypt from Oxford in 1821, shortly after Ramesses's granite head had been rolled out of the Ramesseum.[44]

Wilkinson spent twelve years in Egypt, and along with his academic work he brought the language, ceremonies, and funeral rites of Egyptians to the layman in his five-volume *The Manners and Customs of the Ancient Egyptians*. He even touched on the nature of Egypt, and in this work he weighed in on the ornithological debate about the trochilus:

> Herodotus enters into a detail of the habits of the crocodile, and relates the frequently repeated story of the *trochilus* entering the animal's mouth during its sleep on the banks of the Nile, and relieving it of the leeches whic hadhere [*sic*] to its throat. The truth of this assertion is seriously impugned, when we recollect that leeches do not abound in the Nile; and the polite understanding said to subsist, between the crocodile and the bird becomes more improbable, when we examine the manner in which the throat of the animal is formed. [45]

Wilkinson continues with his explanation of the myth's origin:

> That birds living on flies frequently flit about the crocodile,
> while lying on the sand, we can readily believe: and this cir-
> cumstance, as well as the presence of a small *running* bird, a
> species of *charadrius*, which is often seen on the same bank,
> and which, loudly chirping on the approach of man, may be
> supposed to warn the crocodile of danger, very possibly led
> to the fable of those visits of the *trochilus*, and the friendly
> services it rendered the sleeping crocodile."[46]

As he observed this bird, Roosevelt consulted Wilkinson's ideas
either directly or through his main ornithological source for the
region, the Rev. Alfred Charles Smith's *The Nile and Its Banks.*[47]

In considering the identity of the spur-winged plover, which
is known today as the spur-winged lapwing, Roosevelt sided with
Smith and Wilkinson, recording how "the trochilus, ziczac, or
crocodile bird is <u>the</u> bird of the Nile" and is "the true trochilus
of Herodotus, both because of its present habits and because it
can be seen in the picture[s] on the temples of Egypt."[48] However,
dental service, the most captivating part of the zic-zac's reputed
behavior and the one that interested Herodotus, gets only a passing mention by Roosevelt. In agreement with Smith, he suggests:
"The arabs still give to it the office of Dentist to the crocodile."[49]
Given his lifelong passion for dissecting complex aspects of animal behavior, Roosevelt would have been interested to know that
Herodotus should not have been so easily dismissed by Wilkinson
on at least one count. In fact, leeches do abound in the Nile, and
these bloodsuckers do feed in clusters inside the dental sockets of
crocodiles.[50] The actual taxonomic identity of Herodotus's trochilus is ambiguous; he could have been referring to the spur-winged
lapwing, the Egyptian plover (*Pluvianus aegyptius*), or a related
species. Regardless of the exact identity—whether Roosevelt's "zic-
zac" was the trochilus or not—claims about the dental services of
these birds have received limited confirmation since the time of
Roosevelt's visit, and seem at best rare behaviors.[51]

Roosevelt was most interested in the peculiar cries that Wilkinson suggests generated the bird's name of "zic-zac," and which
serve as a warning device for the animals of the Nile. Even though

he wasn't out for big game on this trip, Roosevelt, now armed with his own shotgun, had quickly absorbed hunting as an element of his identity:

> To the hunter after large game it is most annoying. You are
> nearly within shot of your game, when a ziczac observes
> you. It immediately starts up from the ground, and com-
> mences to utter a series of sharp, clacking cries as though
> a very strong, but cracked watchmans rattle was going off.
> This would be bad enough, even if it flew immediately off,
> but the idea of doing so never enters its head, for it soars
> over your head, wheels rapidly round and runs by the game,
> apparently for the purpose of starting it, brushes by your
> face, and the meanwhile, its shrieks would scare a blind
> donkey.[52]

It would have been easy for Roosevelt to fully agree with Wilkinson's explanation that the pestering shrieks of the zic-zac existed as a warning mechanism for the crocodiles. But he was too good a naturalist to let this kind of storytelling stand without closer investigation. He continued the report in his notebook with an explanation that "this office of watcher is quite involuntary however, for it goes through the same performance, even if no animal is near." Throughout the sites of antiquities Roosevelt continued to collect widely, and he applied his rigorous craft as he communed with the region's great historians.

After returning from their Nile cruise and visiting the Holy Lands, the Roosevelts visited Damascus in mid-March. In the rocky landscape outside this city, Roosevelt's developing skills in hunting, riding, and natural history allowed him to experience a gripping adventure, and the immediate account in his daily journal reflects new spirit and confidence. On that day, Roosevelt went hunting in the plains outside of Damascus and undertook an epic chase:

> Damascus. March 17th 1873 Monday.
>
> Today was showery. We lunched near the beautiful fountain
> of Fijih. Afterwards I had quite a nice hunt. Just as we were

The trochilus, y zic-zac, or crodile bird is the bird of the Nile. Not only is it very c abundant there, but it is also very bold and conspicuous, so that it is almost impossible not to notice. Besides the bold contrast of black, white and brown on its plumage, and its very erect carriage render it a marked and conspicuous bird anyhow. I think that is this is the true trochilus of Herodotus, both because of its present habits and because it can be seen in the pictured on the temples of Egypt, while the Egyptian plover (which is usually given as the Trochilus) has not yet been found there according to Sir. G. Wilkinson, who gives a very exhaustive account of the temples. The arabs

(ABOVE AND FACING) Roosevelt recorded detailed observations and information about the birds he saw and collected in Egypt and in his other travels in two notebooks he labeled "Remarks on Birds." In his account of *Charadrius spinosus*, the spur-winged plover or "zic-zac"—now known as the spur-winged lapwing— he wades into a debate that dates back to Herodotus on whether this bird in fact serves the "office of Dentist to the crocodile." TRC MS Am 1454.33.

still *we* give to it the office of Dentist to the crocodile. Their *name* of Zigzag is derived from its very peculiar cry. It is found indiscriminately ~~on~~ on the sandbanks of the Nile or in the adjacent fields, but not on high ground, for in Egypt there is no high ground except the desert. Its food consists of worms, insects, etc.

To the hunter after large game it is most annoying. You are nearly within shot of your game, when a zigzac observes you. It immediately starts up from the ground, ~~c~~ and commences to utter a series of sharp, clacking cries, as though a very strong, ~~but~~ *cracked* watchmans rattle was going off. This would be bad enough, even if it flew coming on to a plain, Boutross (our under dragman) and myself were far ahead of the rest of the cavalcade, when we suddenly saw a long distance ahead of us a struggling crowd of vultures, and soon made out a couple of jackals. We increased our pace and bore down on them. The jackals made off, and the vultures flew up into the air as we approached, and we reached the remains of the carcass of a goat at the same time with a couple of peasants, who informed us that the goat was theirs, which had been killed by the jackals. We now put our horses to a gallop and made after the jackals who (each with a piece of goat in his mouth) had gotten such a long start of us that, we could not catch up with them. Finally they stopped on a hill, and we got into a valley trying to stalk them. I had just given the gun to Bootrous, while I arranged my bridle when the jackals came in sight and he was off like a flash while I followed, shouting for my gun. He did not hear me and kept on. Bootross was on bad ground and could not get near enough to shoot, but I went much faster and was soon near the beasts. They seperated, and I went after the largest, thinking to ride over him and then kill him with a club. On we went over hills, and through gulleys, where none but a Syrian horse could go. I gained rapidly on him and was within a few yards of him when a leaped over a cliff some fifteen feet high, and while I made a detour around he got in among some rocky hills where I could not get at him. I killed a large vulture afterwards.[53]

Like the shooting of his first bird, this jackal hunt reveals underlying elements that fueled Roosevelt's desire for adventure and his identity as a hunter-naturalist. Although the first traces of adventure narrative had appeared in his early journals and notebooks when he described a bear encounter in the Catskills and recounted stories of Indian battles, in this account from Damascus his writing began to sparkle with narrative detail and the love of the chase. Here, Roosevelt revealed how the challenge and sport of hunting, and the collecting of stories that would later emerge from the chase, also motivated him. The passages also conveyed raw emotion, as in the account of how he took out his frustration on an unlucky vulture. This fusion of natural history exploration, hunting, and writing whetted Roosevelt's appetite for more. Throughout his later life, he repeatedly sought this integrated experience as he ranged over the Badlands, the plains of Africa, and the waters of the Amazon basin.

The adventure in Damascus culminated the active part of the Roosevelts' Old World expedition. The family next sailed through Greece to Dresden, where Theodore would spend the summer studying with a host family named Minkwitz.[54]

Dresden was a departure from Roosevelt's natural history explorations among the awe-inspiring sights of Egypt and the Holy Lands. He studied harder than he had "ever studied before in [his] life."[55] Studies began at 7:30 a.m. and continued until 10 p.m., except for breaks for lunch and coffee and a long pause in the late afternoon. He studied German, French, mathematics, and drawing. At times he was "all most frantic" in juggling the grammar and words of the foreign languages.[56] Even amid his rigorous studies however, Roosevelt found time for action.

He swam the Elbe. He boxed vigorously with his cousin John Elliott, sometimes seeing stars and at others being left with a black eye.[57] The children also had a writing club where they would share poems and stories of their own creation.[58] Ever the naturalist, Roosevelt still labored for his museum—even signing a letter home as "Sec[retary] & Libr[arian] of R[oosevelt] M[useum]"—and worked on expanding its collections.[59]

In June, Roosevelt reported to his father that he had gone on an "excursion" to collect butterflies and beetles on a castle grounds.[60] Later that month he reported progress: "My collection is going on beautifully (40 animals and 220 coins, and a few German Natural Historyies) and so is our club."[61] Despite offering him the opportunity to work on his drawings with a painter named Wegener, the Minkwitz family, like his own, had reservations about being an outpost of the Roosevelt Museum.[62] At one point Roosevelt wrote to his aunt Anna about how his animal husbandry had become an issue: "My scientific pursuits cause the family a good deal of consternation. My arsenic was confiscated and my mice thrown (with the tongs) out of the window."[63] Not without a sense of humor, Roosevelt described his retaliation for the wickedness of these

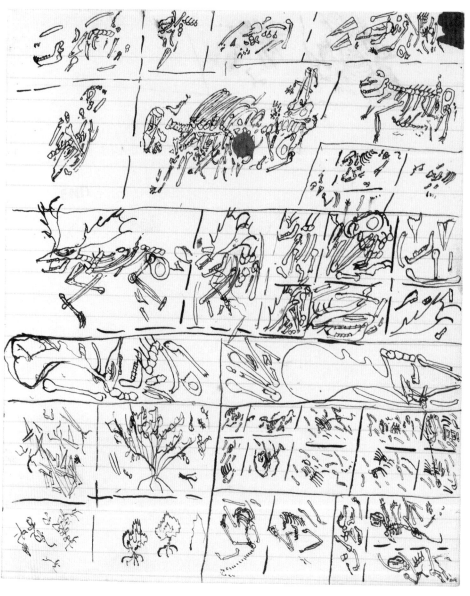

Several pages after he described attending the Great Exposition in Vienna on May 12, 1873, where he viewed "a number of cases of skulls, packets of skins, large models of ships, and miniatures of countries," Roosevelt filled a page of his journal with sketches of disarticulated animal skeletons. TRC MS Am 1454.55 (8).

measures, drawing a sketch of himself waving a mouse in the face of his adversaries.

Roosevelt described his period in Dresden this way: "Health; good. Lessons; good. Play hours bad. Appetite good. Accounts; good. Clothes; greasy. Shoes; holey. Hair; more 'a la Mop' than ever. Nails; dirty in consequence of having an ink bottle upset over them; Library; beautiful. Museum; so-so. Club; splendid."[64] Roosevelt included plenty of humorous assessments and scenes as he melded natural history and daily events in his letters to his family from abroad, but he also revealed that his mind was gravitating toward theory as well. And in the 1870s there was no hotter biological topic than the theory of evolution.

At the end of a letter to his mother on October 5, 1873, Roosevelt drew a sketch of a crane with a fish in its mouth linked by three selective steps to a curly-headed boy named "Theodore" reading a book about fish, in the one-legged avian pose he often assumed while reading.[65] He similarly related his brother Elliott to a bustard, and in a final sequence he showed the transmutational relationships of a wren with "Johnie," his cousin John Elliott. In a second set of sketches he was related to a giraffe, and he culminated the letter with his signature: "Your aff. Son / Cranibus Giraffirus." In these sketches, Roosevelt built upon the ruminations on evolution that he had already brought into his personal worldview in an earlier letter to his sister, with similar sketches.[66]

Charles Darwin had published his views on evolution in the *Origin of Species* the year after Roosevelt was born, and this concept—simple on its surface, and a tangle of unsolved mysteries below—fascinated Roosevelt. Although the theory of evolution by natural selection was only thirteen years old when Roosevelt was in Dresden, it was at the forefront of discussions throughout diverse elements of society. Although not always well accepted, the idea of the process of evolution had been debated for centuries. However, what Darwin (along with Alfred Russel Wallace) put forth was a new mechanism by which that process took place: natural selection.[67] Even though this mechanism was the new scientific element, the main reaction to Darwin and Wallace related to the overall process of evolution; its implications penetrated deep into the collective human psyche. The public debate in the years after

My scientific pursuits cause
the family a good
deal of consternation.
My arsenic was confiscated
and my mice thrown (with
the tongs) out of the window.
In cases like this I would
approach a refractory female,
mouse in hand, corner her,
and bang the mouse very
near her face untill she
was thoroughly convinced of
the wickedness of her actions.
Here is a view of such a scene.

By the way, Mother and
Bamie have gone to Carlsbad.
Aunt Lucy is here and we go to
see her every Sunday Afternoon.

this theory broke often focused on a lingering and inflammatory question: If evolution really had taken place, where did that leave humans? The thought of humans evolving from lowly creatures, and especially of having apes in the bloodline, was truly an uncomfortable idea for many. Theodore Roosevelt, however, was comfortable, even playful, as he engaged evolutionary theory and traced his own origins.

These cartoons about the prehistory of Rooseveltian origins could have been inspired by many takes on evolution that were widely circulating during the 1860s and 1870s. One of most famous was the frontispiece in Thomas Henry Huxley's *Evidence as to Man's Place in Nature,* which cleverly lined up the skeletons of four currently living primates behind that of a human, obviously implying that the human and the other primates shared a common ancestor.[68] Brilliantly, Huxley placed the skeletons in a line that seemed to approximate a time-lapse view of the transmutation of an apelike animal into a man.[69] Roosevelt did one better. Instead

(FACING) During the months that Roosevelt spent studying in Dresden after his trip to Egypt and the Holy Lands, he still maintained his devotion to natural history collecting and his own museum. He even kept live animals, much to the chagrin of his host family. In a letter to his Aunt Anna in June of 1873, he described the conflict over his mice in words and sketches. TRC MS Am 1454.48 (6). (ABOVE) During the 1870s, Roosevelt worked on his illustration skills, including depictions of rodents. TRC MS Am 1541 (288).

of lining up a series of relatives to imply a chain of descent, he drew the intermediate forms.

Although the frontispiece to *Man's Place in Nature* may be the best known of these human evolution images, the many other cartoons and caricatures on evolution that appeared in newspapers and magazines throughout the world were also possible antecedents to Roosevelt's drawings.[70] Those portraying the nested evolution of animate and inanimate objects, such as a woodcut by Charles Bennett that appeared in the *Illustrated Times* in 1863, were similar to Roosevelt's use of the fish coming out of a bird's beak and into a book. In his own sketches Roosevelt also incorporated caricature, which was ubiquitous in many published cartoons. Just as Darwin's unruly beard and bald head were easily exaggerated, Roosevelt's own frazzled hair and spindly frame provided a self-deprecating target. Roosevelt would never have imagined that this sketch would anchor a long tradition of caricatures of his own distinctive countenance, and that in volume and distribution they would rival those depicting the old man of evolution himself.[71]

Following in the footsteps of Darwin and Huxley, Roosevelt embraced the concept of evolution. Over the course of the ensuing decades, the mechanism of natural selection profoundly affected his thinking about the rise and fall of human societies and races as well. Roosevelt repeatedly related the idea of natural selection to his thinking of the growth and development of societies. In his 1895 review of Kidd's *Social Evolution*, there is a striking example of how he used the concept of natural selection to try to make sense of the ontogeny of societies:

> In civilized societies the rivalry of natural selection works against progress. Progress is made in spite of it, for progress results not from the crowding out of the lower classes by the upper, but on the contrary from the steady rise of the lower classes to the level of the upper, as the latter tend to vanish, or at most barely hold their own.[72]

Roosevelt was certainly not alone in applying the ideas that grew out of Darwin's revolution to societies, and his thinking about the struggle for existence was also intertwined with his ideas on race.[73] As we trace back the roots of his writings we can imagine a preco-

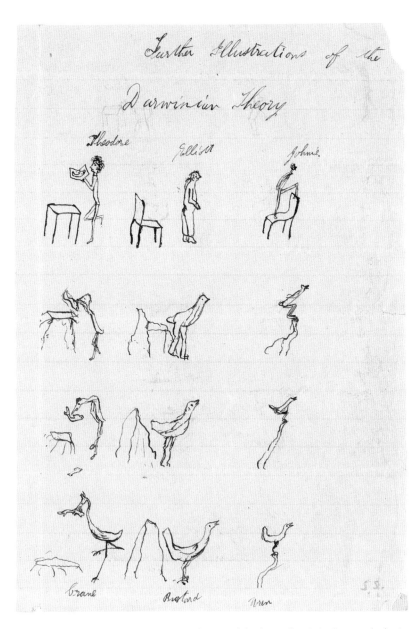

Charles Darwin and Alfred Russel Wallace had proposed the theory of evolution by natural selection the year Roosevelt was born, and it was very much on Roosevelt's mind during the time he was studying in Dresden. In a letter to his mother, he playfully documented the potential evolutionary relationships of himself and his playmates to various animals. TRC MS Am 1454.48 (20).

cious boy—even then one who others predicted was destined for the presidency—rifling through stacks of magazines, newspapers, and notebooks on natural history in 1873 Dresden.[74] And the influence upon him of ideas such as natural selection was powerful partly because he was becoming a true naturalist, a boy who was at home in the field and who, given his firsthand observations, understood how organisms struggled for survival.

Armed with popular media, scientific texts, specimens, pencils, and his own journals, Roosevelt surged ahead in his development during the months he spent in Africa, the Middle East, and Europe. When he again returned to New York Harbor after a long absence, he was ready to undertake an extended run of fieldwork that would allow him to evolve from an interested child into an active contributor in the scientific rendering of the natural world.

Finding a Home

Complete with patched and stained pantaloons, Roosevelt hauled his luggage off the *Russia* in New York Harbor on November 5, 1873. His bags bulged with feathered skins and a set of writings that would provide a starting point for real academic work. After setting foot on the dock, he began a period of his life in which he immersed himself in the nature of the northeast, crisscrossing the corridor between Long Island and the Adirondacks. With his growing set of skills and experiences, he continued to accumulate the knowledge that would lead to his first published work. Although the next several years of his life would include a punishing schedule of preparation for college entrance exams, much of his attention was focused on birds.[1]

During this long run packed with fieldwork, Roosevelt juggled trains, coaches, and ferries as he bounded up and down the Hudson.[2] On April 16, 1875, he was in Garrison, New York, and on May 13 he was back at "Tranquility," the house on Cove Road in Oyster Bay where Roosevelt and his family stayed, and where Roosevelt spent much of the summer collecting.[3] August 2 found him at St. Regis Lake in the Adirondacks, collecting a three-toed woodpecker and grass finch, and on the 25th of that same month he was back down at Oyster Bay, nabbing a yellow-fronted vireo. Roosevelt's diary contained the skeleton of his growing knowledge, and he fleshed out the details in his notebooks. He made concise entries in his diary, as he would for years to come:

January 16, 1875

Garrisons N.Y.

Cloudy. Snow. Crossbills, grosbeaks, redpolls, pine linnets, snowbirds, song sparrows

12 skins[4]

Along with patient study and observation, Roosevelt worked to thoroughly document natural history, and emulated the work of the great ornithologists who were publishing at the time.

If Roosevelt was a sparrow of American ornithology, Elliott Coues was a golden eagle; the shadow of his massive wingspan enveloped even the finest details of the region's birds.[5] Roosevelt neatly packed descriptions on birds into his notebooks following "the classification of Coues."[6] In his work throughout the region, Coues had "made in the field the personal acquaintance of most species of North American Birds" and published two seminal works on the subject, *Key to North American Birds* and *Field Ornithology*, just as Roosevelt was embarking on his serious field studies in the Adirondacks and Oyster Bay.[7] In *Field Ornithology*, published in 1874, Coues appealed directly to the field naturalist and explicitly begged the privilege of "waiving formality, that he may be allowed to address the reader very familiarly, much as if chatting with a friend on a subject of mutual interest."[8] This kind of chat was just what Roosevelt needed, and his voluminous diaries and notebooks highlight his accord with Coues's directions for documentation:

> Don't trust your memory; it will trip you up; what is clear now will grow obscure; what is found will be lost. Write down everything while it is fresh in your mind; write it out in full—time so spent now will be time saved in the end, when you offer your researches to the discriminating public. Don't be satisfied with a dry-as-dust item; clothe a skeleton fact, and breathe life into it with thoughts that glow; let the paper smell of the woods. There's a pulse in a new fact; catch the rhythm before it dies.[9]

(FACING) In the years between Roosevelt's return to the United States in 1873 and his enrollment at Harvard in 1876, he spent much of his time studying natural history and collecting specimens. He kept a range of records, including brief notes and remarks, in his diaries—such as this entry from the spring of 1875, on his collection of recently arrived migratory warblers. TRC MS Am 1454.55 (9).

Magnolia warbler.
Blue yellow back.
Green, & blue black
thr'oated warbler.
5. skins

FRIDAY 14

Warblers very
abundant. Wood
and tawny thrushes,
Prarie and Blackburn warblers
16 skins

SATURDAY 15

Yellow fronted vireo

5 skins

Roosevelt recorded his own observations and ideas on natural history and clothed them with descriptions of plumage and behavior. These were no longer simple accounts of species with information largely gleaned from other sources. Here, Roosevelt synthesized his own observations and collections of each species and earned an in-depth knowledge of its habits and abundance. By accumulating natural history observations in his own original work, he laid the groundwork for his eventual contributions to the ornithological literature.[10]

As he did for many species, Roosevelt rehashed and refined his descriptions of the white-throated sparrow, *Zonotrichia albicollis.* He prowled forest edges and scrubby habitats, often the results of fire and other disturbances, for these inconspicuous sparrows that made nests of pine needles, small sticks, and thick grass. He caught glimpses of the characteristics of their adult plumage—black and white stripes over the crown and eyes, and yellow lores—as they hopped in the underbrush, scratching about in the hopes of finding seeds and even small spiders and snails. As winter approached, he watched as they retired to the southern seaboard and forests. Roosevelt observed and collected the bird many times, and in his diary, journal, and notebooks he composed a Coues-like study of this species that, along with so many others, made him a master of the bird fauna of the region.

Even in the early 1870s, Roosevelt described the white-throated sparrow in his "Notes on Natural History" by calling it an "active sprightly bird" with a song that was "singularly sweet and plaintive."[11] On August 6, 1875, he took his gun into the field near St. Regis Lake in the Adirondacks and recorded in his diary his procurement of a "white throated sparrow."[12] He later returned to this species in his notebook "Remarks on the Zoology of Oyster Bay" and fleshed out his descriptions: "It frequents thickets, hedges, briarpatches, swamps &c" and "continually utters, even in Autumn, its sweet and very plaintive song."[13] In this account he documented the details of eleven specimens he collected, complete with careful measurements of their bodies, bills, and legs. Not satisfied with surface-level records, Roosevelt also included the results of his dissections and noted the contents of the crops. He again returned to this species in his "Notes on the Fauna of the Adirondac Mts."[14]

Index to Mammals.

Sciurus carolinensis
  "   Ludovicia
Tamias striatus
Otomys urucilla
Arctomys monax

In his "Notes on Natural History," Roosevelt used some of the page reserved for an "Index to Mammals" for a set of bird sketches. TRC MS Am 1454.32, TRB, TRCDS.

Along with observing external features of plumage and behavior, and examining internal anatomy, Roosevelt also paid especially close attention to song.

To Roosevelt, as to anyone endeavoring to understand the lives of birds, careful attention to song was absolutely essential in studying their identity and behavior. Roosevelt aspired to be an excellent field ornithologist, and he studied birdsong to identify and understand the birds he observed and collected. Even the most advanced optics may not allow a view of plumage sufficient to identify a bird perched deep within a tree's foliage. Sounds, however—be they extended songs or short calls—can nail down the identity of a bird immediately. Close attention to song can also reveal intricate and subtle aspects of a bird's behavior.

Much of the business of birds is conducted through song as they decorate the air with colorful melodies and menacing signposts. In his critical period of pre-college fieldwork, Roosevelt listened to the complex vocalizations of wrens, many of which we now know are songs that are shared back and forth between individuals, and that are even used in duels between males.[15] He took note of chickadees as they stuttered "dee dee dee"—his "chickaday, day, day"— broadcasts now known to advertise the size of incoming predators.[16] He also heard brown thrashers and catbirds belt out long successions of notes, like sampling deejays—vocalizations that ornithologists now identify as stolen and improvised snippets of sound.[17] Honorable and forthright, Roosevelt not only battled dishonesty and deception in politics but later called out those whose natural history writing gave readers a false impression of how animals acted in the wild. Given his long-standing moral code and his fierce devotion to birds and their songs, he would have appreciated the subtle and sometimes nefarious aspects of bird behavior that modern studies have since uncovered.[18]

Learning the songs of birds and recognizing their significance is hard-won knowledge. But a more vexing problem is how to record these vocalizations on paper. Roosevelt applied plenty of descriptive words to his consideration of songs, like "bright," "cheerful," and "guttural," and he was particularly taken by the "delightful song" of the wood thrush:

Aug 4th Bay Pond. Picoides hirsutus. Common among the pines. Junco hyemalis. Common in opens, and in burnt districts. Entirely a ground sparrow

Zonotrochia albicollis. Common on the edges of the woods, in burnt districts and among bushes. It is ~~very~~ an active sprightly bird, but remains perfectly still while singing. When alarmed it utters. a cluck. The ~~note~~ song is singularly sweet and plaintive. It consists of four bars and may be represented by ⌐ ⌐ ⌣⌣. Sometimes the second note is broken into two as ⌐ ⌣⌣, and occasionally two others are prefixed as ⌣⌐ ⌣⌣.

Dendroica ~~pine~~, blackburniae, virens et coronata. are rather common in the woods. They keep among ~~the~~ higher branches and move in mixed flocks with titmice., creepers and nuthatches

---

The entries in "Notes on Natural History" largely contain information on birds Roosevelt collected in Oyster Bay and the Adirondack Mountains in 1874 and 1875. In his description of the white-throated sparrow, *Zonotrichia albicollis*, collected on August 4, 1875, in the Adirondacks, Roosevelt employed a simple series of dashes to graphically depict this bird's song. TRC MS Am 1454.32, TRB, TRCDS.

Early in July the young begin to sing, and very queer work
they make of it. The bobtailed little minstrel (in posse) usually chooses some very conspicuous twig on which to station
himself, for he shows none of the modesty of his parent;
and from such a perch will give forth his wheezey notes by
the hour. He does not yet try the clear, bell like notes which
are the especial beauty of the song of the older birds, but
confines himself to imatating, with very partial success, the
trills and quavers with which it commences.[19]

To document the songs he heard, Roosevelt also applied the lin-
gua franca of birdsong of the day, an ad hoc system of phonetic
combinations of letters and invented words.[20] These homegrown
onomatopoeias worked better for some songs than others. Some
species, known to birders as the "name-sayers," have songs that
have generated their common names, like the jays, chickadees,
and whip-poor-wills, and even the zic-zac that Roosevelt encountered in Egypt. Birders have translated other songs into convenient
handles, such as the eastern towhee's "drink your tea," or the "wichity wichity" of the common yellowthroat. But for most birds, the
intricacy of their song structure results in long and cumbersome
pseudosentences; Roosevelt packed his notebooks and journals
with just these types of approximations. In his accounts of the
great-crested flycatcher, he described one "loud cry" that sounds
"like 'whoet,' and also another of two syllables like 'wheet-wit.'"[21]
Along with the "curious antics" of a male yellow-breasted chat,
Roosevelt recorded that his song had both "ordinary harsh notes"
and a finer song that he represented as "keck, keck, keck, lüt, lüt,
lüt, jch jch jch jch, whero whero, xic xic, &c."[22] Near the shore,
Roosevelt took note of the spotted sandpiper as it "continually
moves up and down the whole hind part of its body, and often,
especially while on the wing, utters the peetweet."[23]

   As he drilled down on his ornithological studies after returning
to the United States in 1873, Roosevelt added a graphical element
to his descriptions and followed in the footsteps of another wide-
ranging polymath, the seventeenth-century Jesuit scholar Athanasius Kircher.[24] A giant of Renaissance thought who produced
a small library of books on subjects from Egyptology to music to
natural history, Kircher, like Roosevelt, was devoted to the idea

Icteria virens, common. The males still continue their curious antics. In the song, mixed with the ordinary harsh whistling ones notes are sometimes heard some fine whistling ones, that would sound very well by themselves. The song may be represented by "keck, keck, keck, lüt, lüt lüt, gch gch gch gch, whew whew, xic xic, xc.

Setophaga ruticilla. common in the woods. Subsists purely by flycatching. It has a short, quick, lively warble.

Salamandra bilineata. I found several under stones in a small streamlet. They were active and lively. The tail of one having been broken off by accident continued to live for hours.

? Stilla chrysoleuca. Abundant in the small inland ponds.

In Oyster Bay on June 17, 1876, Roosevelt described the song of the yellow-breasted chat, *Icteria virens*, using a series of homemade onomatopoeias. TRC MS Am 1454.38.

of museums and kept his own eclectic cabinet of curiosities, a Baroque-style repository of natural and cultural artifacts.[25]

Kircher was also drawn to the music of the avian world, and had confronted the vexing problem of how to translate the complex pattern of variations in air pressure—sound—to a written form. In keeping with his free-flowing intellectualism, Kircher offered his solution to this problem not in a volume of natural history, but in a book on music. Published in 1650, the musical content of *Musurgia universalis* influenced the likes of Bach and Beethoven, but also provided ornithologists with a new way to record birdsong on paper.[26]

The musical notation Kircher used in his *Musurgia universalis* is one of the first schematic depictions of birdsong.[27] In artistic fashion, Kircher used musical notes to approximate the sounds of a nightingale as well as chickens, a cuckoo, and a quail. He even included a parrot talking in Greek.[28] In retrospect, this was a quantum leap forward as he transcribed songs into graphical patterns of ink on a page. Few ornithologists had the command of the clefs and half notes required to make full use of Kircher's staff method, so, like Roosevelt, most ornithologists in the nineteenth and early twentieth century opted for simpler solutions.

Sprinkled through Roosevelt's descriptions of songs are a series of squiggles, dashes, and lines that are his basic notation of sound. Amid his text he placed between the lines small parallel, angled, and curved lines to depict sounds from such birds as the white-throated sparrow.[29] Grown from the notations developed by Kircher and others, these ornithological hieroglyphs were precursors of the more formal systems of graphical interpretation that came into use in the early twentieth century.

Despite the rigor of Roosevelt's work, the intricate scientific study of birdsong used today had to wait for two major developments. The ability to record bird sounds, first used by the eight-year-old Ludwig Koch in 1889, allowed scientists to replay, share, and examine songs repeatedly.[30] Second, in the 1930s pictorial notations like those used by Kircher and Roosevelt spawned the "sonogram," which amounted to a graph of the frequencies of bird sounds over time.[31] These new graphical representations provided precise documentation of animal sounds, and an opportunity to unlock many secrets of the lives of birds. Roosevelt's work on birds

Athanasius Kircher's 1650 book *Musurgia universalis* included one of the first graphical depictions of birdsong, including a nightingale, a chicken, a cuckoo, and a quail. By permission of the University of Glasgow Library, Special Collections.

in the years before he entered college predated these later develop-ments, but the dashes and lines in his notes are evidence of his ex-tensive efforts to document the richness of bird life and behavior.

Like that of Coues, Roosevelt's primary attention was on birds, but neither man had taxonomic tunnel vision. Roosevelt's work again paralleled that of Coues as he included nonfeathered ani-mals in his studies, digging up runways and shooting scurrying mammals at dusk. He paid special attention to moles, shrews, and weasels as he considered them in his notebooks in words and sketches. Coues also flushed out burrows, warrens, and mounds and published papers on the prairie rabbit and skunk as well as larger monographs on the Mustelidae (wolverines, badgers, skunks, otters, etc.) and the Rodentia.[32] Roosevelt collected a skunk in an unconventional manner: "One fell into our sistern, where it remained for three weeks, to the decided detriment of the water."[33] Aside from these rare departures, Roosevelt followed the methods of Coues and other great working naturalists in America and brought academic rigor to his work. The biological studies he undertook in the field also provided a welcome complement to the serious academic preparation he undertook to gain admittance to college.

Although there was plenty of time for Roosevelt to find what he later termed "ornithological enjoyment and reptilian rapture," he was serious about his academic future and had been preparing for entrance exams since 1873 with a private tutor named Arthur Cutler.[34] The abundant energy he devoted to wrestling with both people and ideas paid off, and he passed his admittance exams and attained his goal of becoming a Harvard man, fit in mind and body.

Roosevelt arrived at Harvard in the fall of 1876 with his guns and arsenic in tow. Avoiding the dusty confines of the college housing in Harvard Yard, he installed himself in a cozy boarding house on Winthrop Street.[35] Roosevelt's idea of a college residential environ-ment was different than those of his classmates, as few would have considered live specimens, bird skins, and shotguns to be homey. But this was just the kind of naturalist's nest that Roosevelt loved, and he plowed ahead at his work on the northeastern fauna even as he began his formal studies. The word got out that there was a field man on campus, and at least one student came to call.

Henry "Hal" Minot learned about Roosevelt's interest in natural history through a family member and gave him only a day on campus before he stopped in at 16 Winthrop Street to talk about birds.[36] Their passionate common interest and long conversations on the finer points of ornithology led to many excursions to the field. Throughout Roosevelt's first year, his extracurricular activities with Minot were a welcome complement to the workaday studies of the Harvard curriculum. As a freshman, Roosevelt did not yet have the freedom offered by the new system of electives implemented by Harvard's president, Charles Eliot.[37] In this year, Roosevelt was stuck in the classic studies such as Greek, Latin, German, chemistry, and physics.[38] Roosevelt muscled through his transition to formal education—the majority of his studies so far had been either self-directed or with private tutors—and, even though he was described as "thin-chested spectacled, nervous and frail," he found a comfortable spot in the hierarchical academic and social scene at Harvard.[39] As his first year came to an end, Roosevelt was back in the field, both with Minot in the Adirondacks and by himself in Oyster Bay. Having spent several years filling notebooks and journals with his accounts of natural history, he now officially entered the tribe of naturalists and made a contribution to the literature. Before he returned to classes for the fall of 1877, he and Minot laid down a modest publication.

The four-page length of Roosevelt and Minot's "The Summer Birds of the Adirondacks" should not cause one to underestimate its gravity.[40] This paper was a checklist of the ninety-seven bird species found in the Adirondacks, including notes on their abundance. On the surface, such a faunal checklist appears simplistic, but in fact documents like it are crucial for those engaged in serious study. In the same way that the checklist in the back of Coues's *Field Ornithology* laid out the 635 species found in North America, Roosevelt and Minot's work captured a snapshot of the birds that inhabited the Adirondacks at that time. Anyone who endeavored to study birds in that region could consult Roosevelt and Minot's paper as a baseline for which birds should be present and how likely they would be encountered. Not only useful when first published, checklists are also invaluable later because they reveal crucial information about the waxing and waning of individual species. Given the expectations for any such checklist,

Roosevelt and Minot's entries were sparse: "White-throated Sparrow. *Zonotrichia albicollis* (Gmelin). Common." But Roosevelt had heaps of observations in his notebooks to back up this account, and having his own checklist in the literature gave him new standing as a naturalist.

The Nuttall Ornithological Club, which had been founded just four years earlier, was one place where Roosevelt engaged his interest throughout his time at Harvard, and they noticed his entrance into ornithological society in their *Bulletin*.[41] Roosevelt's own spelling challenges hopefully allowed him to overlook his name being spelled "Rooseveldt" in this review, as its favorable assessment described a "very acceptable list . . . the first list known to us of the summer birds of this ornithologically little-explored region."[42] It was a fitting honor for the review to be nestled into this volume of the *Bulletin*—which eventually transitioned into the influential *Auk*—because Roosevelt now was literally in line behind one of his heroes. The review appeared just thirty-six pages after a "Note on *Passerculus bairdi* and *P. princeps*," by Elliott Coues.

If Roosevelt had been able to engage Coues in person then, one can imagine how their deep knowledge of ornithology could have led to an intense discussion of seasonal plumage of shorebirds and the cryptic haunts of thrashers, an epic bout of wordslinging that would have dizzied even the most interested birder. It wasn't just that Roosevelt emulated Coues in his fine-grained studies of birds, though; they also shared a multifaceted nature.

Coues had also come to love birds as a youngster. His first dozen years were spent with a zest for the abundant natural history near his home in Portsmouth, New Hampshire. A move to Washington, DC, plucked him from the northern forests, but in a strange way this relocation to the banks of the Potomac landed him much closer to the study of nature. In 1854 Coues's father moved the family to Washington because he had received an appointment in the US Patent Office. Like that of Roosevelt, young Coues's early interest in nature was stoked by great mentors with serious ties. It didn't take him long to come under the tutelage of Spencer Fullerton Baird, then the assistant secretary of the developing Smithsonian Institution.[43] Like John Bell, Baird was an associate of Audubon, and he would have been named along with Bell as part of Audubon's trusted team on the expedition to the Missouri River in 1843, had it not been for a last-minute illness.[44]

Like Roosevelt, Coues did not undertake a professional course in science; he took a medical degree in New York and became an army surgeon during the Civil War. But this profession gave him a long-lived ticket for ornithological adventure. In the postwar years, the commissioned life found him alighting for extended periods at locations including Fort Whipple in the Arizona Territory, Fort Macon in North Carolina, and Fort McHenry in Baltimore, and his identity became not defined by a single professional variable, but developed at the intersection of diverse pursuits.[45]

Possibly because science wasn't his primary occupation, Coues's identity was not bound by it. He was a quintessential field naturalist, believing that "the study of Birds in the field is an indispensable prerequisite to their study in the library and the museum."[46] By defining the field as a place where real ornithology was done, Coues's words spoke directly to Roosevelt as Roosevelt worked to incorporate his love of birds and natural history into his studies at Harvard.

Over his years of outdoor work, Roosevelt earned a great deal of flak for his extensive and seemingly brutal approach to collecting animals. Although it is tempting for some to dismiss Roosevelt's work as that of a gun-crazed maniac, Coues's instructions at the start at of *Field Ornithology* provide a perspective on Roosevelt's mindset. Coues directs his readers to understand that "the double-barrelled shot gun is your main reliance."[47] Economy was not the recommendation; in response to the question of how many birds of each species should be collected, Coues suggests: "*All you can get*— with some reasonable limitations; say fifty or a hundred of any but the most abundant and widely diffused species."[48] Coues continues: "Never shoot a bird you do not fully intend to preserve. . . . Bird-life is too beautiful a thing to destroy . . . unless the tribute is hallowed by worthiness of motive."[49] As we consider the giant game bag of specimens that Roosevelt stuffed to bursting throughout his life, the question of whether he followed "reasonable limitations" in his extensive collecting is still up for debate. Much later, Roosevelt looked back on his early natural history approach to collecting, and recognized that the guidelines for the collection of specimens for scientific study had changed.[50]

In this web of animals, bullets, and science, both Roosevelt and Coues developed their identities. Coues, like Roosevelt, did not atomize his life in the field; he instead stands as another example of how these pursuits can flow from one to another. Being a hunter, field medic, and naturalist can be parts of the same whole. In a passage that foreshadows Roosevelt's experiences in Cuba years later, the multiple facets of Coues's identity were on display outside Fort Whipple, where he was fond of following the plain titmouse:

> This scrubby hillside . . . was a favorite resort of mine, not so much for what I expected to find there in the ornitho-logical line, as for what I very sincerely hoped not to find in the way of the aborigines—for it was in full view of the fort, and much safer than the ravines on either side, where I have gone more than once to bring in the naked and still bleeding bodies of men killed by the Apaches.[51]

Coues had navigated his own path by combining a professional occupation in public service with a massive set of natural history contributions. Although Roosevelt had no interest in medicine, he was barreling down a path similar to the one Coues had followed years before. Both in and out of Cambridge, Roosevelt laid the groundwork for what would become a unique melding of natural history with varied academic studies and professional duties, a mode of responding to diverse forces by taking to the field.

Along with collecting with Minot in the Adirondacks, Roosevelt led an idyllic outdoor life in Oyster Bay during the summer of 1877. He rambled through marshes and coves, watching and col-lecting wildlife. At one point he rowed to Lloyd Neck in "heavy sea, got very wet," and had to dry himself "by lying naked on the dock for an hour."[52] The birds he collected between these aquatic excursions supported an additional publication, printed in his junior year, entitled "Notes on Some of the Birds of Oyster Bay, Long Island."[53] If placed at the forefront of Roosevelt's complete written works, this and his earlier checklist emerge as the starting point for a lifetime of fertile writing that places his intellectual spirit alongside that of Kircher and Coues.

Back in Cambridge for the fall as a sophomore, Roosevelt took

SATURDAY, SEPTEMBER 22, 1877.

Rowed to Loyds neck
to see Miss Boden.
Heavy sea, got very
wet, had to dry
myself by lying
naked on the dock
for an hour. Big
sea running, as
I came home,

In the summer before his sophomore year at Harvard, Roosevelt lived mostly in the outdoors, at Oyster Bay and the Adirondacks. TRC MS Am 1454.55 (11).

a course on scientific prose, along with courses in comparative anatomy and physiology of vertebrates, with William James, and in elementary botany, with George Lincoln Goodale.[54] He found the curriculum's flexibility liberating and described in his diary how "the work is much pleasanter than last year. I like the zoölogical courses very much."[55] These entries record a new momentum as he developed his mind and body in the gym and the classroom: "Gave red-haired Coolidge a tremendous thrashing in the gymnasium, boxing. Have done better than last year in my studies so far."[56] Like most college students, Roosevelt matured as his idealistic pursuits began to collide with professional realities. He wondered how he could square his interest in animals and hunting with the financial demands of a family. Even the harshest aspect of objective existence—mortality—began to find its way into his life. On December 21 he was "suddenly called on to New York" because his father had become very ill, diagnosed with acute peritonitis.[57] His diary reflects that things had turned better after several days: "X mas. Father seems much brighter. Received a double barreled shot gun."[58] He ended the year, as he often did, by adding up his game bag and collections. With a new gun and his father seeming somewhat better, there was ample reason for optimism for what the new year might hold. As he returned to Harvard for spring classes, however, Roosevelt's mettle was tested in a way it had not been before, and the recently published naturalist was jolted into a new phase of adulthood.

Once he heard that his father had relapsed, Roosevelt made a frantic dash from campus and boarded the first available train to New York. The gentle wintery scenes of the eastern seaboard passed by, and the question lingered of how his father's condition had gone from what seemed like stability at Christmas to a grave descent early in February. When he finally arrived home, his father's cries of pain and delirium had already passed away. Roosevelt solemnly recorded the moment in his diary: "My dear Father. Born Sept 23$^\mathrm{d}$ 1831."[59]

The "terrible three days" before his father's burial set in motion a fundamental shift in Roosevelt's mindset.[60] He was no longer a son searching for his place in the world under the guidance of his father; he was in line to be the head of a family. Only halfway through his sophomore year in college, Roosevelt was left to determine his life path without his most trusted counselor.

Roosevelt revered his father. Throughout his own professional life his diaries and letters were filled with names like Burroughs, Muir, McKinley, and Lodge, but he still described his father as "the best man I ever knew."[61] As children, Roosevelt and his siblings would wait in the library for their father to come home at night, and later would "rush out to greet him" and "troop into his room while he was dressing, to stay there as long as [they] were permitted."[62] The childhood image of Roosevelt "eagerly examining anything which came out of his [father's] pockets" and eying "treasures" kept in a small box on his father's dressing table provides a glimpse of the young explorer: early evidence that his father's presence nurtured an uncommon fascination with the secrets and meaning of even the smallest objects.[63]

Although he was never a naturalist or practicing politician, Theodore Roosevelt Sr. had offered a sterling role model to his son. A "big, powerful man, with a leonine face," he was one of the most prominent businessmen and philanthropists in New York.[64] He had carted his children off with him to night schools and lodging houses for the poor to instill in them an ethic of public service, teaching them that one must not only serve the dollar, that wayward souls deserved attention, and that cruelty to children and animals could not be tolerated. At forty-six, Theodore Sr. had been thrust into a contentious nomination for the position of collector of customs to the Port of New York when his first wave of stomach pain hit just several months before his death. Fittingly, Theodore picked up this mantle of service from his father and carried it throughout his own life.

Theodore Sr. had not just provided a moral example; he had also worked to shape his son's life directly. He had arranged for foreign travel, placed him in the company of numerous mentors, read him adventure stories, and even acted as a hunting sidekick. Once the younger Roosevelt had lost this active influence and counsel, he needed to look elsewhere as he reconciled his developing field identity with a choice of professional path.

As Roosevelt returned to Cambridge on February 21, 1878, the loss still seemed "like a hideous dream" as he faced a new life where memories of his father were everywhere.[65] Just getting through

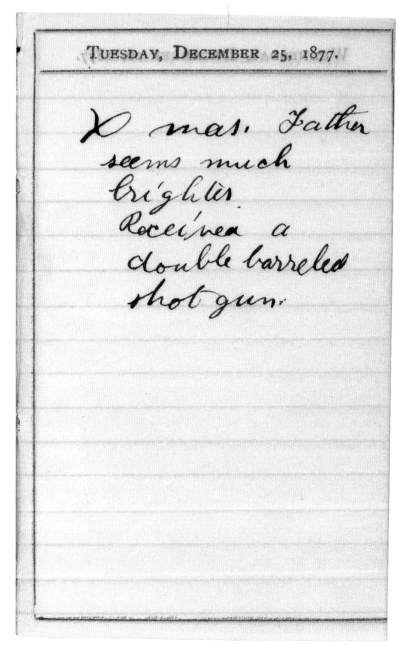

X mas. Father seems much brighter. Received a double barreled shot gun.

At the end of the fall term of 1877, Roosevelt returned from Harvard to New York to spend the holidays at home. His father had been suffering from stomach pain. Much to his delight, Roosevelt received a new double-barreled shotgun for Christmas. Although his father seemed better by the time he left to return to Harvard, Roosevelt was called back home in early February. He did not arrive before his father died of a painful abdominal tumor. TRC MS Am 1454.55 (11).

Looking back on his life, it seems as if mine must be such a weak useless one in comparison.

I should like to be a scientist: oh, how I shall miss his sweet, sympathetic advice!

Roosevelt's father had provided him with guidance and advice throughout his young life. He felt the absence of his father's counsel during college, especially as he worked to reconcile his interest in science with his potential career and life paths. TRP 1878 diary, March 7.

the days in early March was difficult: "It seems brutal to go about my ordinary occupations," he wrote, admitting that on several days he had a "good square break down."[66] He read his childhood journals, and as he reviewed his travels with his father in Egypt, he painfully acknowledged how "every incident is connected with him."[67] In April, however, evidence appeared that the new reality had set in and healing had at least begun: "The days of unalloyed happiness are now over forever. But oh how much I have left to be thankful for!"[68]

Parental expectations loom large for Harvard undergraduates, as they do for most college students, and this was particularly true for Roosevelt, as his father's wisdom and expectations could now only be recalled from memory. Even before he matriculated at Harvard he had been intent on becoming a scientist, and this was no secret to his parents. Fortunately for Roosevelt, his father had not set out inflexible expectations for his son's path; he had instead positioned himself as a responsible adviser.

Theodore Sr.'s own professional pursuits could have easily caused him to dismiss his son's interest in science and natural history, but instead he simply had asked Theodore to carefully consider the possible tradeoffs of such a course. Roosevelt later recalled his father's advice:

> He told me that if I wished to become a scientific man I could do so. He explained that I must be sure that I really intensely desired to do scientific work, because if I went into it I must make it a serious career; that he had made enough money to enable me to take up such a career and do non-remunerative work of value *if I intended to do the very best work there was in me.*[69]

The implications were clear to the younger Roosevelt: "In other words, if I went into a scientific career, I must definitely abandon all thought of the enjoyment that could accompany a money-making career, and must find my pleasures elsewhere."[70] This alone did not make him shy away from science; the idea of staying on a budget was not new to Theodore. His notebooks and journals from his early fieldwork were filled with ledgers and fiscal accounts.

His father's death had put a strange twist on this advice, however, as Roosevelt inherited enough to provide him with a comfortable annual income.[71] As he got back to his coursework, specific concerns about money and comforts were eclipsed by the underlying questions of how he could reconcile his love of the field with the science he was studying at Harvard, and also how he could re-create a loving home life like that of his childhood. In examining the direction of his own life, it was impossible for him not to compare his position to that his father had attained: "Looking back on <u>his</u> life, it seems as if mine must be such a weak useless one in comparison."[72] During Roosevelt's sophomore year, his work improved and his academic plans did not fundamentally change, but the absence of his father's counsel was glaring.[73] His diary reveals a longing to reopen a conversation with his most trusted counselor: "I should like to be a scientist: oh, how I shall miss his sweet, sympathetic advice!"[74] In spite of this wish, Roosevelt would need to seek other influences to help him chart his course.

It must have come as a surprise to Roosevelt's family and friends that he wasn't more inspired by Harvard's science courses and that his instructors were not reeling him in to a professional track. After all, the Museum of Comparative Zoology (MCZ) was one of the hotbeds of natural science in the country, and Harvard even had the chemist Charles Eliot as its president. To those without intimate knowledge of biology or the benefit of hindsight, Theodore's move away from science during his years at Harvard may appear to have been a curious development. However, fundamental change was afoot in the natural sciences in the 1870s, and Theodore's question of how he could fit his field persona into such an academic trajectory was squarely in the middle of it.

Roosevelt studied natural science when the discovery of DNA's structure was still almost a century off, and evolution by natural selection had just begun to be batted about in the literature. At that point there was a widening chasm between those scientists who focused on whole organisms and those who were boring down on questions of physiology and parts of organisms.[75] Unfortunately for Roosevelt, a conflict was also brewing between the MCZ and Harvard College about who should fulfill the responsibility for teaching undergraduates. To solve this problem, the MCZ hired Edward Laurens Mark, a man whose emphasis on microscopy and cytology accompanied his freshly minted doctorate from the University of Leipzig.[76] Roosevelt's hope to become a holistic naturalist did not fit with the emphasis that Mark and his colleagues placed on fractionating organisms. In his *Autobiography*, Roosevelt describes how he had fully intended to make science his "life-work" but the emphasis of instruction was wrong for him:[77]

> Harvard, and I suppose our other colleges, utterly ignored the possibilities of the faunal naturalist, the outdoor naturalist and observer of nature. They treated biology as purely a science of the laboratory and the microscope, a science whose adherents were to spend their time in the study of minute forms of marine life, or else in section-cutting and the study of the tissues of the higher organisms under the microscope. . . . The sound revolt against superficiality of study had been carried to an extreme; thoroughness in minutiæ as the only end of study had been erected into a fetish. There was a total failure to understand the great variety of kinds of work that could be done by naturalists, including what could be done by outdoor naturalists. [78]

What had drawn Roosevelt to biology was the cycle of the naturalist, and interacting directly with organisms in nature. As he butted heads with what is now referred to generally as "reductionism," he could not have imagined the ways in which this disciplinary friction would ignite fires of conflict in the biological sciences well into the future—a conflict nowhere more apparent than at Harvard.

If he were at Harvard today, Roosevelt could study in the Department of Organismic and Evolutionary Biology, and, although he would certainly receive training in the particulars of genetics and molecular biology, he would be encouraged to harness the tools of ecology and evolutionary biology in remote habitats; one could imagine him immediately drawn to the Galapagos Islands to study Darwin's finches. But the very existence of such a department is the result of a bitter reductionist conflict. In the 1950s a group of molecular biologists, led by James Watson, were literally pulling apart molecules and cells to understand the implications of the newly discovered structure of DNA. Others, like Edward O. Wilson and his colleagues in the MCZ, were focused on higher levels like colonies and ecosystems. New paradigms in academia often seek to dominate conversations and resources; this focus on component parts led the encampment of these molecular biologists in the Biological Laboratories and the evolutionary biologists in the MCZ, and the "molecular wars" were on.[79] Thankfully, time and the integration of modern techniques have since dissolved many of the lines of these battles, but a productive tension still persists in biology between approaches that consider wholes and those that seek to understand component parts. Roosevelt learned about the reductionist approaches that dominated the teaching of biology during his time at Harvard, and was not interested in following that path. But a focus on parts of organisms was only one way in which his coursework turned him away from a career in science. Decrying the tedium of dissecting organisms and phenomena, he wanted to spend his time with those who had a better appreciation for the work of the outdoor naturalist. He later returned as an alumnus and bemoaned the absence of fieldwork at Harvard.[80]

To be fair to the institution, there were scientists doing fieldwork while Roosevelt was on campus. Louis Agassiz's son, Alexander, had taken over the directorship of the museum and was exploring the ruins of Titicaca and dredging the Gulf of Mexico for the "minute forms of marine life" that Roosevelt dismissed as uninteresting.[81] But as Edward Laurens Mark became more involved, the instruction of students in natural history was taken over by the college, and the field men of the MCZ were more and more occupied by their own curatorial pursuits.

The natural history professors who taught Roosevelt did little to attract him to a career in science; in fact, his lukewarm assessment of them suggests that they may have pushed him away. With minimal praise, he recorded in his diary that "the Natural History Professors are very pleasant and obliging," and even the more positive assessments of his courses were often conflicted: "One of my Natural History courses this year needs a great deal of laboratory work, which I like but which takes up an awful amount of time."[82] Even those of his professors who possessed field credentials did not seem to inspire his outdoor interests.

When Roosevelt entered his course on the anatomy and physiology of the vertebrates, he met the lanky and intellectual William James. With later influential works like *The Will to Believe* and *Essays in Radical Empiricism,* James's work in philosophy and psychology never made him a hero to naturalists.[83] But early in his career James taught natural science, and he had gone with Louis Agassiz on his famous expedition to Brazil a decade before he taught Roosevelt. One might assume that James would have shown Roosevelt the exotic fishes they had collected—now stocked in barrels and jars in the basement of Agassiz's museum—or shared the yarns of adventure that were recorded in his journals. However, the jottings in James's field notes from Brazil provide one example of why Roosevelt's instructors did not encourage his interest in the field.

While on the Içá River in October of 1865, James had followed members of the native tribes into dense forest to poison ponds and collect fish. Devoid of the sincere interest found in Roosevelt's journals, James sarcastically wrote how "after a most narrow escape from dying of old age at Tonantino we got off at 6 P.M. and went all night."[84] Two days later, his journal records an afternoon nap on the beach and his annoyance with the "awful" mosquitoes. James described his true feelings in a letter to his father: "If there is anything I hate it is collecting. I don't think it suited to my genius at all."[85] Unfortunately for Roosevelt, James had dismissed fieldwork long before the two met as teacher and student.

James's colleague Nathaniel Southgate Shaler was a popular faculty member who lectured and counseled aspiring biologists on field trips and in the laboratories. Although Roosevelt remembered that Shaler had influenced him—Shaler would later be described as a "keen observer, good fighter, good friend, hater of shams"—his acclaimed teaching did not secure enduring accolades from Roosevelt. In Roosevelt's *Autobiography,* praise of his science instructors was notably absent.[86] Roosevelt later reflected that as a student he had gathered the mistaken impression from his instructors that he could not develop a career as a naturalist without becoming a devotee of the microscope. Hawks frequently hunted squirrels in the shadow of the MCZ, and a passage in Roosevelt's zoology notebook suggests that he found more happiness sitting outside the museum taking notes on predatory flights than in section cutting and slide making within its walls.[87]

When he stepped outside the confines of Harvard's curriculum, Roosevelt forged relationships that provided guidance as he mulled over how his field persona could fit into a career path.

Although he loved the chase, was influenced by the lore of the hunter-naturalist, and had a long-standing attraction to physical challenge, up to this point in his life his cycles of adventure—his trips to the field to envision, enact, and render—had largely been related to his desire to understand nature. As his career aspirations began to slowly shift, his underlying motivation to strike out for adventure was not diminished; its applications simply became more varied.

In Cambridge, he and Minot attended the Nuttall Ornithological Club, and his diary reflects that he "very much" valued his interactions with the well known ornithologists William Brewster and J. A. Allen.[88] But Roosevelt did not find his most influential mentors in natural history seminar rooms or lecture halls, and in the fall of 1878 he gained new perspective hundreds of miles north, in the backwoods of Maine.

The warmth of summer lingered in Harvard Yard during September, but as Roosevelt approached his junior year he was not lounging on its green grass, but was instead on a train heading north. The relative isolation of Mattawamkeag Station, Maine, was only a waypoint toward his end goal, and after leaving the train he hopped on the back of a horse-drawn wagon and made his way toward the remote hamlet of Island Falls.

Darkness had already set in when Roosevelt and his cousins Emlen and West arrived in the center of Island Falls and stowed their gear in the warm home of Bill Sewall. The town of Island Falls, some thirty miles east of what is now Baxter State Park, was at the edge of a massive wilderness filled with moose and white-tailed deer. Emlen and West greeted Sewall with familiarity, as they had spent three weeks hunting with him a year earlier, along with Arthur Cutler, Roosevelt's precollege tutor. This time they arrived with a new member of the party: Sewall later described Roosevelt as a "thin, pale youngster with bad eyes and a weak heart."[89] Cutler himself had primed Sewall for Roosevelt's arrival, encouraging him to take it easy on the new visitor because asthma still gripped his lungs and his father's death weighed on his mind.[90] But Roosevelt's uncommon vigor was easy to underestimate, and as he took to fishing and hunting, hiking twenty-five miles on one of the first days of his visit, Sewall realized that "he wasn't such a weakling

SEPTEMBER, FRIDAY 13. 1878.

Rained all day so we stayed in camp — reading, playing euchre and whist and practising with our rifles. I again waited a couple of hours for ducks, getting one long and unsuccessful shot. I killed a bat and a nighthawk.

SEPTEMBER, SATURDAY 14. 1878.

Rained till noon; then it cleared and I took a fifteen mile tramp through the woods with Sewell, but got nothing. I had two shots with the rifle at a couple of foxes about sixty yards off across the river, but missed both; I don't think I ever made as many consecutive bad shots as I have this week. I am disgusted with myself.

Roosevelt escaped to the backwoods of Maine in the fall of 1878 to hunt with his cousins Emlen and West. When he arrived at the remote village of Island Falls, he met William "Bill" Sewall and Wilmot Dow, two rugged Maine guides who would participate in many of his adventures over the next decade. TRP 1878 diary, September 13–14.

as Cutler tried to make out" and was "always good-natured and full of fun."[91]

The hunting guides and the lumbermen who hung around the Sewall cottage were in some ways an unlikely band for Roosevelt to turn to for mentorship. None could relate to Roosevelt's experiences in the British Museum or traveling on a felucca up the Nile River. Sewall called in his nephew Wilmot Dow to guide the rest of the party, and took Roosevelt under his own wing. Sewall and Roosevelt found a common intellectual bond; they were both woodsmen and loved to recite Longfellow. They trekked together on the Mattawamkeag River, and Sewall introduced Roosevelt to his self-reliant concept of the woods. Roosevelt now found the kind of guide who was so influential to characters in the literature of adventure he had consumed as a child. Just as Oliver Edwards had Natty Bumppo in Daniel Defoe's *The Pioneers*, Roosevelt now had Sewall.[92] In such a role, Sewall's assessment was that Roosevelt had a lot to learn, and he recalled that "of course he did not understand the woods, but on every other subject he was posted."[93] There was clearly a lot that Sewall could teach Roosevelt about tracking and hunting. This first trip to Island Falls was a three-week hunting spree, and even Roosevelt acknowledged his shortcomings:

> Sept. 14. "Rained till noon; then it cleared and I took a fifteen mile tramp through the woods with Sewell, but got nothing. I had two shots with the rifle at a couple of foxes about sixty yards off across the river, but missed both; I do'n't think I ever made as many consecutive bad shots as I have this week. I am disgusted with myself."[94]

But Sewall was understanding and encouraging, and Roosevelt even sought Sewall's perspective on his course after college.[95] Although he returned to Cambridge for winter study, Roosevelt was back on the train to Mattawamkeag Station in March of 1879.

On their second trip together, Roosevelt, Sewall, and Dow tracked caribou and deer and collected enough to fill their game bags and their bellies. One day they stopped to pose for a photograph, and the result symbolizes the counsel that Roosevelt found in the woods of Maine. This widely reproduced image shows Sewall, Dow, and Roosevelt standing together in a field of snow.[96] Sewall, bearded and grizzled, grips his snowshoe and leans calmly on the butt of an axe, staring calmly into the lens. In the center, the clean-shaven Dow confidently peers at the camera as he holds his rifle over his shoulder, a hanger for his snowshoes. Roosevelt stands to the right of his companions, leaning one hand on his gun's barrel and the other on his snowshoes. Exposing his bushy side whiskers, Roosevelt's head is turned and, given his short stature, he is literally looking up to his two Maine guides. In the way he later took to the field to build his relationship with John Muir, Roosevelt communed with Sewall and Dow and ruminated on his own future. The balsam fir and glacial crags of the North Woods

During his college days at Harvard, Roosevelt (right) spent much of his time in natural areas. He hunted in Maine with Bill Sewall (left) and Wilmot Dow (center). Sewall and Dow became long-standing companions on Roosevelt's field adventures. TRC 520.12-015.

became a refuge. Here Roosevelt found a haven with mentors and kindred souls who would stoke his field pursuits as a nature writer, rancher, and even as president of the United States.

Tucked away in Roosevelt's bags on his return trip to Boston was a soft and intriguing lynx skin, a prize trophy from his hunts in the North Woods. Back on campus that spring of 1879, he moved further and further away from a career in science as the gap between the nature he loved and the laboratory science of his courses widened, and he gravitated more toward studies of politics and economics. But another element overshadowed this academic tension, and nowhere was this more apparent than in the fate of the lynx specimen, which ended up not in a museum, but at the foot of a beautiful woman.[97] Roosevelt took another trip to Maine in August of 1879, adding the summit of Mount Katahdin to his list of feats, but the urge to create a home like the one in which he had grown up became strong after his father's death.[98] And the opportunity to do so had appeared to him the previous October in the form of Alice Lee.

In his interactions with the opposite sex, Roosevelt was more like Darwin than Don Juan. Like Darwin, he was often ill and had an obsessive interest in nature that took precedence in his early life over being a dapper suitor. But Darwin had completed his field-work early and cemented his scientific trajectory before becoming engaged to his cousin Emma Wedgewood. In Roosevelt's case, the timelines of his choices of a career and of a wife were coincidental, and their outcomes were inextricably linked.

Like points on a bending arc, a pair of facing pages in Roosevelt's diary provide a snapshot of change. In April of 1878, exactly two months after he returned to Cambridge following his father's death, he reminisced: "I have lost the only human being, to whom I told everything." The very next day, he poses a forward-looking question: "I so wonder who my wife will be! . . . one who will be as sweet, pure and innocent as she is wise. Thank Heaven, I am at least perfectly pure."[99] In these passages Roosevelt moved from looking back at the home of his father to the idea of establishing a family of his own. Only six months after he penned these thoughts, he would meet his future wife while visiting the parklike home of his friend Dick Saltonstall in Chestnut Hill. However, he would first consider, and ultimately put on hold, a long-standing friend.

Living next door to Roosevelt as a child, Edith Carow had first known him as "Teedie." Revealing their closeness as childhood playmates, one of Roosevelt's accounts of the day he steamed away on the *Scotia* for his grand tour of Europe includes the comment that "it was verry hard parting from our friend," a statement that historians have interpreted as a reference to Edith.[100] Through-out that trip Roosevelt wrote letters to Edith, and on November 22, 1869, he was in Paris and longed for his dear friend: "In the evening mama showed me the portrait of Eidieth Carow and her face stired up in me homesickness and longings for the past which will come again never, alack never."[101] In some ways prophetic, this remark foreshadows how Roosevelt's relationship with Edith was one of the past and future. In the late summer of 1878, before Roosevelt returned for his junior year in college, his diary suggests that their relationship had temporarily veered toward something more than a tender childhood friendship.

It is not surprising that the simmering days of August found Edith drawn into Theodore's orbit. When she visited him in Oys-ter Bay he was a physical specimen after a long summer of row-ing, riding, and wrestling. It was in this form that he reported an intriguing meeting in his diary.[102] First, Roosevelt took Edith for a sail on the bay, and later that evening they ended going "up to the summer house."[103] The diary is silent on what transpired there, but its accounts of the next several days describe a series of outbursts that suggest a romantic interlude that ended in a clash of two strong personalities.[104] One can only imagine what would drive Roosevelt, a lover of animals, to angrily shoot a neighbor's dog and blast indiscriminately at objects in the sound. Whatever it was, Roosevelt left Edith behind and made his first trip to Maine in September, and although she later would become his second wife, Edith would rarely appear again in his notebooks and dia-ries. Unlike the ones he kept during and shortly after college, Roosevelt's later notebooks contained few intimate accounts of his relationships. Any torment and anger he felt after his interac-tion with Edith in Oyster Bay dissipated quickly, however; only a few weeks after Roosevelt returned from Island Falls, a new flame began to burn.

The first mention of Alice Lee in Roosevelt's diary, made while visiting the Saltonstalls in Chestnut Hill on October 19, 1878, was typical of how Roosevelt portrayed many young women: he described her as "a very sweet pretty girl."[105] However, in this case "pretty" was a clear understatement, as Alice is universally described as having been a fun-loving knockout, with the biographer Edmund Morris calling her "as ravishing a beauty as ever walked across a Boston lawn, or through the pages of any Victorian novel."[106] It is no wonder it only took until Thanksgiving for Roosevelt to predict, in writing, that he would win her hand.

Drama was not lacking in his courtship of Alice. At one point Roosevelt ripped his bold prediction of marriage from the binding of his diary in what one can only imagine was a fit of passion.[107] Despite its rough edges, Roosevelt's sometimes awkward and periodically cramped personality was disarmingly effective, and it only took fifteen months—from the meeting in October, to a premonition of marriage at Thanksgiving, to a family-led campaign the following fall and an ultimate acceptance of marriage on January 25, 1880—for Roosevelt to secure Alice's hand and lay to rest the question of whom he would marry.

Although Roosevelt still focused carefully on his studies in his second two years at Harvard, much of his attention was placed on winning Alice, and passages from his diary exhibit how this courtship played a role as he moved away from a scientific trajectory to a comfortably domestic path of law and public service:[108]

[Diary, September 1, 1878.] I have absolutely no idea what I shall do when I leave college. Oh, Father, my Father, no words can tell how I shall miss your counsel and advice![109]

[Diary, December 26, 1878.] As regards my prospects in afterlife it seems to look more & more as if I was going to be a Naturalist. If so I shall have to study three years abroad—it makes me perfectly blue to think of it.[110]

[Diary, August 18, 1879.] I am thinking pretty seriously as to what I shall do when I leave College; I shall probably either pursue a scientific course, or else study law, preparatory to going into public life.[111]

NOVEMBER, THURSDAY 28. 1878.

spent the day with
"Alice" and "Rose"—
dancing, walking,
playing lawn
tennis &c. I have
gotten very well
acquainted with
both of them; Rose
is a very good pleasant
girl, and as for
pretty Alice Lee,
I think her one
of the sweetest, most
ladylike girls I have
ever met.
They all call me
by my first name
now

DECEMBER, SUNDAY 1. 1878.

Breakfasted as usual
at the Porcellian;
these Sunday break-
-fasts are a great
institution, taking
place about 9.30
The food is capital,
and it is pleasant
to be with the
fellows.

Shortly after he returned from his first hunting trip to Maine with Sewall and Dow, Roosevelt met "a very sweet pretty girl" named Alice Lee. By Thanksgiving he had resolved to win her hand, and he recorded his thoughts in the pages of his diary in the last days of November 1878. At some point in his courtship, however, he returned to his diary and ripped these pages from the binding. TRP 1878 diary, November 28–December 1.

[Letter to Henry Minot, February 13, 1880.] I write to you to announce my engagement to Miss Alice Lee. . . . I have been in love with her for nearly two years now; and have made everything subordinate to winning her; so you can perhaps understand a change in my ideas as regards science &c.[112]

[Diary, March 25, 1880.] I shall study law next year, and must there do my best, and work hard for my own little wife.[113]

Roosevelt graduated from Harvard on June 30, 1880. After the commencement exercises were over, he spent the remainder of the day with his "bewitching queen" Alice Lee and his brother Elliott, whom he affectionately referred to as "Nell." The next day, he recorded tremendous satisfaction with his Harvard days in his diary. TRP 1880 diary, June 30–July 1.

The choice between setting up his beautiful "little wife" using the benefits of a law degree and the possibility of shipping off to Europe for three years of scientific training was simple. As he machinated on his choice of career path later in his college years, Roosevelt sought the advice of one of his political economy instructors, J. Laurence Laughlin, who emphasized the relevance of political and economic studies to those who served in public life.[114] As Roosevelt marched toward graduation, he was clearly satisfied with his decision to move away from natural history as an academic discipline and career.

The day before he received his degree from Harvard, an effervescent Roosevelt described how there were "only four months before we get married! My cup of happiness is almost too full."[115] Once the ceremonies were over and the diploma was in his grasp, Roosevelt looked back to his past: "<u>My career</u> (both in and out of college) <u>has been more successful than that of any man I have known</u>."[116]

This glowing assessment of college did not endure throughout his life, and as he looked back in his *Autobiography*, Roosevelt emphasized what he had learned from books more than his instructors.[117] There was little mention of the elation he had remarked in his journals many times during college. In hindsight, he chalked up his move away from science partly to a lack of deep interest in the subject: "Doubtless this meant that I really did not have the intense devotion to science which I thought I had; for, if I had possessed such devotion, I would have carved out a career for myself somehow without regard to discouragements."[118] However, the honest and passionate diary entries he made during college paint a more complex picture of Roosevelt's choice of life course. Like most of those who struggle to chart their way in college, Roosevelt's quest was influenced by looming expectations from his family as well as by the way in which he tried to fit the complex persona he had developed as a youth into the scientific profession of the day. Ultimately, he nurtured his academic passions in history and economics—he had already been writing a history of the War of 1812—and pursued a course in law and public life that also fit with his overwhelming desire to create a home for himself and Alice.

The summer after graduation, Roosevelt took Alice to Oyster Bay. No longer were his entries peppered with his encounters with other young ladies, like his time spent rowing with Edith Carow in 1878, or teaching "pretty Miss Emily Swan" to play tennis in the summer of 1879.[119] With marriage just months away, Roosevelt focused on his new life with Alice. Although his outdoor skills and persona now assumed a different position in his life with his move away from a career in science, they were not relegated to the past. Instead, Roosevelt's field identity was up in the air, like a feather in a pillow fight, slowly floating down to rest in a place that he could not have predicted at the time. His desire to take to the field for adventure would remain lifelong, but the forces that drove him to the field were shifting. He and Alice walked and picnicked, rowed and sailed, and even trekked to what would later become Acadia National Park, to cement their union on the rocky and romantic coastline of Maine. And then, back home in September, he reluctantly prepared for a hunting trip he had planned with his brother Elliott, and which he thought would be his last trip to the field as a single man.

2

PERSONA *into*

PRACTICE

Tramping West

Suspension was an afterthought on the buckboard wagon that Theodore and Elliott Roosevelt rode in the backwaters of the Midwest as they searched for partridge and hare. Fusing two words with uncomfortable connotations, a "buckboard" is an economical wagon with a flexible board to absorb the shocks of travel. In his *Wild Scenes in the Forest and Prairie*, published in 1843, C. F. Hoffman provides a glimpse into what the Roosevelt brothers experienced: "Let me here initiate the reader into a mode of travelling which is much in fashion about the sources of the Hudson. Did he ever see a teamster riding upon a buckboard? a stout, springy plank, laid upon the bare bolsters of a wagon!"[1] Jounced in all directions, Hoffman describes how his buckboard labored over a rutted road: "As it slammed about among trees and logs, the motion of our vehicle was as much lateral as forward."[2] The Roosevelts had a similar buckboard experience during their six important weeks spent "Midwest tramping" in 1880.

Tired and shot out, the Roosevelt brothers were bumping along the unimproved tracks out of Carroll, Iowa. In the midst of their hunting tour of Illinois, Iowa, and Minnesota, Roosevelt described in his diary how they were on their way to catch the night train to Chicago when they had a brief but dramatic escapade: "We nearly upset over a big rock, both the driver and I being sent flying out of the wagon on our heads."[3] As he got up, luckily "very little hurt," it is unlikely that Roosevelt paused to consider the significance of the event.[4] The image of his head literally passing over his heels, however, is a fitting kinematic projection of his time in the Midwest; one of a developing man whose life was outwardly on track and determined, but of whom much below the surface was still up in the air.

Launching out of a buckboard was only the first of Roosevelt's aerial displays: he later went "head over heels in a mud hole, gun & all," near Moorhead, Minnesota.[5] Taking to the prairies of the Midwest was a brief interlude before he began his professional life, and the relevance of the field identity that had seasoned throughout his adolescent life was now unclear. This time in the field engendered a different kind of experience and brought him perspective on himself, as his eyes were not icily trained through the sights of his gun as they had been in the past. On this trip he was glancing, sometimes staring, back over his shoulder as he considered the new life that awaited him in the East.

The night train out of New York quickly swept Theodore and Elliott past the remaining tracks of deciduous forests in Pennsylvania and out onto the open plains of Illinois as they began their trip. Theodore had ridden camels in Egypt and frolicked in alpine meadows, but this was his first taste of the temperate grasslands that he had long romanticized. He had compared this treasure of America's midlands to the view over the Nile River Valley from the summit of the Great Pyramid in Giza, and when he was on the grand tour he had even looked forward to the time when he would visit Minnesota.[6] Finally nearing these panoramic swaths of grasses, home to prairie dogs and jackrabbits, he and Elliott arrived in Chicago in the midst of a Freemason's convention and had to scramble for accommodations. They eventually "got hold of a man named Wilcox" who agreed to have them hunt on his farm some sixty miles away in Huntley, Illinois. [7]

Not ones to waste time, when the Roosevelt boys arrived at the Wilcox farm they dropped their gear and immediately "took a preliminary tramp through the great rolling fields after prairie chickens."[8] This new kind of "plains shooting" was a challenge for Theodore, and he delighted in the pursuit of grouse, doves, plover, and sand snipe on level fields and open vistas.[9] However, only four short days passed on the farm before Roosevelt was pining for Alice: "In spite of enjoying my hunting so much, I miss Alice dreadfully; I would give up everything just to see her sweet face again."[10] A long distance from her tender touch and soothing countenance, the view from the windswept grasslands put his intense feelings for his beloved in perspective.

| SEPTEMBER, WEDNESDAY 22. | 1880. |
| SEPTEMBER, THURSDAY 23. | 1880. |

Started in tolerably good season, hunting through the stubble fields after chicken and whitebellies; we both of us shot pretty well. At dusk we again camped in the woods in a bend of the Buffalo river; we have no tent or regular outfit, and sleep on the ground; we haven't even a frying pan.

Got off pretty early; it was cloudy all day, raining sometimes. We had only fair success in the stubble fields, but I had capital fun in a big slew, wading about after ducks, until I went head over heels in a mud hole, gun & all. Reached Moorehead in the evening, which we spent with dear old John Elliott. We have had great fun this trip; I have never had a better hunt; but I am awfully homesick for Alice, and shall be too delighted to see her again.

4 sharp tails 3 chicken 2 plover 2 dove — 3 chicken 4 duck 2 dove 4 plover 2 grebe
23 „ „ 7 „ 2 „   7 „ 6 „ 2 „

After leaving Huntley, Illinois, the Roosevelt brothers hunted in Carroll, Iowa, and then made a final stop in Moorhead, Minnesota, a town near the border of the Dakota Territory. In Minnesota, conditions were primitive: the Roosevelts slept on the ground and cooked without even a frying pan. TRP 1880 diary, September 22–23.

The euphoria of graduating from Harvard and starting his life with Alice had been cathartic for Roosevelt, and he had spent the summer months before his Midwest excursion showing her his favorite haunts. When it came time to leave his darling for the Midwest, he confided in his diary "how bitterly I hate to have to leave her for six weeks day after tomorrow."[11] His diary leading up to the trip was bursting with accounts of his "bright, bewitching little sunbeam," and she had even turned the normally logical Roosevelt in contradictory circles: "She grows sweeter and prettier every day—and yet she <u>couldn't</u> be sweeter or prettier than she is."[12] Roosevelt carried these intense emotions along with his gun as he tramped "in sullen silence through the wet prairie grass" near Huntley, and it is no surprise that he "shot very badly."[13] As they prepared to leave the Wilcox farm and board a train bound for the Great Plains of Iowa, Roosevelt summed up the extent of his fixation on home: "Alice is always the first thing I think about in the morning, and the last at night, and I doubt if she is ever absent five minutes from my thoughts—or even from my dreams."[14]

Steaming west through Iowa, Roosevelt penetrated a vast belt of grassland that stretched from the Brazos River in Texas north past the Saskatchewan River in Alberta. Almost a thousand miles wide, this ecosystem was a haven for pronghorn and bison, but on this trip the attraction was the avian refuges. Bitterns, grouse, yellowlegs, and grebes were all fair game as the Roosevelts blasted their way into this beltway of migratory and resident birds. Unknowingly, they were amid one of the most significant ecological transformations in human history, as the Great Plains were being almost completely converted to agricultural lands. In Iowa the change was incredible: two decades before their visit, only 8 percent of the state had been agricultural land, but twenty years after that number was 97 percent.[15] Years after their visit, much of Roosevelt's energy would be consumed by issues of conservation. On his Midwest tramp, however, his attention to the scenic beauty of these plains paled in comparison to his thoughts of home: "Much though I have enjoyed the trip it has not made up to me for being away from my darling; nothing ever could."[16]

With just over two weeks to go, the third leg of their trip took them to Moorhead, Minnesota, several miles from present-day Fargo, North Dakota. In this town on the edge of the great West, saloons were packed with traders and cowboys. Despite the cultural appeal of these watering holes, the Roosevelts had come to see the wilds of the plains, and they quickly tramped into the bush. In the last week of the trip, Roosevelt experienced the romantic adventures he had dreamed about since childhood. On September 19 he and his brother "started early in the morning and drove over thirty miles in a cold, driving rainstorm."[17] Getting lost more than once, they eventually took refuge at the home of a "norwegian settler."[18] That evening the sky partly cleared to reveal the sunset, and Roosevelt described how "we sallied out with our guns, returning with several ducks and grouse."[19] With the wind howling through the cracks that night in the ramshackle house, Roosevelt was enveloped by the field as he slept on the floor under a buffalo robe.[20] In the following days he happily took refuge in even more basic fashion: "We have no tent or regular outfit, and sleep on the ground; we haven't even a frying pan."[21] This cowboy culture of hard ground and buffalo robes would later enshroud him, but at this point even these authentic adventures could not turn his attention fully away from Alice. They left for Saint Paul, and Roosevelt stacked up the experience: "The trip has been great fun; but how glad I am it is over and I am to see Alice!"[22]

Mining his vocabulary for effusive words to describe his love as he looked back east, Roosevelt was in the company of legions of naturalists, hunters, explorers, and even tourists who had gone to the field and found perspective. For some, rugged conditions tested strength. Others found that the absence of distractions brought values into focus. At the same time as Roosevelt was tramping with Elliott that fall, countless other adventurers were finding their own perspectives. Half a world away, one of them had just taken up residence in Waynman Dixon's old tomb—which the Roosevelts had visited less than a decade earlier—and an experience parallel to Roosevelt's was playing out at the foot of the Great Pyramid at Giza.

Flinders Petrie was destined to become one of the most important Egyptologists in history, and in the fall of 1880 he had come to Egypt to survey the pyramids in the Giza complex. Like Roosevelt, Petrie was devoted to the accuracy of descriptions. He arrived at Giza laden with surveying expertise that he had developed by carefully documenting Stonehenge, and he quickly applied that work to the structure and arrangement of the Giza complex. He installed himself in Dixon's tomb, refurbished with as much comfort as could be afforded in what amounted to a stone cave. Suffering from a bad "fever-cold" during his stay, Petrie described a night in the desert far away from his own bed:

> Did not get any sleep till 11 or 12 and then broken by 1st trap down, big rat, killed and reset. 2nd Mouse about trap for long, though bait must have been eaten, got up to see. 3rd Fleas. 4th Mouse let trap down without going in, got up, reset it. 5th Mouse in, got up, killed him, re-set trap.

6th Fleas. 7th Dog set up a protracted conversational barking (just by my door) with sundry neighbours in adjacent
villages; went out and pelted him off. 8th Woke in heavy
perspiration, had to change night shirt and take off sheet.[23]

Sprinkled throughout the pages of Roosevelt's diaries from his
Midwest trip are similar perspectives on field accommodations. At
the Dixon farm he remarked how "both fare and accommodations
here are of the roughest; pork & potatoes being the invariable
meal"; the "miserable old hotel" in Moorhead was not any better.[24]

Both Petrie's and Roosevelt's fieldwork challenged their per-
ceptions and assumptions about people as well. For Petrie, the
workers in the pyramid complex operated in a mode to which he
was entirely unaccustomed: "Nothing seems to be done with any
uniform and regular plan, work is begun and left unfinished; no
regard is paid to future requirements of exploration and no civilized or labour saving re-appliances are used . . . all the sand being
carried in small baskets on the heads of children."[25] Roosevelt's annoyance as they were "still waiting for Wilcox" in Chicago reflects
a similar comparison; he clearly would have liked a man with a
New Englander's punctuality.[26] Neither Petrie nor Roosevelt were
complainers; these passages point out how field conditions can
provide powerful contrasts with home. On his trip to the Midwest,
the cold steel barrel of his gun and thoughts of Alice were strange
bedfellows for Roosevelt, and the distant prospect on his new life
brought him perspective on who he was as a man.

The concept of manhood is an ambiguous idea informed by
personal interpretation and history. Roosevelt's manhood had
plenty of history. Early in his life, he had idolized the strength and
determination of his father and was trained in manly pursuits like
riding horses, shooting guns, and skinning animals. In college, he
soaked in the developing culture of manhood at Harvard. Charles
Eliot had set the stage in his inaugural address as Harvard's president in 1869:

> But there is an aristocracy to which the sons of Har-
> vard have belonged, and, let us hope, will ever aspire to
> belong—the aristocracy which excels in manly sports, car-
> ries off the honors and prizes of the learned professions,

H. ROCHER ——— CHICAGO.

In the late summer and fall after graduating from Harvard, Roosevelt (right) spent six weeks tramping on the plains of Illinois, Iowa, and Minnesota with his brother Elliott (left). Though he enjoyed hunting grouse and other game birds, Roosevelt dearly missed his "bewitching little sunbeam," Alice Lee. TRC 520.12-019.

and bears itself with distinction in all fields of intellectual labor and combat; the aristocracy which in peace stands firmest for the public honor and renown, and in war rides first into the murderous thickets.[27]

Eliot wasn't alone; he had William James and Nathanial Shaler to help him in defining the nature of the "Harvard man."[28] Roosevelt may have agreed with Eliot and Shaler's emphasis on the athletic and academic excelling in manliness, but his view on where women fit in a man's world diverged with that of James. Roosevelt's senior thesis, "The Practicability of Equalizing Men and Women before the Law," argued that women should be not only afforded the right to vote but also brought to equal status in issues of money and education.[29] Given the strength of his fist-pounding speeches and his rides into battle in Cuba, it is no surprise that Roosevelt's public image became an icon of the manhood of his time. His diary from the Midwest provides an intimate view of how the "Victorian codes of bourgeois manliness" and frontier literature that he had been exposed to as a child echoed in the naturalistic struggle of hunting, the vibrating heartstrings of a tortured lover, and the competition of brotherly game bags as he explored the plains of the Midwest.[30]

Facing off with tender utterances on Alice in his diary pages, Roosevelt inserted passages that revealed his struggle to be an alpha male. Although he was the firstborn male in his family, his status was not unchallenged. When the boys tramped together, the testosterone surged and they engaged in one of the oldest forms of human competition: the manly comparison of game bags. Almost daily, Roosevelt compared his own success with Elliott's in his diary, and at the bottom of each page he listed the day's haul with two lines: one for him and a second for Elliott. Less quantitative comparisons also abound, as when he recounted how on the Wilcox farm "I never shot worse, while Elliott hit about everything he fired at."[31] Later in the trip, he "shot pretty well, fully as well as or better than Elliott."[32] Before he left Moorhead, bound for Saint Paul, he listed a "game bag" tally like those that appear periodically in his life's notebooks and journals, but in this table there was column marked "T" for his own birds, directly next to one with an "E" for

SEPTEMBER, FRIDAY 24. 1880.

Spent the day with old Jack. Our bag is as follows.

		E	Total
Sharp tail grouse	26	44	70
Pinnated grouse	69	119	188
Quail	5		5
Dove	8		8
Snipe		1	1
Plover	16	9	25
Shore Snipe	51		51
Rail	1		1
Coot	1		1
Goose	1	1	2
Duck	17	25	42
Grebe	4	1	5
Bittern	2		2
Hare	1	1	2
Rabbit	1		1
	203	201	404

17 duck = 4 mallard 1 wood duck 1 green teal 2 blue teal 2 blue bill 2 dippers 1 widgeon 1 sprigtail 2 red head 2 gadwall 1 hooded merganser

16 plover = 3 upland 5 golden 2 black breast 6 others

51 shore snipe = 33 winter yellowlegs 12 summer yellowlegs 6 sandpipers.

SEPTEMBER, SATURDAY 25. 1880.

Left for St Pauls. The trip has been great fun; but how glad I am it is over and I am to see Alice!

The day Roosevelt finished his Midwest hunting, he tallied his "game bag," using separate columns for himself and Elliott. A practice he had kept at the foot of many of his diary pages, this summation showed Roosevelt edging out his brother by two birds. TRP 1880 diary, September 24–25.

Elliott's. On the trip, Theodore edged out his sibling by a close score of 203 to 201.[33]

It wasn't all competition, however, and Theodore described how it was "great fun to be off with old Nell; he and I can do about anything together; we never lose our temper under difficulties and always accomplish what we set about."[34] Everyone in the Roosevelt family had at least one nickname, and Theodore's use of "Nell" to describe Elliott reflects his affection for his younger brother, who had a very different personality. In contrast to Theodore's oversized grin and bombastic nature, Elliott had gotten a different kind of charm. He had a natural ease with women, and while

Roosevelt doggedly pursued his academic work at Harvard, Elliott traveled the world. When Theodore visited home during college, he heard of Elliott's prowess on the game trail in Texas, and he later returned to hear of him being chased by elephants in Ceylon.[35] Just as Fyodor Dostoevsky was doing in that same fall of 1880 while writing *The Brothers Karamazov*, the Roosevelt brothers were working out the complex tensions of brotherhood.

In addition to his words and deeds, Roosevelt used his apparel to call out his strength and manhood. In the Midwest he reveled in being rough-hewn and dirty: he described how "we are dressed about as badly as mortals could be, with our cropped heads, unshaven faces, dirty gray shirts, still dirtier yellow trousers and cowhide boots."[36] He even joked with his mother that she would likely have disowned him if she had seen him on the trip, because he was "awfully disreputable looking."[37] For him the field was a place to act out his manliness, but it also provided a point of comparison to the image he had adopted in sitting rooms in Chestnut Hill. Just like the heroes he had read about in frontier adventures, he made a point of traveling freely between civilized and undomesticated worlds.[38] He even wrote his sister to make sure that fine clothes would be waiting for him upon his return.[39]

This question of manhood was not only implicit. Roosevelt described his and Elliott's exploits in manly terms: "Nell and I are travelling on our muscle, and do'n't give a hang for any man."[40] He frequently referred to his manhood, as when he wrote to his sister Anna and described how after "three days good shooting" he felt "twice the man for it already."[41] Roosevelt stopped short of self-analysis in his diary, but the passages are dominated by his love for Alice and his hunting exploits. The field as a place for self-exploration and reflection—in this case, on his male identity—was an undeniable element of Roosevelt's experience in the Midwest. He would return to the field countless times in his life for contemplation, and eventually would help set aside wide tracts of land that could be used for similar purposes by all Americans.

When Roosevelt later visited the Grand Canyon as president in 1903, he could not have imagined that at the dawning of the new millennium, more than 275 million people would be visiting our national parks each year.[42] On that day he simply urged the preservation of these national treasures for the benefit of the people:

"I want to ask you to do one thing in connection with it in your own interest and in the interest of the country—to keep this great wonder of nature as it now is. . . . I hope you will not have a building of any kind, not a summer cottage, a hotel, or anything else, to mar the wonderful grandeur, the sublimity, the great loneliness and beauty of the canyon."[43] Throughout his life Roosevelt went to the wilderness to find himself, to appreciate nature, to hunt, and to grieve and seek solace. Early on, these lands shaped his very identity, whose underlying form was in place by the end of his Midwest tramping. Much as his likeness was eventually chipped from a mountainside—Roosevelt's visage on Mount Rushmore, started in 1927 and finished in 1941, was apparent well before it was complete—his identity continued to weather and be refined over decades. On the lumbering eastbound train out of the Midwest in the fall of 1880, Roosevelt moved toward a life dominated at least temporarily by politics, but his underlying field identity was still in place like a stone monument. The question remained, however, of how he would continue to engage in his adventurous mode while undertaking diverse professional pursuits.

As Roosevelt found his way back to Boston in the fall of 1880, his life was at a turning point. He married Alice in October, and they took up residence at 6 West Fifty-Seventh Street in Manhattan just two weeks later. He delved into his law studies at Columbia, and also finished writing his *Naval War of 1812*. Members of the New York elite recognized his potential in politics, and quickly tapped him to run for the New York State Assembly. Only a year out of college and still looking about eighteen, he won a seat in the fall of 1881 and reported to Albany in the cold first days of 1882.[44] Although it didn't take long for Roosevelt's true persona to rise to the surface, he made a first impression that beguiled many of his fellow assemblymen.

A tight-fitting suit and cane were an unfortunate combination with Roosevelt's voice and quirky personality as he walked into the Assembly chamber. Quite the opposite of the masculine Roosevelt who had tracked game with Elliott, he made a more delicate first impression on his new colleagues. This was hard-hitting politics, and people weren't subtle, using terms like "young

SEPTEMBER, THURSDAY 30. 1880.	OCTOBER, FRIDAY 1. 1880.
I am so happy that I hardly know what to do. My own beautiful queen is the same as ever and yet with a certain added charm that I do not know how to describe; I can not take my eyes off her; she is so pure and holy that it seems almost profanation to touch her, no matter how gently and tenderly; and yet when we are alone I can not bear her to be a minute out of my arms. I have been gradually getting frightfully homesick for her; my happiness now is almost too great.	Spent the day with my own hearts darling, my sweetest mistress.

Roosevelt arrived home from the Midwest and was overjoyed to spend time with his fiancée, Alice Lee. He struggled to describe his emotions as he was reunited with his "own heart's darling." TRP 1880 diary, September 30–October 1.

squirt," "punkin-lily," "Jane Dandy," and "Rosy Roosy" as affronts to Roosevelt's masculinity.[45] They even flippantly compared him to Oscar Wilde, the flamboyant literary figure who was lecturing throughout the United States in 1882. Whether in a boxing ring at Harvard or on the floor of the Assembly, Roosevelt was never kept down long; the underlying facets of his persona had a way of rearing up to bite those who trifled with him. Over his first years in politics, descriptions that challenged Roosevelt's masculinity faded, and now only historians remember that he ever was thought of in this way. Eventually, his forceful persona dominated.

Throughout Roosevelt's life, those who described him dipped into an endless well of similes and metaphors and pulled up many comparisons to the field. Some took inspiration from zoology, as he showed that "such a superabundance of animal life was hardly ever condensed in a human [being]."[46] Roosevelt described his own feelings of connection with the animal world; he often felt like a "fighting cock" or "strong as a bull."[47] Others saw Roosevelt's energy as more derived from the physical world, describing his presence as a "gust of wind" or as the spontaneous release of energy from atoms: he was "radio-active."[48] He evoked meteorological forces that shaped the landscape as he spun like a "cyclone" or was "a creature charged with such a voltage," the embodiment of lightning.[49] His words derived their power from the battlefield, like "the bursting of a bombshell," and he similarly described his own experience of ascent: "I rose like a rocket."[50] An opponent's description of Roosevelt evoked a wild-eyed foot soldier in the trenches, a "damn fool" who "would tread on his own balls just as quick as he would on his neighbor's."[51] In Roosevelt's early political life, his true identity rose to the surface: from a first impression as a delicate flower to a more dominant image of exploding ordnance. These symbols of natural strength and power matured throughout the rest of his life in papers, in books, and even in eulogies.

As he so often did, John Burroughs created a naturalistic description of Roosevelt that went straight to the mark. Shortly after Roosevelt died, Burroughs wrote: "There was always something imminent about him, like an avalanche that the sound of your voice might loosen."[52] Burroughs's skill as a wordsmith is only part of what made this reflection on Roosevelt so powerful; if he had hung these words upon another person of strength, it would have only gone part way. The image is believable because the words meshed with Roosevelt's real and perceived identity. It reached into the essence of his character.

No one could mistake Roosevelt's forceful persona in Albany once he had weathered his first year in the Assembly. He became a major part of the cast, taking the stage as he ran for speaker of the Assembly (and lost) or lobbied for bills on fees for liquor licenses. The Assembly chamber's groined ceiling and massive murals loomed over this virtual coliseum of the public good, and the political combat it housed was suited to Roosevelt's irksome charm and underlying tenacity. Roosevelt's outdoor persona was always in his shadow, like a prowling cougar or lumbering grizzly, waiting to step into the light and attack his opponents. To his peers it was clear that he was a forceful politician on the rise. But even celestial bodies are subject to larger forces, and like the moon when it reaches its apogee—the farthest point from earth in its orbit—Roosevelt was slowly pulled back to the field, even more substantially than he ever might have expected.

After the legislative year finished in May of 1883, Roosevelt had a fortuitous encounter at a meeting of the Free Trade Club at Clark's Tavern in New York City.[53] Once the plates were cleared and the cigars came out, Roosevelt was approached by Commander H. H. Gorringe, a retired naval officer who hoped to engage Roosevelt's interest in battle and hunting. Discussion of *The Naval War of 1812* was only a preamble as Gorringe described the land he had recently purchased near the Little Missouri River in the Dakota Territory. Roosevelt's interest was piqued. Gorringe planned to head to this rough terrain in the Dakota Badlands in the coming fall of 1883, and he invited Roosevelt. Many strings pulled Roosevelt west: the lingering taste of his trip to the edge of the Dakota Territory with Elliott, the need to break free from the confines of indoor work, the desire to live out and tell frontier narratives, the urge to hunt buffalo.

Never one who could resist the tug of open places for long, Roosevelt took Gorringe up on his offer. The wheels of his domestic life were spinning fast, with Alice pregnant and plans for a seaside home in Oyster Bay in the works, but none of this could stand in the way of Roosevelt's urge to go west.[54] Gorringe eventually bowed out of the trip, but Roosevelt was determined to go regardless. He hopped a train to Chicago, then to Saint Paul, and then connected to the Northern Pacific Railroad heading west, a line that had printed a thorough description of what its passengers would see on just such a trip: "Beyond the Great Lakes, far from the hum of New England factories, far from the busy throng of Broadway, from the smoke and grime of iron cities, and the dull, prosaic life of many another Eastern town, lies a region which may justly be designated the Wonderland of the World."[55] The Badlands was one of the more extreme landscapes, and the railroad primed passengers using the words of the writer E. V. Smalley: "The change in the scene is so startling, and the appearance of the landscape so wholly novel and so singularly grotesque, that you rub your eyes to make sure that you are not dreaming of some ancient geologic epoch, when the rude, unfinished earth was the sport of Titanic forces, or fancying yourself transported to another planet."[56] Fittingly, Roosevelt followed just a day behind the "Golden Spike Special," a train carrying ex-President Grant and an entourage that was celebrating this newly opened route through the American landscape.[57] Arriving at the Little Missouri stop, Roosevelt gathered his belongings and set foot on the arid soil of the Badlands for the first time.

Roosevelt's own words best describe his first taste of the area: "I first reached the Little Missouri on a Northern Pacific train about three in the morning of a cool September day in 1883. Aside from the station, the only building was a ramshackle structure called the Pyramid Park Hotel. I dragged my duffle-bag thither, and hammered at the door until the frowsy proprietor appeared, muttering oaths."[58] Under the engine of Roosevelt's vigor, much could happen in two weeks.

Once can imagine Roosevelt waking up the next morning, like the rough and tumble characters who surrounded him, with his boots and pants in an accordion lump aside his bed. Ramshackle the Pyramid Park was, and the racket grew as the occupants of the room's fourteen beds pulled on their boots and scraped their faces of whiskers before tracking the smell of bacon to the rough-hewn dining room. Roosevelt knew enough to steer clear of jabs at his "four eyes"; these were men who could kick up a lot more than dust. Roosevelt later described how he found the hard-edged ranchers and cowboys he encountered in the Badlands strangely endearing. These "lean, sinewy" cowpunchers had spurs jangling at their feet and strings of bullets strapped to their waists.[59] Their behavior more than kept up their image, as in this type of men "there was a good deal of rough horse-play, and, as with any other gathering of men or boys of high animal spirits, the horse-play sometimes became very rough indeed; and as the men usually carried revolvers, and as there were occasionally one or two noted gun-fighters among them, there was now and then a shooting affray."[60] Any whiff of the "punkin-lily" would have sunk Roosevelt, so he simply made it known that he was looking for a hunt.

The locals were skeptical of outsiders in general, and Easterners with spectacles especially, so it took Roosevelt some time to find a willing guide for his trip.[61] He started with the grouchy old proprietor of the Pyramid Park, who turned out to be a man named Vine whom everyone called "Captain" in reference to his days at the helm of a riverboat. Mumbling some version of the "ungrateful business of 'trundling a tenderfoot'" to find a buffalo, he reluctantly pointed Roosevelt in the direction of his son.[62] Rotund and rosy-cheeked, clad in a red mackinaw shirt and buckskin pants, Frank Vine was a good bit more accommodating. He walked Roosevelt over to his store, a dimly lit building stuffed so full of boxes and barrels that only a small portion of the space allowed for trade. As Vine had expected, they found Joe Ferris inside.

Joe Ferris was a stocky Canadian who had made his way to the Badlands with his brother Sylvane and their friend Bill Merrifield two years before. Joe Ferris not only had a reputation as a good hunter but also that of a blunt instrument, like "the power end of the pile driver."[63] One employee recalled his methods: "If I happened to be a little slow in jumping when he said the word, for example, it was his idea to pick me up whole and apply me head first as a battering ram against the wall."[64] With some effort, Vine convinced Ferris that Roosevelt had some combination of the grit and cash he would need to be successful in finding a buffalo, and soon enough, Roosevelt had piled his buckboard high with gear and they were on their way to a recommended hunting ground near Gregor Lang's outpost some fifty miles away on the Little Cannonball Creek. Since Sylvane Ferris and Merrifield's ranch was on the way, Roosevelt and Joe Ferris decided to stop there for the night.

The Chimney Butte Ranch that Sylvane and Merrifield worked was a small affair, with only 150 head of cattle. When Roosevelt arrived, it was also an ambiguous place, given that the owners were the only ones who referred to it by the name derived from Chimney Butte, which loomed out on the skyline like a cracked and crumbling smokestack on the horizon. Almost everyone else called the ranch the Maltese Cross, after the brand that was stamped into their cattle.[65]

At the Maltese Cross, Roosevelt met Sylvane and Merrifield, who were in their twenties, were thin and sunburned, and did not warm up to strangers quickly. Roosevelt always had a way of growing on people, and after dinner the group settled into a game of "Old Sledge" on the table. The slow flick of the dealer's hand brought six cards in front of each of the men. In the one-room cabin, the players reflectively assessed their hands and considered the best suit for trump. Suddenly, a bout of cackles and caws came from the henhouse, and in one motion cards fell to the table and chairs scraped back across the dirt floor as the men grabbed their guns and ran outside. A bobcat had been after the chickens, and the ranchers prowled the darkness for any signs of the trail. Unsuccessful, they returned to the cabin. But now the ice was broken, and it was the first of many Badlands bonding experiences among these men.[66]

Joe Ferris determined that he and Roosevelt would head south to Lang's ranch together in the buckboard the next day. Roosevelt had spent plenty of time in a buckboard with Elliott, and his hams certainly remembered the discomfort of that jolting brand of travel. He asked to borrow a saddle horse. Conservative and skeptical, the three ranchers maintained that none were available. Roosevelt persisted, and Ferris later recalled how "he wanted that horse so blamed bad, that when he see we weren't going to let him have it, he offered to buy it for cash."[67] This was only the first time that Roosevelt simply cracked open his wallet and created his "hold" in the Badlands.[68]

The buffalo hunt itself was cold, wet, and ultimately more tiring for Joe Ferris than it was for Roosevelt. Despite being known as one who drove others, Ferris was the one who was driven on this trip. Using Gregor Lang's ranch house as a base, Roosevelt and Ferris headed out looking for the scattered remnants of the buffalo herds that had been plentiful just a few years before. Millions of animals had been slaughtered for hides, for meat, and for sport, and now there were only small bands roaming free. Roosevelt was determined to find one before they were all gone. For more than a week Roosevelt would rise early, and despite Ferris's pleas to wait for the rain to stop, they would ride away from Lang's primitive cabin and out onto the plains. They meandered along creeks and plodded through a greasy slurry of dense mud and clay that the locals called "gumbo."[69] For days they only had periodic shots at deer, returning to the cabin emptyhanded. The hunting pair diverged on their enjoyment of the experience: the supposedly hardy Ferris was "on the point of caving" throughout, but he pasted on some kind of smile as he "was obliged to keep going while trying to look as if he enjoyed it."[70] Roosevelt, on the other hand, was in his element, and when he returned at night, "the grin was still there, being apparently built in and ineradicable. Disfigured with clinging gumbo he might be, and generally was, but always the twinkling eyes and big white teeth shone through."[71]

Not one to turn in early, Roosevelt stayed up late into the night to absorb Gregor Lang's unique perspective on the Badlands. Lang had come to the area to scout out the viability of ranches there for a British investor, so he had thought critically about the prospects.[72] Roosevelt pumped Lang for information on cattle ranching in the Badlands, and weighed his perspective against those of ranchers such as Merrifield and the Ferrises. Even with little sleep and big plans welling up inside him, Roosevelt gulped coffee in the mornings and was again spurring on Ferris to help him find a buffalo.

The days went on with more mud and rain. After six days of methodical searching, hope finally began to rise when they spied fresh evidence of buffalo.[73] There was a rare warmth from the sun that day, and they followed their game up the slope of a ravine, only to catch sight of a shaggy bull lumbering through some bushes. Its giant nostrils caught their scent too early for them to fire as it bounded over a bank and made its way off, never to be seen again. Tracking east that same afternoon, they were encouraged again when through the hot and rippling air on the horizon they made out three small buffalo forms. The riders spurred their horses, but the long days with little water had taxed them. They moved slowly. Within a half mile of the game they dismounted and crept, eventually on hands and knees, to line up a shot only 150 feet away. Roosevelt pulled his trigger, and in an instant a small dust plume rose from the fur of one of the buffalos, but the wound did not prevent the animal from tearing off with the others. Disheartened, Ferris and Roosevelt gathered their horses and set off after the wounded bull. It wasn't until they were amid the crepuscular light of evening when the weary horses brought the hunters again within range of the three buffalo. This time they made straight for them. Ferris charged, and flushed the buffalo toward Roosevelt. Once in close range, Roosevelt took a wild shot as his pony pitched with "violent, labored motion."[74] The bull lowered its nose to the ground and advanced in retaliation, and Roosevelt's frightened pony wheeled around and knocked the rifle into his forehead, cutting a wide gash. With blood pouring down Roosevelt's face, the bull swept past and chased after Ferris's horse with his horns "unpleasantly near the tired pony's tail."[75] The buffalo eventually made off into the night, and the clumsy dance of quadrupeds was over. Tired, bloody, and defeated, Roosevelt and Ferris had no business traipsing back to Lang's in the night. They laid out their bedrolls and tied their ponies to the saddles, which served as pillows for the night.

That night was full of more bad luck. Something spooked the ponies around midnight and they dashed off, ripping the pillows out from under the sleeping hunters' heads. Rubbing the sleep from their eyes, they followed the uneven snakelike saddle tracks in the moonlight, and eventually collected the horses and returned to their blankets. Around three it began to rain, and by morning they were lying in a cold bath of rainwater. With their soggy clothes clinging to their skin, they headed back out in the mud and rain to continue their pursuit. Roosevelt got a shot at a buffalo that day through the thick rain, but missed in a way in which "a man to his dying day always looks back upon with wonder and regret."[76]

There were several more days of discouragement until Roosevelt's shot finally went home. Following the Little Cannonball into the Montana territory, Roosevelt drew a bead on a massive bull and observed through one eye how its "glossy fall coat was in fine trim and shone in the rays of the sun."[77] He let the bullet go from his Sharps .45-120 rifle "not thirty yards from the great grim looking beast."[78] The ball—almost two ounces of metal—entered near the shoulder and went "clean through his body."[79] This time it was the buffalo that was bleeding, and after a short run it expired in a small depression on the other side of a ravine from where Roosevelt had made his shot. Ferris watched as Roosevelt approached the dead bull and his body burst into a motion that Ferris conceptualized as a white man's war dance, gyrating and hollering, releasing the pent-up emotions from many frustrating days. Both pleased and stupefied, Ferris gladly accepted the one hundred dollars Roosevelt handed him on the spot.[80] Ferris was only the first in a long line of individuals puzzled by Roosevelt's actions.

Some have interpreted Roosevelt's desire and ultimate success in killing a buffalo as further evidence of his carrying out the "violent chain of destruction" that he had read about in adventure

small hoofs

Buffalo awful short

2 heads

Buffalo squares up except head

71.782

Roosevelt first traveled to the Badlands in September of 1883 to hunt a buffalo. After a rainy and painstaking hunt, Roosevelt, covered with clinging "gumbo" (mud), shot his first buffalo. Frederic Remington, who would later illustrate some of Roosevelt's Badlands writing, kept notebook sketches of buffalo, which were intricately linked to Roosevelt's story of the West, and ultimately to his efforts in conservation. By permission of the Frederic Remington Art Museum.

books when he was a child.[81] Others have questioned his actions through the lens of conservation, asking how someone so fascinated by nature and so dedicated to conservation efforts could knowingly kill one of the last remaining buffalo "while there were still buffalo left to shoot."[82] As in many of Roosevelt's field adventures, multiple forces had driven him west to hunt buffalo. But here, his urge to engage in the chase and confirm his status as a hunter and hero of Western adventures—with a head for his wall—overshadowed his love of natural history and need for escape. He did not keep the kinds of careful notes on natural history that he had kept when collecting birds as a youth, nor did he dissect the animal to understand its inner workings.[83]

The head and hide in hand, Roosevelt prepared to be off from Lang's cabin. Some of the men he left behind in the Badlands might have stood in disbelief had they known that Roosevelt would later employ them when he was president of the United States. Lang, however, saw through the dust storm that Roosevelt had created: "There goes the most remarkable man I ever met. Unless I am badly mistaken the world is due to hear from him one of these days."[84]

The grand buffalo head procured for Alice to admire was only a piece of what Roosevelt would bring back with him from this first trip to the Badlands.[85] During the nights spent beneath the clay roof of the primitive cabin, Roosevelt had pumped Lang for information, and he now made a decision. He was ready to stake his own claim. The baked soil and scrub grass of the Badlands had infected him, and in a surprising display of guts, bravado, and impulsiveness, he laid down fourteen thousand dollars for a stake in the Maltese Cross ranch. And he didn't even ask for a receipt.[86]

The fact that this sum exceeded his full annual earnings, and dwarfed his salary in the Assembly by a factor of ten, suggests that Roosevelt was serious about adopting the West.[87] Hoping to be back in Alice's arms in just over a week, he wrote to her to explain his decision to make the kind of risky investment that would cause even his uncles to shudder. Roosevelt was earnest in his belief that he would be successful, and he explained to his darling: "It will go a long way towards solving the problem that has puzzled us both a good deal at times—how I am to make more money as our

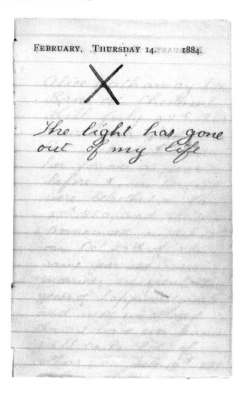

needs increase, and yet try to keep in a position from which I may be able at some future time to again go into public life, or literary life."[88] No doubt Roosevelt was enamored of the land, loved the hunt, and wanted to try his hand at ranching with the three men he had "taken a great fancy to."[89] However, this passing reference to a literary life and the heft of Roosevelt's published Badlands works suggest that his love of narrative—which his mother and aunt had instilled in him in the nursery at East 20th Street—may have been more of a major influence on his decision than he revealed to Alice. Crashing through fields and dried creek beds of the Badlands were

---

(ABOVE AND FACING) Roosevelt married Alice Lee on his birthday, October 27, in 1880. After less than four years of marriage, Alice died of Bright's disease on Valentine's Day of 1884. She had given birth to their only child two days earlier. Just hours before she died in Roosevelt's arms, his mother, Martha Bulloch Roosevelt, had passed away, in the same house, of typhoid fever. He confided in his diary on February 17: "For joy or for sorrow my life has now been lived out." TRP 1884 diary, February 14, 16, and 17.

FEBRUARY, SATURDAY 16. 1884.

Alice Hathaway Lee,
Born at Chestnut
Hill, July 29ᵗʰ 1861.
I saw her first on
Oct 1878; I wooed
her for over a year
before I won her; we
were betrothed on Jan
25ᵗʰ 1880, and it was
announced on Feb 16ᵗʰ;
on Oct 27ᵗʰ of the
same year we were
married; we spent three
years of happiness greater
and more unalloyed
than I have ever known
fall to the lot of
others; on Feb 12ᵗʰ 1884

FEBRUARY, SUNDAY 17. 1884.

her baby was born,
and on Feb 14ᵗʰ she
died in my arms;
On my mother had
died in the same
house, on the same
day, but a few
hours previously. On
Feb 16ᵗʰ they were
buried together in
Greenwood.
On Feb 17ᵗʰ I
christened the baby
Alice Lee Roosevelt

For joy or for sorrow
my life has now been
lived out

bison, cougars, hunters, and cowboys alike. There were stories playing out everywhere in earth and flesh, good stories, and Roosevelt not only wanted to be a character in the cast of these Badlands dramas; he also wanted to be the one to write them.

Western narratives were put on hold as Roosevelt dove back into his work in the Assembly during the fall and winter of 1883. At the dawning of 1884 he was glowing with expectations of fatherhood as Alice was pregnant and getting closer and closer to delivery. On February 6, Roosevelt returned to his lodgings in Albany and penned a letter to Alice that kept her updated on his exploits in the chamber: "I think I made a nice strike in my speech on the aldermanic bill yesterday; I did not do as well as I have sometimes done, but still it was one of my best speeches."[90] He returned home to visit Alice several days later, but after being assured that all was well, he made his way back to Albany on February 12. The next day, he sent out a telegram from Albany that broadcast the news he had just received: "We have a little daughter. The mother only fairly well."[91] Shortly after, Roosevelt received a telegram that made him wince, and he immediately left the chamber on a somber beeline for New York. He arrived in foggy darkness as midnight approached.

Over the next fourteen hours, two of the most tragic events of Theodore Roosevelt's life struck him almost simultaneously, like an unseen uppercut and roundhouse. Elliott Roosevelt described what his brother Theodore found as Valentine's Day 1884 drew near: "There is a curse on this house. Mother is dying, and Alice is dying too."[92] In the darkest hours of the night, Roosevelt took leave from Alice's bedside to say goodbye to his mother, who at 3 a.m. died of typhoid fever. Already exhausted with grief, he climbed the stairs to spend his remaining half day with Alice. Shortly after noon, Elliott's prediction was fulfilled, and Alice died of Bright's disease.

Roosevelt was monotone and somber as he went through the necessary arrangements: the receiving, the funerals, and the burials. Not knowing another course, he turned to his affairs in the Assembly after only four days at home, and spent the spring attempting to bury his grief in political work.

Elliott eventually turned to alcohol to deal with his demons, but Theodore rarely drank; it made him "awfully fighty," not a soothing remedy for grief.[93] Instead, Roosevelt righted his ship in strenuous action. Substantial recovery from this devastating day—a day of which he wrote in his diary, "The light has gone out of my life"— would not happen that spring in the chambers in Albany. It would have to wait for the wide-open landscape of the American West.[94]

The Wilderness Writer

Sullenly pressing into the dust, Roosevelt's boots again connected with the Badlands as he stepped off the Northern Pacific Railroad at the Little Missouri stop. The freedom of this land meant something entirely different now; he arrived after Alice's death more as a devastated castaway than a confident explorer. Although Roosevelt didn't record in his diary exactly what he was looking for, he had come to the Badlands to find it, and he played out multiple factors as he began to focus on the West: to escape the massive loss he had just experienced, to participate in the kinds of frontier narratives he had long embraced, to hunt and to study nature, to become a wilderness storyteller. As he headed out to the Maltese Cross Ranch, his eyes traced the irregular landforms on the horizon and the powerful curves of the horses and cattle. The rugged democracy of this land—where Roosevelt found distraction, recovery, and ultimately healing—was evident in its people and their values.[1] And the fundamental truths of nature, like mortality, were present in the very grains of its course soil.

It wasn't long until Roosevelt eased one dusty boot into a stirrup and kicked the other up over his saddle. He settled his weight down onto his long stirrups and headed out on the roundup, standing almost straight up as the hooves underneath him pounded the cracked earth. It was June 16, 1884, and he had been back in the Badlands only one week, but the abrasion of his flannel shirt and the silk scarf around his neck could now be a soothing comfort, and his chaps had settled into their pistonlike motion against his saddle. The blistering sun glanced off his silver-plated bridle and spurs. His gleaming revolver, too, was a point of pride as it stood ready to shoot rattlesnakes and small game.

Owning the Maltese Cross Ranch didn't skew Roosevelt's concept of democracy. If he had instead been an admirer of feudalism, he would have stayed well back from the dust and grime, pondering ledgers and waiting for reports of the activities of his cowpunchers. However, Roosevelt applied the very fibers of his body—muscle, nerve, connective tissue—to the basic American value of hard work, an application of the strength that was central to his identity as a man. He never wanted to be "the undersize man of letters . . . with his delicate, effeminate sensitiveness"; he would instead be one who found a "man's part among men" and weathered the "winds that harden stouter souls," the type of physical challenge he discovered as he rode along with his crew herding up calves and steers.[2] Few with his resources would have volunteered for such work. But for Roosevelt the roundup had a leveling effect, and anyone who was willing to put up with the conditions could find his role: "As with all other forms of work, so on the round-up, a man of ordinary power, who nevertheless does not shirk things merely because they are disagreeable or irksome, soon earns his place."[3] Like a hero from a frontier story, Roosevelt was a gentleman who could slip into the rough life of the frontier, participating in its hardest challenges while still maintaining his privileged position. With another thousand cattle on the way, this day was just one of many of those rides, and he later described the strenuousness of these experiences: "Once when with Sylvane Ferris I spent about sixteen hours on one horse, riding seventy or eighty miles," or "Another time I was twenty-four hours on horseback in company with Merrifield without changing horses."[4] Although extreme, these weren't even the most extensive rides: "By this time I had been nearly forty hours in the saddle, changing horses five times, and my clothes had thoroughly dried on me."[5]

After a long day in the saddle, he finally ambled back to his cabin for dinner and bed. This was the kind of work that produced satisfying aches in muscles, and calm sleep in the cool night air. Before the day ended, however, Roosevelt sat down to recall the activities of riders, the movements of cattle, and the scurrying of native vermin. He scratched a few short notes in his diary: "One badger; found out on plains away from hole, galloped up to him and killed him with revolver."[6] After thirteen hours of riding the following day, Roosevelt left his diary page blank, and instead wrote a letter to his sister describing his life in the Badlands and his plans for the coming weeks: "Tomorrow my two men go east for the cattle; and I will start out alone to try my hand at finding my way over the prairie by myself."[7] Taking time over the coming days to record his observations in letters and in his diary, and putting much more away in his memory, he found that these moments on the prairie literally became a new chapter in his Badlands experience.

The fading of starlight gave away the sneaking approach of morning as Roosevelt trotted along in the cool air. As he clopped along a river bottom and the crisp night lingered, vision had not yet begun to dominate his other senses. He tasted the dew that still hung in the air and felt its moist residue as the leather of his chaps rubbed his saddle. Banks of wild roses wafted alluring scents, as they had done in June for thousands of years. Hermit thrushes and meadowlarks greeted the morning with the songs he knew so well, and in these dimly lit moments they rang loudly in his ears before his vision began to take precedence.[8]

Roosevelt's horse Manitou picked his way carefully up out of the creek beds, and was met with rosy light in the east, the first "level rays of the cloudless summer sun."[9] Roosevelt could make out the Maltese Cross brand on the meandering lines of cattle as they passed. Lifting their heads as Roosevelt passed by, they briefly met his eyes as they acknowledged the shared experience of a quiet morning.

Much like a sea captain, Roosevelt had a glass slung at his side and he raised it to his eye at intervals, scanning the horizon. He took note of any form; it could be game or approaching wagons or cowboys. Alone on the prairie he found an amorous solitude; as he put it, "nowhere, not even at sea, does a man feel more lonely than when riding over the far-reaching, seemingly never-ending plains; and, after a man has lived a little while on or near them, their very vastness and loneliness and their melancholy monotony have a strong fascination for him."[10]

A group of eight antelope jolted Roosevelt out of contemplation, and he spurred Manitou to full speed in pursuit. Luckily, horse and rider were spry and they ran their prey down on a diagonal. Leaping to the ground as they passed within twenty-five yards of the antelope, Roosevelt raised his gun and emptied both barrels. In the process, he gained another fine buck head for his wall. This

Remington worked as a rancher in Kansas in the early 1880s, and by 1888 he illustrated Roosevelt's article on capturing the boat thieves, entitled "Sheriff's Work on a Ranch," in *Century Magazine*. Remington kept notebooks of sketches and gesture drawings throughout his life, like this page of a cowboy and a hog-tied calf. By permission of the Frederic Remington Art Museum.

trophy was the more minor prize, however, as he would eventually work his diary notes from the day into a full written account of this segment on his Badlands life—complete with revolvers and rattlesnakes, antelopes and badger—entitled "A Trip on the Prairie."[11]

Riding back to the Maltese Cross just five days after he had left it, Roosevelt could see the kind of stories that were playing out every day in the hard-baked country, but he had plenty of logistics to attend to before his ranch would be in shape. There was the question of accommodations and land, as the small cabin at the Maltese Cross was too small for comfortable living and the location was too near the relative bustle of Medora. Fortunately, land was plenty, and he rode north until he found a tract for expansion, which he dubbed "Elkhorn." The land needed a suitable house and people to work it. He had already written to Bill Sewall and Wilmot Dow, his hunting companions from Maine, and asked them to help him fill those needs.

By 1884 the Northern Pacific Railroad had extended long fingers of track across the West, and it was a relatively easy trip for Roosevelt to get back to New York for a bit of politics—he finally gave his full support to the Republican presidential candidate James G. Blaine—and time with his sisters and daughter, and then to collect Sewall and Dow in July. By August, though, he was back in the Badlands.

Upon arriving in the Badlands, Sewall wasn't wholly convinced of the bright future of ranching in a country where a cinnamon brown color dominated the landscape. But he and Dow were as dutiful as they were strong. Roosevelt's generosity didn't hurt, either, as he was rewarding them handsomely for their efforts. The two experienced Maine lumbermen took to the tasks at hand, and first and foremost the Elkhorn Ranch needed to be made habitable. Sewall and Dow planed and joined with skill; they rated Roosevelt's work as being like that of a gnawing beaver, so Roosevelt left the woodwork to the experts.[12] He had other plans on his docket anyway, and once Sewall and Dow were settled, Roosevelt joined up with Merrifield and an "old french halfbreed named Lebo," and headed to the Bighorn Mountains for two months of hunting.[13] It was here that Roosevelt began the extended forays from his ranch that would allow him to add his own contribution to the frontier story, gaining inspiration from the tradition that encompassed the stories of James Fenimore Cooper, the natural history accounts of Audubon, and the legends of Daniel Boone.[14]

Ducking his head under the arched canvas cover, Roosevelt loaded gear into the prairie schooner wagon they had chosen for the trip to the Bighorns.[15] They prepared for over two weeks of travel over rough ground to reach the Bighorns, two hundred miles away in the Wyoming Territory. The wagon's long rectangular bed had ample space for cargo; Roosevelt needed much more than the basic kit he had taken on his prairie jaunt. On August 16–17 he inventoried his gear in his diary: "I cary a buckskin suit, seal skin chaparajos, coon skin overcoat, otter fur robe to sleep in (buttoning into a bag form), oil slicker, boots and moccasins, sombrero, overalls, jersey, 2 flannel shirts, 3 suits of light, 3 of heavy underclothing, heavy socks, plenty of handkerchiefs, soap, towels, washing & shaving things rubber blanket; flour, bacon, beans and coffee, sugar & salt."[16] After he had packed in his clothes and sundries, he catalogued his shells and guns: "My battery consists of a long .45 Colt revolver, 150 cartridges, a no.10 choke bore, 300 cartridges, shotgun; a 45–75 Winchester repeater, with 1000

Roosevelt spent much of the early summer of 1884 preparing his ranch, after which he set off for a two-month hunt in the Bighorn Mountains. He stocked all manner of clothing and gear, assembled a cast of horses, and included an impressive "battery" of guns and ammunition. For a reason he did not indicate, Roosevelt recorded the 1884 hunt in the pages of his 1883 diary. TRP 1883 diary, entries for August 16–17, 1884.

cartridges; a 40–90 Sharps, 150 cartridges; a 50–150 double barrelled Webly express, 100 cartridges."[17]

Like his rifles, the ponies Roosevelt chose had unique qualities worthy of a literary description: "One of these is Blackie, a stout, swift rather vicious pony; Splitear, very enduring; Brownie, willing and swift, but very nervous, and Roachie, quiet and rather small."[18] Even in the rough script of his diary, he painted the scene with vivid and specific details, as any good writer does, before setting off on his adventure.

Two strong workhorses coaxed the prairie schooner across

The most dramatic event on Roosevelt's hunting trip in the Bighorn Mountains was his pursuit of a huge grizzly bear. In moccasins, he tracked the animal up to its bed and "shot him through the brain at 25 feet distance." TRP 1883 diary, entries for September 13–14, 1884.

streambeds and sagebrush bottoms. At times the hail blew so hard that Roosevelt could hardly stand and the horses turned their heads, forcing their feet to find a path alone as they were buffeted in the winds of the angry land. Some days, game was scarce and the grass was poor. At other times the men all bedded down tired and happy, with bellies full of fried duck. Sixteen days of slow and rumbling travel built suspense, and as the trio glided into the spruce forests of the foothills of the Bighorns, they were ready for the chase to begin.

Early on the morning of September 13, Roosevelt slipped his feet into his moccasins and tied their laces snug.[19] At times, he had used this footwear of the Native American as a backup to rugged footwear, as when he had once lost a boot in a stream on his ascent of Mount Katahdin in Maine and completed the trip in moccasins.[20] This day, however, he chose the moccasins on their merits. In his diary he described this choice in a voice normally reserved for his published writing: "In morning took a four hour tramp in moccasins (I wear them walking because they make no noise)."[21] They weren't nearly as clunky as boots, and at times in a chase they allowed him to run at "top speed."[22]

That afternoon, on the tread of his silent second skins, he again set out on foot through the "pine and spruce forests, with their sights & sounds, or more often, absence of sound."[23] Creeping through a dense patch of forest, he found the giant and ominous footprint of a grizzly he and the others had seen signs of the day before. Here, the chase did not have the thundering pace of his earlier horseback pursuits of jackal and antelope. In the dampened light and absorbent acoustics of the forest, Roosevelt "followed the trail noiselessly up, and found him in his bed."[24] Though the grizzly weighed more than a thousand pounds, only a few contractions of its muscles could have propelled its nine-foot frame across the eight yards that separated them. Roosevelt knew he only had one shot. He quickly raised his gun and found the grizzly's head in his sight. Digging deep into the marksmanship he had honed in countless shots at hawks, jays, and deer in his youth, he pulled the trigger.

There was a blind moment directly after the bullet left the gun. A billow of smoke appeared between Roosevelt's eyes and the bear, and Roosevelt reflexively leaped sideways, for if he was to meet the beast he at least wanted to see it coming. But the bear was not coming at him; the engagement was already over. The forest stood still as the massive animal fell to the ground. The long job of preparing the bear's skin would need to wait until morning, as Roosevelt had given enough for one day; but before he turned in that night he recounted the basic facts of the story in his diary. He ended with a gruesome but relevant detail: "I shot him through the brain at 25 feet distance."[25]

Over the next several days the camp was most definitely in meat, although the grizzly was not good eating; the men favored the flesh of the more tender ungulates they had shot. After claiming more bear, they loaded their wagon and wheeled down to Fort

McKinney in the Wyoming Territory. As the spruce trees gave way to sagebrush, the story of the grizzly churned in Roosevelt's mind, and once he reached the fort he wrote an extended account in a letter to his sister Anna. No longer a skeleton of facts, here Roosevelt's letter described a "dense pine forest, fairly choked with fallen timber."[26] Over the thousands of miles to New York, Roosevelt conveyed the vivid experience: "I found myself face to face with the great bear. . . . Doubtless my face was pretty white, but the blue barrel was as steady as a rock as I glanced along it until I could see the top of the bead fairly between his two sinister looking eyes."[27] The narrative picked up speed, and this was only Roosevelt's second telling of it.

Once back at his ranch, and in the company of his long-standing hunting companions Sewall and Dow, Roosevelt surely made another complete and thorough telling of the story. We can imagine that talk also turned to the taking of feathered game like mallard flappers and white belly grouse, as well as to Roosevelt's shots at cougar and white-tailed deer. But the bear story had legs, and it was the one he would "not soon forget."[28]

The letter Roosevelt mailed to Anna from Fort McKinney on September 20 beat him back to the East, but not by much. Roosevelt returned to the Maltese Cross and the Elkhorn briefly before once again heading east to tend to other commitments. Now campaign politics needed his attention. Back in New York for much of October, he gave speeches as a dutiful Republican, trying to keep Grover Cleveland out of the White House. It was a short and in some ways unsuccessful burst of politicking, and by the middle of November Roosevelt was back in Dakota, overseeing construction of the Elkhorn Ranch and working the cattle.

In the early days of this frigid Dakota winter, Roosevelt began to get serious about his stories. None of his early manuscript pages survive, so no one knows the subject of the first words he penned in the Badlands that month. The early strokes of a book are like the first swings with an axe: rough, glancing, and tiring. We can imagine that Roosevelt started with the most memorable event, writing and rewriting the story of his shot at the grizzly. He returned to New York shortly before Christmas and spent the winter months tirelessly writing, conjuring up the men and beasts of the land he had taken ownership of those last two years. By March, he had finished the full manuscript for his first Badlands work, *Hunting Trips of a Ranchman*, and delivered it to Putnam's. Understanding the importance of ending strong, Roosevelt saved the grizzly story for his last chapter.

That chapter, "Old Ephraim," begins by painting a picture of the grizzly's character. Roosevelt first primed the reader's expectations, explaining that the "danger of hunting the grizzly has been greatly exaggerated."[29] The old Eastern hunters, with their small-bore pea rifles, did not have the equipment to deal with the grizzly, but as "restless frontiersmen pressed out over the Western plains," they "taught the grizzly by bitter experience that man is his undoubted overlord," using larger-caliber repeater rifles.[30] In an informative tone, Roosevelt counseled readers that grizzlies would not attack their superiors unless provoked, for this understanding of man's dominance had been incorporated into the very units of their heredity. He knew of only a few men who had actually been hurt; hunting grizzlies wasn't really that dangerous. After comparing Old Ephraim—the name applied to the grizzly by the old mountain men—to others of earth's most formidable beasts, Roosevelt set the stage for his own entrance: "Still, after all is said, the man should have a thoroughly trustworthy weapon and a fairly cool head, who would follow into his own haunts and slay grim Old Ephraim."[31] Here in the amber pages of *Hunting Trips*, Roosevelt draws from his diary, his letters, his retellings, and his traplike memory to weave together a full account of the chase. He passed through burnt forest with "charred tree-trunks and black mould" and felt "an eerie feeling in the silent, lonely woods, to see for the first time the unmistakable proofs that I was in the home of the mighty lord of the wilderness."[32]

The ample space in *Hunting Trips* allowed Roosevelt to add details to the pursuit of the bear: the prints and feeding damage seen at a bull elk carcass the day before his encounter with the bear, his silent movement through the carpet of pine needles, the rearing up of the giant animal on its hind legs before it returned to all fours and stared him down with its "glittering, evil eyes."[33] Throughout the text Roosevelt dropped dramatic and sometimes delicious descriptions characteristic of his genre of field lore, as the "sombre half-light" prevailed on the forest floor and the "shaggy hair" bristled on the bear's back.[34] The climax of the story hit home as Roosevelt's shot struck "as fairly between the eyes as if the distance had been measured by a carpenter's rule."[35] In his quirky style, Roosevelt ended the story with a pedantic footnote, suggesting that the bear's common name arose not from its appearance but from its character, which in its truest form should be "spelt grisly—in the sense of horrible."[36] He had no need to worry that this ending of his treatment of the grizzly might not have been the best one; he returned to his grizzly stories again and again, and in a later book they took up two full chapters.[37]

The grizzly hunt employed moccasin-borne pursuit, and Roosevelt inserted accounts of manly exploits across the pages of *Hunting Trips*. He continually pointed to the tracking of game as the hunter's underlying experience, repeatedly returning to the value of the "chase," a concept that later became a defining feature of the Boone and Crockett club, throughout the book.[38] Although this chasing of game throughout the Badlands cultivated one element of his "manliness," Roosevelt sewed other threads of strenuous self-reliance into the accounts of his Badlands experiences. And despite his unconventional looks, no one was going to push him around.[39]

As Roosevelt rode up to Nolan's Hotel in Mingusville after an exhausting day of chasing lost horses, he heard the foreboding clap of gunshots inside.[40] If it were not so late at night he would have moved on, but he was in no shape to ride home. He would need to make the best of it. He pushed through the door and entered the barroom, easing as inconspicuously as possible into one of the many open seats. Glancing up at the clock, he saw where bullets had pierced its face. It wasn't long until a "shabby individual in a broad hat" found his way over to him, spouting profanity.[41] The man took the most predictable first shot of a bully, calling Roosevelt "four eyes" and suggesting that the newcomer would buy a round for the room. Since Roosevelt had been provoked and the others in the room wore fear on their faces, he could not let the behavior stand. Despite the fact that the "objectionable creature" was waving a gun in each hand, Roosevelt was not intimidated.[42] He looked down at the floor and saw that the man had made a simple mistake: he had stepped well within arms' reach of Roosevelt, and his heels were too close together. In his knuckles and biceps, Roosevelt called up the memory of the hours he had spent boxing with his classmates at Harvard. He later described his decisive response: "As I rose, I struck quick and hard with my right just to one side of the point of his jaw, hitting with my left as I straightened out, and then again with my right."[43] The unlucky brute fell to the ground, out cold. The relieved patrons happily dragged the man out of the bar and locked him in a nearby shed to sober up.

In briefly recounting his leading role in such a great Western story, Roosevelt placed himself amidst the men of the West as he described their habits in his Badlands writing.[44] Here he was amidst a brawling, swearing, gunslinging set of trappers, mountain men, and cowboys. The images seared into Roosevelt's mind were romantic: a fight in the street in front of the Skinner & Dunn Saloon; shots from an amused cowpoke's revolver making a "tenderfoot" dance; a Shaker chair raised overhead, ready to crack to pieces in a barroom melee. Roosevelt's stories burned with the self-reliant voice he had adopted in his rambles through the Badlands, and he collected many more experiences that would stock his writings and build the legends of his time in the West.

There was the time when another rancher, E.G. Paddock, purportedly threatened to kill Roosevelt on sight because of a disagreement over the ownership of the shack at Elkhorn. Manly and direct, Roosevelt galloped up to Paddock's shack near the Pyramid Park, knocked on the door, and, once it was opened, said: "I have come over to see when you want to begin the killing."[45] In another encounter, equally confrontational, a band of four or five "Indians" saw Roosevelt out riding alone on the prairie and "whipped their guns out of their slings, started their horses into a run, and came on at full tilt, whooping and brandishing their weapons."[46] With no time to be scared, Roosevelt hopped off his trusty Manitou and raised his rifle, knowing that it was a fool's errand for them to ride toward a man with a steady gun. It worked like magic. He and Manitou stood firm as the "party scattered out as wild pigeons," and he bagged another story, in this case reinforcing his perspective on the place of Indians in the West.[47]

(FACING) Roosevelt sketched the brand for the Maltese Cross Ranch in his notebook. This ranch, also known as the "Chimney Butte Ranch," was one of his two ranches in the Badlands. His other, "Elkhorn," had two brands: a triangle and a branched horn. TRC MS Am 1454.39.

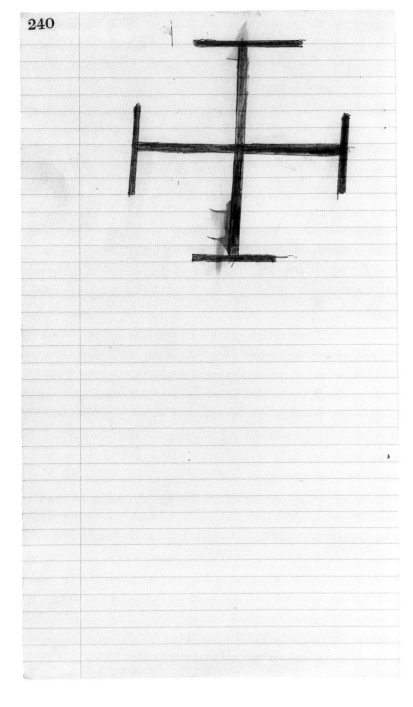

In choosing titles for his Badlands works, Roosevelt advertised their attention to ranching and hunting. Readers who bought these books based on their titles were not disappointed; they contained sketches of all aspects of life on a Western ranch and described the pursuit of virtually every species of big game from the region. Always a keen observer of nature, however, Roosevelt reflexively also included substantial prose on the "ways and habits of the woodland creatures."[48]

As Roosevelt was an author who knew his audience, his natural history descriptions in his Badlands books didn't include the meticulous details he had entered in his earlier natural history notebooks. This was not the forum in which to show off the depth of his knowledge of natural history jargon. He instead called animals to life, describing their habits and haunts in prose that allowed readers to understand their habits as they met them in the woods and on the plains.

In *Hunting Trips*, Roosevelt wove natural history into his chapter-by-chapter consideration of different game. From his accounts, even the naive reader can visualize the behavior of sharp-tailed grouse: "When on the ground it has rather a comical look, for it stands very high on its legs, carries its sharp tail cocked up like a wren's, and when startled stretches its neck out straight."[49] Roosevelt also shared the almost indescribable song of this bird, its "hollow, vibrant sound like that of some wind instrument."[50] Far from describing the grouse's song in the dry style of a natural-history monograph or fascicle, Roosevelt transported readers to the field with him: "I have often stopped and listened to it for many minutes, for it is as strange and weird a form of natural music as any I know."[51] Each species got special consideration: for black-tailed deer he shared details of the forms of their antlers; for buffalo he suggested that recent natural selection had shaped a move away from herding behavior; and he described with passion the predators of elk: a "sly, cunning" cougar that "takes its quarry unawares."[52] The animals were not only in mountains or on plains; they also infested ranch houses, and Roosevelt described having seen "a small revolver, a hunting-knife, two books, a fork, a small bag, and a tin cup" recovered from the nest of a packrat.[53] When reviews of the book came out, many were favorable; the *Overland Monthly and Out West Magazine* even praised Roosevelt's dashing of the trapper's legend that bighorn sheep jumped off mountains to land on their heads unharmed.[54] Roosevelt's "bright and life-like" writing and the beauty of the well-appointed edition also caught attention.

But one publication's reviewer politely took issue with the core of Roosevelt's pride as a natural historian: his accuracy. This criticism would have been much easier to take if the review, in *Forest and Stream*, had been written by a slapdash journalist. It had not. The author was none other than George Bird Grinnell, the editor of the publication and one of the foremost authorities on the nature of the West.

In some ways, Grinnell out-Rooseveleted Roosevelt. Grinnell's childhood had also been steeped in nature study, as he had lived at Audubon Park, on what had been John James Audubon's estate.[55] While there, he had learned the traditions of natural history shooting his first animals with Audubon's grandson, and he had been tutored by Audubon's widow, Lucy. Grinnell's Ivy League experience had been at Yale, but it had shades of Roosevelt's up-and-down performance—he even had been asked to take a year off due to a hazing incident. In his last year, however, he gained a spot on the Marsh Expedition, a paleontological field trip that covered more than six thousand miles in the West.[56] On this trip Grinnell got his first taste of the West, and he returned soon after to begin years of study as he hunted buffalo and studied natural and cultural history in significant depth. Grinnell had accumulated these extended experiences of Western life ten years before Roosevelt would head west—he even had a ranch in the Shirley Basin in Wyoming—so when he took his perch to criticize Roosevelt's writing, he had the lofty view of an authority.[57] Roosevelt read Grinnell's review with anxiety and wanted to know what it was, exactly, that he had taken issue with. In print, Grinnell had vaguely stated that "a number of hunting myths are given as fact," and that Roosevelt was not always able to "distinguish the true from the false."[58] In the same way as he made his natural history observations themselves, Roosevelt wanted to address these concerns directly. The review definitely warranted a visit to its author.

When Roosevelt returned to New York, he called on Grinnell at the offices of *Forest and Stream* to take issue with the criticism.[59] Looking past Grinnell's handlebar mustache and into his modest eyes, he soon found no ill will associated with his comments.

The two talked through the specifics of Grinnell's reservations, and in that and many subsequent visits, Roosevelt discovered how much he shared with Grinnell. Far from becoming enemies, the two would eventually become entwined in the fight to conserve the nature that had brought them together; they even worked together to found the Boone and Crockett Club.[60] *Forest and Stream* later reviewed Roosevelt's *Wilderness Hunter*, and although it took issue with minor points, it had none of sweeping reservations of Grinnell's earlier review. In a further sign that Roosevelt's accuracy issues had been righted, *The New York Times* said of *Wilderness Hunter*: "One may rely upon its information."[61]

Criticisms of Roosevelt's natural history faded—he himself turned into a stickler for accuracy on the subject—but he did not escape other reproaches of his time in the Badlands. Some took issue with the images of Roosevelt that had been taken in New York studios. Others noted that his writing implied that he had spent more time in the West than he actually had. But no one could suggest that he was not an active participant in the life of the Badlands and in the formulation of the lore of the West. One review of his book *Wilderness Hunter* described how Roosevelt developed a unique combination of traits: "To these qualities of brain and heart add a good physique and experience and training in woodcraft, and we have the ideal sportsman, who, after all, is only a gentle man trained in a special way."[62] Ultimately, Roosevelt paid for his stories with grit, sweat, and sometimes even blood. And there were some good ones, stories that allowed him to render his adventures within the overarching narrative of the Western hero.

For Roosevelt, a gun was like an extra appendage. Despite biting criticism and reasoned pleas, he never apologized or backed away from the battery of rifles, shotguns, and revolvers he used in ranching, collecting, and hunting.[63] His writings audibly crackle with their reports. In *Hunting Trips*, however, he articulated an outgrowth of the hunter-naturalist's skill with firearms: "The rifle is the freeman's weapon. The man who uses it well in the chase shows that he can at need use it also in war with human foes."[64] Although Roosevelt would later use his gun in a bloody war, Badlands justice was meted out between small groups of individuals. And in 1886, Roosevelt set off with his rifle to right a human wrong and returned with what is possibly the best short story of his life.

The winter of 1885–86 had been so cold that sharp blocks of ice had damned up part of the river in front of the Elkhorn Ranch, and the flat-bottomed boat that they used to cross the river was tied to one of the trees near the house. It may have been the vigorous wind of the prairies, or just the hard sleep born of a rancher's tiresome day, but Sewall, Dow, and Roosevelt heard no commotion as the boat was stolen on the night of March 23. In the morning, they found a dangling rope with frayed ends.

Cowboys are no strangers to horse thieves—Roosevelt had catalogued the unwritten laws of equine property in his memory and later poured them out in his writings—and although boat thieves in the Badlands were as uncommon as boats themselves, the same principles of justice applied. By way of investigation, the men of the Elkhorn Ranch didn't need to discuss the frayed rope or consider the significance of the red mitten that was dropped at the scene to understand what had happened. They knew that there was a trio of ruffians upriver who were looking to vacate the Badlands, and that they had taken the boat to aid their flight. These men, Finnegan, Pfaffenbach, and Burnsted, could only have gone one way—downstream—and any assumptions they might have made that Roosevelt and his men couldn't follow them, or wouldn't care, were soon corrected.[65]

It was fortunate that Sewall and Dow knew at least as much about wood as they did about horses, and in three days they built a functional craft for their pursuit. Due to a "furious blizzard," they postponed the trip for three days, and in the meantime they piled in buffalo robes and plenty of supplies.[66] Despite the bitter cold, the first two days were relatively easy as the trio periodically stopped to hunt prairie chickens and whitetail deer, ending their days ravenous, as "a man doing hard open-air work in cold weather is always hungry for meat."[67] On the third day, they drifted into view of their original scow, and stopped their boat on the riverbank. With the threat of a fight welling up in their "tingling veins," they stripped off their overcoats and jumped ashore, following the campfire smoke that "curled up through the frosty air."[68] Only one man, Pfaffenbach, known as "the German," was in camp, and he surrendered immediately. Finnegan and Burnsted were walking back to their campsite shortly after, and were met with Roosevelt shouting, "Hands up!" Finnegan hesitated momentarily, but real-

Thieves stole boat; started to build another to go after them

Went out after deer; saw nothing. Boat being built. River very high; ice piled up on banks several feet.

(ABOVE AND FACING) On the night of March 23, 1886, a trio of thieves stole the flat-bottomed boat that Roosevelt and his companions Sewall and Dow had used to cross the ice-clogged Little Missouri River. The next day, the men began work on a new boat to chase the thieves down. After capturing the thieves and transporting them downriver, Roosevelt put them in a prairie schooner wagon and "drove" them the last forty miles overland to the sheriff in Dickinson, walking behind the wagon. TRC MS Am 1454.55 (12).

Shot white tail doe; Dan shot another. Captured the three boat thieves.

Came on with our prisoners till carried off by ice jam.

ized that resistance was ill-advised, as three cocked guns were trained on him. So the men surrendered their battery of "Winchester rifles, Smith & Wesson revolvers, and knives."[69] Although the capture was a bit anticlimactic, the absence of a standoff and gunfight didn't detract from this story. An extended odyssey began as Roosevelt and his men brought the captives to justice, and this would provide plenty of color to the narrative.

With guns instead of antlers, these six men had done what elk and antelope do: they had a struggle for dominance—brief, in this case—after which they all settled into their new roles in the hierarchy as they floated down the Little Missouri together. Fighting can be costly, and unless a wide opening appears for realignment, most animals turn to other concerns after such a struggle.

Eight "irksome and monotonous" days on the river followed as Roosevelt and his men herded the three captives downstream.[70] Practical details lend credibility to Roosevelt's yarn: as it was too cold to bind the thieves' hands without causing them to freeze, the de facto lawmen had the thieves remove their boots—the cactus spines throughout the brush would make flight impossible—and kept a rotating watch. This sheriff's work was most difficult at night when, lying just inside the circle of firelight, one guard watched for movement while struggling to stay awake, and the other two slept with revolvers beneath their heads, watching for a fray.

None came. Captors and captives were civil to each other. After days spent dodging ice on the clogged river and searching for game, all were glad to settle down by a warm fire and turn to their own affairs. An aspiring writer, Roosevelt settled in to Tolstoy's *Anna Karenina*. It held his attention, but he later confessed to his sister some ambivalence about the story.[71] He found Tolstoy a good writer, but something about the morality of the book stuck in his craw. It is possible that the heavy themes of love and death hit too close to home only two years after Alice's death, urging the biting wind and overcast sky to make him feel even more gray. Across the campfire Finnegan, Pfaffenbach, and Burnsted were reading up on literature relevant to their roles as well.

Slowly paging through the tabloid-like pages of the *National Police Gazette*, the captives caught up on the latest in dastardly crimes. An issue of the magazine from just a few weeks before their theft described a gunfight that had broken out at a wedding in Las

Vegas, with two men shooting each other at close range. After the combatants were carted off, the celebration had resumed.[72] Once through these magazines, the men settled into book-length accounts in the *Police Gazette* series "Library of Sensation," which related embellished accounts of criminals and crimes: *The Outlaw Brothers, Frank and Jesse James, Lives of the Poisoners,* and *Billy Le-Roy: Colorado Bandit*.[73] Truth was subjective in these accounts, and the latter mixed fiction with facts from Billy the Kid's early life.[74] Roosevelt didn't look down on the contents of their library—he embraced the glory of the Western literature that he himself both consumed and was creating—but in this particular case, he was simply on the other side of the law. He later even placed himself only one step removed from the demise of Billy the Kid as he became a friend of Pat Garrett, the man who had killed him.[75] By reading his own respective literature, each man refined his role in what became a main act in Roosevelt's Western story.

After days of drifting on the icy river, the provisions began to run low. Roosevelt and his men were not interested in killing the thieves, but they did not want to let them go, either. Sewall struck out onto the land to see if he could find a ranch, but he only succeeded in finding cattle.[76] Then Dow and Roosevelt took their turn, eventually finding a ranch and arranging for transport—a welcome development to the frustrated Roosevelt. A prairie schooner soon arrived, and Roosevelt resolved to take the captives overland himself to the town of Dickinson, with Sewall and Dow attending to the boats. The driver of the wagon, unknown to Roosevelt, had immediately recognized the captives; he shook hands with them and said, "Finnegan, you damned thief, what have you been doing now?"[77] The familiarity not inspiring his confidence, Roosevelt prevented the thieves' escape by loading them into the wagon and plodding behind, armed, in "ankle-deep mud."[78] By the time they had covered the forty-odd miles to Dickinson, his feet were so badly blistered that his second encounter, after handing over the captives, would be with the doctor.

Upon his first glance at Theodore Roosevelt, Dr. Victor H. Stickney pegged him as a fitting apparition for a ghost town. His legs were caked with mud and grit. His eyes drooped from thirty-six sleepless hours. His body movements were slow from physical exertion. As he opened his mouth, however, Stickney found that he was "the most peculiar and at the same time the most wonderful man [he] ever came to know."[79]

As he soaked Roosevelt's feet in warm water and dressed and wrapped the open wounds, Stickney was the first person treated to the full story of the boat thieves. And what a story it had become. It was full of the tensions of the Badlands: hardship and suspense, villains and heroes, justice done. It wasn't long until there were other tellings of the story. From Dickinson and Medora, Roosevelt posted individual letters that told of the incident to his siblings Anna, Corinne, and Elliott, and also one to his friend Henry Cabot Lodge.[80] Although women were largely absent from his narratives of the West, they were central to his early audience, just as his mother and aunt Anna had been among the first to introduce him to the lore of the frontier as a child.[81] Roosevelt was clearly proud of his crime fighting; his letters described the chase and the capture, made in the "most approved western fashion."[82] At this time the "frontier was awash in startling stories of sensational conflicts"—the legends of Wild Bill Hickok, Calamity Jane, and Billy the Kid—and now Roosevelt placed himself as the protagonist in his own Western story of lawmen and outlaws.[83] Word seeped out about the boat thieves story, and *Century Magazine* made a "hasty" inquiry about whether he would consider an article. Roosevelt eventually agreed.[84] During the next year he began to consider how best to tell his story in print. He also opened the pages of *Outing* magazine and identified someone who could add images to his Badlands stories.[85]

A man with a round face and an artistic eye, Frederic Remington was not well known when Roosevelt expressed interest in his illustration services. He had been drawing for weekly publications like *Outing*, but for nothing akin to the widely distributed *Century Magazine*, which Roosevelt had engaged for a series of six articles on the Badlands that were to be released serially in the magazine and then released as a book, *Ranch Life and the Hunting Trail*. Part of Remington's appeal was that he was no stranger to the West. He, like Roosevelt, had traveled widely there, amidst cowpunchers and Indians, and even had purchased a sheep ranch in Kansas in 1883, knowing "more about cow-boys than [he] did about drawing."[86] The eleven drawings that Remington made for "Sheriff's Work on a Ranch," which appeared in the May 1888 issue of *Century Magazine*, brought Roosevelt's words to life.[87] The shadows cast by firelight defined the powerful outlines of guns, boots, and hats. The dark figure of Roosevelt traipsing behind the prairie schooner with gun over his shoulder evoked his singular command of men. All told, the sixty-four illustrations Remington made for Roosevelt's magazine articles, along with the nineteen added in the book version, lit fire to Remington's career because of the way in which they brought Roosevelt's Western life to readers.[88]

Near the end of his life, Roosevelt only included a photograph of the boat incident in his *Autobiography*; he did not retell the story in text.[89] Perhaps he realized he did not need to fan those flames. In the century since his death, many writers who have considered Roosevelt have retold his classic saga of the boat thieves.[90]

Roosevelt's wide-ranging adventures, such as the capture of the boat thieves, stoked his Badlands writing. For readers, these books were a feast of outdoor lore, with tender moments alongside tough passages like flank steak next to gristle. He left all the tales to be consumed in almost one thousand pages of writing: *Hunting Trips of a Ranchman* (1885), *Ranch Life and the Hunting-Trail* (1888), and *The Wilderness Hunter* (1893). In these books Roosevelt wove together narratives with elements of frontier and Western literature. He included descriptions of hunting, natural history, battles with Indians, bar fights and outlaws, along with ruminations on the white conquest of the West. To these personal stories Roosevelt added his four-volume work *The Winning of the West*—a significant historical contribution that illuminates his perspective on race and imperialism, and which shows how his more academic voice affected the developing myth of the American West.[91]

Long after Roosevelt had sold his ranches, his adventures in the Badlands continued to affect how he rendered the West. After he worked with George Bird Grinnell to found the Boone and Crockett Club in 1887, the two men edited multiple volumes of hunting lore.[92] Long into the future, these perspectives on the West, of a hunter-naturalist of the Boone and Crocket Club and a Western hero, would affect both the public's concept of the West and Roosevelt's approach to governance and to conservation.[93] Roosevelt also advised writers like his longtime friend Owen Wister, who authored *The Virginian*, a book that played a major role in defining Western literature and affected how the story of the expansion of

(A) While on the chase after the boat thieves, Roosevelt snapped an image of Sewall (right) and Dow (left) in their new boat. TRC 520.14–001b. (B) Afterwards, Roosevelt sat for a staged photograph of the scene, with Sewall, Dow, and another unidentified man representing the actual thieves. TRC 520.14-001a.

eastern settlers to the West was told for decades.[94] Roosevelt even articulated the thought that in his writings, Wister had "done for the plainsmen and mountainmen, the soldiers, frontiersmen and Indians what nobody else but Bret Harte and Kipling could have done."[95] In hindsight it is clear that Roosevelt's collective narrative leaves out many perspectives—those of women, Native Americans, and African Americans—but there is no question that his rendering of his adventures, and their echoes in both nonfiction and fictional accounts, were significant in shaping the legends and myths of the American West.[96]

Roosevelt's cycles of adventure in the West also added a new facet to his field identity. By allowing him to don chaps and a revolver, they added the role of a manly cowboy and rancher. They provided him with direct experiences that helped develop his ideas on expansion and empire, and his concept of Americanism. Roosevelt himself described how these field pursuits were not historical abstractions, but advanced a synthetic identity. With his rugged eloquence, he laid this out in the preface of *The Wilderness Hunter*:

> In hunting, the finding and killing of game is after all but a part of the whole. The free, self-reliant, adventurous life, with its rugged and stalwart democracy; the wild surroundings, the grand beauty of the scenery, the chance to study the ways and habits of the woodland creatures—all these unite to give to the career of the wilderness hunter its peculiar charm. The chase is among the best of all national pastimes; it cultivates that vigorous manliness for the lack of which in a nation, as in an individual, the possession of no other qualities can possibly atone.[97]

Buoyed by the skills and experiences of his youth, the adventures Roosevelt collected around his Badlands ranches were direct experiences that fundamentally affected his worldview and also provided stories he would tell the rest of his life.

After Roosevelt captured the boat thieves in the spring of 1886, the parts of his complicated whole slowly began another major realignment. Just as he had ruminated on his career during college, he now was considering his future aspirations. As the summer of 1886 began, he continued with his ranch life, spending five weeks on the roundup, rarely had "breakfast as late as four oclock any morning," and found himself "tough as a hickory knot."[98] He spent several days writing for each day of riding and hunting, and relished the "wild, half adventurous life of a ranchman."[99] In early June he hunted for elk with Bill Sewall. After the Fourth of July, he returned to New York for several weeks to finish writing his biography of Thomas Hart Benton, and on August 2 he returned to the Badlands and continued to relish the freedom his field life offered. As fall approached, however, the questions about his next steps became more glaring, and he confided his worries about the future to Henry Cabot Lodge: "It is no use saying that I would like a chance at something I thought I could really do; at present I see nothing whatever ahead. However, there is the hunting in the fall, at any rate."[100] Two days later, Roosevelt embarked on a hunt in the Coeur D'Alene Mountains for white goat, pondering his future options, one being a possible run for mayor of New York. He returned to his ranch in September, and then to Oyster Bay in October. The massive home he had built in Oyster Bay was no longer named after Alice; he now called it Sagamore Hill, after the Native American chief who had signed away the land more than two centuries before.[101] In many ways, this return marked a shift, with the locus of Roosevelt's personal and professional life moving away from the field.

Just as a web of forces had pulled him West to establish his hold in the Badlands, now a different set of forces pulled him back to civilization. Only shortly after he returned to New York, he wrote to Elihu Root and William Bellamy on October 16: "I accept the nomination for Mayor tendered me by the Republican Convention."[102] It was a short campaign, and by November 1 Roosevelt wrote to Henry Cabot Lodge that he had "but little chance" in the election, but he was already looking to future political activity in battles against those who had acted with "dishonesty and un-truthfulness" in the campaign.[103] In his letter to Lodge, he closed: "May Providence in due season give me a chance to get even with some of them!" This letter also revealed to Lodge a shift in his personal life, with Roosevelt explaining that he was sailing to England within the week to finally marry Edith Carow. After Alice's death Roosevelt had seen little of Edith until the early fall of 1885, when they met again in New York. They entered into a quiet engagement on November 17, 1885.[104] Even his 1886 diary references to her were guarded: she first appears as "E. K. C." and then just "E."[105]

This began a decade in which a significant part of Roosevelt's attention focused on growing his own family with Edith, and creating the kind of home his parents had provided for him. This was already in evidence when he returned from his honeymoon in Europe in March of 1887. Theodore Jr.—technically Theodore Roosevelt III—was born on September 13, and joined Alice, Roosevelt's daughter from his first marriage to Alice Lee Roosevelt, as part of the family. More offspring soon followed, with Kermit in 1889, Ethel in 1891, Archibald in 1894, and Quentin in 1897. Unbeknownst to Roosevelt, another shift was in motion while he glowed in appreciation of his new wife and the sights of Italy on his honeymoon: in the Badlands his ranch and cattle were suffering terribly.

Lincoln Lang later described the winter of 1886–87 as "the Cataclysm."[106] Many of the Badlands cattle and people could not survive as the temperatures dipped past forty below zero that winter and a "swift-driving ice dust" swept the land.[107] When the thaw finally came, "carcasses were being spewed forth in untold thousands by the rushing waters, to be carried away on the crest of the foaming, turgid flood rushing down the valley."[108] Thankfully, Sewall and Dow, also with new children in the fall of 1886, had left the Badlands for good to return to Maine. Roosevelt would return to his Badlands property periodically over the coming years, but after this "winter of the blue snow," his ranching operation was slowly being dismantled; it would no longer be much more than a short-term hunting and vacation outpost.[109]

Although Roosevelt likely kept some field notes in the decade between 1887 and 1897, no diaries, notebooks, or journals survive.[110] He certainly published furiously during this time on both biographical subjects and natural history in order to augment the income from his modest and uncertain political posts. Over this span, Roosevelt's time in the wilderness was largely confined to late-summer hunting trips in the West. But he did not leave the field behind. Instead, the long trail he had traveled over the previous years—in Loantaka, the Catskills, the Adirondacks, Egypt, Maine, the Midwest, and throughout the Badlands—had impressed upon him both the value of nature and its fragility. The awareness of environmental change he had exhibited as a boy observing populations of house sparrows had now expanded in light of many new examples from his travels in the East and the West.[111] Lincoln Lang recognized that the environment in the Badlands had changed during his time there: "The glorious buttes were becoming more and more scarred and defoliated." He also saw how migratory birds and game animals were becoming scarce.[112] Lang explained that Roosevelt knew this too: "In the light of Roosevelt's powers of close observation directed through his nature studies, none of this had escaped him."[113]

In the last days of 1887, Roosevelt laid the groundwork for another shift. No longer would he simply indulge himself in what he recognized as the natural treasures of the United States; he would work to save them from destruction. One of his first steps was his founding, with George Bird Grinnell, of the Boone and Crockett Club. This effort was controversial in some circles, because one of its aims was to save natural land for sportsmen. The approach to the environment that Roosevelt developed through it, however, provided a flexible template, and over the coming decades he worked to set aside land for hunting, agriculture, appreciation of nature and antiquities, reintroduction of endangered species, and forest recreation and use.[114] This was a phase in Roosevelt's life in which his body spent less time in the field but his mind was deeply devoted to the pursuits that happened there. Roosevelt developed his standing and political power in ways that would later allow him to convince the American people to save large swaths of land for intertwined uses, including "the Yosemite, the groves of giant sequoias and redwoods, the Canyon of the Colorado, the Canyon of the Yellowstone, the Three Tetons . . . for their children and their children's children forever, with their majestic beauty all unmarred."[115]

It would be some time before Roosevelt would spend significant time with his own children in the West. In 1890 they were still small, providing the domestic amusement typical of a loving home. Ted and Kermit were two "sturdy little scamps" who, as little bears, raccoons, or badgers, would confront their "very big bear" father, crawling on the floor or latching onto his leg.[116] At tea, Alice would "sidle hastily round" to Roosevelt's chair, where he would give her a scoop of icing from the cake, if he could distract Edith long enough.[117] But in that year, Roosevelt took the opportunity to set off with Edith and a small entourage—including his sisters Anna and Corinne and their husbands, and Henry Cabot Lodge's sixteen-year old son George—to visit his ranch country and Yellowstone Park.

On this trip Roosevelt was no longer traveling in a professional capacity as rancher and writer. Instead, he was a family tour guide intent on sharing what he had found in the West. The group tramped in rainstorms through "glutinous slime," met Western legends like "Hell-Roarin'" Bill Jones, and took in the scenery of Yellowstone: "the wonderful shapes of the rocks, some like peaks and turrets, others broken in strange fantastic jags, and then the marvellous colors of them all."[118] Although unusually rustic, this family recreation in America's wild lands impressed their value upon Roosevelt. And he relished the joy they could bring: "I have rarely seen Edith enjoy anything more than she did the six days at my ranch, and the trip through the Yellowstone Park; and she looks just as well and young and pretty and happy as she did four years ago when I married her."[119] Revelry in nature was an exception in this period, during which Roosevelt toiled to advance the aims of the Civil Service Commission and the New York City Police, and continued to develop his political skills.[120] The time went quickly, however; and only seven years later, he again prepared to play out his professional aspirations in the field.

Into Murderous Thickets

The "new-fangled" desk in the assistant secretary of the Navy's office did not suit Theodore Roosevelt as he took up his new post in April of 1897. With his robust field persona and a deep appreciation for the history of the Navy, he rummaged around the back rooms of the department to locate a work surface that was in sync with his love of power, solidity, and symbolism. A desk with just those characteristics turned up—one that had been used by the Civil War–era assistant secretary, Gustavus Fox, which had an ironclad warship carved into its side panel, representing the most modern part of Fox's fleet. The desk was squeezed through the door of Roosevelt's office and it seems likely that he would have paused to appreciate the set of columbiads—early Howitzer canon—that were carved into the solid oak face of the center drawer. Now he had a fitting place to add his own mark to the story of the United States Navy.[1]

Installed in his new office, Roosevelt had an opportunity to consider the impressive string of accomplishments that had allowed him to transition out of his Badlands life and into his new appointment. Only three years after he corralled the boat thieves on the Little Missouri, and after his unsuccessful run for mayor of New York City, he had begun a six-year term as US Civil Service commissioner in 1889, in which he worked to "withdraw the administrative offices of the Government from the domain of spoils politics, and thereby cut out of American political life a fruitful source of corruption and degradation."[2] In addition to this professional work under President Benjamin Harrison and then President Grover Cleveland, he had also continued to crank out books. Following up on his previous biographical work *Thomas Hart Benton*, Roosevelt had offered a rendering of the peglegged womanizer and Founding Father of the United States, Gouverneur Morris.[3] During the mid-1890s he had also finished his four-volume history *The Winning of the West*, along with his hunter-naturalist narrative *The Wilderness Hunter*. And there were collaborative literary works: *Hero Tales from American History*, with Henry Cabot Lodge, and three volumes of hunting narratives edited with George Grinnell for the Boone and Crockett Club.[4] Upon being appointed police commissioner in New York in 1895, Roosevelt had grabbed the horns of another organization in which it was "most difficult to accomplish anything good, while the field for intrigue and conspiracy was limitless."[5] Here again, he had applied his will to excise politics and favoritism from an institution, and even incorporated elements of his field approach. Late some nights he would walk the beat himself, to rid sleeping and negligent officers from the police force. At other times he would summon reporters with his "Hi yi yi" cowboy call from the open window of his office on Mulberry Street in Manhattan.[6] Then, as the apple blossoms emerged in Washington in the spring of 1897, President William McKinley had somewhat reluctantly plucked him from state government and appointed him assistant secretary of the Navy.[7]

Roosevelt's hawkish sensibilities and credentials from his first book, *The Naval War of 1812*, made him a fit for such a post. Diving into his new responsibilities, he settled on certain guiding principles. For example, he was convinced that war to deal with the "murderous oppression" of the Cubans was unavoidable, and he also believed that the American military was simply not prepared for conflict.[8] In his outsized fashion, Roosevelt lobbied for immediate construction of new battleships and cruisers. He even spent three days with the fleet, remarking that he had "never enjoyed three days more" as he saw for himself the powerful movements of turrets, and how the bright searchlights scanned the seas for drifting targets at night.[9] With carrier pigeons floating overhead, transmitting messages to shore, Roosevelt took time to stand on the deck of the *Iowa*—his teeth and gums rattled by its blasting guns—reinforcing his dedication to naval muscle and firsthand experience.[10]

Roosevelt's knowledge of the benefits of strong leadership in battle guided his efforts to install Commodore George Dewey as the commander of the fleet headed to the Philippines. Roosevelt's immediate superior, Navy Secretary John D. Long, was taking some time away from the office to deal with his wracked nerves. Long was apprehensive, however, about an absence that would leave Roosevelt in charge, and rightfully so: Roosevelt made an end run around him and placed Dewey in charge of the Asiatic fleet.[11] As Roosevelt pushed for war, others, like McKinley and Long, hoped for a peaceful solution.[12] On February 15, 1898, however, a horrendous crunching sound and deafening roar rocked Havana harbor, and the American battleship *Maine* sank into the murk. Despite investigations and attempts at diplomacy, war seemed imminent. Dewey had already left the Western Hemisphere and was in place to keep the Spanish fleet from leaving Asia; the rattling of sabers grew louder as the wreck of the *Maine* was investigated—with most fingers pointing to enemies encamped in Cuba.[13] By April 19, McKinley's reluctance could no longer stand, and war was declared. Roosevelt was relieved by these developments, and had no intentions of seeing the impending campaign from the deck of a boat or from his Washington office. He felt that the Navy was in "good shape," and he wanted his part of the war to be as close as possible to the action.[14]

Behind the scenes, many of Roosevelt's colleagues couldn't understand his impulse to place himself on the field of battle. To some, this was wholly different than what had drawn him to the hunting field, where his body was also placed in peril, whether from the charge of an angry grizzly or from doing a somersault over a fence while on horseback.[15] The safety of the homeland and the importance of wielding power in a more significant political post should have outweighed any of his omnipresent drive to find places away from the confines of home and office to connect with the world directly. That is, why would Roosevelt give up such an influential post at the Navy to be dodging bullets with enlisted men? His friend Winthrop Chanler went straight to the mark: "I really think he is going mad. The President has asked him twice as a personal favor to stay in the Navy Department, but Theodore is wild to fight and hack and hew."[16] As rain poured down in Washington on April 25, Secretary Long confided his own caustic assessment to his journal: "He has lost his head to this unutterable folly of deserting the post where he is of most service and running off to ride a horse and, probably, brush mosquitoes from his neck on the Florida sands. . . . Without exception every one of his friends advises him, he is acting like a fool." However, Long provided a caveat: "And, yet, how absurd this will sound if, by some turn of fortune, he should accomplish some great thing and strike a very high mark." Scratched onto this document in Long's hand is a postwar admission that Roosevelt's good fortune had indeed come about.[17]

Refusing to be sidetracked by his superiors, Roosevelt was convinced of the way forward. He had made a promise to himself and to the people that if war ever came, he would fight:

> I had always felt that if there were a serious war I wished to be in a position to explain to my children why I did take part in it, and not why I did not take part in it. Moreover, I had very deeply felt that it was our duty to free Cuba, and I had publicly expressed this feeling; and when a man takes such a position, he ought to be willing to make his words good by his deeds. . . . He should pay with his body.[18]

Surely the fact that Roosevelt's father had hired a soldier to serve for him in the Civil War lingered in his mind.[19] The expansionist rationale for war also fit with his own philosophy: the United States would simply be continuing the work that had been started by the colonists and backwoodsmen who had moved across the continent.[20] As was the case with the other soldiers who lined up to fight in Cuba, multiple factors had led Roosevelt to volunteer.[21] In response to a letter in which his old friend Bill Sewall expressed reservations about the wisdom of his going to Cuba, Roosevelt replied: "I thank you for your advice, old man, but it seems to me that if I can go I better had. My work here has been the work of preparing the tools. They are prepared, and now the work must lie with those who use them."[22] Ultimately, Roosevelt was never content to experience life as a witness from an armchair: in his studies of biology he had eschewed the relative comforts of the laboratory for study of animals in their natural environment; as a writer he had taken to the West, collecting narratives as he ranged throughout some of the harshest territory in North America; on hunts he had followed even the most ferocious animals to their burrows and dens. Roosevelt had always worked to be in the middle of the action.

Ever watchful for political intrigue, *The New York Times* had caught wind of Roosevelt's motivations, and kept public tabs on him in late April of 1898 as he contemplated his most daring field excursion to date. On the nineteenth of the month, they considered Roosevelt's ambitions: "He still refuses to say whether he will leave the Navy Department for service in the field."[23] Two days later, one of their headlines asked: "Will Mr. Roosevelt resign?" They wondered if he was ready "to take the field in a capacity that will give him opportunity for more active work for the Government."[24] A few more days passed before headlines explained that "Assistant Secretary Roosevelt is not talking much about his plans for the war, but they are gradually leaking out. . . . He is restless and is determined to render his country such aid as he can in the field.[25] Finally, the *Times* came out with the resignation on April 29: "It is understood to-night that Theodore Roosevelt will actually sever his connection with the Navy Department to-morrow. . . . He completed the purchase of his Cuban outfit to-day, and he expects to start West to help enlist his cowboys to-morrow."[26]

Just as he had mistakenly dismissed Roosevelt's zeal to get to the front, Secretary Long also overestimated the reservations of Roosevelt's friends. At least one, Leonard Wood, had been ready to tread into battle with Roosevelt for almost a year.

The story of Wood's friendship with Roosevelt—and the history of the Rough Riders—begins at a dinner party in Washington on June 18, 1897. Otherwise without auspices, Roosevelt described meeting a "very interesting Dr. Wood of the army" at the dinner.[27] There was an instant bond between the men, and they walked home that night finding how common their experiences with Indians and cowpunchers had been in the West.

Roosevelt and Wood shared a toughness that was fired in the same kiln. Wood had gone west in the 1880s; and just a month after Roosevelt captured the boat thieves on the Little Missouri, he had been part of the military contingent that chased the Apache leader Geronimo. On that chase, Wood had earned a reputation for possessing the extreme vigor that Roosevelt respected and embodied. At one point, Wood continued the chase despite having a severe fever and a massively swollen wound on his leg that he needed to lance repeatedly; he was "so sick and dizzy that [he] kept falling down while on foot."[28] Wood had dodged plenty of bullets and danger in his time in the West as well, once narrowly avoiding being shot as he approached a ranch wearing only his underwear, moccasins, and a ragged handkerchief and hat on his head, and was mistaken for an Apache.[29] Though they never overlapped, Wood's and Roosevelt's parallel Western experiences cemented their shared perspective on expansion and Indians, and their devotion to the grassroots attributes of honesty, gristle, and fearlessness in bold actions. Now in Washington, Roosevelt and Wood shared thoughts on how they might apply these strengths in the honor of their country as they walked together in the woods surrounding Washington or kicked a football together in a vacant lot.[30] As 1897 waned, their conversations turned more and more to the imminence of war with Spain in Cuba. They agreed that "war would be as righteous as it would be advantageous to the honor and the interests of the nation."[31] Roosevelt later summed up how they felt that spring: "As soon as war was upon us, Wood and I began to try for a chance to go to the front."[32]

Bouncing from office to office and friend to friend, Roosevelt and Wood machinated and plotted about how they would get to Cuba. Although Roosevelt was high up in the Navy and Wood was medical adviser to both the president and Secretary of War Russell Alger, neither had a natural path to the front lines. They certainly could have found staff positions with Army generals, but there they might not be much closer to the fight than they would be in Washington. They also pursued avenues of enlistment, Wood in Massachusetts and Roosevelt with his friend Colonel Francis Greene, but they were not able to secure places in these regiments. Roosevelt was at points distraught: "I shall chafe my heart out if I am kept here instead of being at the front."[33] Luckily, Congress provided a unique opportunity when it authorized the formation of three cavalry regiments made up of the kind of "wild riders and riflemen" these two Western-loving men understood.[34] President McKinley and Secretary Long agreed with those who felt that Roosevelt was mad in leaving the Navy, but they did not prevent Alger from offering Roosevelt the colonelcy of one of these regiments—a group that would become known as the "Rough Riders."[35]

Surprisingly, Roosevelt refused the colonelcy. Not known for calmly putting his ego aside—Roosevelt's image in this period is

MAY, 1898.

THURS. 5.

FRI. 6. Commissioned as
Lt- Col, X, 1ˢᵗ U. S
Volunteer Cavalry.
Wood as Col, my
choice, the Colonelcy
was offered me.

SAT. 7.
The delays and shortcoming
of Flager & the ordnance
Dept surpass belief.
The Quartermaster Dept
is better, but bad.
The Commissary dept

APPOINTMENTS.

is good, There is no
head, no management-
whatever in the War
Dept, against a good
nation we should be helpless.

On May 6, 1898, Roosevelt completed his transition from
assistant secretary of the Navy to lieutenant colonel of the First
Volunteer Cavalry, known as the "Rough Riders." Although he
was offered the colonelcy at the beginning, he elected to serve
under Leonard Wood instead. Partway through the campaign,
however, he was elevated to the rank of colonel after Wood was
promoted. TRC MS Am 1454.55 (12a).

MAY, 1898.

THURS. 19.

The drilling is *incessant*, & the progress of the regiment wonderful

FRI. 20.

The Harvard & New York men & are getting on capitally with the cowpunchers

SAT. 21.

The blunders & delays of the Ordnance Bureau surpass belief. They express us stuff we don't need, and send us the rifles by slow

APPOINTMENTS. freight! There is no head, no energy, no intelligence tsk in the War Dept, the President is of course really to blame.

Roosevelt arrived in San Antonio, where the Rough Riders were assembling to drill. The regiment included men from a wide range of backgrounds, including many "cowpunchers" from the West, and "Harvard & New York men" from the East. TRC MS Am 1454.55 (12a).

generally rendered as that of a fearless leader or wild-eyed soldier—
he instead accepted a position as lieutenant colonel under Wood,
a decision that stands as a testament to Roosevelt's maturity and
practicality. He confided in his diary: "Wood as Col, by my choice.
The Colonelcy was offered me."[36] Wood had extensive experience
and perspective on the command of regulars and Indians from the
Geronimo campaign. Roosevelt realized that he had some of the
skills needed to make a great leader of the soldier-cowpunchers,
but also that he needed to add at least a short burst of military management to his resume. Serving under Wood was just the solution.

For many men, serving as Roosevelt's superior would have been
disastrous. Roosevelt was bursting with charisma, and along with
being drawn in by Wood, many of the Rough Riders had signed
up because of Roosevelt: to see him, hear from him, and serve
under him.[37] Even at this point in his life, Roosevelt was already
something of a celebrity. Well after the Rough Riders had been
assembled and they were rolling along the tracks to the port in
Tampa, a passenger train squeaked past theirs, with men chant-
ing, "Hallo, Teddy! Speech! Speech! We want Teddy Roosevelt!"[38]
To his credit, Roosevelt stayed in his car, and Wood, at least outwardly, made nothing of the incident. Despite the tension in the
somewhat inverted leadership structure of the Rough Riders, the
respect and professionalism of both Roosevelt and Wood allowed
them to provide effective leadership.

His new Army uniform in hand, and his distinctive campaign hat
in place on his head, Roosevelt returned to his office in the Navy
Department after he was commissioned as a lieutenant colonel in
the First United States Volunteer Cavalry on May 6, 1898.[39] Once
the formalities were out of the way, he and Wood took on the
critical task of selecting their men. Estimates of the number of
applications that stacked up on Roosevelt's desk reached twenty-
three thousand, stiff competition for the one thousand–plus spots
in the Rough Riders.[40] The wide arc of Roosevelt's persona was a
beacon to hardy men throughout the country. Each man lobbied
to get a spot in the Rough Riders; a piece of each one of them was
in Roosevelt.

Roosevelt sought men with outdoor talents and the kind of
vigorous manliness he had championed in his outdoor writing,

and in his writings he recounted them with the color and style he had used in his wilderness verse. There were athletes: "Dudley Dean, perhaps the best quarterback who ever played on a Harvard Eleven"; "Waller, the high jumper"; "Craig Wadsworth, the steeple-chase rider"; "Joe Stevens, the crack polo player; . . . Hamilton Fish the ex-captain of Columbia crew."[41] Other Rough Riders were Native Americans from the "Cherokees, Chickasaws, Choctaws, and Creeks."[42] There were, of course, plenty of African American cowboys and soldiers in the West as well, but they were concentrated in other regiments.[43] Other hunters, horsemen, cowboys, and office workers rounded out the mix:

> There was tall Profitt, the sharpshooter, from North Carolina—sinewy, saturnine, fearless; Smith, the bear-hunter from Wyoming, and McCann, the Arizona book-keeper, who had begun life as a buffalo-hunter. There was Crockett, the Georgian, who had been an Internal Revenue officer, and had waged perilous war on the rifle-bearing "moonshiners." There were Darnell and Wood of New Mexico, who could literally ride any horses alive. There were Goodwin, and Buck Taylor, and Armstrong the ranger, crack shots with rifle or revolver.[44]

More than a decade earlier, Roosevelt had remarked from Medora that there was "some good fighting stuff among these harum-scarum roughriders out here."[45] Now, some of those men made incredible efforts to join up. Just before his seventeenth birthday, Jesse Langdon hopped a train in North Dakota, bound for Washington, having heard that Roosevelt was raising a regiment to take to war. When Langdon was a child in the Badlands he had met Roosevelt briefly, a glimpse that had convinced him that Roosevelt was the kind of man to follow onto the battlefield. Once in the capital, Langdon tracked down Roosevelt and hailed him as he was coming down the stairs outside the recruiting office.[46]

Langdon: "I'm Jesse Langdon from North Dakota, and I've beaten my way here on the train to join your Rough Riders."
Roosevelt: "Well, can you ride a horse?"
Langdon: "I can ride anything that's got hair on it."

That certainly fulfilled one of the main conditions for the Rough Riders—skill in horsemanship—and since he could shoot well and his waist wasn't bigger than his chest, Roosevelt brought Langdon into the Rough Rider fold.

To Roosevelt, raising such an interesting and competent band of men would become a lifelong source of pride. Immediately, however, the task of equipping and transporting these men became a festering sore on his hide. The day after his commission, he began to rant in his diary about the "delays and stupidity" in the Ordnance Department, and warned: "Against a good nation we should be helpless."[47] This would become the tension that underlay Roosevelt's story of the Rough Riders, with the best men rising to glory in the midst of inexcusably poor infrastructure and preparation by their nation—although others would have their own perspectives on the root causes of these logistical challenges.[48]

The Rough Riders were instructed to gather in San Antonio, Texas, and Wood went there directly as Roosevelt lingered in Washington to finagle any last arrangements he could, drawing on his abundant connections to ensure that his regiment had proper weapons and transportation. It would be a calamity if they missed the fight due to logistics.

With as many preparations in place as possible, Roosevelt made his way to San Antonio. He endured three days of travel before he was in the presence of his men, but then he began to pull the eclectic and talented band of soldiers together. They drilled incessantly in clouds of dust, both on horseback and on foot, and the work paid off.[49] After only several days, the lieutenant colonel observed: "The progress of the regiment wonderful."[50] They all "possessed in common the traits of hardihood and a thirst for adventure. They were to a man born adventurers, in the old sense of the word."[51] Roosevelt pulled together the disparate unit, as the Harvard and New York men got on "capitally with the cowpunchers."[52]

A furry band of mascots also helped unite the regiment. These mascots were not simply icons sewn on flags or patches; the hurly-burly Rough Riders kept the real things. The Arizona men had brought an unruly cougar cub named Josephine. From New Mexico had come a golden eagle. A scruffy dog named Cuba rounded out the band. The scraps between the eagle and the cougar exhilarated the men, like miniature boxing matches, and there was much

effect of cavalyman
equally + every
thing jolling +
flying

The Rough Riders gathered with many other military contingents in Tampa, Florida, to be transported to Cuba. Roosevelt's old illustrator friend, Frederic Remington, had also traveled to Tampa in hopes of gaining a post as a war correspondent. While there, Remington sketched the cavalry's movements. By permission of the Frederic Remington Art Museum.

pride in Josephine's feline tomfoolery: later in the campaign she stole off one night and entered the bed of a Third Cavalryman.[53] Common bonds were formed instantly; these men, despite their wide differences in upbringing, could all speak the language of the field.

To the troops Roosevelt exuded confidence and discipline. But in his diary he continued to boil with frustration: "The blunders & delays of the ordnance bureau surpass belief. They express us stuff we do'n't need, and send us the rifles by slow freight!"[54] The fault did not sit in any of the boots on the ground; Roosevelt ultimately laid the blame at the feet of the president.[55]

As the Rough Riders set off by train for Tampa on May 29, the conditions continued to be intolerable. The day after they left, the train broke down. Only a short time after it was fixed, it broke down again. Horses and men alike suffered from these long delays, as the men had to unload the horses to water and rest them, and then load them back up. The train lurched forward and slowly passed the Florida panhandle. Unfortunately, the trials would continue when they arrived in Tampa.

Roosevelt settled on the word "confusion" to describe the scene in Tampa. Upon his arrival, he observed the "railway system in wildest confusion."[56] Three days later, as he again observed regular breakdowns of freight trains and supply chains, he fumed in his diary: "No words can paint the confusion."[57] For three more days the Rough Riders drilled in the open areas as admirably as they could, but around them chaos reigned as plans, if there were any, changed on a dime. Finally, on June 8 they were ordered to depart by train to the docks in order to board a transport ship, but they waited all night by the side of the railway for a train that never came.[58] Wood and Roosevelt finally succeeded in getting their troops space in some empty coal cars for the trip down to the wharf. Roosevelt noted in his diary: "No allotment of transports, utter confusion."[59] Once in sight of the transport boats, Wood commandeered a small vessel and took possession of a transport that had been intended for the Seventy-First New York regiment. The Rough Riders double-timed aboard just before the Seventy-First arrived. Even amidst this disorganization in Tampa, morale didn't fade. Roosevelt wrote Edith's name in his diary—a rare occurrence—as evidence of a short visit she paid him in Tampa.[60]

Edith had recently undergone surgery, and some had even taken Roosevelt's departure while his wife was ill as additional evidence of his wild attraction to war. His good friend Winthrop Chanler had even suggested that Roosevelt had surrounded her with "a lot of perfectly incompetent doctors, taxidermists and veterinaries."[61] Even so, Edith's visit lifted his spirits, and the Rough Riders had their earnest and inspiring leaders to keep them strong.

After further delays, the transport *Yucatan* split the waters of the Gulf of Mexico with the Rough Riders aboard as they steamed "southward through a sapphire sea . . . under an almost cloudless sky."[62] There were still delays and mishaps—Roosevelt wrote in his diary that he found it "idiotic" that the fleet was being slowed to tow a schooner—but they slowly made progress into tropical waters.[63] The men drilled in the manual of arms by day, and the officers met to sharpen their own skills by night. After a week at sea, the men sighted the mountainous outline of the Cuban coast on the horizon. Far from being discouraged by the logistical failures, Roosevelt was thrilled by the opportunity to approach battle. He stood with his men on the deck of the *Yucatan* as the red sun set in the west, and as the band played "The Star Spangled Banner" they prepared themselves for the ultimate test of their wills.

If not for the battle, Roosevelt the naturalist would have been delighted to wander through the dense tropical forest and open expanses of palms and grass after they arrived in Cuba. As it was, the two-day march to Las Guasimas gave him only a brief opening to experience the nature of the neotropics and make a few observations. There were the feathery leaves of acacia trees on the trailside, and land crabs "almost as big as rabbits" scurrying along the ground.[64] Some spiders were spinners of orb webs like those in the Adirondacks, but others were palm-sized tarantulas. Vultures soared high overhead, and the men listened to nefarious "bird-notes," like the "cooing of doves and the call of a great brush cuckoo."[65] Along the trail, some of the men exchanged sightings with Roosevelt, "pointing out unfamiliar trees and birds."[66] As they made camp amidst this lush scene on June 23, Roosevelt trained his powers of observation on human life. In his sergeant and captain, Hamilton Fish and Allyn Capron, he saw men whose "frames seemed of steel, to withstand all fatigue; they were flushed with health; in their eyes shone high resolve and fiery desire."[67] Around

JUNE, 1898.

THURS. 23.

Marched

FRI. 24.

*Fight a las Guasimas.
We drove enemy
in fine shape. Lost
60 men killed &
wounded; 20 slight.*

SAT. 25.

Rested.

APPOINTMENTS.

The Rough Riders' first battle began as they were ambushed at Las Guasimas, but they eventually pushed the Spanish back. Although Roosevelt did not remember enjoying this battle, he wrote in his diary that they "drove [the] enemy in fine shape." TRC MS Am 1454.55 (12a).

a crackling fire the men, brimming with the best of health, shared a pregnant moment of calm and consideration.

The tropical sun rose quickly the next morning as the Rough Riders moved up the ridge into a tangled mass of foliage.[68] Capron and Fish struck out ahead to look for signs of the enemy position, and Capron returned to meet the advancing regiment only an hour later with news of a dead Spanish soldier just ahead. Scores of nervous eyes tried to make out human forms in the muggy green mosaic of leaves and vines in the forest slope ahead. As Roosevelt would later learn in South America, using vision to hunt mammals in a tropical forest is often futile. They could see nothing, but all at once the air burst with sounds as bullets rained down from Spanish snipers hidden in the trees. Lieutenant Fish, the steely, dashing man of the Columbia crew team, was the first man of the regiment to die as the battle began. Capron fell next. Another man was shot dead while he stood next to a tree with Roosevelt.[69] The Rough Riders fanned out in the jungle and inched their way toward an unseen enemy. Screaming Mauser bullets whizzed past their heads, sliced deep into tree trunks, and sometime found flesh. These bullets—smaller, faster, and more merciful than those shot by the Americans—made disconcerting sounds.[70] Overhead they made a "zir-ah-ah"; when they came near the sound was more like a "zip." A noise akin to that of a fist punching into a pillow indicated that a bullet had penetrated flesh.[71] One man leaned down to the forest floor and scooped up his hat, bugle, and haversack, all of which been knocked off by bullets, keeping them as potential curiosities should he be lucky enough to return home.[72] The foliage and smokeless powder concealed the snipers—much as natural camouflage patterns concealed the stick insects and moths that rested on tree branches around them—and allowed the ambush. This became a persistent theme in Roosevelt's account; he repeatedly returned to the effects of smokeless powder, describing it in terms of his own firsthand experience with disguise in the natural world, a topic that would become a long-standing interest for him.

Pushing forward through the hail, Roosevelt's remaining men saw the canopy give way to an open view of an upward slope on their right. They could see General Samuel Young's troops firing at Spanish troops on the slope. With a target finally in view, the Rough Riders let loose with an angry and accurate flurry of their

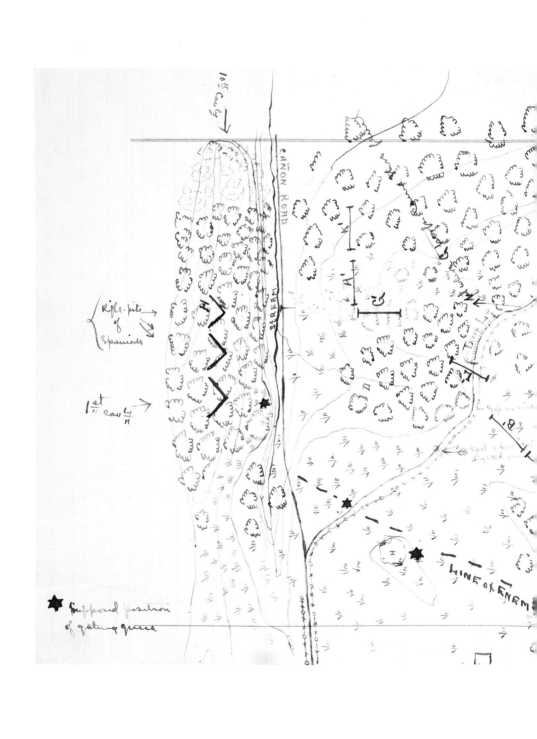

10ᵗʰ Cav.ᵣ

CAÑON ROAD

STREAM

Rifle-pits
of
Spaniards

1ˢᵗ Cav.ᵣ

K'

A'

G

F

D

I

B'

H

LINE OF ENEMY

Supposed position
of gatling guns

Leonard Wood was colonel of the Rough Riders during the battle of Las Guasimas, and he recorded the field of battle in a sketch. Leonard Wood Papers, Library of Congress.

own bullets and joined the advance of all of the regiments. After less than three hours of battle, the remaining Spaniards began to fall back, and any animals that had taken refuge behind logs or under leaves could creep out of hiding.

The natural beauty of Cuba was instantly recast that morning; the curious crabs became sinister as they circled the dead; the vultures reviled as they took to their ugly work. The Rough Riders had been selected for their hardihood, however, and those who survived accepted the realities of war. Even in his estimate of the butcher's bill, Roosevelt was pleased with the exploit: "We drove enemy in fine shape. Lost 60 men killed & wounded; 20 slight."[73] So ended the battle of Las Guasimas.

They attended to the grim task of collecting and burying the dead in a big trench the following morning.[74] The whole regiment joined in a round of "Rock of Ages" to honor their fallen; with vultures darkening the sky overhead, few lingered. They only moved a few miles the next day and the men continued to rest and recover, readying for a push toward Santiago. Despite having slept on the ground and not having removed his clothes in four full days, Roosevelt was full of vigor. He prowled their makeshift camp and found food wanting, so he galloped back to the coast to haggle for bags of beans.[75] Meanwhile, the men of the regiment found ways to use the culinary ingredients available.[76] One solider, Kirk McCurdy, wrote his father and recorded a firsthand account of how they were making the best of their conditions:

> We have become experienced cooks, and have several varieties of things—mango boiled in sugar, which is fine and like apple sauce; fried in sugar, it is like sweet potatoes; we also have hardtack fried in bacon grease which is about as good as anything toasted, we also soak about four hardtack in water until it is dough, add salt, then mix in coffee, fry in bacon grease, put a little sugar on top and enjoy it to its full extent.[77]

Their bellies were fortunate to receive even these unconventional mixes, as the days to come would leave little time or materials for cooking. Their stomachs, though not pierced by bullets, were serially strained by the anxiety of battle and the ensuing effects of disease.

Including the dead and wounded, many of those waiting for the siege of Santiago were not having as good a war as Roosevelt. Despite Brigadier General Young's old school credentials as one of the few in Cuba who "had given and taken wounds with the saber," he was forced to miss the main fight when he was struck down with fever.[78] This misfortune furthered Roosevelt's goals, however, as Colonel Wood was immediately promoted to the head of the cavalry brigade, and Roosevelt, to his "intense delight," was hoisted up to full command of the Rough Riders.[79]

Roosevelt's old illustrator friend, Frederic Remington, was also having a miserable time in Cuba without much success in getting to the front. The scene in Tampa had been much the same for Remington as it was for Roosevelt: long days of waiting in the presence of almost complete confusion. He had come seeking a role as a war correspondent, and he eventually found sponsorship with General Young. After weeks of lounging and drinking in Tampa, he had made it to Siboney and then past Guasimas, but only after the fighting had occurred. Unfortunately, this was to be Remington's story of the war, as he wandered among the fallen behind the lines, eventually succumbing to fever himself. In possibly his best written contribution of the campaign, Remington channeled Rudyard Kipling as he described the oppressive heat that sat over the troops like a steaming wool blanket: "And the heat would make your blooming eyebrows crawl."[80] As Roosevelt was poised to lead the Rough Riders on the charge, Remington was far to the rear, dodging shrapnel and Mausers, straining for a glimpse of the battle. He was short on food, as they all were, but even his hunger and deprivation did not keep him from capturing enough of the general scene to eventually paint one of the most enduring images—*The Charge of the Rough Riders*—of what happened next.[81]

Roosevelt put on his spectacles in the 4 a.m. darkness of July 1. The orders had come to advance, and he made sure all was in readiness. This was to be his day. One can imagine that every pair of eyes in the regiment was on him that morning, watching his movements and stance, taking in the subtle cues that good leaders give off before they march into battle.[82]

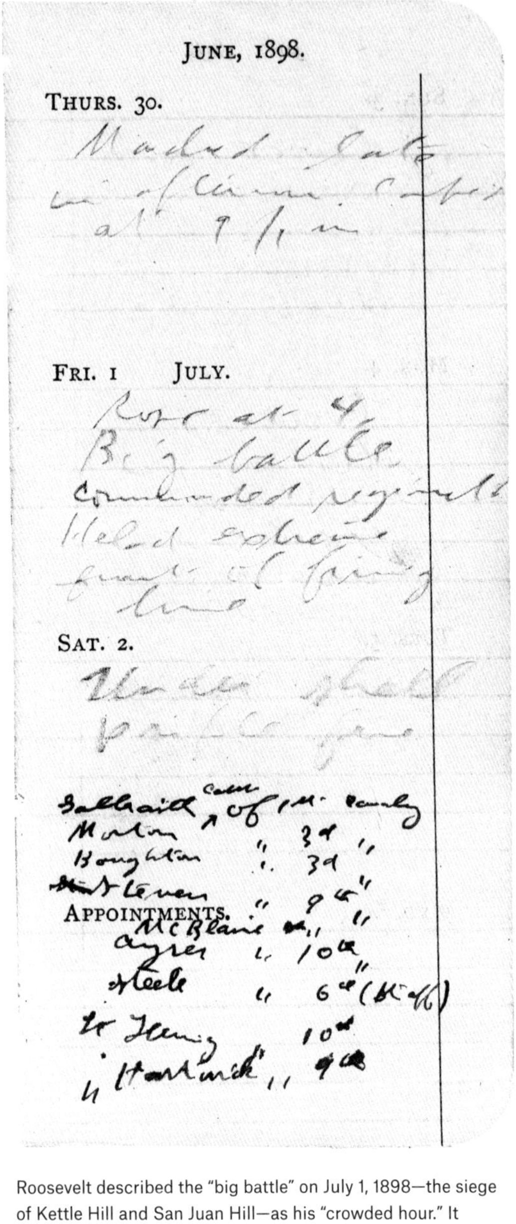

JUNE, 1898.

THURS. 30.

Marched late in afternoon, camped at 9 pm

FRI. 1 JULY.

Rose at 4. Big battle. Commanded regiment. Held extreme front of firing line

SAT. 2.

Under shell & rifle fire

Galbraith, capt. of 1st cavalry
Morton " 3d "
Boughton " 3d "
Stevens " 9th "
McBlain " "
Ayres " 10th
Steele " 6th
Lt Fleming 10th
" Hartwick " 9th

APPOINTMENTS.

Roosevelt described the "big battle" on July 1, 1898—the siege of Kettle Hill and San Juan Hill—as his "crowded hour." It became one of the defining moments of his life. TRC MS Am 1454.55 (12a).

As the sun rose over their backs, the theatre of war came into view. The Rough Riders marched down the road, heading in a straight line toward San Juan Heights, a bluff that lay in front of Santiago. A wide expanse of waist-high grass lay in the low areas, and they turned right and followed San Juan Creek, which ran along the base of the hills. Despite the whizzing bullets and bursting fire, Roosevelt was atop his horse, Little Texas, leading his regiment with an iron will. He had fixed the blue polka-dotted handkerchief—which became a symbol of the regiment—under his hat so that it flowed back over his neck. With a headdress somewhere between that of a sheikh and a cowboy, Roosevelt stood out on the battlefield as other regiments fanned out at the base of the heights, and the Rough Riders prepared to attack a second hill, now known as Kettle Hill, where there was another Spanish stronghold.

Prancing back and forth atop Little Texas while the rest of the regiment was hunkered down, he jeered and joked with the men, at one point yelling, "Are you afraid to stand up when I am on horseback?"[83] In the thick stew of battle—the heat, the smoke, and the explosive noise—each man had a decision to make. As they were paused at the bottom of Kettle Hill waiting for the order to charge, each one weighed the options to follow their leaders into battle. There was trepidation among the other regiments lying in the grass, even though it was clear that the main charge had started up the bluffs in the distance. Roosevelt later recounted how he could see no other colonel and therefore gave the order to charge. In front of him the others hesitated, so he barked, "Then let my men through, sir."[84] With this posturing the Rough Riders filed through, picking up members of the regulars like a magnet collecting iron shavings, and the siege of Kettle Hill began.

Some like snakes and some like groundhogs, the soldiers split the high grass as they ran up Kettle Hill. Atop his steed, Roosevelt was more like a gazelle, splashing through a small creek and bounding up through a horizontal rain of bullets. Men running next to Roosevelt were whipped to the side and back as bullets sunk home in their arms, legs, and heads. The soldiers reached a fence and Roosevelt dismounted, sending Little Texas back, and led the rest of the charge on foot. After furious steps through waves of coarse and slender leaves, a Spanish soldier met the advance. Roosevelt pulled from his belt a Colt .45 military revolver that had been raked up from the wreck of the *Maine* in Havana Harbor, and used it to fulfill his earlier promise to kill a Spaniard himself. The young Spaniard fell to the ground as he absorbed the bullet, while the rest of his countrymen were in retreat.[85]

A fair prospect from the hill, Roosevelt could easily see the progress of the troops who were sieging San Juan Hill, off to their left, and he realized they could use help. A few hasty conferences and attempts to organize the troops ensued, and then he was off like a Mauser himself, down the side of Kettle Hill and into the low-lying grass, before he realized that the troops weren't following: the men either hadn't heard his call to charge or hadn't obeyed. Frantically retracing his steps back up Kettle Hill, he barked new orders, and the assault began anew. There weren't nearly as many Rough Riders left now, but Roosevelt ran out in front, revolver waving and kerchief streaming. This was not an uncommon scene during the battle, as one Rough Rider remembered how at one point "Roosevelt went on and overran the trenches, and he was maybe seventy-five yards ahead of us—he was *always* ahead of us."[86]

Once Roosevelt made it atop San Juan Hill at last, the most dramatic day of his life was beginning to wane. Despite the grim remains of the battle, he was "revelling in victory and gore."[87] It was an emotional release much like his buffalo dance in the Wyoming Territory fifteen years before. In macabre joy he pointed out the bodies, caked with the deep crimson of recently spilled blood: "Look at all these damned Spanish dead!"[88] Then came the less glorious part.

There was still some shelling and fighting during the final siege of Santiago, but the remaining maneuvers were mostly political and diplomatic. Just over two weeks later, on July 17, the Americans took control of Santiago. No longer were bullets and shrapnel screaming past their heads; now, unbeknownst to them, the real threat was buzzing in their ears.

Roosevelt only makes passing reference to mosquitoes in his *Rough Riders*, but the specter of malaria, and more so yellow fever, was very much on his mind as the troops were in their holding pattern after the battle was won. Roosevelt himself was in fine form—he even swam three hundred yards through a school of sharks to stand on the wreck of the *Merrimac*—but his troops were suffering.[89] The sick list grew, with festering wounds and the onset of

One evening, the Rough Riders gathered and considered the fate of a Spanish prisoner. Frederic Remington captured the scene. By permission of the Frederic Remington Art Museum.

exhaustion and fever, and a rage began to grow in Roosevelt about the lack of action in removing the troops. Although he couldn't have known that mosquitoes vectored the dreaded yellow fever, he could see that conditions were ripe for disease to decimate his men.[90] On the last day of July he wrote to Henry Cabot Lodge, bitterly rebuking Secretary Alger's reluctance to remove the troops from Cuba. Despite being in good health, Roosevelt recognized his own mental strain: "Perhaps you think I write too bitterly. I can only say, old man, that what I have seen during the last five weeks has been enough to make one bitter."[91] Four days later, Roosevelt resorted to a surprisingly public act of insubordination to remove his troops from harm's way, as he banded together with other officers in a joint letter: "The army is disabled by malarial fever . . . [and is] in a condition to be practically entirely destroyed by an epidemic of yellow fever, which is sure to come in the near future."[92] A public flap ensued, but the letter worked: the army was sent to recover in Montauk, on Long Island, within three days.[93]

"It was a plain case of hug" that General Young applied as Roosevelt stepped off the gangplank onto Iron Pier at Montauk.[94] First grabbing Roosevelt's hand in a firm shake and then wrapping a bearlike arm around his neck, he stood together with him, the two

After the Rough Riders finished fighting in Cuba, they returned to Montauk Point on Long Island. While there, their colonel posed for a photograph while writing in his tent. TRC.

making a fair contrast: the battle-hardened and sunbaked colonel with the home-front general. As they held the embrace for a full thirty seconds, it is likely that Roosevelt conveyed to Young a version of what he said to the press just after: "Well, I am disgracefully healthy. Really, I am ashamed of myself, feeling so well and strong, with all these poor fellows suffering and so weak they can hardly stand. But I tell you we had a bully fight. This is a fine regiment, all a lot of crack-a-jacks."[95]

As Roosevelt returned a hero, hundreds of boisterous onlookers joined Young in marveling at the fact that he had not been struck by a bullet or blown apart by a shell. And as Roosevelt the storyteller publicly launched into yarns that would soon become part of the Rough Riders canon—the religious and ethnic diversity of the regiment, the gallant fighting of Capron and Fish at Las Guasimas, the assault on San Juan Hill—the spotlight slowly began to turn back onto the unique constellation of attributes that had made Roosevelt a success on the battlefield. Those who were there tried to sum up what made him so effective: "There was nobody quite like him. . . . Men were drawn to him because they knew he was the right man."[96] Roosevelt even described himself as uniquely qualified to lead the Rough Riders: "In my regiment nine-tenths of the men were better horsemen than I was, and probably two-thirds of them better shots than I was, while on the average they were certainly hardier and more enduring. Yet after I had had them a very short while they all knew, and I knew too, that nobody else could command them as I could."[97] Others attempted at the time to identify the parts that made up this identity. Before Roosevelt had left for Cuba, *The New York Times* had made a prediction of success based on the synthetic nature of his persona: "Mr. Roosevelt has been a hunter of big game in the West, is accustomed to hardship and peril, and is one of the best shots in the country. Thus officered, this regiment of cowboys ought to make a name for itself in the annals of the war with Spain."[98] At this small but raucous gathering on the coast of Long Island, it was clear that this prophecy was fulfilled. With his triumphant return, Roosevelt successfully completed another turn in his cycle of adventure, and it was only months until his rendering of the campaign appeared in *The Rough Riders*.[99] Although it met with popular approval at the time, Roosevelt's version of events, like his Western writings, has exposed him to much later criticism that he fashioned his account to fit with a narrative of Western heroes and empire, with groups like the African American soldiers of the cavalry left to the side.[100]

The newspapers of the time weren't content to dwell on Roosevelt's recent exploits with the Rough Riders, however, and rumors were already circulating that he would run for governor that fall. On August 16, with the whiff of a soon-to-be candidate managing his image, Roosevelt told reporters from several papers, including *The New York Times*: "I want you all to bear witness that I have not said a word except about the regiment, and that is worth while talking about."[101] The reporters may have not been able to get Roosevelt to open up, but in the *Times* Roosevelt's potential candidacy for New York governor was heralded as the best Republican nomination since the end of the Civil War.[102]

As the Roosevelt candidacy started to unfold, one description framed it as "one of the most picturesque canvasses the State has ever experienced."[103] The campaign embraced many voices, even the impassioned endorsement of one Rough Rider who spoke at a gathering to provide his perspective on Roosevelt's worth as a leader: "My friends and fellow citizens, my colonel was a great soldier. He will make a great governor. He always put us boys in battle where we would be killed if there was a chance, and that is what he will do with you."[104] Although Roosevelt's initial resistance may have been a necessary formality, it did nothing to quell his rise. In less than three months, just after his fortieth birthday, he was elected governor of New York.

The door was locked when Roosevelt returned to the Executive Mansion at 11 p.m. in the subzero cold of inauguration day. It was the Roosevelt's first night in the governor's residence, and Edith and the children were already in bed. The wind had been howling in from the east ever since he had left the Parsons' home on Elk Street in his carriage. He knocked on the door and waited for someone to emerge from the darkened building, but the door stood still. This simple conflict with an inanimate object might have flummoxed other politicians, but physical contests—with animate or inanimate opponents—had always been a source of exhilaration and satisfaction for him. Roosevelt did not worry that the press might cast him as a "housebreaker" on his first day in office; he simply smashed a window, opened its latch, and entered.[105]

Roosevelt carried this aptitude for approaching confrontation head-on with him as he trod up the massive staircase of the Capitol in Albany, and his battle-tested instincts made for a successful transition back into politics. His cache of experiences since he had last roamed the Assembly chamber was impressive, but even so he quickly became enmeshed in complicated entanglements linking the governor, the legislature, and the people. Roosevelt found himself wedged between big business and the "Boss" of the New York Republican Party, Thomas Collier Platt, but he soon found adroit ways of getting what he wanted.[106]

Early in his second year as governor, Roosevelt stood up to the weight of influence wielded by the insurance business as he sought to rid the state of the superintendent of insurance, Louis F. Payn. Roosevelt and many others had never liked Payn's backdoor dealings and the spoils he gained from his post. The fact that Roosevelt stood up in the face of a blistering wind of influence was not new;

it was how he did so that was novel. In a letter to his old friend
Henry Sprague, he confessed:

> I shall not feel real easy until the vote has actually been
> taken, but apparently everything is now all right. I have
> always been fond of the West African proverb: "Speak softly
> and carry a big stick; you will go far." If I had not carried
> the big stick the organization would not have gotten behind
> me, and if I had yelled and blustered at Parkhurst and the
> similar dishonest lunatics desired, I would not have had ten
> votes. But I was entirely good-humored, kept perfectly cool
> and steadfastly refused to listen to anything save that Payn
> had to go, and that I would take none but a thoroughly
> upright and capable man in his place.[107]

Here Roosevelt applied this "proverb"—more likely a saying he had
picked up—to describe a natural phenomenon that he himself
employed and embodied. As he hurtled toward the presidency,
this was just a first articulation of his stick-swinging mentality.

Governor Roosevelt also dealt blows in the name of conservation. In January 1900 he employed his Annual Message to place
the stewardship of nature front and center: "Forest preservation is
of the utmost importance to the State."[108] He lobbied for the preservation of the Adirondacks and Catskills, and increased measures
to protect their waterways from fouling by sawmills and wood-pulp
mills. He wanted more and better game wardens to protect the
populations of fish and game. He also wanted ordinary birds, like
songbirds, to be protected and never sacrificed for ornaments and
headwear. Some lumbering and reservoir making would be permitted, but only by using "scientific" principles that would prevent
the "ruin of the great woods and the drying up of the sources of
the rivers." Further explicating the complicated combination of
preservation and use that he would use to justify his policies well
into the future, he added: "Hardy outdoor sports, like hunting,
are in themselves of no small value to the National character and
should be encouraged in every way. Men who go into the wilderness, indeed, men who take part in any field sports with horse or
rifle, receive a benefit which can hardly be given by even the most
vigorous athletic games." In Albany, Roosevelt laid the groundwork

for his future efforts in conserving forests and birds with Gifford Pinchot and Frank Chapman.[109]

The New York governorship, like his post as assistant secretary of the Navy, was a relatively short link in a chain of causality that led Roosevelt to the White House. Much later, when he returned to North Dakota to lay the cornerstone of a new library at Fargo College, Roosevelt would have a chance to reflect on the steps that had led him toward the presidency. In a speech introducing him, the president of the college, C. C. Creager, would suggest of Roosevelt: "Had he not lived on the cattle ranch there, there would have been no Rough Rider regiment, and the events that followed Roosevelt's career in that regiment would not have taken place." Roosevelt would follow with words of agreement: "I never would have been president had it not been for my experience in North Dakota."[110] John Long, too, later added: "His going into the Army led straight to the presidency."[111] The lessons he extracted from cattle ranches and hunting trips in the Badlands had contributed to his success with the Rough Riders. Now, unquestionably, the characteristics that had been emboldened in Roosevelt by his success on the battlefield were propelling him through the New York governorship.

Before Roosevelt had been governor a full year, a potential link to the US presidency emerged. Vice President Garrett Hobart died in November of 1899. Initially, Roosevelt estimated the chance of a vice president accomplishing anything in office as "infinitesimal," and thought that the position would be a "bore."[112] He wrote to his sister Anna in February of 1900 with a stark assessment: "It would be an irksome, wearisome place where I could do nothing."[113] There was also the question of money, as he worried about how he could support his family on a more modest salary than he was receiving in the New York governorship. Eventually, however, the finesse of "Boss" Platt and Henry Cabot Lodge—each with their own agenda—set the stage for Roosevelt's eventual acceptance of the vice-presidential nomination in June. In the end, some considered this a "shelving" of Roosevelt, while others thought of him as being "kicked upstairs."[114]

Decision made, Roosevelt broke "all records as a campaigner" as President William McKinley's "field marshal" in September and

October of 1900.[115] Although Roosevelt's efforts in campaigning and speechmaking weren't like his nature study, hunting, and soldiering, some elements of his outdoor persona applied. For someone who had once spent more than a day in the saddle without sleeping, making seventeen presidential campaign stops in Kansas on September 28 and ten speeches in Kentucky on October 15 simply constituted two honest days' work.[116] Roosevelt's old field companions found him seemingly everywhere on the trail, with Rough Riders cheering him on and helping to chase off egg-throwing supporters of the opposition presidential candidate, William Jennings Bryan.[117] Luckily, the fact that one of the "harum-scarum" Rough Riders shot a newspaper editor who had made an "unfavorable estimate" of Roosevelt's character did nothing to prevent McKinley's landslide victory.[118] On November 6, the Rough Riders' colonel, now a true national leader, assumed the title of vice president–elect.

In Tooth and Claw

In his new status as vice president–elect, Roosevelt had a window of time, starting in January of 1901, in which he was relatively free from political responsibilities. His cache of specimens and the heads that hung on the wall at Sagamore Hill—bison, antelope, wapiti, sheep, and goats—revealed his relative neglect of the elusive felids of North America. He knew his life would not get less complicated after inauguration on March 4, so he seized the moment to temporarily return to the life of a hunter-naturalist and to track cougar in Colorado.

After absorbing the impact of forty-five miles of ruts and bumps in the road as they drove from the railroad station, Roosevelt and his hunting companions Philip Stewart and Gerald Webb stopped for the night in Meeker, Colorado.[1] It wasn't just Roosevelt's buckskin shirt and double-layered socks that kept his blood warm; he had the anticipation of the chase welling up inside him. Darkness had already blanketed the White River when he arrived, and the subzero temperatures gave the air a familiar bite as he walked through the doors of the two-story Meeker Hotel. That evening in Meeker allowed for a rendezvous with a prominent hunter, John Goff, who would guide Roosevelt for five weeks in the mountainous land north of town. After a night's sleep, the party gathered in front of the hotel and headed north to Goff's ranch. By afternoon, the guns were already out.

Goff made an immediate and lasting impression on Roosevelt as one of the best hunters he had ever encountered, but even he was a supporting character on this adventure. The leading roles were taken not by humans, but by Goff's colorful pack of dogs.[2] As the men mounted horses and headed north toward Coyote Basin, Roosevelt evaluated each dog and learned its name and unique habits, developing the characters of his next story. Ahead ran the eight hounds, led by Jim, the biggest and most formidable of the lot. Once Jim picked up the scent of a cougar or bobcat, he would charge off in the lead of the hounds and use his loud bark to force it up a tree. Next came Boxer, an older and smaller dog that "never gave up" and made up for his size with tenacity.[3] Boxer could not keep up with Jim in the chase, but when Roosevelt laid out the remains of game for the dogs to eat, Boxer scrapped for his share, as he "devoured it eagerly . . . always looking as if he had swallowed a mattress." And on they went: Tree'em, with a remarkable staccato bark; Lil and Nel, "two very stanch and fast bitches" with "shrill voices"; Pete, a female, a great hunter; and Pete's brother Jimmie, the young apprentice. Far back from the hounds were the four professional hunting dogs that stayed with the horses and men. It was only after the hounds had surrounded a cougar that these brutes jumped into the fray, locking onto the cat's head with their jaws, keeping it from biting and slashing with its teeth.

Despite their powerful muscles and sharp teeth and claws, cougars are afraid of dogs. Goff's pack exploited this aspect of their behavior, having chased down hundreds of cougars over their many years in the mountains. Hunting cougars without hounds is futile: humans rarely lay eyes on them; instead, the cougars are usually the ones that do the observing.[4]

Of the many feline eyes that likely watched Roosevelt on his first day out, those of only one bobcat had the misfortune of being seen by the hunters. The hounds picked up the cat's scent and the hunters followed behind, eventually collecting their first specimen. A doe carcass left after a kill was the only evidence of cougar that day, but it still made for good conversation that night at Goff's ranch house. The next morning the men were back on the trail, headed toward the Keystone Ranch, where they would base their operations. Along with running down another bobcat on their second day, the dogs also located a cougar trail. Frantically running back and forth, they were puzzled by evidence that they couldn't quite place. The trail had gone too cold for even their keen eyes and noses, and on their first night at Keystone Ranch they had yet to see a cougar.

The next morning, there was no reason to be off at the break of dawn; the hounds could not take the dawn-until-dusk pace that Roosevelt adopted in many of his other pursuits. So once the men

Ther.   SUN. JAN. 13, 1901   Wea.

Hunted all day. Dogs
worried another lynx, ♀
Pack puzzled by cold
cougar trail, spent night
at Keystone ranch.

Ther.   MONDAY 14   Wea.

Knifed a cougar which
the dogs held. Four of
them were more or less hurt;
were over 2 hours on trail. Cougar
a fullgrown but small ♀; length
nearly 6 feet; weight a little over 80 lbs.

Ther.   TUESDAY 15   Wea.

Knifed another cougar
while the dogs held him,
He had 3 killed in cave in cañon
bank; a few days old, ♂ length
6 feet 7 inches. Weight 118 lbs
Pack rather used up.   118

Shortly before he was sworn in as vice president, Roosevelt took a trip to Colorado to hunt
cougar and bobcat. His guide, John Goff, had a colorful pack of hunting dogs that would chase
down the cats and immobilize them.

Ther.　　WED. JAN. 16, 1901　　Wea.

Rode all day — 5th day.
shot lynx in piñon
after excellent run;
weighed 21 lbs. ♀

Ther.　　THURSDAY 17　　Wea.

Webb shot lynx, 29 lbs. ♂
Rode from 9 a.m. to 6 p.m.
Two good runs after lynx,
climbing very rugged
mountains to the top.
Big lynx had killed an
8 months fawn; could kill
a yearling deer.

Ther.　　FRIDAY 18　　Wea.

Stewart sick. Webb killed
cougar; tree small, on cliff face;
6 ft 5 inches. weight 107 lbs. ♀
I killed lynx, 25 lbs ♀

Hunting big cats provided an exciting chase for Roosevelt as he rode on horseback after the pack of dogs, which "worried" the game over long snowy trails in the mountains. TRC MS Am 1454.55 (13).

and dogs had eased into their third day, the hunters set off again to home in on their elusive prize. For two hours there were plenty of dead-end trails, old prints left from previous days. The hounds needed encouragement to keep on track, and Goff nudged them back from the trails of bobcat, focusing attention on the large prints of cougar. Suddenly, there was the loud blast of a hunting trumpet. Roosevelt turned on his mount and saw Goff with his horn to his lips, calling the pack to a recent cougar trail and inducing a frenzy of sniffing. Back and forth along the trail, Jim led the chase, following loops and backtracks through the lightly packed snow. The hounds moved out of sight into the next valley, and soon Goff muttered, "Barking treed!" in his low voice as he identified a distant transition in the hounds' barks which indicated that a cat was in a tree.[5] Immediately, the four fighting dogs charged off to join the hounds, arriving to find a small female cougar perched in a pinyon pine surrounded by barking hounds. After several moments, the cougar leapt from the tree, ran ahead of the growling pack, and climbed another tree. As the rest of the hunting party came close, the cougar again jumped to the ground to try to escape, but this time the dogs caught up, and "after running a couple of hundred yards, the dogs seized it. The worry was terrific; the growling, snarling, and yelling rang among the rocks."[6] The hunters jumped off of their horses and ran up to the wriggling mass of fur and teeth. The dogs had immobilized the cougar's head, so Roosevelt was able to dispatch the cougar with his knife.

What happened next was less like Roosevelt's conquest of his first grizzly, and more like his childhood examination of the Broadway seal. The dogs were cleared back and the animal was laid out in the snow. Stewart took a photograph of Goff, Roosevelt, and the cougar ringed by the hounds. Then the important work began. Roosevelt had been anxious not only to track and kill cougars, but to send data and specimens to C. Hart Merriam at the Smithsonian Institution for scientific study. As Roosevelt brandished a tape measure, Goff pulled from his rifle scabbard not a gun but a steel yardstick, and the two men took measurements of the animal from nose to tail, "between uprights."[7] In his diary, Roosevelt recorded the events and information that would then be passed to Merriam: "Knifed a cougar which the dogs held. Four of them were more or less hurt; were over 2 hours on trail. Cougar a full grown but small ♀; length exactly 6 feet; weight a little over 80 lbs."[8] In taking stock of the dogs, the hunters noticed that Boxer had taken a solid bite in the leg from the cougar and thereafter ran on only three legs, with one of his hind legs "packed" or held up.[9] Roosevelt was adamant that "every hunter *ought* to be a field naturalist, and *must* be an observer, if he is to be a hunter in anything but name."[10] Too often, the precious facts and observations that pieced together the knowledge of species were lost "by the time the trained scientific man comes upon the field."

Lying on the ground in the midday sun, the specimen allowed careful examination of the aspects of the cougar that make it so formidable. Just down from the ruffled fur of its legs where the dogs had clamped on, its leathery footpads were soft to the touch. In this flesh was the evidence of how the cougar had silently crept through the woods, claws retracted for maximum stealth, waiting for a chance to pounce. Roosevelt opened the cat's maw and examined the long teeth that allowed it to make a quick and dramatic strike at the neck of prey, either suffocating or cracking the vertebrae of the deer, elk, and porcupine that are a cougar's main sources of food.[11] In this specimen, the worn teeth provided the hunter-scientists with evidence of advanced age, but even in this older individual of the species known as cougar, mountain lion, and puma throughout its wide range in North and South America, a quiet stealth had been backed up by quick and overwhelming power. Roosevelt had an opportunity to consider this combination of attributes—walking softly but being able to instantly unleash a fury of strength—as he continued his hunt.[12]

Through a succession of ranches—Keystone, Mathes, Judge Foreman's— the hunters went, bringing in new cougar specimens that built a picture of the variation in size and coloration that the species displayed in this habitat. Over five weeks of hunting they tallied fourteen cougars and nine bobcats. Roosevelt killed twelve cats himself, some with a knife and others with a gun. He related to Merriam one of the more sensational collections on the hunt, specimen "No. 2", which weighed 164 pounds and was seven feet, eight inches in length: "I hung over a cliff by moonlight and brained it as it lay on a ledge below me."[13] It "made a pretty complete smash" of much of the skull, Roosevelt wrote, but the teeth were still worthy of study.[14] Along with long days of hunting, the hunters took target practice and prepared their specimens, hanging up the skins to dry in the winter sun.

By February 15 the men rode back to Meeker with a sizable cache of carefully bundled specimens, and a trove of data scrawled in Roosevelt's diary. In addition to his daily accounts, the twelve pages at the rear of his diary labeled for "memoranda" and "cash account" contained stories and facts Roosevelt had absorbed from Goff and the other ranchers. This material provided background and color to the data, highlighting the interface between humans and the wild that had so captivated him in his Badlands life. Roosevelt even recorded a yarn about how a bobcat was fond of the house cat of a rancher named Haywood. After the bobcat chased his cat into his house while he was reading the paper, Haywood shot the intruder, but the house cat "would not leave house for three days afterwards."[15]

The train ride east found Roosevelt pondering what he had learned about cougars and planning an article on the trip for *Scribner's Magazine*. He grinned when he remembered that settlers near Meeker referred to him as "Johnny Goff's tourist" and not as the vice president–elect of the United States.[16] As Roosevelt click-clacked back east to Washington and turned to a new role in politics, he reveled in the fact that he could slip in and out of Western life as a normal citizen. But, as usual, he did not leave the ways of the field behind.

Second in line was a position that did not fit Roosevelt's disposition, but he did his best to support President McKinley and turn to the relatively workaday vice-presidential docket as the four days of inauguration ceremonies concluded. In March, he reined in political scraps and rows as he oversaw the US Senate. In April, once Congress had adjourned, he visited Boston to attend the Home Market Banquet and hobnob at Harvard, also taking time to be sure that his Colorado cougar specimens made their way to C. G. Gunther's Sons in Manhattan to be mounted.[17] Late spring found him laying the cornerstone of the New Methodist Episcopal Church on Long Island, and helping to open the Pan-American Exposition in Buffalo. As the heat of summer arrived, he was back at Harvard for commencement, after which he took a fishing trip with his sons. In late summer he went west to Colorado with a speech to help the state celebrate its quarto-centennial, and then, never one to miss a hunting opportunity, he met up again with Goff and Stewart to run down coyotes. As September dawned, Roosevelt was off to another fair, this time in Minneapolis. After shaking hundreds of hands, he made an address there that ranged over familiar ground on wealth and wages, and on the unity of the country.[18] But he also publicly brandished a metaphorical weapon for the first time:

> A good many of you are probably acquainted with the old proverb: "Speak softly and carry a big stick—you will go far." If a man continually blusters, if he lacks civility, a big stick will not save him from trouble; and neither will speaking softly avail, if back of the softness there does not lie strength, power. In private life there are few beings more obnoxious than the man who is always loudly boasting; and if the boaster is not prepared to back up his words his position becomes absolutely contemptible. So it is with the nation.[19]

Despite his high-minded ruminations on national power, Roosevelt ambled through the hinterlands in early September of 1901. After giving a short speech at the fair in Rutland, Vermont, he paid a visit on September 6 to the Vermont Fish and Game League on Isle La Motte, a sizeable island in Lake Champlain, directly between Vermont and New York. On this remote and unlikely island, his life changed course.

Roosevelt's voice careened off the ceiling of the tent set up next to the house of the state's former governor, Nelson W. Fisk, as Roosevelt entertained the guests with anecdotes, including stories of his recent cougar hunt.[20] Afterwards, his hosts thought that some refreshment and a chair might suit him, so they stepped inside Fisk's library for a brief rest.[21] Roosevelt loosened his necktie and sat down to change his clothes for dinner. One more speech, and he had reached hundreds more ears. Outside, preparations were being made for him to reappear for the customary barrage of glad-handing. An urgent phone call, however, interrupted the

Rode all day — 8th day Stewart killed cougar, young ♀ (8 months ?) length 40½ weight — 47 lbs. Two baits, killed in open, had been dragged (not carried) some obj[...] under trees,

Rested. Nailed up skins; shot at target; bathed.

Rode all day, Stewart shot a bobcat on a rock. ♀ 22 lbs

The long days of chasing cats through the snow-covered trails in the mountains tired both the hunters and dogs. On some days they rested at one of the ranches where they based operations, nailing up skins to dry in the sun.

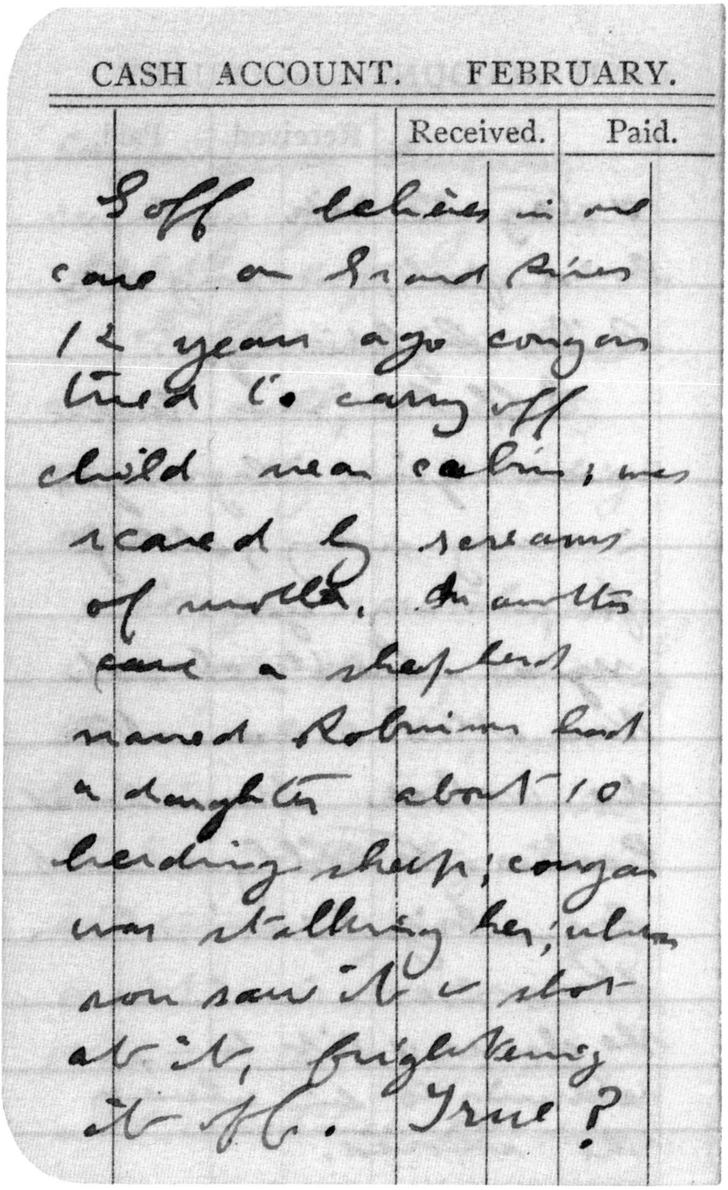
CASH ACCOUNT. FEBRUARY.

	Received.	Paid.

Goff tells in one
case on Grand River
12 years ago cougar
tried to carry off
child near cabin; was
scared by screams
of mother. In another
case a shepherd
named Robinson had
a daughter about 10
herding sheep; cougar
was stalking her, when
son saw it & shot
at it, frightening
it off. True?

In the notes section at the back of his 1901 diary, Roosevelt recorded a story of how the ten-year-old daughter of a shepherd named Robinson had been stalked by a cougar. Roosevelt noted his ambivalence about whether he should believe this yarn with a single word: "True?" TRC MS Am 1454.55 (13).

quiet moment and jolted Roosevelt out of his perceived irrelevancy: McKinley had been shot by an anarchist in Buffalo. The president was stable, but his wounds were serious.

A rare stunned expression blanketed Roosevelt's face; then tears welled up in his eyes. Collecting himself, he asked Redfield Proctor, US senator from Vermont, to make brief remarks that would inform the crowd of the grave state of the nation. Meanwhile, the vice president "paced nervously, but not excitedly, up and down the room," exchanging only "a few appropriate remarks in conversation" with the few friends who lingered.[22] Soon enough, news came that McKinley's wounds were not fatal, and Roosevelt rushed to the veranda and attempted to reassure the crowd, asking them to spread calming words to the others who had already boarded the ferry *Chateaugay*, which was readying to embark for Burlington. Roosevelt left for Burlington that evening on the yacht *Elfrida*, and made for Buffalo in the "Grand Isle" car of the Rutland Railroad. He arrived at 1 p.m. on September 7 to shouts of "Teddy" along the streets, and was relieved to find the president doing relatively well.[23] After spending several days in Buffalo, Roosevelt was assured that McKinley was stable, so he decided to avoid the appearance of a hovering would-be successor and continued with his family plans, leaving for their vacation in a remote location in the Adirondacks.

It would be hard for a scriptwriter to concoct a more dramatic entrance to the presidency than what happened in the following week.[24] Roosevelt first joined Edith and his children at a remote lodge in New York called the Tahawus Club on September 11. The next morning, an entourage including Edith and the children hiked up rain-soaked paths to a cabin at Lake Colden. Feeling satisfied with their tramp and having had their fill of campfires and stories, Edith and the children were escorted back to the club the following morning. Roosevelt then made for the summit of Mount Marcy, in no way expecting that by afternoon, he himself would be the one being pursued.

The somber message that tracked Roosevelt that day began as telegrams sent by McKinley's secretary George Cortelyou and Secretary of War Elihu Root, both of whom were with McKinley in Buffalo, watching him slip into a coma. Roosevelt's personal secretary, William Loeb Jr., was waiting at North Creek Station, the closest train stop to Tahawus, and received the messages that made it clear that McKinley was deteriorating. Loeb immediately telephoned the camp's Lower Club House, the farthest that the telephone line reached into the woods, with the news. David Hunter, the club's superintendent, carried Loeb's message by wagon to the Upper Club House, where he met a crew of guides who were casually telling stories by the fire. Hunter announced: "Boys, there is bad news from the President. Who will carry the message to Mr. Roosevelt?"[25] The task quickly fell to the "tall, thin, weather-beaten" Harrison Hall, who powerfully strode off into the mist toward the summit.[26]

Meanwhile, newspapermen conjured up a more romantic scene for the public, in which "the far-reaching megaphones and the rifle-cracking signals of the mountain-climbing guides . . . marked the passage of the searching mountaineers."[27] In reality, the others involved at Tahawus were recruiting relay teams of horses to stand ready to transport Roosevelt from Tahawus to North Creek Station.

Roosevelt and his guides were at the summit of Mount Marcy at 11:52 a.m., at which point the mist cleared and they were able to gaze out over the landscape. Shortly after noon they descended to Lake Tear of the Clouds, the source of the Hudson River, where Roosevelt sat down with his trusted guide Noah LaCasse for a lunch of canned ox tongue next to the lake. In his usual way, Roosevelt entertained the party with stories of his time in the West. Accounts differ as to what was said when Hall emerged from the mist at 1:25 p.m. and approached Roosevelt. Whatever it was, the yellow slip of paper Hall handed him seemed only a formality. Roosevelt read the message: "President's condition causes gravest apprehension."[28] There was no question as to what he had to do. He solemnly started back down the mountain.

That small slip of paper set in motion Roosevelt's emergence from the woods of the Adirondacks into the presidency. He had returned from the field countless times in his life after communing with nature: after studying birds, hunting, and ranching. He had emerged from Maine with a lynx pelt that helped him secure Alice Lee's hand in marriage. He had repeatedly emerged from the Badlands for activity in New York politics. He had emerged from a Cuban battlefield to almost immediately become the governor of New York. This time, the world was watching his emergence from New York as President McKinley lay on his deathbed.

Back at the club that evening, LaCasse was scrubbing Roosevelt's pants and boots in the stream when a message came in reaffirming McKinley's peril. By late evening, another communication arrived that shifted Roosevelt's plans to immediate departure. Roosevelt left the Tahawus Club in a buckboard, and disappeared into the "almost impenetrable darkness" of the night of September 13.[29] It was a harrowing nighttime ride as he and David Hunter, the driver, exhausted three teams of horses, coursing over roads blanketed with a thick slurry of mud. At one point a horse stumbled, losing its footing on the slippery road, but it soon righted itself and continued the frantic pace toward North Creek Station. At 5:20 a.m. on the fourteenth, Roosevelt arrived. Loeb immediately handed him a telegram from Secretary of State John Hay: "The President died at 2:15 this morning."[30] With this news, Roosevelt bounded into the private car of the vice president of the Delaware and Hudson Company, which then steamed off to Saratoga and then Albany. The six minutes Roosevelt's train car spent at Albany, from 7:56 to 8:02 a.m., only allowed time for the porters to snatch Roosevelt's breakfast from the station restaurant, and for the private car to be hitched to burly engine 908 of the New York Central.

Roosevelt's old friend Ansley Wilcox met him at the station in Buffalo with a contingent of twenty-three mounted police, an escort that stopped briefly at Wilcox's house for lunch.[31] At two-thirty, Roosevelt put on a black frock coat and top hat, clutched a pair of tan gloves, and somberly entered the Millburn house, where McKinley's body was resting, surrounded by family. There were quiet condolences. Roosevelt then returned to the Wilcox house for his oath.

Light trickled in through the stained-glass bay windows onto the towering bookshelves in the library of the Wilcox house, the place chosen for Roosevelt's oath. Secretary Root began to speak, but he broke down and wept for two full minutes. Finally, Judge Hazel of the US District Court stepped forward and uttered the Constitutional oath of office in eerie silence. Roosevelt presented his right hand, raised "as steady as if carved from marble," and concluded the back-and-forth recitation with "And thus I swear."[32]

The next day, boarding a train that also carried McKinley's earthly remains, Roosevelt completed his zigzag migration south

to Washington to officially become the twenty-sixth president of
the United States.

Roosevelt's first two years in the White House presented him with
plenty of opportunities to apply his strong persona to national
politics. Front and center was the question of European interven-
tion in the Americas. One of his predecessors—President James
Monroe—had clearly articulated a doctrine in 1823 which asserted
that European colonization would not be tolerated in the Western
Hemisphere. In the winter of 1903, though, Germany, Britain, and
Italy were blockading the Venezuelan coast in order to pressure
the government there into making reparations for damages their
citizens had incurred in the Venezuelan civil war.[33] Tensions slowly
grew as the Venezuelan president did not back down. As the US
Navy moved closer, President Roosevelt involved himself directly
in the negotiations, most of which took place out of the earshot
of inquisitive reporters.

Technically, these European nations were not violating the
Monroe Doctrine, as they were not colonizing; they simply wanted
to be compensated for damages. Roosevelt, however, felt that this
type of meddling still fell under the category of European inter-
vention, especially after Germany had sunk several Venezuelan
boats. Roosevelt did not bark out threats to Germany in the press;
he instead quietly and diplomatically issued a dated ultimatum:
Either compromise and desist, or risk war with the United States.
Roosevelt's threat set off a popcorn series of cablegrams, diplomatic visits, and wires between the States, the kaiser, and others.
At the last minute, the Germans realized that Roosevelt's softly
articulated warning was no bluff; he was ready to use the force
of US gunboats to clobber the powerful, but widely dispersed,
German navy. Bringing the metaphorical "big stick" he had introduced in Minnesota onto center stage, this moment branded
it onto Roosevelt's public image.

The "big stick" became Roosevelt's constant companion in the
articles and images that portrayed him in the press. Occasionally
he was shown in formal dress, carrying a stick to beat political ri-
vals, but much more often the stick was combined with the other
icons of power and identity he had picked up in his adventures—

Roosevelt's interest in mountain lions dates back to his time in the Badlands. Although he never exclusively hunted them in his early days in the West, he included an illustration entitled "Mountain Lions at the Deer Cache" in his book *Ranch Life and the Hunting Trail*. Like all images in that book, the illustration was created by Frederic Remington. Possibly in preparation for that illustration, Remington made this sketch. By permission of the Frederic Remington Art Museum.

his campaign hat, revolver, and riding gloves—to create an easily identifiable icon of Roosevelt's approach to power.[34]

Over time, Roosevelt's "stick" became a symbol for a specific political ideology. But even more, it evolved into a symbol of a philosophy he adopted and embodied: the quiet and confident wielding of power that tweaked the approach of George Washington, and even more basally mirrored the quiet tread of cougars on the hunt.[35]

Roosevelt engaged in literal stick-swinging at the White House. Leonard Wood would often appear at six o'clock in the evening to exchange beatings with the president. Roosevelt wrote to his son to describe the unusual scene in White House as he and Wood played "singlestick":

> We put on heavily padded helmets, breastplates and gauntlets and wrap bath towels around our necks, and then we turn to and beat one another like carpets. Now and then

by an accident one or the other of us gets hit where there is no protecting armament. We are not very good at it yet and consequently are able to hit far better than we parry. Ted insists that each one simply "swats" the other in turn like the medieval "biding a buffet." . . . We look like Tweedledum and Tweedledee in *Alice through the Looking Glass*.[36]

Despite this apt comparison, the image of Roosevelt projected in media cartoons never latched on to the Lewis-Carroll–style bundles of towels and crude armor. But in the midst of the wrangling over judicial appointments and amendment of the Cuban treaty in the spring of 1903, part of Roosevelt's mind, as it often was, was focused on the cycle of the field. And Roosevelt the writer wrapped himself up in his symbolic garb and employed his "stick" in defending the purity of science and natural history.

A newspaper headline from 1907, "Roosevelt Whacks Dr. Long Once More," called appropriate attention to another way in which Roosevelt had been using his "big stick."[37] The recipient of this metaphorical thrashing was no senator, viceroy, or chancellor, but instead a natural history writer, the Reverend William J. Long.

The beating started quietly when, only seven days after the March 1903 issue of the *Atlantic Monthly* had been published, Roosevelt wrote to tell John Burroughs he had long wished that someone would pen something akin to "Real and Sham Natural History," an article by Burroughs in that month's issue, which called out the amalgamation of fact and fiction in the work of Long and others.[38] Roosevelt had long been interested in helping to police the natural history and hunting literature, and he felt that those who went to the field should be dedicated to accuracy when they returned and rendered their observations and adventures in print. He had pointed out the fable of the "darning needle" dragonfly in one of his earliest notebooks, he had called into question explanations of the zic-zac's vocalizations in Egypt, and he had responded to George Bird Grinnell's questions about his own accounts of his hunts in the Badlands. Five years before Burroughs's article appeared, Roosevelt had even written to the African game hunter Frederick Selous and pointed out how some of the old time hunter-naturalists had "stretched the long bow" in their accounts.[39] One story Roosevelt found particularly preposterous was that of "Colonel Pollok," who had related a tale of how an English army major had been captured by a native chief and forced to battle a gorilla in hand-to-hand combat. Roosevelt scoffed at the tale's ending, in which the man recognized a bulge in the gorilla's side—obvious evidence of an enlarged spleen—and successfully targeted it with his fist. The gorilla immediately began spitting blood and then fell over dead, the story concluding with "dates, names and places being left vacant."[40] The publication of Burroughs's article in the *Atlantic* inspired Roosevelt to broaden his own commentary on this type of mythmaking.

Burroughs's beard was now considerably longer and whiter than when he had first met Roosevelt in New York City more than a decade earlier, and the expanse of exposed scalp on his head was far wider, but this aging had done nothing to dampen his fire for writing natural history.[41] Burroughs by then was arguably the leading bard of American natural history writing, feeding narratives of nature to the lay reader in books like *Wake Robin*, his first book of nature essays, published in 1871. Like many Americans, Roosevelt loved to read Burroughs's stories of plants and animals. But the sympathy between the two men ran much deeper: they agreed on the fundamental practices of the observant naturalist. Burroughs, like Roosevelt, walked constantly, and he described how this methodical pace allowed him to pay proper attention to his surroundings: "I am not going to advocate the disuse of boots and shoes, or the abandoning of the improved modes of travel; but I am going to brag as lustily as I can on behalf of the pedestrian, and show how all the shining angels second and accompany the man who goes afoot, while all the dark spirits are ever looking out for a chance to ride."[42] Far from just being opinionated pedestrians, Burroughs and Roosevelt felt that communicating these primary observations on nature was a noble responsibility. Honestly rendering experiences as a "keen-eyed observer" was the responsibility of any adventurer.[43] By 1903, however, Burroughs had had enough of what some other so-called naturalists were publishing as accurate observations on natural history. So he started a little war on nature.

By Burroughs's measures, only a minority of the natural history writers active at the turn of the twentieth century were going about their work in the tradition established by the likes of Gilbert

White, Charles Darwin, and Alfred Russel Wallace. The demands of the market encouraged many to produce widely consumed books that inappropriately combined "the love of nature and the love of fiction."[44] The majority of this poor lot, however, were not as troubling as the Reverend William J. Long's work, such as his *School of the Woods.*[45]

Degrees from Harvard, Andover Theological Seminary, and the University of Heidelberg buoyed Long's general academic standing—he was no backwoods hermit—and his book delved into the role of nature and nurture in animal behavior. The knowledge Long had gained in years of looking through rifle sights and wedging his svelte frame into bird blinds allowed him to act as a minister of nature.[46] Long was especially enamored of the lore of trappers and Indians, so much so that at the back of many of his books he included glossaries of Indian names. This love of narrative and interpretation, not his underlying fascination with instinct and learning, is what caused him to run afoul of Burroughs and expose his works to criticism for blurring the line between fiction and fact. Burroughs articulated this tension, which was a danger for all natural history writers: "the danger of making too much of what we see and describe,—of putting in too much sentiment, too much literature,—in short, of valuing these things more for the literary effects we can get out of them than for themselves."[47]

In the text of his 1903 *Atlantic* article, much of Burroughs's thrashing of Long related to the role of instinct and facts—whether birds teach their young to sing and build nests, whether red squirrels have cheek pouches, and whether great blue herons fish with frog legs as bait—but below it was a central claim: Long was a "false prophet" of natural history who "has really never been to the woods, but who sits in his study and cooks up these yarns from things he has read in Forest and Stream, or in other sporting journals."[48] Burroughs didn't stop with simply casting Long as a liar; he even ruminated on a root cause, wondering what Long had eaten for dinner on the evenings when he dreamed up his fancies of natural history.

Long was aghast at the content and tone of Burroughs's criticisms, and he came out with a personal and passionate defense of his own writing, a philosophical articulation of his views on the non-overlapping domains of science and natural history:

First, the study of Nature is a vastly different thing from the
study of Science. . . . Above and beyond the world of facts and
law, with which alone Science concerns itself, is an immense
and almost unknown world of suggestion and freedom and
inspiration, in which the individual, whether animal or man,
must struggle against fact and law to develop or keep his
own individuality. . . . This upper world of appreciation and
suggestion, of individuality interpreted by individuality, is
the world of Nature, the Nature of the poets and prophets
and thinkers. Though less exact, it is not less but rather more
true and real than Science, as emotions are more real than
facts, and love is more true than Economics."[49]

Needless to say, Burroughs did not endorse the insertion of this
kind of "suggestion and freedom and inspiration" into the recounting of natural history. But others came to Long's defense, and one
of them published a response to Burroughs in *Forest and Stream*
under the pseudonym "Hermit."[50]

Starting with a blast at Burroughs for his own "false natural
history," Hermit launched into Burroughs's sweeping generalizations regarding the lack of learning in birds.[51] Less than a month
after Roosevelt had read Burroughs's original *Atlantic* article, he
found Hermit's tirade in *Forest and Stream*. Having no interest in
avoiding battle, Roosevelt took up the issue with a private letter to
the editor of the publication, his old friend George Bird Grinnell.

First, Roosevelt chastised Grinnell for publishing an unsigned
article with dubious content. More important, though, Roosevelt
brought the heart of the debate into focus: "Now any writer will
occasionally err, and it is a dishonest and disingenuous thing to
attempt to blast a man's whole character because of an error or
an inaccurate observation, or more than one, even if fairly important."[52] In a second nod to accuracy, Roosevelt informed Grinnell
that he had already written to Burroughs to address his overreach-
ing generalizations on instinct. But this was beside the point. It
was Long's work that needed to be addressed, because it was far
outside the range of occasional inaccuracies. Roosevelt felt that
Long's tales were "simply preposterous."[53] When it came down to
it, the issue was not accuracy; it was honesty. Roosevelt asked Grinnell to keep the contents of the letter private, as he did not feel it

was proper for him to use his influence as president to weigh in on the debate publicly. But as the back-and-forth battle ground ahead for the next four years, Roosevelt's resolve to remain out of the public debate was scraped away. By the fall of 1907 he could no longer resist, allowing himself to take some swings at Long in an interview and follow-up article printed by *Everybody's Magazine*.[54]

And whacks they were. Roosevelt came out of his corner boldly: "William J. Long is perhaps the worst of these nature-writing offenders."[55] He struck again as he assessed the value of Long's works: "It is grotesque to claim literal truthfulness for such a tissue of absurdities."[56] These weren't the fictional fables of Mowgli and Bagheera in Rudyard Kipling's *Jungle Book*; those myths, which explained things like why tigers had stripes, had been presented as fiction. What rankled Roosevelt was the supposed natural history offered by writers like Long.[57] These impostors conflated fact and fiction in the manner of the "quaint little books" of the Middle Ages which described observations of basilisks and unicorns as actual animals: "I am not speaking of ordinary mistakes, of ordinary errors of observation, of differences of interpretation and opinion; I am dealing only with deliberate invention, deliberate perversion of fact."[58]

Several of Long's "inventions" were particularly glaring. In *Northern Trails: Some Studies of Animal Life in the Far North*, Long described how a white wolf had chased down a stag caribou. As the young buck reared back, the wolf made a "quick snap under the stag's chest just behind the fore legs, where the heart lay."[59] The stag stumbled for a few steps and fell down dead. Long's implication that a wolf could, in one bite, rip through the tough hide and ribs and into the heart of such a large animal defied principles of anatomy and physics. But in his introduction to the book, Long clearly claimed the story's veracity: "Every incident in this wolf's life . . . is minutely true to fact, and is based squarely upon my own observation and that of my Indians."[60] Indignantly, Roosevelt claimed that no such bite had been made by a terrestrial carnivore since sabertooth cats roamed the earth.[61] He felt sure that his many years of firsthand observations in the field had him on solid ground in rebuking Long's claims. Similar fiction appeared in Long's description of a fantastically constructed oriole nest, put together as birds tied three sticks together in a "perfectly measured triangle" and fastened them using a "reversed double-hitch, the kind that a man uses in cinching his saddle."[62] Surely orioles build elaborate nests, but it was clear to anyone who, like Roosevelt, ornithologically inclined that this was well beyond even the oriole's astounding weaving abilities.

Impossible occurrences Long described in supposed eyewitness accounts, such as the savage wolf bite and the marline-manipulating oriole, were places in which it was easy to pin him down as a faker. Many of his other claims did not involve clear-cut examples of observation, but were instead wild interpretations of facts. For example, he described how animals performed "surgery" on themselves.[63] A woodcock that had a broken leg with a dirt clod on it was taken as evidence of a bird applying a cast. Beavers and muskrats that had amputated their own limbs (by chewing) to escape from traps had supposedly also applied resin to stop the flow of blood and help them heal. Burroughs and Roosevelt disputed these far-reaching interpretations as well, but their point had already been made and was well hashed out in the press. Although the debate was complicated, it was clear that much of Long's work was not good natural history, and the debate eventually faded.

Roosevelt wasn't finished with his natural history policing. In 1909, an author who considered the inherently deceptive concept of animal camouflage came under his shadow. Nervous, eccentric, and a genius with a brush, Abbott Thayer was well established as a portraitist and landscape painter when he turned his professional attention to interpreting nature. From his childhood days he had immersed himself in nature, even dabbling in taxidermy as Roosevelt had done. As a painter and naturalist, he had a keen eye for detail and had long been intrigued by the complex ways in which animals employ camouflage. He started with an accurate observation, finding the graded pattern of countershading—a light belly and dark upper side—to be ubiquitous in animals. With sketchpad and canvas, he harnessed his ability to render animals against natural backgrounds, and eventually considered the evolutionary reason for this pattern.[64]

Darwin's idea of adaptation by natural selection had penetrated deep into Thayer's psyche, spurring him to find an explanation for the pattern of countershading. As an artist, he found it obvious

When Abbott Thayer and his son Gerald published *Concealing Coloration in the Animal Kingdom* in 1909, Roosevelt took issue with how they portrayed and explained animal color patterns. The book included an image, painted by Abbott Thayer, that showed the hues of a blue jay's wing blending into a patch of snow, thereby implying the reason for the bird's coloration. By permission of the Smithsonian Institution American Art Museum.

that the advantage of this pattern arose from a simple physical fact: three-dimensional objects cast shadows. A uniformly-colored object in sunlight will appear lighter at top and darker at the bottom as a result, but a countershaded object will appear uniform, the balance of the lighter bottom in effect canceling out the shadows. This mechanistic explanation for how countershading helps conceal animals was captivating to Thayer, and it seemed to provide an explanation for why animals show this pattern. Unlike so many other scientific ideas percolating at the time, the idea of deception and camouflage in nature could be grasped by all manner of lay people. And now Thayer felt that he had cracked the code of one of the most common color patterns in the animal kingdom. He published his ideas in two science journals, the *Auk* and *Nature*, receiving significant accolades from the esteemed British scientist and entomologist Edward B. Poulton.[65] Poulton's approval fanned Thayer's zeal to explain protective coloration in animals, and Thayer began to believe that virtually all patterns in animals were the result of protective coloration. He just needed to show it.

Thayer's copious color plates, alongside pages of thorough text provided by his son Gerald Thayer, were meant to make *Concealing-Coloration in the Animal Kingdom* a lavish explication of his idea.[66] In the end, however, they became an example of how it is easy to invent explanations, or tell stories, about nature without reasonable evidence to back them up.

By the time Roosevelt got hold of Thayer's 1909 book, he had enough time on his hands to publish a 113-page rebuke of his argument.[67] Despite his acknowledgment that Thayer was not the kind of lying "faker" that he took Long to be, he rapped Thayer repeatedly for his wild explanations of animal coloration. Roosevelt had been thinking about the idea of "protective coloration" for several years, his interest piqued by discussion of the phenomenon by the great African hunter Frederick Selous in his *African Nature Notes and Reminiscences*.[68] In his review of the Thayers' work, Roosevelt took on their sweeping explanation of all animal coloration as concealing: "In its extreme form as stated by these gentlemen, the doctrine seems to me to be pushed to such a fantastic extreme and to include such wild absurdities as to call for the application of common sense thereto."[69]

Thayer's questions were reasonable. Why are a blue jay's wings blue and gray? Why are flamingos pink? But he had stumbled into the quagmire that faced Long and every other curious naturalist who tried to explain patterns in nature: How can inquiries about facts and observations, the "what" questions, be supported in positing explanations and interpretations, answers to the "why" questions? Thayer picked apart the subtle blues and grays of the blue jay with his eyes, and then reconstructed them against a blue patch of snow with his palette of pigments. Words were not even necessary for readers to grasp his explanation that the reason for a blue jay's coloration is to blend in against a wintry background. Another of Thayer's examples came from the tropics, where the colors of flamingos, in both their pink- or white-color forms, arose to blend into a sunset or white sky to avoid the predators of the saltpans. The Thayers, in paint and ink, became master storytellers on the "why" questions of camouflage.

But Roosevelt thumped away in response. For the blue jay, he considered it "a simple impossibility that the blue jay's coloration can have been developed in order to make the bird invisible under the almost never-occurring conditions when it happens to strike a small patch of shadow on the snow which is of the same bright blue color as its own bright plumage."[70] As evidence, he pointed out that other species of blue jays live in areas where snow never falls. Roosevelt ranked Thayer's explanation of the even more gaudy colors of flamingos high among the "erroneous statements, wild guesses, and absurd interpretations of facts" in *Concealing Coloration*, because for each instance in which "the brilliant coloring of a flamingo or a spoonbill or a scarlet ibis tends to disguise it, there are probably ten thousand occasions, or many more, when this coloration is of the most highly advertising quality."[71]

As he had done with his reaction to reductionism, Roosevelt was in on the early stages of another persistent debate in biology. At his alma mater, decades later in the late 1970s, the evolutionary biologists Stephen Jay Gould and Richard C. Lewontin would pick up on a similar thread. In a now classic paper entitled "The Spandrels of San Marco and the Panglossian Paradigm," Gould and Lewontin made the case that biologists were good at publishing papers that heralded convincing evolutionary explanations for behaviors and anatomical structures even when there was little or no evidence to back them up.[72] Many times, they felt, biologists didn't consider

(ABOVE AND FACING) Abbott Thayer's most infamous paintings on animal camouflage depicted his idea that the pink color of flamingos was an adaptation to blend into the sunset. Roosevelt described this and other interpretations Thayer made in his *Concealing Coloration* as an example of "absurd interpretations of facts." By permission of the Smithsonian Institution American Art Museum.

alternative hypotheses that could also account for the observed phenomena. In a style that we can imagine Roosevelt would have loved, Gould and Lewontin made an analogy: What biologists were doing was like saying that the "spandrels" in Saint Mark's Cathedral in Venice—the small spaces that were a by-product of mounting a dome atop a frame of rounded arches—had been created as spaces to hold the paintings they now contained.[73] In this case, the explanation of causality was reversed. The "spandrels" had emerged as a result of architecture, and they happened to provide a nice place for paintings. Turning to the natural world, Gould and Lewontin called out the sensational hypothesis that human sacrifice and cannibalism in the Aztecs had arisen because of a lack of meat in their diet—again, the kind of red-meat story that Roosevelt would have cherished. Here again, though,

Gould and Lewontin chastised scientists for not considering alternative hypotheses (for example, that perhaps the cannibalism was just a ritual). This kind of "just so" philosophy—embraced in Voltaire's *Candide* by Dr. Pangloss, who believed that the reason for the existence of noses was to provide a place to rest eyeglasses—highlighted this pitfall, now known as adaptationist storytelling, or the "Panglossian paradigm." This problem was at the heart of what Roosevelt had seen in Thayer's explanations of concealing coloration in animals six decades before.

Although Roosevelt's use of his rhetorical weaponry was not as severe as it had been with Long, it still contained caustic comments on Thayer's work: "I have no question that Mr. Thayer intends to put his facts honestly; but in actual practice he is evidently unable to study facts with the sincere desire of finding out what they are, and of making proper deductions from them."[74] Others stepped in to parry the blows, as when F. H. Allen wrote in the *Auk* of Roosevelt's victim: "Even if we don't agree with him, it is not necessary either to cut him into little pieces or to break every bone in his body with the 'big stick.'"[75] For Roosevelt, though, his experiences in the field allowed him to make a defense of natural history that deserved the same dogged devotion to honesty and accuracy that he applied in politics; any deviation was met with a willingness to bear arms in defense of what he felt was honest and right.

The Field President

In the same 1903 letter in which Roosevelt applauded John Burroughs's opening salvo of the nature faker war, there was an invitation: "I would like to visit the Yellowstone Park for a fortnight
this spring. . . . I wonder whether you could not come along?"[1]
The developing notion of this trip—one that would take him first
to Yellowstone and then to the West Coast for countless speeches,
banquets, and appearances—nested comfortably into Roosevelt's
bailiwick. He had ridden trains deep into the Midwest and up the
Eastern Seaboard many times in his youth, and he had proven
himself a historically good campaign traveler for the McKinley
ticket in 1900. Roosevelt could toggle with ease between the quiet
wilderness and raucous crowds at whistle-stop speeches. But he was
worried that this would not suit Burroughs. He assured Burroughs
that he would be comfortable: "I would see that you endured neither fatigue nor hardship."[2]

Although he was most comfortable in his natural habitat at
Slabsides—the primitive backwoods retreat he had escaped to in
upstate New York for many years—and although his most comfortable mode of travel was his feet, Burroughs accepted the president's invitation. To milk the full experience, he even decided to
board the train in Washington and be part of the entire trip to
Yellowstone.

Throughout March, Roosevelt envisioned a general itinerary for
his trip, planning to accept many of the invitations for visits and
speeches that piled up on his desk. He assured the press that it was
not meant as a political trip: the Western states he was to visit were
a lock for him for in his upcoming bid for reelection. He instead
hoped to start with some relaxation in Yellowstone and then meet
as many of the Western people of the United States as he could.[3]

As for any president, however, it was impossible to disentangle politics from any other aspect of life.

Letters rolled into Roosevelt's office with invitations as his trip plans developed; he responded with missives and requests for arrangements. The letter Roosevelt sent to the superintendent of Yellowstone Park, Major John Pitcher, revealed that he wasn't exactly forthright about all of his motives for the trip. His enjoyment of his Colorado cougar hunt had left him itching to return to the chase with hounds, and he explored his options for a low-key hunt in Yellowstone. His conversations with Elihu Root, however, had him concerned that he might not be able to make the Yellowstone trip work: "Secretary Root is afraid that a false impression might get out if I killed anything in the Park, even though it was killed, as of course would be the case, strictly under Park regulations."[4] He wondered if he could arrange for some of Goff's dogs to be sent for a hunt outside the park. He could even send his gun along separately in order to deny that he had any firearms aboard the train. He recognized it was a long shot, but again appealed to Pitcher on March 2: "But I of course would greatly like a week or ten days during which we could hunt mountain lions."[5]

While considering how he might use the wilderness for a hunt—in the park or out—Roosevelt was also thinking about forests. Two days before he penned his note to Burroughs, Roosevelt wrote to the lumber baron Frederick Weyerhaeuser to inquire whether they could meet along with Gifford Pinchot, his chief of forestry: "I earnestly desire that the movement for the preservation of the forests shall come from the lumbermen themselves."[6]

It was within the same week that Roosevelt sent letters to Pitcher, Weyerhaeuser, and Burroughs. For him, there was no reason why he could not consult lumbermen, foresters, and naturalists and even consider a bit of hunting as he looked forward to Yellowstone. However, he knew better than to attempt a nuanced explanation to the American people that there was simply a good bit of the nature loving of John Muir, the nature study of John Burroughs, and the hunting of John Goff in him, and that those pieces got along quite nicely.

As Roosevelt's elaborate train chugged out of Washington toward the West on April 1, Burroughs began to take in the rolling Roosevelt spectacular. It was a never-ending procession of speeches and handshakes as they steamed through Chicago, Milwaukee, Madison, Saint Paul, and Minneapolis. Many of the eight to ten speeches that Roosevelt gave each day were small affairs, but some, like the blowout in Chicago, placed the people's adoration of Roosevelt on display. The five thousand people who composed the "great, shouting, seemingly half frenzied audience" there cheered on Roosevelt's sputtering about "that piece of 'unrecognized international law' known as the Monroe doctrine," accompanied by his now characteristic wielding of the "big stick."[7] In his quiet way, Burroughs sat by and observed Roosevelt's interaction with the public, which he recalled as "one of the grandest human spectacles I ever witnessed."[8] The crowds became smaller as they moved out of Minneapolis and made a short stop at Medora, North Dakota, where Burroughs applied his gift for description to the Badlands landscape: "flayed, fantastic, treeless, a riot of naked clay slopes, chimney-like buttes, and dry coulees."[9] After a week for the public, Roosevelt's closely packed life gave way to big sky and crisp sounds of wildlife as finally, on April 8, he was on his way out of Gardiner, Montana, toward Yellowstone.

As he rode into the park, Roosevelt certainly looked like the field president, atop a muscular gray horse named Bonaparte.[10] There was, of course, an associated entourage, including Major Pitcher and an "ambulance"—a term Burroughs used for the horse-drawn wagon, a somewhat embarrassing mode of transportation he was offered instead—that composed a threadlike tail against a backdrop of mountains that jutted out of Paradise Valley.[11] On Roosevelt's explicit instructions, the entourage left the Secret Service, the press corps, his private secretary, and all others behind so that he could find the solitude he desired.[12]

Roosevelt had also left his earlier aspirations for a hunt behind. This was not a place to mix messages on hunting and conservation; he realized instead that it was a time to engage in rigorous exertion and natural history observation with Burroughs. Unbeknownst to many, Burroughs even felt a twinge of regret that there would be no hunting. He stemmed the desire of his own inner predator: "I was then cherishing the secret hope that I might be allowed to shoot a cougar or bobcat; but this fun did not come to me."[13] Since Roosevelt had decreed that there would be no hunting, the men set off instead as observer-naturalists.

The trek from Gardiner to the fort at Mammoth Springs was a chance to see a procession of wildlife: hundreds of prongbuck antelope, the carcasses of deer and antelope killed by cougars, throngs of black-tailed deer by the trail and, surprisingly to Roosevelt, in the parade grounds at the camp, not more than feet from the houses. The naturalists in the party continued to make careful observations over the next several days. At one point Roosevelt, Burroughs, and Pitcher spent four hours with binoculars on Bison Peak, carefully counting elk—about the three thousand—that were in view. Another observation was foisted on Roosevelt at an inopportune time. The party had seen a band of sheep feeding high up on a perpendicular rock face, and they wondered how in the world the animals could negotiate the almost vertical trail down to the river for water. "Would they try it while we were there to see?"[14] As the afternoon slackened, word came to Roosevelt, who was in his tent shaving, that the sheep were on the move. He burst through the flaps with a towel around his neck, one half of his face clean-shaven and the other half lathered. "The shaving can wait, and the sheep won't," he cried.[15] The attentive naturalists were treated to a view of the sheep's delicate descent over the loose rock.

A new closeness developed between Roosevelt and Burroughs during the trip as they bunked together in cabins with the windows open wide, sharing their delight in a frigid night's sleep.[16] Burroughs helped the president identify the call of Townsend's solitaire, a song that neither had heard in the wild before, but which Burroughs had hoped to compare to its relative, the song of the West India solitaire.[17] The absence of guns did not prevent Roosevelt and Burroughs from delighting in the chase as they quietly tracked a pygmy owl, again a new species for Roosevelt, and watched a golden eagle descend on a yearling elk and make it its meal.[18] In contrast to their serious study, there were also moments of levity that deepened their bond, like when they were skiing in deep snow near "Geyserland." As they careened downhill, they lost control and ended up in a comical pair of "headers," both men with their noggins stuck in the snow.[19] To their amusement, Roosevelt even used his horse in chasing down and herding a group of elk.[20] These cherished moments of communion caused Roosevelt to mine his Dutch heritage for a moniker of affection. There was no more "My dear Mr. Burroughs"; it was "Oom John" now.[21]

The days in the park progressed, and as the men moved southward, ascending the terrain toward the upper geyser basin, they changed from horseback to skis and sleighs. Here, Roosevelt's resolve momentarily weakened one afternoon as he leapt from the sleigh and pounced on a dark scurrying form on the snow. It turned out to be a montane vole, his only collection in the park.[22] That afternoon, while the others went out to fish, Roosevelt prepared the skin and skull for Hart Merriam at the Smithsonian as best he could, emptying a salt shaker for preservative in the name of science.

Each day that Burroughs spent with the president in the field seemed to reveal a different aspect of Roosevelt's persona—hunter-scientist, naturalist-observer—confirming Burroughs's assessment that he was a "a man made for action in a wide field." In the evenings, when Roosevelt put his complex persona on display, a "picturesque stream" of words came from his mouth: "anecdote, history, science, politics, adventure, literature; bits of his experience as a ranchman, hunter, Rough Rider, legislator, civil service commissioner, police commissioner, governor, president." Around roaring campfires, Roosevelt entertained the men as he drew on his old yarns of adventure, like the story of the bar fight at Nolan's Hotel and the dramatic siege of Kettle Hill. He knew how to draw laughs, too, and recounted a plea he had received as president from a jailed Arizona Rough Rider: "Dear Colonel,—I am in trouble. I shot a lady in the eye, but I did not intend to hit the lady; I was shooting at my wife."[23] As his trip with the president wound down, Burroughs stored away his affectionate impressions of him, which he would later formalize in his book *Camping & Tramping with Roosevelt*. (Surprisingly, Roosevelt never wrote a thorough account of his time with Burroughs, though he would recount its effects in speeches.)

This part of the trip came to an end with Roosevelt's speech at the dedication of the Yellowstone Arch. It was the best April day that Montana weather could have provided, as Roosevelt held forth at the dedication of the new arch at the northern gate of Yellowstone. A large crowd, some of whom were Masons, had been ferried out to the site on special trains to oversee the ritual in the fashion of that organization; there was even a nugget of Montana gold with a Masonic symbol for the president. The speech began with Roosevelt's awe of the "tract of veritable wonderland" and the need for its preservation: "The scheme of its preservation is note-worthy in its essential democracy. This Park was created and now is administered for the benefit and enjoyment of the people."[24] Yes, part of the purpose of such a park was to keep the wilderness pure. But in his remarks Roosevelt returned to the "rugged and stalwart democracy" of the wilderness that he had explicated almost a de-cade before, in his preface to *The Wilderness Hunter.* In addition to national lands as pristine playgrounds, he also highlighted how the preservation of forest was important for utilitarian purposes like hydroelectric power, and also to impart "much of the old-time pleasure of the hardy life of the wilderness and of the hunter in the wilderness."[25] Here, at the new gate of Yellowstone, Roosevelt wove together diverse and sometimes conflicted approaches to natural lands. He, like Burroughs, wasn't a strict preservationist. He believed in the importance of wilderness for aesthetic pur-poses, jibing with the spiritual and romantic arguments of John Muir. But he also saw how forests were important for use, and he was sympathetic to the view of his chief forester, Gifford Pinchot, who felt that forests and land were important to use and manage scientifically, providing "the greatest good to the greatest number for the longest time."[26] Roosevelt understood the value of forests as feeds for reservoirs, and for stocks of creatures that could be available for sportsmen, a need he felt personally. He had lamented privately to Burroughs in Yellowstone: "I feel as if I ought to keep the camp in meat. I always have."[27] Roosevelt wasn't an outsider; instead, he was a participant in the multifarious pursuits of the wil-derness.[28] Along with being president, he was part of a food chain.

The Yellowstone tramp behind them, Burroughs and Roosevelt parted ways as Burroughs boarded a train for a trip to Califor-nia and Washington State, and Roosevelt resumed his breakneck schedule of speeches through America's western midsection: Saint Louis, Kansas City, Topeka, Denver, Santa Fe, Albuquerque, and then to the Grand Canyon.

Using the word "awful" to describe his emotional reaction on beholding the Grand Canyon for the first time wasn't Roosevelt's most effective rhetorical flourish.[29] Though he quickly clarified it to mean "full of awe," perhaps "moved," "inflamed," "exhilarated," or even "thunderstruck" might have been more fitting. But the

Roosevelt's work to conserve the natural resources of the country was highlighted on his fourteen-thousand-mile swing through the western United States in 1903. In the first part of the trip, Roosevelt (in front, right) brought the naturalist and writer John Burroughs (in rear, with beard) for a trip into Yellowstone National Park. Burroughs and Roosevelt reveled in the natural wonderland that the park provided. TRC 560.51 1903-031.

sentiment was clear—this was a place to sanctify—and he made a passionate plea for preservation: "I hope you won't have a building of any kind to mar the wonderful grandeur and sublimity of the canyon. You cannot improve on it. The ages have been at work on it, and men can only mar it. Keep it for your children, and your children's children, and all who come after you, as one of the great sights for Americans to see."[30] While urging preservation of the canyon for an American escape, Roosevelt, as he had done in Yellowstone, harped on his larger philosophy of land use and returned to the importance of irrigation in the West. His water policy later pitted him against preservationists when he supported damming the Hetch Hetchy valley of Yosemite as a reservoir. But to this pledge on the Grand Canyon he remained faithful. After his famous Act for the Preservation of American Antiquities, he was able to make national monuments by presidential proclamation.[31] He later established the Grand Canyon National Monument, and he even carried out his vision of passing the canyon down to his children when he later returned to its rim for a cougar hunt with his own sons Archie and Quentin.[32]

California was next as they rolled past ten thousand cheering well-wishers at Redlands. The president's sight and smell were awakened by the orange groves and ranches of the Santa Clara Valley, and also by the lush flowers that were placed in "every nook" of his personal car as he arrived at San Jose.[33] The fruits of this agricultural oasis touched his belly as well. At a luncheon in Felton, Roosevelt received at least anecdotal reassurance that his growing fears of "race suicide"—the idea that Americans were not procreating enough—were not immediately relevant.[34] Exhibiting a robust American fecundity, Mrs. J. M. Gesetterest, mother of thirty-four children, served him her special Spanish beans for lunch. Even this kind of vitality couldn't match the two hundred thousand wildly cheering people who were ready for his electrifying presence in San Francisco. But after his appearance there, Roosevelt headed out, with his thoughts turning to conservation, to a long-awaited meeting with another sage of the wilderness in the Yosemite Valley.[35]

In many ways besides the length and fullness of their white beards, John Muir and John Burroughs were very similar. They both loved nature and had spent the majority of their lives rambling through wild lands. They had even spent time in the field together, on the Harriman Expedition to Alaska in 1899, and would later jointly tour the Grand Canyon and Yosemite.[36] But on more careful examination there were important differences between the men. On the surface, Burroughs had a rounded midsection, whereas Muir was rigid and slender. Burroughs may have been more eloquent in writing, but Muir proved a better bipedalist, at one point walking the entire way from Kentucky to Florida.[37] They were different in their outlooks as well. While Burroughs was accepting of the utilitarian uses of natural areas, as when he itched to enjoy both hunting and nature gazing in Yellowstone with Roosevelt, Muir was more of a romantic purist. While Muir accepted that some lands had to be used for agriculture, he fiercely lobbied

Roosevelt also visited Yosemite National Park in his 1903 loop tour, and there he was accompanied by the naturalist and preservationist John Muir. Although Roosevelt was not as close personally with Muir as he was with Burroughs, the Yosemite trip gave the men the opportunity for a backwoods summit meeting on issues of conservation. Muir was satisfied that Roosevelt had heard his strong views on the importance of preserving forests, and remembered that he "stuffed him pretty well" on the issues. TRC 560.51 1903-118.

for national lands to remain pure.[38] The men also diverged in their taxonomic preferences; Burroughs was more keen for birds, where Muir gravitated toward plants. Possibly because Muir was connected with the rhythms of the green world while Roosevelt was in some senses an über-animal, it took Muir longer to warm to Roosevelt's invitation to an outing than it did Burroughs.

The diplomatic outreach to convince Muir to join the president for a tramp in Yosemite began as early as 1902, when Robert Underwood Johnson, editor of *Century Magazine*, wrote to him expressing his hope that Muir would provide a tour so that Roosevelt would "not fall into the hands of the Yosemite crowd."[39] Then Benjamin Ide Wheeler, president of the University of California, took up the mantle by writing Muir and then calling him on the telephone. It seemed that Muir was hesitating partly because he would need to postpone a long-planned trip to Europe with Charles Sprague Sargent, the director of Harvard's Arnold Arboretum. Sargent himself weighed in by suggesting to Muir that he could spend several days with the president and still make the journey to Europe. Sargent—like the secretary of the Sierra Club, William Colby, who also phoned Muir—saw a meeting of Muir and Roosevelt as a chance to advance the causes of nature preservation.

As in many aspects of his life, Roosevelt thrived on direct connection, and here he wanted to experience Yosemite with Muir himself. Roosevelt even wrote to Muir directly, expressing his desire to see Yosemite with Muir and Muir only: "I wish to write you personally to express the hope that you will be able to take me through the Yosemite. I do not want anyone with me but you, and I want to drop politics absolutely for four days and just be out in the open with you."[40] Muir finally relented, and the arrangements were made for Muir to board the president's train on May 14, just across the bay from San Francisco at the Oakland Mole. Later that evening, the train headed out into the night.

It was clear that Roosevelt was approaching the topographic grandeur of Yosemite when his train began to tax the engines of the Southern Pacific Railroad. The train was eventually divided in two, the president's portion sent speeding ahead and the other cars with the sleepers following behind, with both parts reconnecting at Raymond, California at 7:30 a.m. on the fifteenth. There, the president's party paused for a hearty breakfast and a brief speech by Roosevelt on the porch of a store. Then they embarked on a dry and dusty stagecoach ride, rolling through the tangled backdrop of manzanita bushes toward the grove of massive sequoias. Aside from being grimy, the trip was uneventful save a moment when a small forest fire blazed at the side of the trail, drowning the air in smoke. As the stagecoach passed through, the president hoped that the smokescreen would allow him to disappear from public view for four days and into the great Yosemite Valley, with an intimate tour from that habitat's most knowledgeable guide.[41]

Once the party arrived in Mariposa Grove, the president paused for a photograph under the towering canopy of bark and leaves provided by the Grizzly Giant, the oldest of the grove's giant sequoias. Scooting their carriage through a tunnel in the Wawona Tree, some members of the party looked back to be captured for posterity in another photograph. With the formalities over, Roosevelt dismissed everyone in the party except Muir, two park rangers named Charlie Leidig and Archie Leonard, and one Army packer. Not even the Secret Service officers were allowed to tag along. Finally at peace under the huge swaying branches, Roosevelt hungrily devoured a dinner of fried chicken and beefsteak, guzzled strong black coffee, and enveloped himself in the pile of forty blankets that had been laid out for him, his sole shelter for the night.

After a good night's sleep they headed north the following morning, doing their best to avoid the throngs of civilians at the Wawona Hotel. The snow got deeper as they trudged over the Empire Meadows Trail; at one point Roosevelt was so mired in the five feet of snow that Leidig had to use a log to pull him out. With snow whipping in their faces, they descended to a somewhat sheltered camp at Glacier Point and bedded down for a historic night. Finally, Roosevelt and Muir had a wilderness tête-à-tête in which Roosevelt could benefit from Muir's kmowledge of how to read the glacial history of Yosemite in its granite pages.[42] Although neither of the men could be accurately described as a gasbag—both were known for the substance of their words—the gusts whipping past Yosemite Valley weren't the only winds blowing that night. Leidig, well back and out of the way, observed that fronts of words occasionally collided, as "both men wanted to do the talking."[43]

Muir and Roosevelt spent their first night in Yosemite under the towering forms of the giant sequoias in Mariposa Grove. Muir's journals teem with sketches, including a rendering of these majestic plants. John Muir Papers, Holt-Atherton Special Collections, University of the Pacific Library. © 1984 Muir-Hanna Trust.

The roar of the campfire waned as the night wore on; the men's conversation turned to pressing questions of the use of forests and how best they could preserve the kind of American wilderness that surrounded them.

Roosevelt's third day in Yosemite, despite the beautiful surroundings, was more like a political procession than a wilderness romp. The party stopped briefly for photographs at Glacier Point in the morning, and once they made it to Little Yosemite Valley for lunch, a crowd had gathered for a glimpse of the president. Down the trail they clopped after lunch toward Camp Curry, but into view came an obstruction lining the path. As the party approached, they made out a line of people, all women, blocking the way in hopes of shaking hands with the president. This kind of obstruction violated the "not anyone with me but you" idea that Roosevelt had intended for Yosemite, and he indicated his dissatisfaction to Leidig. With his Winchester rifle and six-shooter waving, Leidig spurred his horse and charged, parting the onlookers. As a consolation to them, Roosevelt provided a presidential wave of the hat as his party went by. The party then gained the Sentinel Bridge, and Roosevelt needed to employ a more diplomatic technique in putting off the entourage that had assembled there: a band of commissioners and administrators who had a very different idea for his Yosemite tour, complete with firework displays and dinners. Roosevelt dismounted and entered the cabin-studio of the painter Chris Jorgensen, which had been reserved for his use, politely gazing at a few paintings and curtly offering his apologies for refusing their kindness. After fifteen minutes he was off again for his last night in the park, at Bridalveil Falls.

It was "a big string of people on horseback, in buggies, surries, and others on foot," whom Leidig estimated to be upwards of a thousand, who met the president's party in the meadow near the falls.[44] With his patience thin and a ravenous hunger in his belly, Roosevelt barked: "Those people annoy me. Can you get rid of them?"[45] After Leidig cleared the onlookers, some of whom left on respectful tiptoes, Roosevelt settled down for a last night of conversation with Muir and his party, entertaining them with some of his time-tested campfire stories of cougar hunts and Western adventures.

When the rustic conservation summit concluded, Roosevelt

parted with Muir and rumbled out of Yosemite on into Nevada, and then back into California to Sacramento, north to Oregon and Washington, and then eastward for various stops in Utah and Wyoming, finally wrapping up his trip with a flurry of visits in Illinois. There is evidence that even before Roosevelt completed the last leg of his winding loop tour, his time in Yosemite had helped advance his conservation agenda. Muir provided his take on this effect to Merriam at the Smithsonian, almost boasting that in his nights with the president, he "stuffed him pretty well regarding the timber thieves, the destructive work of the lumberman, and other spoilers of the forest."[46] Unlike Burroughs, Roosevelt did not recount these trips in an article or book. Instead, the major outcome was in his political actions. Only days after his time with Muir, on May 19, Roosevelt had written from Sacramento to Ethan Hitchcock, secretary of the interior: "I should like to have an extension of the forest reserves to include the California forests throughout the Mount Shasta region and its extensions. Will you not consult Pinchot about this and have the orders prepared?"[47]

Roosevelt's return to the White House proved that it wasn't only in the wide-open West that he could fulfill his fundamental need to be engaged in all manner of outdoor pursuits. After the completion of his fourteen-thousand-mile journey, his re-entry to Washington showed that, despite endless meetings and paperwork, the field was a presidential state of mind.

While Roosevelt was still wrapping up his trip, paying homage to the Land of Lincoln, preparations were already underway for additions to the White House menagerie. The Roosevelt children had gotten word of the "mountain lions, raccoons, prairie dogs, wildcats, deer, and numerous other specimens from the plains and mountains" that had been acquired on their father's trip.[48] They studiously sketched out diagrams of pens and enclosures for these new inhabitants that could be built behind the White House. Far from prim and stately, at times the Roosevelt White House was like a field station; more often it bordered on a state of bedlam. Granted, any large or ferocious acquisitions—like two ostriches and an Arabian zebra sent by the king of Abyssinia, and the lion cub from the African savannah—were sent to the National Zoological Park. But on site, the children were delighted to experiment with "almost every American small animal capable of being domesticated."[49] There was "Slippers" the six-toed cat, a family favorite; a Mexican parrot that yelled "Alice" in the corridors; and a sizeable macaw named "Eli Yale" that spouted raspy remarks, "probably most personal and ill-natured, if one could have interpreted them properly." Kermit housed kangaroo rats; Quentin tended guinea pigs.[50] Mostly these were causes of color and amusement in the White House, but occasionally they created consternation among the adult inhabitants and guests.

The newspaper headline "BANISHED FROM THE WHITE HOUSE: Man-Eating Bulldog in Exile" rolled from the presses after Archie's bulldog "Pete," normally "satisfied to chase members of the President's lawn tennis cabinet, and take a bite or two of a foreign ambassador," champed down on the leg of an intolerant telephone lineman and was ejected from the grounds.[51] A larger example of an unwelcome inroad into the White House was when Algonquin, the darling pony of Ethel, Archie, and Quentin, was smuggled into the home and up the elevator to cheer the spirits of the children, who were suffering from measles.[52] However, possibly the most radical, and certainly the most serpentine, occurrence in the Roosevelt White House occurred when Quentin took his two ailing pet snakes to a "snakeologist named Schmitz" for medical attention. Upon learning that the snakes would need inpatient care, Quentin flashed a downtrodden look that convinced Schmitz to provide three loaners that would keep him occupied during his own snakes' recovery. With new life, Quentin zoomed toward Pennsylvania Avenue on roller skates with three serpents twined around his arms.[53]

After entering through the outer office and careening toward the conference room, Quentin had a brief, twirling exchange with the president's personal secretary, William Loeb:

Loeb: Where are you going?
Quentin: Going to show my father my new snakes.
Loeb: But the Attorney General is with him, and they may not want to see the snakes.
Quentin: Oh, yes, they will. My father likes snakes.

It was on into the conference room as Quentin, still on his skates

WHITE HOUSE,
WASHINGTON,

June 12th 1904

Blessed Quenty-Quee,

The little
birds in the nest in
the vines on the
garden fence are
nearly grown up.
Their mother still

(ABOVE AND FACING) When the children were off for the summer in Oyster Bay while Roosevelt stayed at the White House, he wrote to them and described the growth of birds in their garden. By permission, Sagamore Hill National Historic Site.

feeds them.

You see the mother
bird with a worm
in her beak, and
the little birds with
their beaks wide
open!

and with snakes slithering, responded as the president and Attorney General Charles Bonaparte turned in surprise and beheld the gaping serpents:

Bonaparte: This question of infringement . . .
Quentin: . . . What's the matter? Aren't they lovely snakes?
Roosevelt: Quentin, I don't believe Mr. Bonaparte is much interested in snakes. Suppose you go into the next room. Pete Hepburn and Lacey are in there and they are very fond of snakes.

Quentin then skated into the presence of the waiting congressmen, Colonel Pete Hepburn and Major John F. Lacey, in the next room.

Quentin: See what I've got?
Lacey: Look at what the boy has, Pete. Toy snakes twined round his arm. Wonderful, isn't it? How lifelike they make the things nowadays. Come here, son, and let me—holy Moses!

Lacey jumped onto a table as the president, peering into the room with a grin, witnessed Quentin asking Hepburn to help him secure one of the snakes that had slithered up the sleeve of his coat. With a personal affection for childhood snake husbandry born of his own enterprise in his Harvard days, Roosevelt quipped: "Fond of snakes, Pete?"

In the midst of churning out a copious stream of letters to political friends and foes, Roosevelt took time to romp and play with his children and the curiosities in their natural history cabinet. His letters to them sometimes recounted the natural pageantry. When one much-loved pet died, Roosevelt wrote to Kermit—who was studying at the Groton school at the time—recounting the funeral, in which "Archie, in his overalls, dragged the wagon with the little black coffin in which poor Peter Rabbit lay."[54] After Quentin and Archie left the White House for their own summer ramblings in 1904, the president kept them apprised of the natural occurrences on the grounds. "Blessed Quenty-Quee: The little birds in the nest in the vines on the garden fence are nearly grown up. Their mother still feeds them."[55] With similar affection, he wrote to "Blessed Archie-kins" on the same day: "All kinds of live things are sent me from time to time. The other day an eagle came; this morning an owl. (I have drawn him holding a rat in one claw.)"[56] Roosevelt directed much of this infusion of nature toward his own children, but occasionally the naturalist-in-chief widened his reach, at one point replying to the daughter of a family friend who had wished him a happy birthday: "Dear Little Miss Sarah, I liked your birthday note *very* much; and my children say I should draw you two pictures in return." He continued: "The children have very cunning pony. He is a little pet, like a dog, but he plays tricks on them when they ride him. He bucked Ethel over his head the other day. Your father will tell you that these are pictures of the UNPOLISHED STONE PERIOD."[57]

Along with his involvement in the breeding and bucking of the children's pets, Roosevelt also stole moments in which he could connect with nature near home. There were periodic jaunts to his satellite field site at Oyster Bay, where he chased kids and ponies. He escaped to a new rustic retreat Edith had given him, called Pine Knot, near Keene, Virginia. He also took visitors and friends on his rambles to Rock Creek Park in Washington. These weren't stately walks; instead, as one participant recalled, these were more like games of follow the leader, with Roosevelt leading in climbs "along the sheer face of a rock which overhung Rock Creek."[58] Afterwards, Roosevelt "plunged into the stream and swam to the other side with all his clothes on."[59] Others had similar swims in the park while dodging floating blocks of ice.[60] But even on the White House grounds, Roosevelt found moments to let his mind escape into the natural world. At one point he wrote to Burroughs and remarked: "Most of the warblers were up in the tops of the trees, and I could not get a good glimpse of them; but there was one with chestnut cheeks, with bright yellow behind the cheeks, and a yellow breast thickly streaked with black, which has puzzled me."[61] Roosevelt even kept field notes on White House stationery, recording the birds he had seen on his ramblings on the grounds and in nearby Washington.[62]

Roosevelt's field mindset was not simply personal and playful; he applied his love of animals and open spaces in his work at the White house as well. Accelerating the pace of the initiatives he had started in the Boone and Crockett Club and as governor of New York, Roosevelt worked with advocates such as Gifford Pinchot

June 21, 1904.

Dear Quentyquee;

The other day when out riding what should I see in the
road ahead of me but a real B'rer Terrapin and B'rer Rabbit.
They were sitting solemnly beside one another and looked just
as if they had come out of a book; but as my horse walked
along B'rer Rabbit went *lippity lippity lippity* off into the
bushes and B'rer Terrapin drew in his head and legs till I
passed.

Your loving father,

Theodore Roosevelt

Master Quentin Roosevelt,
Oyster Bay, N. Y.

Roosevelt wrote to his son Quentin in June of 1904 to describe his real-life encounter with B'rer
Terrapin and B'rer Rabbit as he rode on horseback in Washington. By permission, Sagamore
Hill National Historic Site.

Theodore Roosevelt. March 27th 1908.
Birds seen around Washington, 1901-1908.

(X denotes a species seen on White House grounds)

THE WHITE HOUSE,
WASHINGTON.

Night Heron. Five spent winter of 1907 in swampy
Dove.   country west ½ mile west of Washington monument.
Quail.
Ruffed grouse. One seen on Rock creek.
Sharp shinned hawk.
Red shouldered hawk.
X Sparrow hawk. A pair spent the last two winters on or
            around the White House grounds, feeding on
            its sparrows — largely, thank Heaven, on its
            English sparrows.

X Screech Owl. Steady resident on White House grounds.

X Saw whet owl. A pair spent several weeks by the
            south portico of the White House in
    Kingfisher.   June 1905
X Yellow billed cuckoo.
    Hairy wood pecker.
X Downy wood pecker
X Sapsucker.
X, Red headed „ Nests (1 pair) on White House grounds.
X, Flicker. Nests (several pair) „ „ „ „ .
    Whip poor will.
    Night hawk.
+ Chimney swallow.
+ Hummer
    Kingbird
    Great crest
    Phoebe
    Wood peewee.
    Horned lark
+ crow
+ Fish crow

Although Roosevelt had numerous field experiences while he was president, he also paid close attention to the nature on the White House grounds and in the surrounding areas of Washington. As any serious naturalist would, he kept track of birds that he sighted during his time as president. TRC MS Am 1454.33.

and Congressman John Lacey to establish various types of parks, preserves, and refuges. In 1902 he created Crater Lake National Park and thirteen reserves that set aside more than fourteen million acres of land.[63] Motivated by his long-standing love of birds and his disgust with their slaughter in Florida for plumes and decorations, he realized that there was no legal barrier keeping him from using his position to unilaterally preserve wildlife.[64] In March of 1903 he established the first National Bird Reservation on Pelican Island in Florida, with his oft-quoted "I so declare it."[65] In 1904 he added Sullys Hill National Park in North Dakota, and another bird reservation on Breton Island in Louisiana.[66]

After a relatively uneventful reelection bid, Roosevelt was inaugurated for his second term in March of 1905. Now he could count as political accomplishments his resolution of the anthracite coal strike, the successful wrangling with Germany over Venezuela, the groundwork for an isthmian canal, and his campaigns against large trusts. Given the time and effort he had spent on these endeavors, bears and cougars had gotten a reprieve from Roosevelt's guns during much of his first term.[67] But shortly after he had secured his new term—even in the midst of heightened tensions between Russia and Japan—Roosevelt turned his rifle sights back toward the West.[68]

In April 1905, Roosevelt headed West for a hunting loop through Oklahoma and Colorado.[69] The trip began with a swing through the Midwest, with stops for speeches, and then a Rough Riders reunion in San Antonio.[70] Although Roosevelt shook plenty of hands and harped on his usual themes in speeches, he was able to focus on the true purpose of his trip when he arrived in Frederick, Oklahoma on April 8.[71] As a good naturalist, he always trained his powers of observation on the essence of what made something unique, whether it was variations in birdsong or in the way a cowboy roped a steer. And Roosevelt knew well before he arrived in Oklahoma what the most interesting part of the story there would be. Unlike John Goff in Colorado, whose the dogs had stolen the show during a cougar hunt, here the guide, Jack Abernathy, was the prime attraction.

One of Roosevelt's old Rough Riders, Cecil Lyon, had witnessed Abernathy's ability to catch a coyote with his bare hands at a celebration shortly before Christmas. This display had amazed the crowd—especially after endless greyhound races—and Lyon related the details of this man, known as "Catch'Em Alive Jack," to Roosevelt.⁷² Now, Abernathy had accepted an invitation to help Roosevelt find game, and was now on his way to Lyon's ranch. It was easy for any accomplished hunter to earn Roosevelt's respect, but there were other reasons why Abernathy entranced Roosevelt from the moment they met. Like Roosevelt, Abernathy had a rich Western persona. He was a kind of plains polymath, and he could enact the ballads of the West just as easily as he could call them out on the harmonica and fiddle. He also shared with Roosevelt a sense of range justice, once having single-handedly brought a stagecoach robber and murderer back from the Wichita Mountains. At 2 p.m. on April 5, Abernathy rode up to the grandstand in Frederick as Roosevelt was discussing the imminence of Oklahoma's statehood in his welcome speech. As a first greeting, Roosevelt paused and called out to Abernathy a crowd-pleasing welcome: "You look like a man who could catch a wolf."⁷³

It wasn't long before Roosevelt and Abernathy ranged over the pancake-like prairies that lay at the foot of the Wichita Mountains as they and a pack of greyhounds ran down coyotes. Roosevelt's hunting companion and personal physician, Alexander Lambert, rode alongside to capture the scene in photographs. After catching some coyotes in the more conventional fashion, with greyhounds chasing down and immobilizing them until the hunters arrived, Roosevelt got to see the Wild-West–style work of Abernathy.

The group shogged over the plains, carefully navigating the holes that belied a continuous web of prairie dog burrows. Suddenly, the hunting dogs caught sight of a coyote and sprang into action. The rumbling herd of hunters spread out on the chase, and after ten miles of hard riding many cowpunchers in the group slowed with fatigue. But Roosevelt shot past them and caught sight of Abernathy and one of his hounds. As he pulled closer, he saw the coyote approach a clear creek bed and cut back across Abernathy's trail, narrowly avoiding being run down. Then, Abernathy went to work as he leapt from his horse and onto the coyote:

> Abernathy, who had ridden his horse right on them as they struggled, leaped off and sprang on top of the wolf. He

Bowy Moore

Wea. Thur. Apr. 6, 1905 Ther.

Bowy Moore

John Abernethy

Jesca

Oklahoma,

Moore is the coyote; held it aloft on horseback.

Abernethy held up coyote by jaw.

Uncle Ed Billing, the former cowboy of the 4 R ranch; now a separate ranchman

Dr. Taylor (who skinned coyote) the rare very good fellow. Burnett such a fine fellow; & his son

(ABOVE AND FACING) Shortly after his second presidential term began, Roosevelt went west on a hunting trip. His first aim was to hunt coyotes with Jack Abernathy in Oklahoma. Known as "Catch'Em Alive Jack," Abernathy would ride up to a coyote on horseback and then jump off his mount to grab the animal in his arms. He would quickly shove his fist into the coyote's mouth to subdue it. TRC MS Am 1454.55 (14).

Abernethy the
homesteader &
wolf catcher; he
catches them with
his hands; his
grayhounds; they
will hold but not
kill a big wolf;
the biggest one of
the latter he ever
killed weighed 97 lbs.
It has only killed a few.
Thinks there are half
breeds or grades between
them & the coyote. Black
70 pound wolf; about
2 sizes larger than
the first coyote.

held the reins of the horse with one hand and thrust the
other, with a rapidity and precision even greater than the
rapidity of the wolf's snap, into the wolf's mouth, jamming
his hand down crosswise between the jaws, seizing the lower
jaw and bending it down so that the wolf could not bite
him. He had a stout glove on his hand, but this would have
been of no avail whatever had he not seized the animal
just as he did; that is, behind the canines, while his hand
pressed the lips against the teeth; with his knees he kept
the wolf from using its fore paws to break the hold, until it
gave up struggling.[74]

It didn't matter that Abernathy had lost the wire he normally used
to keep the coyote's mouth shut. He simply threw the coyote across
the front of his saddle with one hand, still immobilizing the jaw,
and rode on. Roosevelt gazed in amazement, and appreciated a
new and literal display of the power of an alpha male. Despite being "very stiff & sore" after this ride, he continued to hunt coyote
and bobcats over the next several days.[75] Roosevelt reveled in the
beautiful combination of man and nature, and along with his notes
on Abernathy's feats, he rendered the rustic scenery in his diary:
the cottonwoods and mesquite; cardinals, jays, and fork-tailed fly-
catchers; black-tailed jackrabbits.[76] It was a scene reminiscent of
his roundup days, and he jotted the brief note "All day out with
chuck wagon," a reminder to ask his *Scribner's* readers, "Where does
a man take more frank enjoyment in his dinner than at the tail end
of a chuck-wagon?"[77] He considered the full canvas of Abernathy's
coyote-catching spectacle—"as remarkable a feat of the kind as I
have ever seen"—and he knew his readers would eat it up, too.[78]

With a fond farewell to Abernathy on April 13, Roosevelt continued on into Colorado with Lambert. Two days later, they met
up with the old cougar crew of John Goff and Philip Stewart, along
with another guide from Kentucky named Jake Borah, to begin to
look for bear at their camp near Divide Creek, about twenty miles
from Newcastle. Roosevelt had always been proud of the bear hunts
that were a standard part of his hunting lore. But on this hunt he
was trying to make a bear-hunting rebound: it was his first major
hunt since one of the worst outdoor experiences of his life.

In November of 1902, Roosevelt had escaped Washington and

made for the Mississippi canebrakes to hunt for the Louisiana black bear.[79] Roosevelt would never write an account of that trip for *Scribner's,* and no field notes from the trip survive. However, Roosevelt surely did not forgot the searing headlines after that trip. The *Atlanta Constitution* began its trip postmortem with an unforgiving assessment: "That President Roosevelt did not bring down a black bear during his hunt in the Mississippi bottoms was his own fault."[80] It continued to describe how bears were common in the area but "too fat and logy to run far." No doubt part of the harshness of this coverage was because much of the south, at least the non-blacks, were incensed with Roosevelt for having had Booker T. Washington dine at the White House a year before, the first African American to ever do so. Even still, his trip had been an ugly scene.

The Mississippi hunting party had relied on the formidable skill of the legendary African American hunting guide Holt Collier. The kind of complicated character Roosevelt had always loved, Collier had started hunting when he was ten years old and was thought to have killed more than three thousand bears in his lifetime.[81] Even with the help of Collier, though, the trip was full of near misses for Roosevelt. Despite the fact that bears were in the area, throughout the trip they had vanished when Roosevelt was near. Roosevelt painted the scene in a letter to Philip Stewart: "But my kind hosts, with the best of intentions, insisted upon turning the affair into a cross between a hunt and a picnic, which always results in a failure for the hunt and usually in a failure for the picnic."[82] And a failure it became. Finally, Collier chased a bear into a pool of water, eventually subduing it with a forceful blow with his rifle butt. He then managed to get a lasso around its neck before the president arrived. Roosevelt waded into the water but couldn't possibly shoot the lassoed bear himself. It would go against everything he and the Boone and Crockett Club stood for in hunting.

The dark scene ended with the bear being dispatched with a knife, but, amazingly, this is not the rendering that has persisted. The press has the power to pivot and spin public perception, and in this case a cartoon in *The Washington Post* portrayed an image of a compassionate Roosevelt. The cartoonist, Clifford Berryman, portrayed the president, in characteristic Rough Rider regalia, sparing the bear with his hand up, and with his face turned away from a white man holding a young bear with a lasso.[83] Despite the inaccuracy of the image—the bear had been an adult, and it was Collier who had held it—the image of Roosevelt's dignified restraint and the cute bear were seared into the mind of the public.[84] Soon enough, toy companies were producing stuffed bears called "Teddy bears." Adults and children alike were taken with them, and these toys soon became a fixture of American culture. Although he disliked being referred to as "Teddy," there was an even wider transfer of his persona, as it was applied to living animals as well.[85] *The Washington Post* later reported how "Teddy" had become a worldwide namesake: the name had been given to ten thousand camels in Egypt, one-third of the dogs in Chicago, "three live 'Teddy' bears, a 'Teddy' wolf, and canaries, roosters, parrots, horses, and tomcats innumerable."[86] In keeping with his persona, the *Post* felt it was important to clarify that "the name 'Teddy' is especially suitable for spike-collared watch dogs." The bear is what became forever linked with Roosevelt, however, and Berryman's cartoon overshadowed the ugly and unsuccessful hunt of 1902 in which Roosevelt never had shot a bear. Now, in the snowy Colorado spring of 1905, he had a chance to prove that he had not become passive and soft during his time in the White House, especially when it came to bears.

As the hunters rode out from their camp near Divide Creek, the dogs locked onto the trail of bobcats, cougars, and bears amid the biting snow of the Rocky Mountains. As Roosevelt surveyed the animals that yipped and galloped beside him, he recognized some characters from his hunt with Goff in 1901—Jim, Tree'em, and Bruno—while others he was meeting for the first time had names like Badge, Bill, Rowdy, Bruise, and Skip.[87] Roosevelt noted during the trip that Skip especially fought the "bear & bobcat hard," and he was amused that the dog begged to ride "home on horseback."[88] Roosevelt obliged, and became so fond of Skip that he would later bring him to the White House.

One of the horses also attracted Roosevelt's attention as "atavistic"—exhibiting characters of bygone days of evolution—because of wide black and "zebra-like" stripes on its back.[89] Roosevelt's imagination whirred as he considered how this animal looked "much as the horses must have looked which an age or two ago lived in this very locality and were preyed on by sabre-toothed tigers, hyenadons, and other strange and terrible beasts of a long-vanished era." When one member of the party ribbed the horse's owner that the horse should be called "Fossil" because it was "a hundred thousand years old," the owner replied: "Gee! and that man sold him to me for a seven-year-old! I'll have the law on him!" As it often did on the hunt, Roosevelt's intellectualism jibed nicely with the folksy ways of his compatriots.

On April 17, Roosevelt set off with twenty-six hounds and four terriers, and shot a 330-pound male bear from sixty yards, "breaking his hips."[90] A second bullet from thirty yards hit the bear's neck. The next day, Roosevelt "rode 6 hours, mostly in snowdrifts; saw nothing," save "sand hill cranes; eagles; ravens; jays & c."[91] Then there were more snowstorms, Roosevelt had a fit of malarial fever, and there was a flurry of communications with Washington on the situation with Russia and Japan, which would cause the trip to be shortened. Roosevelt felt better by April 24, and the hunting party rode for eleven hours. Finally, Roosevelt found evidence of a bear and "put dogs on old she's trail," sending it up a spruce. He recorded the result in his field notes: "I shot her dead through heart."[92] The bear was a female of 175 pounds, and it only had rosebuds in its stomach.

Despite the mountains of snow, the nature of spring was chirping in his ears: white-crowned sparrows and towhees, Say's flycatcher and Western meadow larks. There was delight in the appearances of rodents and lagomorphs, with the white-footed mice and pack rats running through camp, and squirrels and snowshoe rabbits on the trail.[93] As the hunt ended in early May, he certainly had enough stories and observations to reaffirm his bear-hunting ability in *Scribner's*, and the trip had provided him with a successful diversion from the growing Russo-Japanese conflict. And it would not be his last chance for bear.

In 1907, Roosevelt returned to the southern canebrakes to finally bag his Louisiana black bear. Collier was again called in for the hunt, and Roosevelt scratched some hasty, undated field notes that allowed him to later paint the scene of this cathartic hunting experience for his readers.[94] He noted the bear's place in the context of the hunter—"Major Hamblin killed by bear"—which he later expanded into the story of Dr. Monroe Hamberlin's fatal wrestling match with a large black bear.[95] He also documented how another

Brick Wells, the rider & hunter.

Left Newcastle,
Colorado, with Phil
Stewart, Aleck Lambert
and the guides
John Goff and
Jake Borah (a
Kentuckian). Rode
about 20 miles to
our camp on upper
waters of east
Divide creek. Very
comfortable. Three
good horses for any
one use, 30-40 Springfield,
30 odd hounds & curs.

Snow in drifts. High,
rugged country. Freeze at
night.

(ABOVE AND FACING) After his adventures with Abernathy on the coyote hunt in Oklahoma, Roosevelt traveled to Colorado to hunt bear. Despite having had a complicated bear hunt in 1902—the event that inspired the "Teddy Bear"—Roosevelt was ready to try for bear again in 1905. This hunt was successful, and on his third day he killed a 330-pound male bear after an almost two-hour chase. TRC MS Am 1454.55 (14).

Went out after
the bear, with 2 & 6
hounds & 4 terriers.
In very high & difficult
country. Lots of snow,
Precipitous canyons.
Found his last night's
track. Got him after
chase of 1 3/4 hours.
♂ 330 lbs. Stomach empty.
Would not tree; stood
off dogs; made a
walking bay. Hard
scramble to where he
way. Hit him in chest as
he walked away, at 60
yards, breaking his hips;
broke his neck at 30 yards.
He killed one terrier; &
wounded 6 or 8 dogs.

southern hunter, Ben Lilly, soon joined their camp. Roosevelt recorded Lilly as a man who "comes up through swamp, lies out over night," and was equal to "Cooper's Deerslayer in woodcraft."[96] He made more general cultural assessments in a letter to his daughter Ethel, as he remarked how two women of Native American and African American blood had ridden by on a horse, their heritage reminding him of "Voodoo Tales."[97] Roosevelt then turned his attention to the overall environment, in which the "swamps" were thick with plants: "hackberries, cottonwoods, tupelo gum."[98] In the water there were the menacing alligator and gar, but he was most intrigued by the amphibious swamp rabbit.[99] The air was teeming, too; he even saw two of the increasingly rare ivory-billed woodpeckers. Roosevelt applied his special attention to documenting birdsongs using hieroglyphics reminiscent of his childhood notebooks: the barred owl uttered a "uugh—uugh—hoo!"[100] His writings from this trip even revealed the same kinds of longings as he had had in the field during his Midwest tramp in 1880: he wrote that he was "very homesick" for his "darling sweetheart" Edith.[101] At this point he wasn't optimistic about his chances for success on the hunt, but he soon absconded into the brush with Collier and shot a 202-pound she-bear. Ever the naturalist, Roosevelt opened the bear's stomach and recorded that it had been feeding on beetles, acorns, and palmetto berries.[102] In the end, he summed up the unique cornucopia of wildlife they had shot in the canebrakes: "We got three bears, six deer, one wild turkey, twelve squirrels, one duck, one opossum, and one wildcat. We ate them all except the wildcat, and there were times when we almost felt as if we could eat it."[103] He was so excited by his first bear on that trip that he hugged every member of his party.

Even at the time, not everyone embraced the president's love of hunting. When Mark Twain, a one-time supporter of Roosevelt, read of the Louisiana bear hunt, he fumed about the "wonderful dime-novel performance" in his notebooks: "There it is—he hugged the guides after the kill. It is the President all over; he is still only fourteen years old after living half a century; he takes a boy's delight in showing off. . . . Nothing would do this lad but he must kill her and be a hero."[104] Roosevelt's hunting was too much even for Muir, who asked Roosevelt at one point: "When are you going to get beyond the boyishness of killing things?"[105] The breadth of Roosevelt's actions were easy to criticize or parody, but much harder to place into context.

Journalists were often content to poke fun at Roosevelt's outsized contradictions. The humorist Hugh Herdman's column in *The Pacific Monthly* conjured an image of how one of Roosevelt's diary accounts from a day on the hunt, accompanied by his secretary William Loeb, might look. A condensed version of Herdman's column follows.

Camp Roosevelt, Colorado, May 1.

4:55 a.m.—Turned out. Took a snow bath. Ran one mile as an appetizer.

5:00—Built the fire. Waked the cook. Chucked a snowball down Loeb's neck to wake him up.

5:05—Curried all my horses and fed the whole bunch.

5:10—Getting pretty hungry by this time. Think I'll have to have another cook, this one being too slow; can't get breakfast in less than twenty minutes.

5:15—Threw the cook into a snow drift and got breakfast myself.

5:20—Breakfast. Had lost my appetite by this time, and ate only two bear steaks, three plates of potatoes, two cans of tomatoes, sixteen flap-jacks and four cups of coffee.

5:35—Ran down a wolf on foot. Caught him by the throat. Then the dogs caught up with me. Ate the wolf—the dogs did.

5:40—Whole party rode down the mountain for bear. Thought out that Denver speech. Loeb made suggestions, but I vetoed them.

5:50—Shinned up a pine tree and licked a bob cat. He reminded me of Castro. . . .

6:25— . . . Had a wrestling match with a mad she-grizzly. Won the first fall.

6:30—Skinned the grizzly. Ordered a pair of chaps made of the pelt.

6:35—Dictated the outline of the story of the bear hunt that we shall make to-morrow. Loeb seemed worried and couldn't follow dictation very well.

6:40—Ran foot races with the crowd. Loeb was last. I beat him anyhow. . . .

6:50—Pulled a cougar out of his den by the tail and broke his head against a tree. . . .

6:55—Snow storm. Started a little game of draw. Busted Loeb. Guess he'll have to walk home. Changed itinerary of our return at Loeb's request. Wonder why he wants the change.

7:00—Am beginning to tire of this inactivity. Wish something would turn up.

7:05—Tried to run down an antelope. He ran even better than I did last November. . . .

7:20—No more bears to-day. Started a wrestling tournament in camp. These fellows don't know anything about the game. Loeb thought he did, but has changed his mind.

7:30—Started a boxing tournament. I used that kangaroo side step that Fitz taught me and that corkscrew uppercut that I learned from Jeff. Turned camp into a hospital. Sent to town for a doctor. The probabilities are that I'll need a new secretary.

7:35—Too busy nursing the wounded to write more.[106]

Thankfully, the kind of unusual energy and direct action that Herdman identified also applied to Roosevelt's work at the White House. Settling into his second term, Roosevelt was ready to begin a new flurry of conservation initiatives.

When the summer of 1906 began, it had been more than a year since Roosevelt's last major trip to the field, and it would be another year before he would experience anything more adventurous than respites at Sagamore Hill and Pine Knot. Part of the outcome of Roosevelt staying close to home during this period, however, was that he worked to set aside places for the general public to experience the natural and cultural wonders of the United States.

With the help of Congressman John Lacey and the archaeologist Edgar Lee Hewitt, Roosevelt signed "An Act for the Preservation of American Antiquities" into law on June 6. Although its title sounded quaint, this new law gave Roosevelt another unprecedented mechanism to protect a wide range of national treasures.[107] Unlike the process for establishing national parks, which required the involvement of Congress, this act gave the president the sole power to establish national monuments by proclamation. It gave the president the ability to set aside not only "historic landmarks, historic and prehistoric structures," but also "other objects of historic or scientific interest." Roosevelt seized this language and interpreted it expansively, as he did with the qualification that the lands should be "confined to the smallest area compatible with proper care and management of the objects to be protected." To Roosevelt, "smallest" was a relative term, especially when used in reference to the treasures of the American West like the Grand Canyon. Once the Antiquities Act was passed, Roosevelt went straight to work. In 1906 he established national monuments at Devil's Tower in Wyoming, El Morro in New Mexico, and Montezuma Castle and the Petrified Forest in Arizona. The next year, there were new monuments at Chaco Canyon and the Gila Cliff Dwellings in New Mexico, Lassen Peak and Cinder Cone in California, and Tonto in Arizona. Roosevelt continued on with monuments in 1908, including Muir Woods in California, Jewel Cave in South Dakota, and the Grand Canyon of Arizona.

Roosevelt wasn't done with national parks and reserves for forests and birds either, and on only a few choice days in June of 1906, July of 1908, and February and March of 1909 he worked to establish two national parks and set aside thousands of acres of land for national forests and bird reservations.[108] He not only worked with small groups for conservation but also convened a summit of state governors in 1908 to promote the aims of conservation.[109]

As Roosevelt toggled between using his presidential power to establish wildlife reserves, refuges, and parks and absconding for hunts in Mississippi, Louisiana, Oklahoma, and Colorado, the tension of the hunter-naturalist came to the fore. Along with Roosevelt's enjoyment of hunting as a pastime, which was very common in his day, the naturalist tradition he followed—practiced earlier by Darwin, Audubon, and Coues—involved many forms of hunting and came to life through direct action, in holding specimens in the hand to observe their structure, color, and anatomy. Although some aspects of Roosevelt's hunting were nestled in the traditions of the naturalist, legitimate questions emerged about how his love of the chase and of hunting as a pastime on its own related to his efforts to study nature, as well as to conservation and preservation.

How could someone who had shot birds so freely in his youth be such a forceful opponent of the plume hunters in Florida? How could a hunter who opposed the hunting of deer with dogs in the Adirondacks have so freely used canines to hunt bear and cougar in Colorado? How could a man who danced in delight after shooting one of the last free-ranging buffalo be so dedicated to reintroducing this species into a preserve in the Wichita Mountains?

Some of these contradictions are ones of context. For Roosevelt, the status of the animal as a "varmint," its relative abundance, and its eventual fate as a scientific specimen might enable him to rationalize aggressive hunting for sport or science.[110] Other aspects of this contradiction can be resolved by Roosevelt's own development. Over the course of his life he began to realize that his early freedom in shooting birds, following the instructions of Coues, was no longer appropriate.[111] Some aspects of his behavior, like his drive to hunt a buffalo, and later the white rhino, may simply stand as true inconsistencies that lack a compelling rationale.[112]

The contradictions, complexities, and some of what now seem

to be clear mistakes in Roosevelt's life as a hunter-naturalist need to be placed into the same context as other areas of his life where, in hindsight, he did not achieve success, like the negative environmental impacts of his water policy and his mishandling of the racial incident at Brownsville.[113] But the question remains: Would Roosevelt have been able to effect such a massive amount of conservation—winning the support of so many diverse constituencies—had he not been a hunter, regardless of whether or not his hunting was always optimal? If one removed his intimate interactions with other influential sportsmen, his deep knowledge and love for organisms he gained in the chase, and his processing of specimens, would he still have made such strides in conservation? In this light, it is indisputable that Roosevelt—as an entire individual—made remarkable achievements in his efforts to conserve the natural world.

On December 8, 1908, Roosevelt submitted his eighth and final annual message as president. The pages were stuffed with his feelings about conservation. He chastised Americans for thinking that all of their resources, be they water, coal, or forests, were limitless.

> Short-sighted persons, or persons blinded to the future
> by desire to make money in every way out of the present,
> sometimes speak as if no great damage would be done by
> the reckless destruction of our forests. It is difficult to have
> patience with the arguments of these persons. Thanks to
> our own recklessness in the use of our splendid forests, we
> have already crossed the verge of a timber famine in this
> country, and no measures that we now take can, at least for
> many years, undo the mischief that has already been done.
> But we can prevent further mischief being done . . . especially as regards the national forests which the nation can
> *now*, at this very moment, control.[114]

Ever the historian, Roosevelt drew on the observations of Marco Polo in twelfth-century China, where vast forests and groves of mulberry trees provided food for silkworms. By Roosevelt's day, those forests and the agriculture they supported were gone. Similar degradation could be seen in North Africa and Europe, and the wonderlands of the United States would share the same fate unless action was taken. These were not the words or sentiments of a crazed animal killer or thoughtless capitalist; they were the words of a man who knew and loved the field in all of its incarnations.

Roosevelt's assessment of his contribution was brief: "I am happy to say that I have been able to set aside in various parts of the country small, well-chosen tracts of ground to serve as sanctuaries and nurseries for wild creatures."[115] All told, Roosevelt's assessment was a vast understatement.

Surely Roosevelt's field-hardened characteristics were important in trust busting, political rows, and extended travel in political campaigns. But, much more important, the strength of his persona furthered an unrivaled accomplishment in conservation and preservation. His scorecard was stunning: he created or enlarged 150 national forests that accounted for 150 million new acres in the public domain, and he established fifty-one federal bird reservations, four national game preserves, five national parks, and eighteen national monuments.[116]

What he accomplished in conservation was clearly prodigious. But how he achieved it was unique. His field credibility allowed him to gather together people with widely diverging viewpoints— naturalists, scientists, nature lovers, hunters, and utilitarians like ranchers and foresters—so that he could listen to them and comprehend their perspectives. He was not simply able to understand these diverse perspectives. Like the cowpunchers and Ivy leaguers he embodied when he donned his Rough Riders hat, there was, nestled in his robust persona, a vital part of each of these constituents of conservation.[117]

With his substantial work as president completed in March of 1909, Roosevelt handed the White House keys to William Howard Taft, and turned his attention back to the field.

3

RETURN
to the FIELD

{CHAPTER TEN}

African Syzygy

It was as if Roosevelt had been plunked down into a life-size diorama of the Pleistocene, its walls somewhere over the distant horizon and its inhabitants given life by his boyish imagination. Through this landscape he started on a fantastical journey, riding on a specially made bench atop the cowcatcher of a locomotive, steaming westward from the azure coast toward the heart of Africa. The scene was as magnificent as it was surreal; Roosevelt was a figurehead splitting the African air, as in a scene from a movie yet to be filmed. It was "literally like passing through a vast zoological garden," a moving picture of wildlife so captivating to Roosevelt that he perched in front of the train from dawn until dusk, only taking leave for a short lunch.¹ Others had described this part of Africa as a place to witness nature's superlatives—its longest horns, biggest tusks, and most interesting geography—like a "zoological gardens let loose."² It was just a few years earlier that Roosevelt had been awed by thousands of elk as he rode into Yellowstone, but such memories were now dwarfed by this scene: massive herds of wildebeest, strutting ostriches, and galloping impala, and the brachiating antics of monkeys. Birds flitted in the air—sunbirds, bee-eaters and weaverbirds—and bustards and francolin prowled over the stubbly earth. The wildlife was mostly at a safe distance, but it occasionally came near the hurtling train. At one time, a stillbuck jumped from a ditch and came just two yards from the train.³ At another, a black and white hornbill swooped so close that Roosevelt and his companions "nearly caught it with [their] hands."⁴

Roosevelt imagined that he was on a trip back in time. The relative civilization of Mombasa faded as the line of his horizon bounded a vast quantity of life that could be sighted, touched, and hunted like none he had ever seen. In this natural land, he did not simply connect with the experience of early naturalists like Audubon and Coues; here he felt he was experiencing the life his human ancestors had led thousands of years before.

It was the land of great animals, the lion, the elephant, and the horse—animals whose own recent ancestors had been the most important and formidable creatures ever to walk the earth with humans. To Roosevelt, the lion represented the ferocious cats that had terrorized early humans.[5] The tusks and towering forms of elephants evoked the mammoths that had provided humans with food. In zebras, Roosevelt could see traits of the horses that had originated in the New World and gone extinct there, only to repopulate and become the work animals he had ridden on his ranch in the Badlands. Even the people he saw in Africa—which he unfortunately conceptualized as "savages"—seemed to him to be living examples of how early humans had lived in the days when they "lived in caves and smote one other with stone-headed axes."[6] He truly felt he was on a railroad chugging through the Pleistocene, with the raw and dangerous roots of the human experience laid bare.

Roosevelt had first envisioned African adventure in his parent's library on East 20th Street, by paging through the dramatic woodcuts in Livingstone's *Missionary Travels*, his young eyes bulging as the protagonist fought off angry hippos or was mauled by a lion.[7] Less than a decade later, he had his first experience in Africa as he cruised the Nile, observing plovers and crocodiles in watery pools. But these sights were just rough sketches of the Dark Continent; much more of Roosevelt's life passed before the most fantastic of earth's creatures came into better resolution. While president he began his in-depth study of Africa, as he so many times had with his investigations, by learning from the great naturalists of the region. And with Livingstone long gone, there was, at least in Roosevelt's mind, no more prominent African naturalist and explorer than Frederick Selous.[8]

Along with many other people, including Roosevelt, Selous had dreamed about exploring Africa since childhood. About the time the preliterate Roosevelt was carrying around *Missionary Travels*, Selous was dreaming of Africa as he fell asleep on the hard floor of a British boarding school in Northamptonshire. It wasn't that

Roosevelt left the White House in 1909 after completing his second term, and turned his complete attention to a yearlong safari in Africa. Just after arriving in Mombasa, in what was then British East Africa, Roosevelt met up with his friend, the legendary African hunter Frederick Selous. Roosevelt and Selous sat atop a specially-designed cowcatcher on a locomotive that steamed westward out of Mombasa and into the plains of Africa, which teemed with impalas, wildebeests, ostriches, and monkeys. TRC 560.61–185.

Selous was without means; like Roosevelt, he grew up in a wealthy family. But he eschewed his bed in preparation for the hard life of an African explorer and hunter in the style of Livingstone.[9]

By the time Roosevelt first wrote him in 1897, Selous had proven that his youthful activities were in fact not eccentricities but forward-thinking preparations. Selous had lived much of his adult life hunting and exploring in Africa, and he immortalized his travels in works like *Travel and Adventure in South-East Africa* and *A Hunter's Wanderings in Africa*.[10] With many shared interests, Roosevelt and Selous began a warm correspondence on hunting, politics, and even the personal challenges of attempting to remain active in the field despite the needs of parenthood.[11] Roosevelt revealed his longing for Africa in his letters to Selous, at one point calling it "the other wilderness, which I have never seen, and never shall see, except through your books."[12] After years of letters, Selous visited Roosevelt at the White House in 1905, bringing about Roosevelt's long-awaited meeting with the man he later described as "the foremost of all hunter naturalists."[13]

The visit began with a rigorous outing as Roosevelt rounded up four additional companions—including Gifford Pinchot—for a "good scramble and climb" in the rocks and fields of nearby Washington.[14] Legs stretched and bellies rumbling, they returned to the White House in the late afternoon as dinner was being prepared (likely a good deal of red meat for the occasion). Archie, Quentin, and Ethel naturally began to hover, intrigued by the rugged, dashing British guest in their home. Such a living trove of stories could not be squandered; Roosevelt politely inquired if Selous might share some of his experiences with the family.

The shadows that lengthened in the room framed Selous and revealed that he was not an ordinary storyteller; he had tracked, wrestled with, and killed some of the most dangerous creatures alive. From behind the whiskers of his pointed beard emerged delightfully terrifying stories about lions and hyenas. At some point the children were shuffled off to bed, but Roosevelt certainly stayed up to hear Selous's full tale: "A lion story is usually a tale of adventures, often very terrible and pathetic, which occupied but a few hours of one night; but the tales of the Tsavo man-eaters is an epic of terrible tragedies spread out over several months, and only at last brought to an end by the resource and determination of one man."[15] It was a tale that reinforced the colonial perspective that whites and colonists were brave people who battled Africa's beasts while those lower on the hierarchy of races turned and ran—but in its conclusion it provided a cautionary story on the perils of Africa, even for British and American hunter-naturalists like Roosevelt and Selous.[16]

Selous's story began with the construction of the Uganda Railway, a connection between Mombasa and the great lake then known as Victoria Nyansa.[17] In the late 1890s, engineers from Britain converged with laborers from India to lay the track and construct the bridges that would allow penetration of the continent by locomotives. These men—such as James Patterson, who was hired to oversee the construction of a bridge over the Tsavo River—arrived knowing they would face risks. But none envisioned the terror that would emerge from the African nights.

As the work clanked along in Tsavo, rumors began to emerge that men were disappearing into the night. At first, Patterson was skeptical. There was no question of the veracity of these abductions, however, when one of the leaders of the Indian work crew was dragged from his tent in the middle of the night, in full view of his horrified tent mate. The next morning, the survivor followed two lines in the sand—left by dragging heels—to find his friend's body. Much of the skin had been licked from the body, the veins were devoid of blood, and the limbs evidenced the characteristic feeding of lions. After this ugly event, Patterson stood watch, set traps, and laid bait laced with strychnine. But it was in vain. The "reign of terror" continued.[18]

One night, two men were carried off from the railhead. A few days later, lions returned to the same place and absconded with two more men. One man was killed outright and eaten; the other was so badly mauled that he died after a few days of agony. Weeks passed and yet another man was seized by lions, which brought his body so close to Patterson's shelter that Patterson vividly recalled how he "could plainly hear them crunching the bones, and the sound of their dreadful purring filled the air and rang in my ears for days afterwards."[19] It would have been futile for Patterson to head into the night after the man-eater. The man was already dead, and it was too dark to hunt. Patterson lay there, trying to sleep amidst the terrible feast. Patterson was not the only one disturbed by these lions, however. Stories of the man-eaters trickled out to the media as far away as the United States. Some journalists suggested that the "terror inspired among the Indians was so great that they flung themselves on the line in the track of advancing engines, so as to leave the engineers no choice but to run over them or to transport them to Mombasa."[20]

After a series of mishaps—including a misfire when a group of Indians flushed one man-eater from a thicket with clanking cans, and a dreadful night spent alone atop a wobbly twelve-foot structure being stalked by one of the lions—Patterson finally killed the two man-eaters of Tsavo. This allowed him to finish the bridge, but it didn't eradicate the lion problem. Later, a man-eater showed up in Kimaa, 120 miles closer to Nairobi on the Uganda railroad line. Three men, Mr. Huebner, Mr. Parenti, and Mr. C. H. Ryall, were in the area and decided to address the situation. They pulled their train car onto a siding, and after an unsuccessful afternoon hunt they bedded down for the night in the train car. Ryall, who was the superintendent of police for British East Africa, took the first watch. The only notable occurrence in the first part of the evening was "what they took to be two very bright and steady glow-worms" in the darkness, a misinterpretation that would later haunt the survivors in hindsight.[21] Ryall then dozed off in the early part of his watch. Fatefully, all three men were painfully jolted from sleep when a lion slipped into the car, stepped on Parenti with its front paws, and got Ryall in his jaws. Huebner miraculously leapt over the lion's back to safety, and Parenti also wriggled away. But Ryall had no such luck, as he was carried off into the night, his mangled body found the next morning.

Roosevelt was electrified by Selous's story, and later that week he wrote Kermit at the Groton School and described the scene, letting him know that the stories of lions "so enthralled the little boys that the next evening I had to tell them a large number myself."[22] Selous's lion stories clearly enraptured the children, but the meeting had the biggest effect on Roosevelt. He immediately requested that Selous send him the articles written by Patterson in the British hunting magazine *The Field* so that he could read and reread the original narratives.[23]

Roosevelt kept up his correspondence with Selous, and his interest in African hunting continued to grow. He even encouraged Selous to continue his own writing, and penned the foreword to Selous's 1908 book *African Nature Notes and Reminiscences*.[24] So when in the spring of 1908 Roosevelt began to more seriously imagine a grand safari, he consulted Selous.[25]

"Now, can you give me some advice?" Roosevelt wrote. "A year hence I shall stop being President, and while I can not be certain of what I shall do, it may be that I can afford to devote a year to a trip in Africa, trying to get into a really good game country."[26] Roosevelt was so "hot to be on the ground" that he was having trouble focusing on his work as president.[27] He summed up his growing infatuation and goal: "In short, I want to take a trip back to the Pleistocene." Selous quickly began to provide aid, serving as trip planner and consultant for the developing expedition.[28] He sent Roosevelt maps and possible itineraries, and there was back-and-forth consultation about details of guides, food, and equipment. Selous felt that the safari should be run by Richard John "R. J." Cuninghame, a seasoned English guide, rather than by native Africans. Roosevelt initially confused Cuninghame with D. J. Cunningham, a person he understood was "gouty, infirm and corpulent." But R. J. Cuninghame was known by others as the opposite: his "short stature and otherwise slender frame are burdened with a pair of shoulders so massive in depth and breadth as to incline any one to feel sorry for his legs."[29] Roosevelt was wise to eventually accept Selous's advice. He also would have preferred to travel with his old campaign hat, but Selous suggested a helmet. Many foods from the Old World—like French plums and marmalade—were struck from Selous's lists by Roosevelt in favor of New World alternatives like California peaches and strawberry jam. In response to the listing of a tin of "Marrowfat," Roosevelt bristled: "What is Marrowfat? Can't we have Boston Baked Beans instead?"[30] Roosevelt relished the thought of returning to the staple fare from his roundup days, where in hot and dry lands canned tomatoes were "about the nicest things there were" and Boston baked beans provided a few days' sustenance if there was ever "a lack of meat."[31]

In the year leading up to the safari, Roosevelt widened his consultations on planning and equipment to include several other authorities on African hunting. Questions, answers, and materials were shuffled in and out of the White House in letters and parcels. Along with food, Roosevelt considered the finer points of bullets, colored glasses, Zeiss lenses, iron pans, enameled tableware, cameras, and "flashlights."[32] When considering his clothing, he allotted ample space to field pants and shirts, but he also consulted the lieutenant governor of the East Africa Protectorate, Frederick Jackson, on whether he should pack any more formal attire, which seemed in contrast to his cotton and canvas to be the "hideous canonical garb of civilization."[33] One of Roosevelt's main correspondents, the British politician, conservationist, and hunter Edward North Buxton, provided advice on where Roosevelt should hunt and how he should select the safari leader. Buxton patiently engaged in an extensive and literal exchange regarding selection of the Roosevelts' footwear, including boots, mosquito boots, leather stockings, and slippers. James Patterson and Sir Alfred Pease fielded Roosevelt's questions on his anticipated chase for lion. From the AMNH, Henry Fairfield Osborn sent relevant zoological books, and he also made edits to a lecture Roosevelt planned to give after the safari. Roosevelt appealed to his editor at Scribner's, Robert Bridges, to arrange for a "portfolio to contain the two dozen pads, two dozen pencils, envelopes, and carbon of a kind that will stand the rough treatment of a year's African trip."[34] Carl Akeley, the eminent collector and taxidermist who had been an early supporter of Roosevelt's safari plans, sent a camp table and a plaster head of an elephant that allowed Roosevelt an up-close examination of the best spots to place a bullet. Some hunters even made the trek to the White House to provide their perspectives in person, with Patterson and Akeley being two of the more prominent naturalists to attend Roosevelt's "African hunters" dinners there.[35]

Roosevelt was more self-sufficient in carefully planning for what he would do in the evenings. He would of course have his writing to attend to—he had signed a contract for a series of articles for *Scribner's* that would also be published as a book, which would help fund the trip—but his ravenous appetite for books was just as intense in the field as it was at home. Space was tight, however, and normal book bindings were too frail for a lengthy safari. His sister Corinne later recalled a conversation with Roosevelt about a solution.

"Theodore, I want to give you a *real* present before you go
away. What do you think you would like?" His eyes sparkled
like a child who was about to receive a specially nice toy,
and he said: "Do you really want to make me a *real* present,
Pussie? I think I should like a pigskin library." "A pigskin
library," I said, in great astonishment. "What is a pigskin
library?" He laughed, and said: "Of course, I must take a
good many books; I couldn't go anywhere, not even into
jungles in Africa without a good many books. But also, of
course, they are not very likely to last in ordinary bindings,
and so I want to have them all bound in pigskin, and I
would rather have that present than any other."[36]

The following day, Roosevelt provided Corinne with a long list of
books, of course starting with the Bible, and also including authors
like Shakespeare, Homer, Longfellow, Dante, Euripides, and Dickens. The order was sent to a bookbinder, and the resulting volumes
were wrapped in a case made of oilcloth and light aluminum in
preparation for the trip.[37]

After Roosevelt had reviewed important logistical materials
from Selous, he sent them on to his son Kermit at Groton: "I en-
close you letters from Buxton and Selous, and maps. . . . I shall not
answer them until I have consulted with you."[38] Roosevelt adopted
Kermit as his trusted partner from the earliest stages of the expedition, and he worked to orchestrate a meaningful experience
for his son. Along with involving him in the preparations, he appointed him expedition photographer and consulted with Frank
Chapman at the AMNH on the best way to help Kermit prepare
for the role.[39] There were also even more serious topics, such as
making sure Kermit understood that after this year of "holiday"
was over, he would be expected to do hard work.[40] The most serious topic of all, however, concerned the fact that their lives would
be frequently in danger during the trip.

To friends, Roosevelt laughed off the perils of hunting wild
game in Africa. He was amused by a quip in the *Public Ledger* that
it would be fitting for him to meet his end in Africa, and he even
called up the image of Mrs. Gummidge, the grumpy and naysay-
ing character in Charles Dickens's *David Copperfield*, to deflect the
specter of these dangers. He began a letter to his friend Cecil

Spring Rice: "Oh, you beloved Mrs. Gummidge! . . . I laughed until I almost cried over your sending [Edith] the pamphlet upon the 'sleeping-sickness.'"[41] And Akeley assured the public that the places Roosevelt was to visit in Africa were at least as safe as Oyster Bay, and probably safer than Chicago.[42] Others realized how dangerous African hunting could be, however, and when John T. McCutcheon, a cartoonist with the *Chicago Tribune,* covered Roosevelt in Africa, he kept "an unnecessarily large quantity of Indian rupees" with him at all times "in case anything serious happened to the colonel" and he needed to report it to the world.[43]

Roosevelt privately revealed his concerns about how his physical shape after his years in the White House related to the demands and dangers he would face in Africa. To Patterson, he worried that he was "not fit for the hard work of the genuine African explorer type."[44] To his son Ted, he observed how his friend Leonard Wood was still "built like a gorilla," and was a "horrid example to sedentary creatures" like himself.[45] Roosevelt was more direct in his self-description to Pease: "I am old and fat."[46] Even one of the primary aspects of his identity—his manliness—seemed challenged, as he felt "effeminate" and worried that he would be mistaken for a "Cook's tourist," given the relative luxury of the safari being prepared to accommodate him.[47] He was especially concerned about how the lingering effects of a leg injury he had sustained in a collision with a trolley car would heal in time for the strains of the trip.[48] He understood, however, that part of what would compensate for his physical condition was teamwork, and perhaps it was because Kermit hadn't heard Selous's lion stories in person that Roosevelt privately made sure there was no misunderstanding between them about the potential perils in Africa: "It is no child's play going after lion, elephant, rhino and buffalo," he wrote to Kermit. "We must be very cautious; we must be always ready to back one another up."[49]

To Roosevelt, backing up meant being at the ready with a good battery: "I think I shall get a double-barrelled 450 cordite, but shall expect to use almost all the time my Springfield and my 45-70 Winchester. I shall want you to have a first-class rifle, perhaps one of the powerful new model 40 or 45 caliber Winchesters. Then it may be that it would be a good thing to have a 12-bore shotgun that could be used with solid ball. Perhaps you should also have a spare rifle."[50] As he had done regarding the other aspects of equipment, Roosevelt wrote Selous and Buxton letters that serially refined his choice of weaponry. Never one to settle for secondary interactions, he also engaged the Winchester Arms Company directly, and at one point they sent a sharpshooter to visit with him and adjust their "beautiful weapons."[51] In the cold first days of 1909, Roosevelt even planned to have a shooting range installed in the attic of the White House, "such as they use in the Navy."[52]

With the logistics and equipment lists developing, Roosevelt turned to the fate of the significant number of specimens these efforts would generate. He wrote to Charles Doolittle Walcott, then the secretary of the Smithsonian Institution, to propose a joint expedition.[53] He wondered if they together could form a larger expedition that would collect a wide range of birds and small mammals alongside the large game he was planning to bag. Roosevelt could afford to foot the bill for himself and Kermit, but he wondered if Walcott could provide "one or two professional field taxidermists, field naturalists" to go along.[54] He and Kermit would of course do the shooting of the big game, but there would be far too much skinning and preparing for them to do alone. A sharp political tactician, Roosevelt closed his thoughts by introducing a bit of competition: "If the National Museum won't do anything in the matter, I may communicate with the American Museum of Natural History of New York." He ended more softly: "But of course, as ex-President, I should feel that the National Museum is the museum to which my collection should go."[55] Little more compelling was needed, and with a few taps on the typewriter Roosevelt set the stage for a massive influx of specimens to the National Museum.

One can imagine charting on a giant aerial map the origin of all of the specimens that were in the National Museum of Natural History on March 22, 1909, the day before the joint expedition left Hoboken Harbor on the SS *Hamburg*. Red lines would connect the location where each specimen was collected with a small dot a few blocks west of the US Capitol, representing the NMNH. The pattern that emerged would appear like the bent and irregular spokes of a giant bicycle wheel. Some of these lines would even evidence Roosevelt's earlier collecting, like cougars brought in from Colorado and finches from the Adirondacks. If the specimens for the next year were charted, however, the museum would appear like a vortex of natural history, with fine lines flooding small African villages and railroad stations, thicker ones flooding Mombasa and Khartoum, and throbbing lines passing through various ports on their way to warehouses in New York Harbor, where the specimens sat in wooden crates labeled with the massive and unmistakable initials "T.R."[56] Then, a final line of migration down the coast to Washington would complete a historic syzygy—like a lining up of heavenly bodies—of once-living specimens at the National Museum of Natural History.

Two weeks on the *Hamburg*, calling at the Azores, Gibraltar, and then Naples, allowed Roosevelt ample time to get acquainted with the three naturalists sent by the Smithsonian to collect and prepare specimens. Edgar A. Mearns, retired from his post as Army surgeon, carried an impressive resume of collecting, mostly of birds, undertaken on his many posts throughout the United States and the Philippines. His short stature, slight build, and mild medical manners could be deceiving: in field pursuits he was "fearless and intrepid," and might be seen systematically "slaughtering humming-birds, pursuing them from bush to bush."[57] Mearns had been recommended to Roosevelt as "the best field naturalist and collector in the United States."[58] He became known to the Africans first as "doctor," then as "the man with the big mustache," and finally as "the man who never sleeps," given his habits of nocturnal collecting.[59]

For big mammals, Edmund Heller was selected. Heller was a native of Illinois who had migrated to California as a teen. By the time he visited Roosevelt at the White House in February of 1909, he had vast field experience, having participated in expeditions to the western United States, Mexico, and Central America. He had collected in Africa two years earlier with Carl Akeley's expedition, and the previous year in Alaska on Annie Alexander's expedition with the Museum of Vertebrate Zoology.[60] Pairing his clean-shaven face (the other naturalists were mustachioed) with a dry sense of humor, Heller focused his efforts on skinning the large animals—so much so that he eventually earned the title "Bwana Engose," the "skin master," from the native Africans.[61] His task in the expedition was in some ways the largest, with the skinning and salting of massive skins that sometimes took days.

Finally, John Alden Loring, also a lifelong naturalist and a veteran of the US Biological Survey and the New York Zoological Park, was charged with the smaller animals and became known as "mouse man" to the local residents.[62] Like the other naturalists on the trip, Loring's study of nature was fueled by childlike wonder, and he even wrote books and articles on the curious habits of mammals. Like Roosevelt, he contributed articles to *St. Nicholas Magazine*, such as his "Interesting Observations of Prairie-Dogs," in the interest of shaping the minds of American boys.[63] Also like Roosevelt and the others on the expedition, Loring was dedicated to the naturalist's tradition of field notes, and he had indicated its importance to youth in his 1906 *Young Folks' Nature Field Book*, in which he left every other page of the book blank, with the heading "Notes."[64]

The information flowing out of the safari was to be tightly controlled, and Roosevelt made the general guidelines clear to his naturalists. The shooting of big game was to be done by "two rifles," Kermit's and his, and any renderings of the travels other than his own were to be delayed until after his own account was published.[65] Roosevelt found himself irritated by an "appalling proposition" from Loring, who requested permission to write while on safari. Roosevelt responded with a clear articulation that nothing could be published by others until his own articles and book were out, and he even suggested that the naturalists should be careful that their letters home were not adapted for early articles.[66]

Roosevelt's worries about how the safari would be portrayed to the public was not limited to his own naturalists; during his preparations he regularly fretted about the newspapers knowing his whereabouts, with the fear that these "enterprising apostles of sensationalism" would "be literally an intolerable nuisance."[67] In a note to Heller, he revealed the extent of his concern about how outside parties could affect his goals: "We shall be much hampered by people trying to find out our plans. . . . Please be very careful not to give a hint of any kind as to any of our movements."[68]

At Naples, the expedition transferred to the SS *Admiral*, bound for Mombasa in British East Africa. Selous was already aboard, and the band of hunter-naturalists had more than two weeks together to share their well-worn yarns. Each had something to offer, but Selous's stories were unmatched, and the men gathered to hear him tell the gripping highlights of his many years in Africa. Cutting the Indian Ocean toward Mombasa, Roosevelt wrote to Corinne of his approval of the men: "My three naturalists are trumps." They already had skins drying in his room, a nostalgic reminder of his youthful days collecting on the Nile.[69] Despite the highlights he was experiencing with Selous, Roosevelt was irked by sea voyages, but he found a way to approach the days philosophically: talking, reading, and listening to Kermit strum soothing melodies on his mandolin.[70] At least in Mearns's medically trained eyes, the Roosevelts were more than ready for what lay before them; in a letter to his mother, he wrote: "Colonel Roosevelt has been in fine fettle and Kermit is the real stuff!"[71]

The *Admiral* docked in Mombasa on April 21 as a torrential downpour came on, transforming their initial view of the city's green foliage, huge baobab trees, white houses, and ancient Spanish fort into something somewhat less scenic than it otherwise might have been.[72] The men's spirits were brightened, however, as Cuninghame—the safari's principal organizer—bounded aboard the ship with their refined itinerary, and Acting Governor Jackson welcomed them with a dinner at the Mombasa Club that evening.[73] Within hours of arriving in Africa, Roosevelt had a taste of its raw and authentic nature: he heard a firsthand account from Mr. Huebner, "one of the actors in a blood-curdling tragedy"—the same one that had been related by Colonel Patterson in *Man-Eaters of the Tsavo*. Heubner described to Roosevelt how he had watched from a bunk as a man-eating lion slipped into the railway car, stood on Parenti with his hind legs, and locked Ryall in his maw.[74]

Roosevelt had time the next day to replay this epic fable in his mind as he sat atop the cowcatcher, chugging out of Mombasa. Newspapermen were largely excluded from the safari, but Warrington Dawson, one of the few who gained direct access at points over the course of the expedition, described Roosevelt's travel: "Very special indeed, this train,—extra special, it might be called. It has special inspection carriages, it starts at a special time, it has a special seat fixed on to the cowcatcher."[75] Dawson was offered a spot next to Kermit, Frederick Selous, and Roosevelt, and he observed how they were strapped into this structure, which was like a "garden bench" with a slat of wood that protected riders from the smoke and sparks that spewed from the locomotive's engine.[76]

African Wanderings of a Hunter Naturalist 7

Naturalist.

[margin notes: Is the title all right? Would you prefer "An American Hunter Naturalist in Africa?" etc.?]

I

A Railroad through the Pleistocene.

The great world movement which began with the voyages of Columbus and Vasco di Gama, and has gone on with ever increasing rapidity and complexity until our own time, has developed along a myriad lines of interests. In no way has it been more interesting than in the way in which it has resulted in bringing into sudden, violent and intimate contact two phases of the world's life history which normally would be seperated by untold centuries of slow developments. Again and again, in the continents new to peoples of European stock, we have seen the spectacle of a high civilization all at once thrust into and superimposed upon a wilderness of savage men and savage beasts. Nowhere, and at no time, has the contrast been more strange and more striking than in British East Africa during the last dozen years.

While on safari in Africa, Roosevelt devoted significant time to writing chapters of his book *African Game Trails: An Account of the African Wanderings of an American Hunter-Naturalist*, which would first appear serially in *Scribner's Magazine*. Roosevelt sent chapters off to his editor in New York, Robert Bridges, in small batches. The first page of chapter 1 reveals that Roosevelt was still considering his title for the full book. TRC MS Am 1454.28.

Others passengers, like Loring, frequently sat further back on the roof of a train car, with the advantage of being able to see the whole horizon, and with the associated disadvantage of having cinders burn holes in his clothes.[77] The train chugged over the very bridge that Patterson had helped build on the Tsavo River—a landmark that was only a waypoint on Roosevelt's voyage to the Kapiti Plains Station, where he would begin his safari. Once he arrived there, Dawson and Selous returned to Nairobi with the train while Roosevelt and Kermit began to review the porters and equipment.

It took several days to get the safari sorted out at the Kapiti Plains Station, and Roosevelt quickly found his life on safari to be "quite a contrast to life on the round-up," as he had his own tent with a canvas floor and a cot. To the rear, he also had a tub in which he had a hot nightly bath—"a tropic necessity."[78] An American flag flew prominently above his tent as a sign of reverence by the native people who first dubbed Roosevelt "Bwana Tumbo" (portly master), and rapidly revised it to "Bwana Mkubwa" (great master).[79] Two native attendants, referred to as tent "boys," saw after his material belongings; two gun "boys" saw after his battery; and two horse "boys" made sure his transports were always fed and ready.[80] Roosevelt pulled back the heavy tent flap and observed the commotion as his equipment was packed and divided among the more than two hundred porters who would carry the load on safari. It was no easy task to keep such a large group in line, given the strenuous conditions, and it sometimes involved brutal modes of enforcement of which Roosevelt was unlikely to approve.[81]

In describing a safari to others, Roosevelt made sure they understood that in this context the term "safari" referred to one of two meanings. Here, it meant the caravan of an expedition; it could also, however, refer to the expedition itself.[82] The preparation of this caravan was a scene of purposeful chaos, much like ants gathering hundreds of irregularly shaped breadcrumbs. Boxes of scientific "impedimenta" were shuffled and sorted; tents were bundled.[83] Parcels, some knobby and some smooth, were filled with blankets, ammunition, bathtubs, canned peaches, strawberry jam, portions of the four tons of salt that was being brought to preserve specimens, and every other item that would render the men who would do the hunting both prepared and comfortable. The ox carts and wagons that served as transports for expeditions in many other parts of the world were often absent from African safaris; usually, all manner of equipment, provisions, and gear was picked up by a long line of native Africans who carried it on their heads and shoulders.

It was an amusing scene as the safari shuffled out of Kapiti. A blast came out of an antelope horn. Someone began banging on an old can that served as a drum. Others carried "queer stringed instruments."[84] Then more than two hundred people lurched forward.[85] Ahead marched the armed guards, askaris, followed by their leader, carrying a dirty white umbrella. The American flag came next. Then the long line of porters filed by. In addition to wearing a loose shirt and shorts, each porter carried a blanket and a personal article, like a worn coat. Their heads were often topped with a red fez, a form of headgear Roosevelt considered useless because it provided one with no sun protection.[86] A fez did provide for decoration, however, and many were adorned with feathers, zebra skins, and tails of squirrels. One fez was "really too intricate for description because it included the man's natural hair, some strips of skin, and an empty tin can."[87] There was no reciprocal cultural assessment: none of the porters recorded what they thought of Roosevelt's attire as he stood in his khaki trousers, army shirt, and sun helmet, periodically raising his field glasses, looking ahead of the winding string of porters, and pondering his impending journey back into human history.[88]

A massive theater of the hunt opened before Roosevelt on the Kapiti Plains. The rainy season was late, and the heat waves made it hard to judge the distance over the flat ground, which teemed with gazelles, wildebeest, and hartebeest. Roosevelt opened his game bag on April 24 with a shot at a Thompson's gazelle, which he referred to with a hunter's affection as a "Tommy" as he shot it "stone dead" at 225 yards.[89] Moving on for more desirable specimens, he singled out a bull and cow of the brindled gnu, or blue wildebeest—"creatures of queer, eccentric habits. . . . shaggy manes, heavy forequarters, and generally bovine look."[90] He shot the bull first at 400 yards, following with the cow at 350. On this day, the style of his diary entries changed. Previous pages had only single lines and mundane facts. But the lines under "April 24, 1909" erupted with descriptions, measurements, and Paleolithic-like red lilies; white flowers like narcissus

Wea.   WED. APRIL 28, 1909   Ther.

Tommies everlastingly
shaking their tails, not
Grants.

Gentle humped cattle; the two
boers; the wild natives; ostriches
mincing along.

Jessamine. sweet. Many flowers;
brilliant sun birds. Yellow
flowered mimosa, Yellow flowered
vies, Flat topped mimosa,
Euphorbia. Fig tree. Hartebeest
Out with Heller. Wildebee=
con, 250 yds, facing me; shot les
thigh face, broke neck. Zebra
mare, very large, quartering, 160
yards, between neck & shoulder.
Grants buck, 220 yds, underside shoulder,
Steynbok, 180 yds,   "   " .
Hartebeest weighed 320 lbs.
Immense herd of mixed game.
12 cartridges; smallest under for game
I have got. Barking "qua-ha" of zebra.

abt 4, quarters of hartebeest
lying down; very fine zebra

Roosevelt's first week of hunting included shots at Thompson's gazelle, brindled gnu (blue wildebeest), Grant's zebra, and hartebeest. Along with his descriptions of game, Roosevelt also recorded his observations on plants and birds.

On April 29, Roosevelt hunted lion with Sir Alfred Pease, the owner of the ranch where he stayed periodically during his safari. After Roosevelt and Kermit killed two lion cubs, they shot "the tawny, galloping form a of big maneless lion." Roosevelt made drawings of the lions in his diary, along with notes on the contents of their stomachs. TRC MS Am 1454.55 (15).

sketches as he recorded the safari in the field notes in his diary.

Two more days passed with shots at hartebeest, gazelle, and zebra. In this early part of the safari Roosevelt pondered the intriguing patterns that nature had painted on the hides of these beasts, animals he was seeing for the first time. He wondered how so many people could assume that the patterns of animals that rarely made attempts to hide could have evolved for protective coloration. Given the black and white stripes of a zebra specimen, he considered the absurdity of how some thought this pattern could be concealing. "If any man seriously regards the zebra's coloration as 'protective,' let him try the experiment of wearing a hunting suit of the zebra pattern; he will speedily be undeceived."[91] To his readers, Roosevelt pointed out how a naturalist who directly experiences nature earns a fundamental understanding of its principles. Soon, his thoughts shifted away from theoretical aspects of evolution to the dangerous game of a Pleistocene-like world.

In chasing great cats, Roosevelt knew he could change from predator to prey in an instant, with a misfire or missed glance spelling a grisly death. Roosevelt was not paralyzed by the thought of being hunted—even potential assassins who circled him in his loop tour of the American West hadn't prevented him from regularly shaking hands with thousands of strangers. However, he had no intention of tempting fate with close meetings with the paws of lions, at least not until after the lions were bagged.[92]

In Roosevelt's diary, the twenty-seventh was a "blank day after lions;" the twenty-eighth brought notes on "Tommies everlastingly shaking their tails" and on "brilliant sun birds" and "flat topped mimosa."[93] Sketched at the foot of his diary page for the twenty-ninth, however, are drawings of feline forms that document his first victory over the lords of the plains. That day, Roosevelt rode out on a lion hunt with Sir Alfred Pease, the owner of the ranch where he stayed periodically during the first several weeks of safari. Just after lunch, the dogs caught the scent of lion and, their hair bristling, led the men to a patch of bush just on the other side of a small ravine. Roosevelt fired just after he saw movement, killing a small lion cub. Almost simultaneously, Kermit shot another cub. Disappointed by having found only cubs, they pressed on. By afternoon, they locked onto the trail of two big lions. With Pease providing instructions, the group eventually gave chase and forced the lions into hiding in a patch of brush.[94] Roosevelt jumped from his horse and raised his gun in anticipation. Would the lions charge? Would they run? There was a brief pause, and then movement only thirty yards away as he saw "the tawny, galloping form of a big maneless lion."[95] His hunter's instinct allowed no additional pause:

> Crack! the Winchester spoke; and as the soft-nosed bullet ploughed forward through his flank the lion swerved so that I missed him with the second shot; but my third bullet went through the spine and forward into his chest. Down he came, sixty yards off, his hind quarters dragging, his head up, his ears back, his jaws open and lips drawn up into a prodigious snarl, as he endeavored to turn to face us. His back was broken; but of this we could not at the moment be sure, and if it had merely been grazed, he might have recovered, and then, even though dying, his charge might have done mischief. So Kermit, Sir Alfred, and I fired, almost together, into his chest. His head sank, and he died.[96]

A group of porters brought the lion skins back to camp, strapped to long poles, amidst dancing and singing—a feature of the safari that was a "weard sight" in Loring's view.[97] Roosevelt made sketches in his diary of the first big male, with a series of three bullet holes indicated in order from hind to front, and of the second lion, with only two. He added beside his drawings, as he often did, notes on the contents of the animals' stomachs.

The next day, Roosevelt lunched with Selous, a periodic visitor to the safari, but aside from accommodating a short hunt that day, he had other work to attend to. He needed to make progress on his first article for *Scribner's*, especially because he had negotiated a sizable contract.[98] Along with making notes in his diary, Roosevelt began rendering his experiences in the field for his readers as they were happening.[99] The life-and-death nature of the land conjured up dramatic words as he penned the first two paragraphs: sudden, violent, intimate, savage. He imagined the far-off woodlands, "forests of deadly luxuriance," and "great trips of exploration and adventure."[100] On May 12 Roosevelt wrote to his editor, Robert Bridges: "Here is my first article. I have had great luck; the game has come quicker than I thought."[101] He titled the article "A

THE MISSIONARY'S ESCAPE FROM THE LION.

He came on steadily—ears laid back and uttering terrific coughing grunts

Drawn by Philip R. Goodwin from photographs and from descriptions furnished by Mr. Roosevelt

As a young child, Roosevelt had been inspired by adventure narratives such as David Livingstone's *Missionary Travels and Researches in South Africa*. The dramatic figures in this book, like the image of Livingstone being mauled by a lion (A), are similar to those that Roosevelt used in his book on his safari, *African Game Trails*. Here (B), Roosevelt depicts the charge of a large male lion.

Railroad through the Pleistocene." By the twenty-third, a second article, "On an East African Ranch," was added and mailed off to Bridges in New York. Roosevelt told Bridges that he had "material for six chapters now," his use of the term "chapters" indicating the plan for the articles to be bundled into book form only shortly after his return. With these first two pieces off his wilderness "desk," he could turn his attention back to lions.

It wasn't just Patterson who had stories of man-eating; it seemed to Roosevelt that at every turn, there was evidence of maulings. In fact, the first person who met Roosevelt as he got off the boat in Mombasa bore the scars of a bad mauling. In Nairobi, Roosevelt visited the graves of seven people killed by lions. And his safari didn't escape these ravages; at one point several members were mauled, and Dr. Mearns could only save one of them.[102] There was no question in Roosevelt's mind that in Africa "the lion was lord and that his reign was cruel."[103] It wasn't long before he was scratching out a third installment for *Scribner's*: "Lion Hunting on the Kapiti Plains."

After five weeks of hunting, Edmund Heller knelt amidst an array of bones as he organized the first batch of specimens for shipment.[104] They were the fruits of a large loop out from the Kapiti Plains Station and round to Nairobi. Heller gazed forward over the stinking skulls of warthog, giraffe, gazelle, and hartebeest lined up on the ground. Behind him lay disarticulated skeletons sorted into individual heaps. The skinning and sorting was exhausting work; large animals like rhinos sometimes took days to process. At times during the safari, Heller could be found "suffering from a bad case of 'rhinocerositis,'" showing little patience for the birds and small furry creatures that Mearns and Loring were adding to the haul.[105]

As the safari continued, it fell into a pattern it would follow throughout the remainder of the expedition, moving among field camps and farms between periodic trips to Nairobi.[106] The hunters spent several weeks "on safari" in the Mua Hills hunting lions, and then lodged for a week at Juja Farm. Even when they stayed at ranches and farms they kept hunting, their game bag filling with "Lion, Leopard, Hyena, Rhino, Hippo, Giraffe, Eland, Zebra, Waterhog, and various kinds of Antelope."[107] Then they marched to

In morning killed 2 bull buffalo; one surely mine; one probably Kermit but first; I finished it. Got 3d bull in swamp; shot about heart.

Why dah birds; dance; cut off grass with their bills, put down, dead, trodden down grass; will erect clump in centre; 14 ft. will wings out spread; in early a.m. males zig behind; new flock; flies.

head back

The African buffalo ranked high on Roosevelt's list of the most dangerous game to hunt. Given its size and unpredictable nature, it was difficult to bring down. While hunting buffalo on the plains west of Nairobi in May 1909, Roosevelt also paid attention to the dance of the whydah bird.

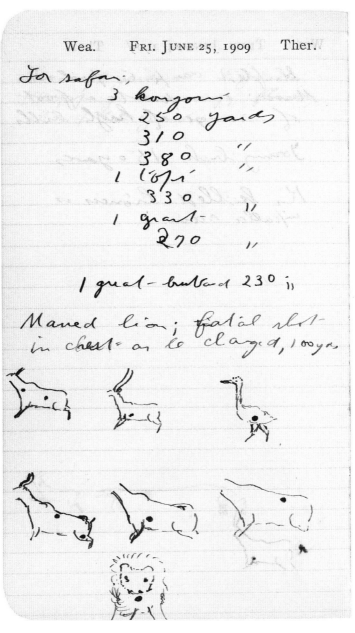

For safari;
  3 kongoni
    250 yards
    310
    380   "
  1 topi
    330   "
  1 grant   "
    270   "

1 grant-bustard 230 "

Maned lion; fatal shot
in chest- as he charged, 100 yds

Roosevelt spent much of June on safari in the Sotik, a capital hunting ground in the plains east of Nairobi near the Guaso Nyero River. While there, he reveled in some of the best hunting of his entire trip. In his notes for June 25, he continued his practice of carefully documenting exactly where his bullets struck the animals he shot. He took particular note of a "fatal shot in chest" of a lion, taken as it charged him, and he included a telling sketch. TRC MS Am 1454.55 (15).

Kamiti Ranch for another week, and after several days in Nairobi to send off specimens, they departed again on safari. The next loop began southward through a dry and desolate wasteland, known as "the thirst," which would lead them to the Sotik, a plentiful hunting ground on a limestone plateau.

"The thirst" was a three-day obstacle of grass and dust. The men and the oxen took a last drink of water on June 1, and by 12:30 p.m. the safari moved south. As night fell, the party halted for a dinner of bread and cold meat; it was off again by 8:30. And so it went. At midnight, the travelers stopped. At 3 a.m. the horns blew and they rose and walked on. By 7 a.m., it was time for another rest. The travel at night—illuminated by the moon and the Southern Cross—was the most pleasant. Baked and tired, the safari eventually reached the relative oasis of the Guaso Nyero River. Mearns and Loring set up a collecting outpost, and the Roosevelts and Heller began four weeks of wandering on the trail of big game.

The Sotik provided some of the best hunting and most romantic safari travel of the entire trip. After the difficult walk across the thirst, this "luxurious" safari life offered warm days and cool nights. Roosevelt reported to home that he and his party had experienced no hardships; he was "in burly health."[108] He even questioned whether with "tent boys" waiting on him, he "was having rather more luxury than was good for" him.[109] The Sotik teemed with game, and the hunters' prodigious collecting came to a head when within three days they collected three rhinos and six antelope—evidence that the Roosevelts' rifles "tended to get ahead of the taxed resources of the naturalists."[110] The never-ending flow of specimens made Mearns feel that his work would never be finished, but at this point Roosevelt took a brief respite from hunting in which he could write letters and polish off more articles. Despite the idyllic conditions, worries crept in.[111]

Roosevelt had watched his son Kermit grow from a timid boy into a manly and confident hunter. On the safari, Kermit's aim was improving by the day, and he was proving himself an excellent rider. But Roosevelt found him reckless and bold. He wrote to Corinne that although Kermit had shot a large rhino—"he was as cool as if it had been a rabbit"— he didn't fully understand the danger.[112] Their regular encounters with the graves of people killed by animals seemed to have no effect on him; the maimed and crippled men they saw gave him no pause. In exasperation, Roosevelt wrote to Corinne that "since I have been out here twelve men have been killed or mauled by Lions, and, naturally, when Kermit shows a reckless indifference to consequences when hunting them, I feel like beating him."[113]

Even though Roosevelt often found his writing a source of enjoyment, it too was challenging on safari. The conditions and his fatigue made it "not always easy to write in the field."[114] He fretted over the questions all writers confront: Were the chapters too short or long? Were the breaks between chapters "natural?"[115] Ultimately, he pondered quality: "I think they are good, but of course I can't judge."[116] Sometimes he simply couldn't face the writing, and instead took solace in selections from his pigskin library.

As it moved northward to Lake Naivasha in search of hippos, the safari literally took a page from one of David Livingstone's adventures in *Missionary Travels*. Roosevelt knew that he and his companions had already collected much of the range of specimens they wanted for this species, but he needed a good bull to complete the series. Livingstone's woodcut *Boat Capsized by a Hippopotamus Robbed of Her Young* encapsulates aspects of a dangerous experience Roosevelt would have at the lake.[117] In this image, a large hippo rears up below a long boat, with men flailing and diving over the sides. It is easy to underestimate the ferocity and power of these animals as they placidly munch water lilies, filling their huge jaws like buckets. A better cue is taken from the dominance struggles between powerfully muscled males. Hippos are mysterious, too: they slowly submerge themselves in the murky water of lakes and swamps, periodically breaking the water's surface with their eyes and nostrils for a breath, only to slowly descend and lurk somewhere below.

On July 15 the Roosevelts stood in a small rowboat, straining to discern the details of a hippo on the shore. The rowers pulled their small vessel closer as they watched the animal step into the water to bask briefly among the water lilies. After a few moments the hippo came back into full view as it crunched over the crusty papyrus on shore. Was it a bull? It was full and stout and it looked like one. Pulling the boat to within one hundred yards, Roosevelt

BOAT CAPSIZED BY AN HIPPOPOTAMUS ROBBED OF HER YOUNG.

Charged straight for the boat with open jaws, bent on mischief
Drawn by Philip R. Goodwin from photographs and from descriptions furnished by Mr. Roosevelt

(A) Hippopotamuses are extremely dangerous to hunt, given that they can remain submerged for long periods of time, can surface directly below a boat, and are powerful enough to capsize a small craft. Such an image, entitled "Boat Capsized by a Hippopotamus Robbed of Her Young," had been included in Livingstone's *Missionary Travels*. (B) Roosevelt immortalized his own experience of a hippo charge in his book *African Game Trails*, which included a color drawing by Philip R. Goodwin.

fired a shot, and the bullet pierced the animal's shoulder. In agony, the huge hippo spun toward the water and flung itself in, splashing and bobbing toward the boat. As it came nearer, Roosevelt fired again and again, hoping to stop its erratic charge. Kermit watched through his jiggling viewfinder, snapping photographs that he hoped would immortalize the adventure for *Scribner's*. Nearing the boat, the hippo opened its jaws so wide that it appeared to onlookers as though it might actually swallow the small rowboat.[118] Roosevelt fired directly into the hippo's mouth, which snapped shut with "the clash of a sprung bear trap."[119] The animal went still, the ripples on the water attenuated. The lake was placid again. Of course another hippo could be submerged anywhere, but for the moment the danger had passed.

After the excitement, there was again disappointment. As the hunters attached ropes to the hippo's body and dragged it behind the boat toward shore, it became clear that the animal was a cow. Heller had a full day's work of skinning ahead of him. Dawson looked on with perverse amusement as he watched the porters yell and jump upon noticing leeches on their legs, and lose their footing on the slippery mud before falling into the water.[120] Exhausted, and feeling the onset of one of the periodic recurrences of his Cuban fever—malaria—Roosevelt spent the next several days resting.

Although the men knew he had been ill, Roosevelt's absence at dinner on July 20 caused concern among the members of the party. He had been seen heading out on a hippo hunt earlier that day. There was little of the usual levity at the meal, given the unknown status of their leader; the dinner of mud duck and hedgehog being even more "reciprocally reminiscent of mud and hedges" than it would have been otherwise.[121] Dawson was back with the safari and joined the meal, but he had a hard time hearing Loring and Mearns describe all of the unpalatable items that they had removed from the guts of the animals they were consuming.[122]

At six o'clock the next morning, Dawson's tent boy shook him awake. For one of the few reporters who had found a way to penetrate the safari, such an early summoning was ominous. Roosevelt had kept a strict press ban, but Dawson had been slowly brought into the fold to assist Roosevelt in letter writing and press matters. With whatever clothing he could grab, Dawson stumbled out of his tent to find Ali, Roosevelt's tent boy, looking very grave. As they ran toward Roosevelt's tent, he breathlessly asked Ali if Bwana Mkubwa had had an accident. "No; no accident," he said. "Bwana Mkubwa kill *minge kiboko*." The boss had killed many hippos.

A remorseful Roosevelt sat in his tent, showing signs of "sleeplessness and exhaustion." He had returned only three hours earlier, and as Dawson entered, he said: "Warrington, a most awful thing has happened. And I didn't intend to. Ali has told you?" He recounted to Dawson an unintended slaughter that had taken place on the previous day, when he was out looking for his bull hippo. He had been alone in a rowboat with two native Africans when a school of hippos surrounded the boat. The Africans were frightened, and they had urged Roosevelt to shoot. Drawing a bead on one hippo he thought was a bull, he fired, and the hippo sank. A miss? Roosevelt fired at another large head, but it seemed that this shot was also a miss. Suddenly, an unsettling jolt came from under the small boat, and he knew that a hippo was surfacing directly beneath them. Was this a Livingstone moment? Amid splashing and shouting, Roosevelt blindly fired a burst of bullets into the water in hopes of scaring the whole group of hippos away. Then silence. After several minutes passed, a rounded form slowly broke over the surface of the water. With the appearance of this gray hulking mass, the hunters' sense of danger began to change into the satisfaction of a successful hunt. They fixed ropes to the animal and began slowly dragging it to shore. But then another form appeared—and another, and yet another. Roosevelt's gun had been far too effective. What was he doing? What would he tell the press? This would do nothing to convince them that the "great deal of game" he had collected was not in fact the result of a game-slaughtering expedition.[123] He entered only spartan field notes on his diary page for that day. Below "5 hippo" he scrawled simple lines for the nose, head, and ears of each animal; bullet holes were marked with dark black circles.[124]

Another brief pause in the safari followed, in which Roosevelt was able to recover from the hippo mishap. He attended to his writing and went to Nairobi to give a speech on education. Kermit participated in the festivities of Nairobi's "race week," a festival of "cricket matches, tennis tournaments, concerts, amateur theatricals, dances, and dinner parties" in addition to horse races;[125] he rode happily on "poor horses, generally near the tail of the procession."[126] Then, as the safari headed northward and upward to Mount Kenya for elephant, Roosevelt began to worry that his long litany of hunting stories would begin to bore his audience, especially general readers.[127] However, the elephant hunt brought him new excitement and insights.

While trudging up the approach to Mount Kenya, Heller scurried after mice and shrews while Roosevelt eyed old elephant tracks. At this point in the safari, Roosevelt pondered the placement of the elephant on his scale of natural history superlatives, and he determined that, on the basis of its enormous bulk, the value of its ivory, and its intelligence, it was, "not only to hunters, but to naturalists, and to all people who possess any curiosity about wild creatures and the wild life of nature, the most interesting of all animals."[128] It certainly ranked with the lion and the buffalo as the most dangerous of African animals as well.

With periodic glimpses of the snowy peaks of Mount Kenya, the elephant hunters hacked through dense forests of tree ferns and giant figs. Black-and-white monkeys swung in the trees, their long hair trailing as it protected them from the cool temperatures. The fine spines of urticating stems stung the hunters' hands as they pushed through drenched foliage and climbed over massive downed tree trunks. In and among the tangled foliage that carpeted the forest floor, the hunters found cracked limbs, tracks, and droppings—elephant spoor—that provided evidence that they were getting close to "the great lord of the forest."[129]

After another twist in the winding trail, Roosevelt caught a glimpse of a pair of massive white tusks resting on a branch. He started to close the thirty yards that separated him from the massive beast, but then paused and evaluated the potential specimen. The elephant's tusks were certainly large enough. Roosevelt then made out features that assured him that the animal was a bull. He raised his gun and sighted the elephant's right eye, after which he moved his trajectory slightly to the left in hopes of finding the elephant's intelligent, but very small, brain. The rifle spoke and the bullet struck the head, but the bull only stumbled. Roosevelt again sighted the brain, and this time he hit his mark. The great animal fell with the sounds of a towering tree: rustling leaves, cracking

In July, Roosevelt and his entourage traveled to Lake Naivasha to hunt hippo. After taking a shot from a small rowboat at a cow hippo on shore, the angry and wounded animal bounded into the water toward his boat. As the hippo came closer, Roosevelt shot repeatedly at the animal, with one of his bullets entering its open mouth, which then snapped shut like "the clash of a sprung bear trap."

5 hippo.

The simplicity and relative silence of Roosevelt's diary entry for July 20 at Lake Navaisha underscores a somber occurrence. Roosevelt went out in hopes of finally getting a bull hippo to complete his collection. A school of hippos surfaced all around his small boat, and the other men in the boat encouraged him to shoot to scare them away. At one point the boat began to rise: a massive hippo was surfacing beneath them, threatening to overturn the craft. Roosevelt shot repeatedly in the splashing confusion. After the water settled, he sadly realized that he had killed five hippos. TRC MS Am 1454.55 (15).

branches, and then a massive thud. But there was no time to celebrate: a loud sound came crashing through the foliage as another
huge elephant tramped toward Roosevelt, coming so close that he
could almost touch its tusks and trunk as it passed by. Roosevelt's
brush with death was seemingly over before it started. He threaded
his way through the tangled growth and, finally next to the great
animal, he put his hands on its still warm hide. A feeling of pride
welled up inside him.

"Then, chattering like monkeys, and as happy as possible, all,
porters, gun-bearers, and 'Ndorobo alike, began the work of skinning and cutting up the quarry."[130] The camp was ecstatic to be
in such meat. Heller oversaw the carving, and soon "they were
all splashed with blood from head to foot."[131] One tracker even
stripped down and climbed inside the carcass to better slice strips
of meat for his meal.

The stars gleamed brightly that night as the elephant hunters
gnawed and chewed on the delectable game. Roosevelt recorded
how he connected with this primal experience of the hunter, em-
bracing a Pleistocene-like meal: "I toasted slices of elephant's heart
on a pronged stick before the fire, and found it delicious; for I
was hungry, and the night was cold. We talked of our success and
exulted over it, and made our plans for the morrow; and then we
turned in under our blankets for another night's sleep."[132] The
meal was a ritual communion of eating the flesh of the conquered
that followed cultural and religious traditions that Roosevelt considered primitive and advanced. In consuming meat from this
beast, Roosevelt found both nourishment and strength. In the
morning Heller returned to the cadaver: he faced more days of
bloody work to get the skin and bones in shape for shipment while
Roosevelt was off for more elephant. After this, Rooosevelt spent
three months tracking eland, rhino, giraffe, and lion in N'gouga
Crater, Guaso Nyero, and Naivahsa; and then, just before Christmas, he headed by boat across Lake Victoria to Uganda.

Relatively few points of reference from the outside world penetrated Roosevelt's safari life. There was at least some attention to
the calendar, as there was a passing observance in camp as Roosevelt turned fifty-one in October. In November, Roosevelt received
a telegram that stated: "Reported here you have been killed. Mrs.
Roosevelt worried." Roosevelt replied: "I think I might answer that

by saying that the report is premature."[133] John T. McCutcheon, a journalist who was traveling with Carl Akeley's safari—a group that had happened upon Roosevelt's safari and hunted elephant with them on the Uasin Gishu Plateau in November—documented in his diary that Roosevelt's party was "jolly" and that Roosevelt in fact was in "great form."[134] Then, Christmas Day came and went as they tramped into Uganda with only a modest observance of the holiday; there was little point to a large celebration without the "hopping expectancy" of little children awaiting their stockings and gifts.[135] Newspapers were completely absent from the first two months of the safari, and afterwards much of Roosevelt's interaction with current events took place through letters. He was certainly interested in weighing in on things like the veracity of Robert Peary's claim about reaching the North Pole. After all, Peary had visited him in Oyster Bay on his ship, named the *Roosevelt*, before his quest. He had also sent the Roosevelt family treasures like fox skins and narwhal horns, and Roosevelt considered him a "national asset."[136] Peary had even cabled Roosevelt while he was in Africa: "Your farewell was a royal mascot. The Pole is ours."[137] Even then, Roosevelt fashioned himself as a naturalist explorer and hoped to someday add geographical exploration to his adventures. Roosevelt also found himself being sucked into intellectual debates, such as what he perceived as the absurdity of former Harvard University President Charles Eliot selecting "the list" of books for his forthcoming *Dr. Eliot's Five Foot Shelf* (later the fifty-one-volume *Harvard Classics*). Roosevelt had little tolerance for those who attempted to determine a finite list of the world's best books.[138] What about the selections in the pigskin library that were absent from Eliot's list?

Aside from being a commentator on current events, Roosevelt was an event unto himself. His distance and isolation from the United States fueled speculation on his future in politics. He tried throughout the trip to fend off the rumors as best he could: "Of course I shan't make a prediction of any kind about my future. . . . The chances are infinitesimal that I shall ever go back into public life, but it would be the height of folly even to talk of the subject in any way. My destiny at present is to shoot rhino and lions, and I hope ultimately elephant."[139] As Roosevelt's return to the United States came closer, though, more and more people wondered

In October of 1909, as the safari processed toward the Uasin Gishu Plateau, Roosevelt worked to fill the remaining holes in his collection, hunting giraffes and oryx.

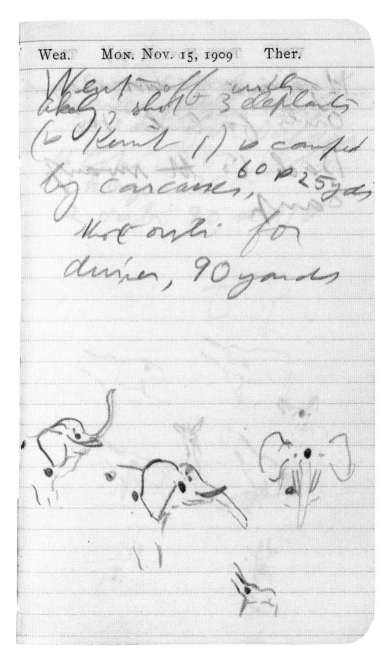

Went off with
likely shot 3 elephants
(6 "Kent 1) & camped
by carcasses, 60 & 25 yds;
shot oribi for
dinner, 90 yards

After having hunted elephants on Mount Kenya in August, Roosevelt collected additional specimens on the Uasin Gishu Plateau in November. Afterwards, he and his party "camped by carcasses." TRC MS Am 1454.55 (15).

During the African safari, Roosevelt encountered the eminent collector and taxidermist Carl Akeley. After a hyena got itself caught inside the abdomen of a prize elephant specimen the expedition was preparing, Roosevelt captured the scene with his camera. In turn, Akeley photographed Roosevelt. TRC 560.61-111.

about his intentions. He made it clear that any reception for his return should not be political in nature, but instead should be open to everyone. In his mind, however, the door for another run for the presidency was clearly still open. After all, his public statement that he would not run again was not really a "promise."[140]

In the first days of 1910, the expedition traded hooves and footsteps for the meandering and peaceful pace of a natural history flotilla that consisted of "a crazy little steam launch, two sail-boats, and two big row-boats."[141] The hunters floated past distant foothills that obscured the Congo forest, and through the crocodile-filled streams that fed Lake Albert. Finally they descended northward into the White Nile. Roosevelt pawed through his pigskin library, past the small copy of *Nibelungenlied* that bore a dark blood stain from a puff adder—it had been stowed with a specimen in his saddlebag one day—and settled on Poe's *Tales*.[142] The story "Silence," set by the river Zaire, brought Roosevelt close to the scene he was experiencing, and he used Poe's words to begin the next chapter of his adventure, "The Great Rhinoceros of the Lado." Although to many readers the outcome of this hunt made this "dreary" and "ghastly" literary reference fitting, the landing at Lado was beautiful: "herons, flocks of beautiful white egrets, clamorous spur-winged plover, sacred ibis, noisy purple ibis, saddle-billed storks, and lily trotters."[143] Fish eagles, snakebirds, eagle owls, and kingfishers squealed and swooped in the air. Most amazingly, the aerial dances of nightjars with their foot-long tail feathers provided a lush zoological backdrop as Roosevelt explored the Lado, a small enclave on the west bank of the White Nile, north of Lake Albert. It was here they went looking for the rare square-mouthed—"sometimes miscalled, the white"—rhinoceros.[144]

By this point there were few new things to collect; Roosevelt had already shot representatives of virtually all of the African mega-fauna. But the white rhino was an exception, and although lions and elephants had been at the top of his list of the animals he most wanted to shoot, the white rhino had been in his sights since the early days of the safari as the "great prize of the trip from the zoological standpoint."[145] Roosevelt had intimated to Buxton that he would "accept the certainty of fever" for the chance to bag a white rhino, and had looked forward to following in the footsteps of Winston Churchill in doing so.[146]

The casual observer could miss the apparent differences between the white and black rhinos. The white is on average larger, has a differently shaped mouth, and has a large hump on its back. Roosevelt knew that these rare rhinos were absent in natural populations from southern Africa, and that only a few poorly known populations existed in the region he was exploring. From a conservation perspective, Roosevelt felt that "it would certainly be well if all killing of it were prohibited until careful inquiry has been made as to its numbers and exact distribution."[147] However, the enthusiastic hunter and collector in Roosevelt overruled the conservationist.[148] As when he had chased his first buffalo in the Badlands, he wanted to make sure that he hunted the white rhino before it was gone—this time in the name of the United States and science. Here he sidestepped the obvious conservation issue and focused on providing specimens to the NMNH and AMNH,

(10-355)

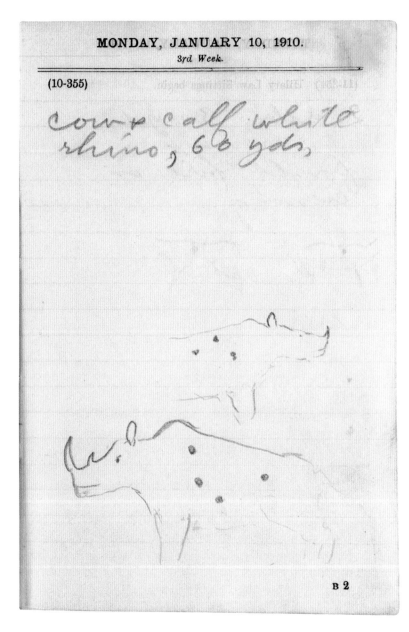

cow + calf white
rhino; 6 0 yds,

B 2

After crossing Lake Albert and heading down the White Nile on what amounted to a small natural history flotilla, Roosevelt stopped to hunt the square-lipped, or "white," rhino in the Lado. A rare and endangered species at the time, Roosevelt recognized its fragile status but still collected specimens for several museums in the United States. Edmund Heller, the mammalogist on the safari from the Smithsonian Institution, used these specimens for a thorough study and description of the species.

(22-343)

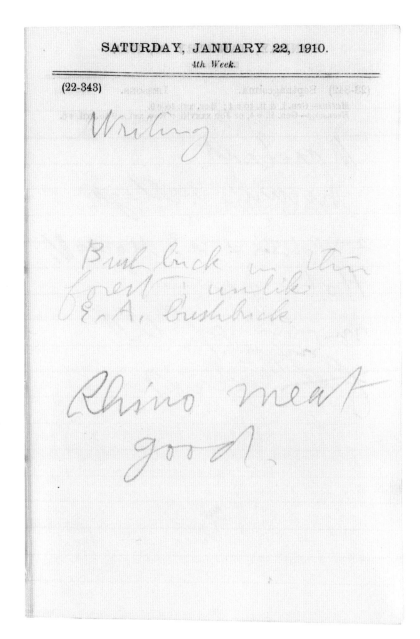

Writing

Bush buck in the forest — unlike E. A. bushbuck.

Rhino meat good.

Throughout the safari, Roosevelt hunted animals both for specimens and to keep the roughly two hundred porters and attendants "in meat." In Lado, Roosevelt described a delicious meal, revealing how his psyche, at least, had traveled back in time: "Rhino meat good." TRC MS Am 1454.55 (16), TRB, TRCDS.

as well as a head to the Heads and Horns Collection at the Bronx Zoological Park.[149]

Roosevelt and his party found their first white rhino sleeping like "an enormous pig."[150] When it sensed their approach it sat up on its front feet like a dog; Roosevelt's Holland bullet pierced into its chest. Four other rhinos scattered; Kermit shot another bull, while Roosevelt hit a calf. As usual, Heller descended with his team to take to the grim task of getting the skins. Stench and flies soon followed. These massive specimens required a full thirty-six hours to prepare, and on the second night the meat attracted a group of lions that circled the camp in the darkness, hoping for an easy meal. So the three weeks of rhino hunting continued: more bulls, cows, and calves. Roosevelt's mind was still deeply immersed in the world of early humans while in the Lado. A diary account Roosevelt wrote after a particularly good meal seemed to reveal a president-turned-caveman: "Rhino meat good."[151] Well satiated, and with their collections complete, the hunters boarded their makeshift flotilla and continued to float down the White Nile.

The white rhino hunt was the culmination of an expedition Roosevelt had envisioned for years, in which he collected thousands of specimens and explored diverse habitats, all the while recording his observations in field notes. He was also completing his rendering of the trip in what would eventually be published as *African Game Trails*, a volume he would add not only to his own burgeoning list of books, but also to the long-standing literature in which white naturalists and hunters recounted their safaris.[152] Like many of the hunts recounted in those stories, Roosevelt's hunting in Africa was motivated by diverse forces—and in his descriptions of his hunting more generally, Roosevelt had provided multiple justifications for his love of the hunt.[153] Before leaving for Africa, he had done his best to distinguish himself from the "game butchers" he so reviled, who went to Africa only to get heads for their walls.[154] Other authors, like William J. Long, would make no such distinction between Roosevelt and those other hunters.[155] However, there would be trophies from the safari; Roosevelt considered his house "small," and had described how it had contained so many animal heads as to look "too much like a taxidermist's shop" before he had cleared many of the heads away to make room for the specimens from the safari.[156] As the results of the safari became permanently wedged between his love of the hunt and his dedication to conservation and natural history, Roosevelt focused his attention on the scientific value of the specimens that would be lodged in museums throughout the United States.[157]

There was little flourish or closure as Roosevelt's safari ended in Khartoum. In the last words of *African Game Trails*, Roosevelt would leave his readers with a marginal discussion of whether liquor should be consumed in the tropics, remarking that his own consumption over the eleven months of the safari was a mere six ounces. He penned a foreword to the book, opining about "the joy of wandering through lonely lands; the joy of hunting the mighty and terrible lords of the wilderness."[158] Roosevelt's accounts, although sometimes dramatic, weren't as sensational as other accounts of his adventures that were being prepared at the time, which described his "thrilling, exciting, daring and dangerous exploits" and his "miraculous adventures and wonderful feats with his rifle."[159] Although *African Game Trails* was not the most spectacular account of Roosevelt's trip, it was favorably reviewed.[160] The conundrum of Roosevelt's enthusiastic and bloody pursuits in Africa lingered, however, and a "Rhymed Review" of the book framed this problem for posterity:

> I read the Nibelungenlied,
> Euripides and scraps of Pickwick,
> Bestrode again my gallant steed
> And slew a melancholy Dik-wik.
>
> How slow and tame a life! Methinks
> No more the Elephant I'll mangle.
> I guess I'll go and ask the Sphinx
> About this Conservation wrangle.[161]

Meanwhile, despite the contradictions implicit in the hunt and how it was rendered, Roosevelt had now reached Khartoum, at the arid convergence of the Blue and White Nile Rivers, having completed another loop in his cycles of adventure.

Edith was waiting for him in Khartoum, and now that the safari was over he traveled with her to Thebes and the Great Pyramid,

While hunting black rhinos early in the safari, Roosevelt also shot a "greater bustard." TRC.

retracing the steps he had taken as a child.[162] Then he spent April and May sightseeing, making speeches, and doing diplomacy in Naples, Rome, Vienna, Budapest, Paris, Berlin, Oslo (for his long-overdue Nobel Prize speech), and London. Roosevelt had written his major speeches well before he had left, and in the one he gave at the Sorbonne—often referred to as his "Man in the Arena" speech—he began by returning to his earlier frontier narratives, describing how conquering the wilderness meant "to wrest victory from the same hostile forces with which mankind struggled in the immemorial infancy of our race."[163] Now, after the "Pleistocene" experiences he had gained in his many months blasting away in

Britain's African empire, these words delivered in visits to European powers reinforced Roosevelt's reputation as an imperialist.[164] And, despite his long absence from active politics, he was quickly pulled back into his role as a public figure.[165] Finally, after a week at sea, he entered New York harbor on June 18 aboard the SS *Kaiserin Auguste Victoria*.

As the ship rounded Sandy Hook through the early morning mist into New York Harbor, Roosevelt began another dramatic reemergence from the field. The scene conjured up an image Dawson had described, of Roosevelt emerging from the Sotik onto the shores of Lake Navaisha as a "conquering hero coming" out of the wilderness.[166] Roosevelt's appearance also had elements of his earlier return to the United States from Cuba: he was the much-loved figure coming home after a dangerous adventure, and there was intrigue as to his future plans. Many in the crowd that gathered at the harbor's edge were hoping that he would run again for political office. But the most striking aspect of this new scene was its magnitude. On Iron Pier at Montauk in August of 1898, the crowd of people who had come to see Roosevelt and the other Rough Riders return from Cuba had been measured in the hundreds. But this return from Africa was different. Roosevelt hadn't even passed the blue-clad sailors who lined the decks of torpedo boats and destroyers that stood at attention in the harbor—boats that Roosevelt himself had had built—before those numbers were reached. The battleship *South Carolina* thundered a twenty-one-gun salute. Roosevelt strode from the *Kaiserin Auguste Victoria* onto the cutter *Manhattan* to greet his family, and then onto another cutter, the *Androscoggin*, for the slow procession to shore. He scaled the *Androscoggin*'s pilothouse and stood waving and bowing to the crowds as he neared Pier A. In the crowd there was no mistaking that this was a time to celebrate Roosevelt and Roosevelt alone. One man sarcastically quipped, "Who is this Roosevelt, anyhow?" Swiftly and forcefully, he was shoved into the water.[167]

Roosevelt made a few brief remarks at Battery Park, and then gave a yell to the 144 Rough Riders who had come to lead his parade. They and the two horses affixed to his open carriage clopped forward shortly before noon, beginning the parade route up Broadway. There was a jog up Fourth Avenue to Washington

Square, and then up Fifth Avenue toward Central Park. The press struggled to find hyperbole fit to describe the scene. To a reporter from the *Detroit Free Press*, it seemed that "all the sirens and whistles and automobile horns and brass bands and throats in the entire world burst loose." The *Chicago Daily Tribune* chimed in: "A solid yell traveled with him. . . . The bandsmen might have ceased from tooting, for none heard their toots as the colonel passed. Here was two hours of uninterrupted cheering from five miles of humanity." *The Washington Post* added: "Everything imaginable was waved alow and aloft. Whirls of descending ticker tape . . . filled the air with spirals." Were there a million in attendance? Half again as many? The papers couldn't agree.[168]

Each person in the crowd had a different story of how and why they had come to see Roosevelt. No stories, however, were more dramatic than those of Temple and Louis Abernathy. The sons of "Catch 'Em Alive" Jack Abernathy of coyote-catching fame, the two boys, ages six and ten, had ridden alone on horseback all the way from Oklahoma to welcome Roosevelt home.[169] Ultimately, the Abernathy boys joined the rest of the frenzied crowd in viewing the conflicted icon of leadership, hunting, conservation, and adventure that Roosevelt had become.

Just over two years later, Roosevelt was embroiled in another presidential campaign.[170] Despite considerable internal support, the Republican Party bosses had engineered the nomination for William Howard Taft, so Roosevelt formed his own Progressive Party, which came to also be known as the "Bull Moose Party." It was looking as though Roosevelt would split the Republican vote with Taft and thus hand the presidency to Woodrow Wilson, the Democratic candidate—but he was still campaigning hard. On the evening of October 14, 1912, Roosevelt emerged from the Gilpatrick Hotel in Milwaukee, heading for the car that would take him to the Milwaukee Auditorium, where he would make his speech. The weather was cool, and he wore a thick military overcoat. As Roosevelt stepped into the roofless car and stood, this normal scene gave no indication to him that a set of objects—two bodies, a bullet, an eyeglass case, and a folded stack of paper—were beginning a historic alignment, a vile syzygy that would test what some viewed as Roosevelt's inflated persona as a war hero and manly hunter.

Pushing briskly through the crowd toward Roosevelt was a red-haired man with a slightly puffy face. His name was John Schrank. He was a New York bartender who had been following Roosevelt through eight states, over two thousand miles, for his chance at this moment. Now only six feet from his target, he aimed his .38 caliber revolver at Roosevelt's chest and took a shot. Roosevelt stumbled. Elbert Martin, his stenographer and an ex-football player, wrestled Schrank to the ground. Righting himself, Roosevelt displayed a strange tenderness as he called to Martin and the other men who were preparing to pummel and strangle Schrank: "Don't hurt him. Bring him here. I want to look at him."[171]

After taking in Schrank's disturbed countenance, Roosevelt slipped his hand inside his coat and pulled it out bloody. It was clear that the bullet had gone well into his chest. But he refused his attendants' calls to go to the hospital to have the wound dressed. He insisted instead that they head straight to the auditorium.

The crowd in the building buzzed with nervous energy and rumors. As Roosevelt took the stage, his spoken words diverged from the remarks he had prepared.

> Friends, I shall ask you to be as quiet as possible. . . . I
> don't know whether you fully understand that I have just
> been shot, but it takes more than that to kill a bull moose.
> (Cheers.) But fortunately I had my manuscript, so you see I
> was going to make a long speech (holds up manuscript with
> bullet hole) and there is a bullet—there is where the bullet
> went through and it probably saved me from it going into
> my heart. The bullet is in me now, so that I can not make a
> very long speech, but I will try my best.[172]

Roosevelt proceeded to speak for more than an hour, at one point pulling open his jacket to reveal a stain of blood that covered much of his shirt.[173] "I give you my word. I do not care a rap about being shot not a rap."

Possibly the most extreme of Roosevelt's extremes, his response to this assassination attempt was telling to those who believed that Roosevelt the hunter and soldier was a mollycoddled pretender, a man who had fashioned his Western image in New York photographic studios, or a Brooks Brothers Brahmin who loved to play tough guy. Today, one could explain his decision to continue with the speech as a mixture of delirium and underlying psychology. But in action, Roosevelt showed that he was willing to pay with his body and continue his fight, just like the Rough Riders who had fallen into stinking trenches next to him. If he had backed away from this challenge, what would he have told his fellow veterans?[174] When Frederick Selous sent Roosevelt a worried note several days after the assassination attempt, Roosevelt expressed a similar sentiment:

> I could not help being a little amused by your statement that my "magnificent behavior, splendid pluck and great constitutional strength have made a great impression." Come, come, old elephant hunter and lion hunter! Down at the bottom of your heart you must have a better perspective of my behavior after being shot. Modern civilisation, indeed I suppose all civilisation, is rather soft; and I suppose the average political orator, or indeed the average sedentary broker or banker or business man or professional man, especially if elderly, is much overcome by being shot or meeting with some other similar accident, and feels very sorry for himself and thinks that he has met with an unparalleled misfortune; but the average soldier or sailor in a campaign or battle, even the average miner or deep-sea fisherman or fireman or policeman, and of course the average hunter of dangerous game, would treat both my accident and my behavior after the accident as entirely matter of course. It was nothing like as nerve-shattering as your experience with the elephant that nearly got you or as your experience with more than one lion and more than one buffalo. The injury itself was not as serious as your injury the time that the old four bore gun was loaded twice over by mistake; and as other injuries you received in the hunting field.[175]

In Roosevelt's view, men of the field saw the world differently. They had come to understand the cycle of nature and the Darwinian struggle for survival through direct experience, and its painful and malicious course did not surprise them. They expected, and embraced, its painful and bloody reality.

To the Amazon

Even making a dramatic speech with a bullet recently lodged in his chest was not enough to secure the 1912 election for Roosevelt and his Bull Moose Party. Shortly before midnight on election day—Tuesday, November 5—Roosevelt set a few more logs ablaze in the fireplace of his study at Sagamore Hill. In just a few minutes, a group of reporters would file into the room to hear his remarks. As the first of them arrived, he finished sending a terse telegram to Woodrow Wilson to concede defeat: "The American people, by a great plurality, have conferred upon you the highest honor in their gift. I congratulate you thereon."[1] Roosevelt put on his best face for the press, and after only a bit of chatting he ushered them out with the assurance that he was taking defeat in stride and that he would be in his office at *The Outlook* on Friday.

Roosevelt had been using his position as contributing editor at *The Outlook* to have his ideas, mostly political, heard for the past four years.[2] So as he began to recover from his electoral defeat, he took solace in his writing. There was of course plenty of healing to do, as not only had damage been done to his ego and his body; his relationships also suffered. It had been an election of Republican Party chaos, and Roosevelt's characteristic vigor and fight had lost him more than a few friends. In the cold December evenings he returned from his office to Sagamore Hill and trudged through wet snow down to the bay, catching sight of the black and white forms of buffleheads and mergansers bobbing up and down on the water. His thoughts turned to the past, and he lumbered back up the hill to his study to begin work on his *Autobiography*. By late February his childhood reminiscences, the first of his "Chapters of a Possible Autobiography," had already appeared in *The Outlook*.[3] A single book project wasn't enough to consume Roosevelt, how-ever, and he was also working on a massive tome, *Life-Histories of*

African Game Animals, with Edmund Heller.[4] As summer came, he fell back into his well-worn pattern of following bouts of politics by escaping to the wilderness, and he was off for a cougar hunt on the rim of the Grand Canyon with Archie and Quentin. And as he added three chapters on these Southwestern adventures to his workload for *The Outlook*, his attention began gravitating toward a more substantial adventure further south.[5]

South America—the land of explorers like Charles Darwin and Alexander von Humboldt—was still teeming with untold stories of nature in 1913. Roosevelt's small tastes of Cuba and Panama had only whetted his appetite for the neotropics, and since Kermit was living and working in Brazil, it seemed an opportune time to explore the region. And, as from most places, Roosevelt was receiving invitations to give lectures there. As he considered a potential trip, his African safari served him as a template: it had been a fusion of father-son exploration, museum collecting, natural history writing, and public appearances, all supported by a massive infrastructure of material and logistical support by native peoples. These elements began to align again in Roosevelt's mind, and this time he hoped to explore the rivers of central South America and Amazonia.

An offbeat and slightly stooped priest named Father John Augustine Zahm had been hounding Roosevelt for years to join him in a South American expedition.[6] When Roosevelt began to seriously consider such a trip, he scheduled a lunch with Frank Chapman, the eminent ornithologist at the AMNH, to discuss possibilities for a collaborative venture. To Roosevelt's surprise, Zahm had already been in touch with Chapman and showed up at the meal. Zahm had plenty of pluck and enthusiasm to compliment his fatherly demeanor. Before the check arrived at the table, Zahm had wiggled himself into Roosevelt's developing expedition.[7] At its conception, the idea was a relatively tame float-and-shoot on the Paraguay and Tapajos rivers, a joint expedition that would collect bird and mammal specimens for the AMNH. Chapman began to assemble the team of scientists who would support Roosevelt in his collecting efforts, and Zahm focused his attention on logistics.

As these preparations began to churn in 1913, other explorers were also preparing expeditions. While Roosevelt contemplated the jungles of South America, the British explorer Ernest Shackleton was looking much farther south. In 1909, Shackleton had led an expedition that traveled to the furthest point south ever reached by explorers, less than one hundred miles shy of the South Pole. Not long after that, the Norwegian explorer Roald Amundsen reached the South Pole and claimed that prize for Norway. Looking for unachieved feats he could still claim for England, Shackleton considered a bold trip across the entire continent of Antarctica, which some felt would be "the most daring journey ever undertaken by man."[8] In the contemplation phase of any such expedition, careful planning is essential and, most importantly, success rests on the brave people entrusted to envision, equip, and execute it. An often reprinted piece of lore that has endured about the Shackleton expedition includes a claim that Shackleton took out an advertisement in a British newspaper that read: "Men wanted: For hazardous journey. Small wages, bitter cold, long months of complete darkness, constant danger, safe return doubtful. Honour and recognition in case of success."[9] Whether or not Shackleton actually articulated this sentiment as he chose his men, it should have been heeded by anyone considering a serious exploring expedition at the turn of the twentieth century. It was even more relevant to the Roosevelt expedition than to Shackleton's; despite the fact that Shackleton's ship, the *Endurance*, became stuck in an ice floe and was eventually crushed, leaving the men casting about the Antarctic, dodging icebergs, and hiding under lifeboats, everyone who set off in the *Endurance* returned home alive. Roosevelt's expedition could make no such claim.

In planning the South American expedition, Roosevelt began the preparations with his African playbook. He would write about his adventures along the way, sending a series of articles to Scribner's that would be published in their magazine and then in book form. He had enlisted a museum man, this time Chapman, to provide legitimacy and to support aspects of natural history collecting. Chapman did his job well by choosing two excellent naturalists. George Cherrie was approaching fifty, with graying hair and a weathered face that advertised the years he had spent accumulating vast experience in the New World tropics. On more than twenty-five trips to Central and South America, he had collected thousands of specimens, mostly birds, for museums throughout

the world. Chapman also chose an up-and-coming AMNH naturalist named Leo Miller to accompany Cherrie and attend to mammals. Despite his slicked back hair and boyish face, Miller was a
tenacious collector, ready to begin to make a major contribution to
the museum. As competent field men, collectors, and, most of all,
excellent zoologists, Cherrie and Miller were similar to the naturalist team of Heller, Loring, and Mearns, from Roosevelt's African
adventure. But when he turned to logistics, Roosevelt anointed
Zahm to deal with the nuts-and-bolts aspects of gear and travel.
And Zahm was no Frederick Selous.

After Roosevelt had enlisted Selous in his arrangements for
Africa, Selous in turn had chosen R. J. Cuninghame for on-the-
ground logistics.[10] Like Selous, Cuninghame had decades of experience in organizing safaris in East Africa: he knew exactly what to
pack, where to go, and with whom to interact. Zahm, on the other
hand, had only spent a few tourist trips in South America and had
never done any serious exploring. With Roosevelt's attention occupied by political affairs and his hunt in Arizona, however, the job of
equipping the expedition fell almost exclusively to Zahm—at least,
that is, until Zahm was rummaging through the sporting goods
section of Rogers Peet Company in New York, where he "fell in"
with an employee who seemed to have the kind of experience that
would help him equip Roosevelt's trip.[11] This man was Anthony
Fiala, a former polar explorer who, after hearing about Roosevelt's
expedition, said to Zahm, "I would give anything in the world to
go with you." Zahm replied, "Come along . . . I am sure Colonel
Roosevelt will be glad to have you as a member of the expedition."
Zahm left Fiala to deal with the details of equipment with what
he assumed would be "rare intelligence and dispatch." But Zahm
didn't quite grasp that Fiala wasn't exactly a respected explorer—
nor did he understand that Fiala's conception of the needs of tropical exploration came only from Zahm's own meager insights.[12]

Despite shaky foundations, the Roosevelt expedition moved forward. With an ambiguous itinerary and countless boxes filled with
equipment and stores, Roosevelt joined Cherrie, Fiala, Zahm, and
Jacob Sigg, an ex-Army nurse and cook who would travel as Zahm's
attendant, on the SS *Vandyck* as they left New York Harbor on October 4. They were bound for a short stop in Barbados, where they

were to pick up Miller, who was waiting to join what he understood would be "a rather short and not too difficult trip up the Paraguay River and down the Tapajos, having its prime object the study of the fauna and collection of zoological specimens."[13] The same day the *Vandyck* left New York, Brazilian officials were also preparing for the arrival of Roosevelt and his team.

Colonel Candido Mariano da Silva Rondon had just returned from inspecting a remote section of telegraph line when he received an urgent telegram from the Brazilian minister of foreign affairs, Lauro Müller, asking him to participate in Roosevelt's expedition. Not much past five feet tall, with bronze skin that revealed his native heritage, Rondon was a veteran leader of the Brazilian Strategic Telegraph Commission, which was working to string a telephone line across Brazil. His carefully groomed white mustache stood out against his dark skin, a stark contrast that symbolized his reputation for exacting and strict leadership. Müller's message to Rondon was clear: he wanted him to provide Roosevelt with every assistance in his upcoming expedition. Rondon immediately snapped into action. With a military appreciation of contingencies, Rondon arranged for canoes to be prepared on several possible routes that the expedition might take. Shortly after that, however, he learned that Roosevelt intended to take the Tapajos and Arinos Rivers, a course that he felt "could not offer anything new to an Expedition whose object was to unravel the unknown aspects of our wilds."[14] He promptly sent off a set of options to Müller that could be presented to Roosevelt for consideration. He was sure to indicate that the alternative with the "greatest unforeseen difficulties," and of course the greatest possible rewards, was the route down the Rio da Duvida.[15] Rondon was not without his own motives: he had discovered the Duvida on one of his own previous expeditions.[16] He had even given it its ominous name, translated "River of Doubt," due to its uncertain course out of the Brazilian Highlands and into the unknown of the Amazon basin.

When the *Vandyck* arrived in Rio de Janeiro, Roosevelt met with Müller in person and was quick to accept the opportunity to descend the Duvida, feeling that the "trip could be made of much scientific value, and that substantial addition could be made to the geographical knowledge of one of the least-known parts of South America."[17] Whether the expedition primarily involved collecting or exploring was not of primary concern to Roosevelt; his underlying motive was to take to the field. Cherrie and Miller used few words to record in their journals what proved to be a monumental change in plans, but one can only imagine their thoughts about the shift from a natural history expedition to a more geographical one.[18] Back in New York, Chapman did not hide his reservations about this change to a much more dangerous journey. But in reply Roosevelt quipped: "If it is necessary for me to leave my bones in South America, I am quite ready to do so."[19] He did acknowledge that on such an expedition the men would have a "horribly uncomfortable time," but to him it still seemed "a feat worth doing."[20] Not easily deterred, especially at such a distance, Roosevelt continued with the new plan with the full support of the Brazilians. In Rio de Janeiro, Cherrie was handed a letter that instructed all military and civilian personnel in Brazil to provide every form of assistance that the members of the expedition would need.[21] Ultimately, Roosevelt was confident that they would be successful. After discussing the potential perils in a letter to Henry Cabot Lodge, he assured him: "But I am inclined to think we shall come through all right."[22]

Roosevelt left Rio de Janeiro for a six-week speaking tour in major cities throughout Brazil, Argentina, Uruguay, and Chile on topics like "American Internationalism" and "Democratic Ideals."[23] Meanwhile, the other expedition members looped around on the *Vandyck* to Buenos Aires, after which they started up the Paraguay River toward Corumba, at the foot of the Brazilian Highlands, where they would reconvene around Christmas.

While Fiala, Zahm, and Sigg waited for a freight boat to bring the expedition's "rather appalling amount of luggage" up the Parana to the town of Asuncion, where the Paraguay River begins, Cherrie and Miller took the railroad overland to Asuncion so that they could immediately begin collecting.[24] Cherrie exclaimed, "At last real collecting has begun," as he and Miller began to revel in the naturalists' paradise surrounding Asuncion.[25] They investigated the teeming bird life, "vivacious tanagers, creepers, and finches," and paid special attention to the transformation of the white ani.[26] The gorgeous turquoise eggs of this species were covered with a "lace-work deposit of calcareous material" that, when cracked by the emerging hatchling, revealed what Miller dubbed the "ugliest creature imaginable."[27] Their eyes turned from the air

Friday 7 Nov 1913   { Gran Hotel del Paraguay
                     { Asunción, Paraguay.

Today, this morning, I tried to begin our collecting and succeeded in getting seven birds representing five species. I took my gun and went out above the hotel where there are a couple of vacant lots. Birds were not abundant and what there were, were wary. I might however have added a few more specimens to what I had if the police had not interfeared! and asked me not to shoot any more within the city limits.

Asunción
Tram. Light & Power Co.
67½ Cts.
Este boleto será entregado al Inspector, cada vez que sea exigido. En su defecto pagará por el viaje, el doble de su valor.
Série 4
59190

D No. 40251
Intransferible
REGRES...
T. V. M
$ 1.00

Two samples of the street car tickets one is expected to hold as long as they continue on board a car.

Miller and I went out to Trinidad (a suburb of Asunción) today at 11 A.M. as guests of Prof. Fiebrig of the Colegio Nacional. He had invited us to lunch. Their home is at what was formerly an (Prof. Fiebrig has a wife) agricultural experiment station. It is a fine large estate, the house on a slight elevation that overlooks the surrounding country including the city of Asunción. Tomorrow Miller and I will go as Prof. Fiebrig's guests to remain for three or four days collecting.

George Cherrie, a seasoned neotropical ornithologist, was one of two naturalists selected to accompany Roosevelt on his expedition to South America. Cherrie kept a detailed journal throughout the trip. As he continued collecting specimens into late November 1913, he took notes and eventually recognized that the expedition was not well organized or prepared. By permission of the Department of Ornithology Archives, American Museum of Natural History.

to the water as Miller became fascinated with the piranhas that quietly schooled beneath the water's surface. An inquisitive scientist, he wondered why at certain times piranhas swarmed and devoured animals, including humans, and at others left them alone. He fished with raw meat—which the fish eagerly devoured—and then moved on to throwing large specimens he had collected, like skinned monkeys, into the water. They, too, were eaten directly. Interestingly, however, stunned piranhas and unplucked birds were not devoured. Even Miller himself became part of the experiment as a piranha chomped a piece out of his fingers as he washed his hands in the river. In the evenings, the naturalists took shelter beneath their net-covered hammocks, carefully discerning the subtle differences of pitch in the sounds of different biting insects. The angry sounds that surrounded them were "not unlike the sound produced by a swarm of enraged bees."[28] There were ten days of sweltering and blissful collecting in the areas surrounding Asuncion; Cherrie collected more than 150 birds, and Miller 50 mammals.[29] Unfortunately, the work of the naturalists then began to slowly descend in the priorities of the trip; instead, the efforts of the expedition members would often be focused on survival.

After a trip up the Paraguay River on the SS *Asuncion*, Cherrie and his contingent arrived in Corumba. To a seasoned tropical explorer it was already clear that there were major problems with the preparations for this expedition. Cherrie railed on the planning in his journal: "I have not written anything about the organization of our expedition, but now I'm going to record my opinion that a greater lack of organization seems hardly possible!"[30]

December still provided Cherrie with some good collecting in Corumba—his count of bird skins topped five hundred, and he began to have trouble adding new species to his list—but already the expedition was changing. Rondon had met Roosevelt in Ascuncion on the twelvth, and they steamed up the Paraguay; the whole expedition group gathered in Corumba on the sixteenth. Once there, Roosevelt went off with Rondon for just over a week's jaguar hunt. But upon arriving back in Corumba at 5 p.m. on the twenty-fourth, he was ready to move ahead with what had become the expedition's main purpose.

Roosevelt anxiously paced the dock where the riverboat *Nyoac* was moored on this night before Christmas.[31] His emotions had nothing to do with stockings or presents; he simply wanted to get moving. In response, Cherrie and Fiala got a "hustle on," placing all manner of gear and supplies aboard the boat.[32] At the same time, Kermit was frantically developing the last photographs he would bundle with Roosevelt's article, "A Jaguar-Hunt on the Taquary" in the outgoing mail to New York. There was a particularly nice photograph of Roosevelt kneeling next to his first jaguar, his left hand on his rifle and his right holding the jaguar's head in his lap. These images simply had to be included. Finally, at 10 p.m., the photographs were finished and the supplies were in order. The *Nyoac*'s whistle echoed out over the river as the full cast of the expedition left Corumba. As sun reemerged over the treetops on Christmas morning, they were well on their way in the ascent of the Paraguay and Sepotuba Rivers to the port of Tapirapuan, where they would begin the 375-mile overland journey to the headwaters of their unknown river.

After a few stops to beat for jaguars and hunt deer, peccaries, tapirs, and monkeys, the expedition reached Tapirapuan on January 16, meeting a somewhat wild scene of 180 pack animals—mules and oxen—that Rondon had arranged for the expedition's use.[33] It was no simple task to whip this terrestrial transport into shape. In Rondon's words, the "organization and expedition of the various lots of this baggage train, with a cargo of 360 large packages, besides many other smaller ones, took five days of incessant toil."[34]

Up to this point the trip had been relatively leisurely. But now they reached their first major challenge as they left Tapirapuan and started to scale and cross the Brazilian Highlands. Covering a vast expanse on the eastern half of South America, its northern slopes descending into the Amazon Basin, this massive geological formation constituted an expansive plateau that the expedition needed to cross. Roosevelt remarked how it was an intriguing and almost endless pastureland, with grasshoppers that seemed the size of sparrows, spiders that seemed to float in midair, and vampire bats that came out when the sun disappeared over the horizon. On this slow and grinding crossing, the men would hunker down in their tents at night and engage in the age-old tradition of explorers: storytelling. Fiala spun tales of long polar nights in which he was quietly stalked by polar bears. Roosevelt dipped into his vast repertoire of African tales. But Cherrie had by far the most extensive experience of the Americas, and his stories brought to life the spirits that lurked in neotropical jungles. It helped his presentation that, along with his status as a professional and proficient scientific collector, he also harbored a belief in the supernatural. His stories riveted the men as he conjured up not only the real-life dangers of the jungle, but also ghosts and werewolves, beneath the blanket of the dark South American night.[35]

As the days of plodding through the scrubland wore on, several motor wagons from the Telegaph Lines Commission passed by, carrying some of the expedition's baggage. Father Zahm, seeing an opportunity to be freed from the uncomfortable mules, convinced Roosevelt that he should join the motorcade. Cherrie and Miller also hitched a ride to more quickly reach Utiariy, their next stop, and have more time to collect.

While in camp on January 27, Roosevelt plunked himself down in his folding chair, placed his writing pad on a simple folding table, and began to write his account of the first part of the overland journey, "Through the Highland Wilderness of Western Brazil." On that day he told Rondon that the title of the expedition had officially changed. It was no longer "Colonel Roosevelt's South American Expedition for the American Museum of Natural History." He had adopted the "Roosevelt-Rondon Scientific Expedition," the title printed on the crates of equipment Rondon had brought with him.[36] Although Roosevelt outwardly supported his collaborators, he was not entirely happy with the expedition's progress. His published account of the march over the plateau only acknowledged the hardships of overland travel. Privately, however, he told a different story, of how seriously the expedition began to shed equipment and people only shortly after leaving Tapirapuan.

After he returned from the expedition, Roosevelt wrote a letter to John Keltie at the Royal Geographical Society to make sure he knew "the truth" about the overland part of the trip.[37] After leaving Tapirapuan, the mule train quickly began to break down under the weight of the equipment. The first pieces of equipment jettisoned were some of the extremely heavy tents Rondon had brought along. Even though the mules and oxen were clearly overburdened, Rondon did not want Roosevelt and his men to dismount so that the animals could carry supplies. Confidentially, Roosevelt attributed this poor decision to Rondon's "Latin-American mind"—a signpost of Roosevelt's complicated views on race. Despite Rondon's assurances that he had packed everything necessary for the trip, Roosevelt realized that several loads of rations had been left behind in favor of more splendorous items like a silver appointed saddle and bridle meant for Roosevelt's use. There was blame to go around, however: others in the party had already pointed out problems created by the inept planning of Zahm and Fiala.

In spite of the beautiful and interesting things they encountered upon arriving at the village of Utiarity—a thundering waterfall and a group of Pareci Indians playing an intriguing game of "head ball"—it was clear to Roosevelt that he needed to make significant personnel changes to preserve some possibility of the expedition's success. On the block was Father Zahm. To his readers, Roosevelt described his decision offhandedly: "From here Father Zahm returned to Tapirapoan, accompanied by Sigg."[38] Cherrie, however, penned a more honest assessment in his journal: "Dr. Zahm had gotten much on 'T.R.'s' nerves!"[39]

It wasn't just that Zahm had exhibited his frailty by insisting on riding in the motor trucks for much of the overland journey's first leg. As he looked toward a more difficult journey from Utiarity to the headwaters of the River of Doubt, he had been trying to arrange for a team of Pareci to carry him "across the wilderness on a chair fastened to two long rods which would serve to keep it upright and at the same time rest on the shoulders of four men."[40] Met with protests, Zahm argued that in Peru, carrying a member of the clergy in this manner was considered an honor. Rondon, himself of indigenous blood, saw Zahm as absurd. Unfortunately for Zahm, every other member of the expedition agreed with Rondon. Each signed his name beneath a statement that it was "essential to the success and well being of the expedition that Father Zahm should at once leave it and return to the settled country."[41]

Roosevelt also orchestrated a further division of the expedition. He had already arranged for a split with the naturalists when they reached the headwaters of the Duvida, with Miller heading down the Gy-Parana River, and Cherrie staying with Roosevelt. But the day after they left Utiarity, Roosevelt told Fiala that he would not be on the descent of the Duvida either, but would explore the course of the Papagio River instead.[42] The winnowing of the expedition

Utiarity
Feb. 1st 1914

Every member of the expedition has told me that in his opinion it is essential to the success and well being of the expedition that Father Zahm should at once leave it and return to the ~~coast~~ settled country ~~civilization~~

Theodore Roosevelt

The above statement is correct —

Leo E. Miller

Candido M. S. Rondon
J. S. Lyra
José A. Cajazeira.
Euzebio Paulo de Oliveira

Geo K. Cherrie
Jacob Sigg
Anthy Fiala
Kermit Roosevelt

was apparent to all, and Cherrie remarked in his journal: "Of the North Americans only four of our original party are left!"[43]

As Fiala, the now teary-eyed former polar explorer, turned back, an expedition with ironic parallels was developing elsewhere.[44] Crackling over the wireless telegraph from England to the remote Marconi Station on Cape Cod, special to *The New York Times*, came Shackleton's announcement of the men who would carry out his Antarctic expedition.[45] He had picked people like Frank Wild, a veteran explorer who had proven himself on three other daring polar expeditions. Wild had the kind of grit and fortitude that would eventually allow Shackleton to entrust him to remain stranded indefinitely on a desolate Antarctic island in charge of twenty-one men. Meanwhile, Roosevelt sat waterlogged on a sagging mule, thinking about Fiala and Zahm and wishing that he had chosen better. At this point in the journey, however, he had no conception of how much further the problems with his crew would descend.

Fiala wasn't all the expedition left behind as it continued its overland voyage to the headwaters of the Duvida. Also left were the boat motor with its fuel, and many zoological and anthropological collections to be sent back to the United States. Every remaining member of the party looked over his equipment and discarded all but the most important items. Even so, the pack train was overtaxed, and the expedition periodically left a suffering mule behind, its bones soon to join the bleached skeletons that littered the remote telegraph line—grim reminders of previous hardships. Many of the trails were so slick that the men and mules perilously slopped along. Game was scarce, but unfortunately more miniature wildlife was abundant. Various species of biting insects circled everything with hair, and stingless bees swarmed the men's eyes. The agitated explorers cursed the small black flies, or "Pium (blackflies)" as a

---

(FACING) After a difficult overland journey across the Brazilian Highlands, where many pack animals and much equipment was left behind, Roosevelt decided that to preserve any chance of success, more equipment and personnel would have to be cut. Father John Augustine Zahm, an aged priest who had been an early proponent of the expedition, was sent back to "the settled country" after he tried to convince members of the native Pareci people to carry him on their shoulders in a chair for the remaining overland journey. Roosevelt recorded this action in a hastily written document, signed by him and the other memebers of the expedition. Kermit and Belle Roosevelt Papers, Library of Congress.

Throughout Roosevelt's voyage leading to the River of Doubt and down its rocky and meandering path, he wrote about his adventures for *Scribner's*. As he had done in Africa, he sent his manuscript back in sections; it was published serially in the magazine, and then in book form under the title *Through the Brazilian Wilderness*. Writing in the neotropical forests challenged Roosevelt, as he was pestered by all manner of biting insects. He used "fly dope" for the first time in his life, and covered himself in long sleeves and pants, a head net, and gauntlets as he sat down to write at a folding table. TRC.

"perfect torment that one cannot get away from."[46] Despite the relentless pests, Cherrie still collected birds new to science, and Roosevelt took to his writing, pulling a mosquito net over his hat and covering his entire body with clothing. Even his hands were covered by leather gauntlets, with long, fringed covers well up his arm, as he worked to provide an intimate view of the expedition to his readers in *Scribner's*.

Less than a week after Fiala's departure, ominous news found the Roosevelt-Rondon party. On Fiala's first day out, his canoe had capsized in the rapids and he had almost drowned. As Roosevelt's party reached the small streams that fed into the Duvida on February 25, Miller prepared to break off to explore the Gy-Parana.[47] Rations were divided further, decreasing the stores that were already low. Roosevelt and his team finally arrived at the first navigable section of the Duvida and prepared their boats. In the back of their minds, they all hoped they could avoid a fate similar to Fiala's.

Miller snapped a photograph as Roosevelt's dugout canoe rushed away from the shore and down the River of Doubt.[48] It was February 27. A paddler was standing in the rear of the canoe, keeping it in the center of the swollen river, away from the scraggly branches that reached out from the shore. Although the expedition had purged equipment several times, the remaining cargo pulled the gunwales of the canoes perilously close to the water line. Roosevelt's significant experience in navigating small craft—college crew on the Charles River, rowing in Oyster Bay, and canoeing the Mattawamkeag in Maine—told him of the peril. The boats were not ideal: "One was small, one was cranky, and two were old, waterlogged, and leaky. The other three were good."[49] Given that no other boats were available, however, the Roosevelt-Rondon Expedition began its exploration of the Duvida with seven dugout canoes and twenty-two men. Roosevelt took the lead, exuding all the confidence he could muster.

The main aim of the expedition was now the mapping of the river, and Kermit's canoe floated ahead of the others with a sighting pole.[50] Rondon's team followed behind, with a telemeter and compass to record measurements. The first day was grueling, with Kermit landing on the bank more than one hundred times to set up measurements amid all manner of biting and stinging insects. Given the slow pace of work, the travelers made just over nine kilometers. But they pushed on through three more days of slow travel before they came to their first rapids. The roiling water stretched out for almost a mile, and there was no way the primitive boats could run them. The only option was to pull the boats from the water and portage.

The camaradas—Rondon's men—first carried the heavy gear downstream, chopping a crude path as they went, and then dragged the boats over the uneven ground past the rapids. Placing a long line of logs ahead of the boats as rollers, the men heaved and pushed the boats past the rapids for three days. Here the battle with insects became even more dogged. No longer was Roosevelt brushing aside the "slight tickling" of the small stingless bees.[51] With the numbers and diversity of these insects, his skin began to crawl, and it often swelled noticeably; the itching was intolerable. Roosevelt finally reached into his kit for a bottle of "fly dope,"

Roosevelt's son Kermit, his right-hand man on the Brazilian expedition as he had been in Africa, kept a detailed diary throughout the trip. As the men of the expedition loaded their canoes and descended "into the unknown" on February 27, 1914, Kermit made observations on natural history. Kermit and Belle Roosevelt Papers, Library of Congress.

which in all his field travels he had never needed to use before, and applied it to his skin.[52] Other insects, such as termites, took aim at the men's clothing, and Cherrie's poncho was munched out from under him while he slept.[53] Finally, after almost three days of slow terrestrial movement around the rapids, the explorers were back underway.

Late the next day, they found themselves at the start of a sequence of three more rapids. Again they hauled their heavy gear from the canoes and carried it and their boats downriver, a process taking several more days. This time the unladen canoes could run the rapids. On March 10 there was another small set of rapids, but that night all the men went to bed exhausted, for a hard and oblivious sleep in the muggy forest air.

Cherrie began his journal entry for March 11 with: "'Broken Canoes' Rapids.' This morning our first serious <u>misfortune</u> faces us!"[54] During the night, the river had swelled and pulled the two large and waterlogged canoes into the river, where they ran down and were smashed to pieces on rocks. For any explorers who depend on boats for survival—whether in surveying a Brazilian river or in navigating Antarctic ice—seeing a boat reduced to splinters by roiling water is a depressing event. Deep in the Brazilian wilderness, now down to five canoes, the men of the Roosevelt-Rondon Expedition faced just such an experience. With no other options, they turned to the disheartening task of sizing up tree trunks in the forest to find the raw material for a new canoe.

For more than three days, the bronze-bodied camaradas chopped and scraped, employing axe and adze to carve out the long tree they had selected for their new dugout. Once the canoe was finally finished, they immediately loaded it with gear and headed downstream.

The extremely slow progress of the first two weeks of travel brought hard realities to the fore. Just like the animals that lived in the lush but merciless jungle, Roosevelt and his men had to weigh risks and make decisions based on an assessment of energy and time. Starvation was a real possibility, but any time spent hunting and foraging increased their exposure to other hardships. The decision to make an arduous portage that taxed the men's energy and brought them additional exposure to insects and injury was weighed against the risk of running the canoes through rough waters. Just past the "broken canoes' rapids," they approached another rapids and decided that they couldn't face another portage. They decided to take the chance of running them. Although they had to furiously bail water from the canoes, their gamble paid off and they safely made it to the calm water beyond the rapids.

When the morning of the fifteenth dawned, however, luck was no longer running with the expedition. Rondon could see the telltale signs of rapids coming up, and he pulled his canoe off to the edge of the river. He signaled to the leading boat, which carried Kermit and two *canoeiros*, João and Simplicio, to do the

10 Mch 1914 (Camp 9)

The two last of the canoes are dragged around the last carry of "8th of March Rapids" and our outfit and supplies are loaded by noon. ¶ Our present camp is only about a mile below the last, on the right bank of the river. However it is below another series of three rapids. We get out and walk around all. The cargoes are removed and carried around the first and third but the loaded canoes run the second. Seeing the men run third rapids in the empty canoes was quite exciting. The smaller of the two "balsas" was run but sank and would have been lost but for the boatmen springing into the water and towing it ashore. The two old canoes forming the second balsa were carefully passed near the shore and down below the rapids

11 Mch 1914 Camp 9 "Broken canoes Rapids"

This morning our first serious misfortune faced us! The two old big canoes forming the larger of the two balsas broke away last night and are smashed on the rocks! There is nothing for us to do but stop and build one or two new canoes. That means time and the eating into our limited supply of provisions! ¶ Evening. A suitable tree was soon found, and felled. Eight meters was measured off from the base, for the canoe and work has gone on satisfactorily. It is too early to predict but it looks as though the work might be finished

On March 11, 1914, the expedition met with its first major setback when Roosevelt and his men realized that during the previous night, two of their dugout canoes had been carried away as the river swelled over its banks. The canoes were smashed on rocks downstream, and the men promptly searched the forest for a suitable tree that could be fashioned into a new boat. Cherrie recorded the event in his journal. By permission of the Department of Ornithology Archives, American Museum of Natural History.

same. Accounts differ on why Kermit's boat moved out into the river—Kermit may have simply disregarded Rondon's order—but after stopping briefly at a small island, it was caught in a strong current and it shot down the rapids.[55] The men made it to the foot of the rapids wthout falling out of the boat, but the boat was slowly sinking below the surface. As the men attempted to reach the shore, the canoe was sucked into a swirling eddy and it capsized. João jumped in and tried to tow the boat to shore, but could not. Simplicio disappeared into the water. Kermit grabbed his gun, his favorite Winchester from Africa, and attempted to keep his balance atop the boat as it continued to sink. The boat sank to the bottom and was lost. Kermit was pulled into the water as well, but he was able to fight his way up from the rocky bottom and struggle his way to shore on the side of the river where Rondon had stopped. Dripping and cold, he looked across to the other bank where he saw a man going ashore. He assumed that the two other men had survived. Kermit met an angry Rondon as he was tramping back to where the other canoes had stopped, hearing him bark: "Well, you have had a splendid bath, eh?"[56] Reaching the rest of the party, Kermit found João, but no Simplicio. While the others, still upstream, unloaded their canoes and prepared to portage, Kermit went downstream to search for Simplicio, but could not find any trace of him. He attempted a meager salvage operation, swimming back into the river to rescue a box of food and a paddle still floating on the water's surface. With the recognition that Simplicio was lost, the men made a humble memorial—a simple wooden sign—and also mourned the loss of another canoe and its contents: ten days' rations, one rifle, and a set of boatbuilding tools. All the men had known the risks of the expedition, and there was no use in brooding. Cherrie spent the latter part of the day collecting. He and Roosevelt eagerly examined the crop of a black and white hawk he had shot, carefully noting its unusual diet of seeds and insects.[57]

No one died the next day, March 16, but it was equally "dark and gloomy."[58] It began with evidence of hostile Indians. Rondon had been out along the trail when he heard his dog, Lobo, yelping. Once he caught up with the dog, he found it dead, its body penetrated by two arrows. Knowing that he had not yet befriended these Indians, Rondon shuddered to think what would have happened if he and not his dog had been in the lead. Soon the expedition lost another canoe as the men attempted to coax it down the rapids. Precious rope and tackle were also lost. These unfortunate events necessitated more sober calculations. The explorers had used a third of their food, but had only traveled a fifth or less of their planned distance. Only four canoes remained, not nearly enough to carry the crew of twenty-one men and the remaining gear. Either the expedition could make camp in hostile territory to fashion more canoes, or it could proceed with most of the men threading their way along the shore on foot. The men chose the latter.

As Roosevelt and Cherrie set off in the canoes with six camaradas, the remaining thirteen men walked along the shore. It was another moment of equipment purging. The last of the big tents were left behind, along with some of the heavy surveying equipment. After two days of mostly walking, the expedition had cleared several rapids. Feeling better about the threat from Indians, the men stopped to begin work on two new canoes, smaller and lighter than the one they had built previously. Once they were finished, they continued to pass the "uninterrupted succession of rapids."[59] They were very tolerant of risk; they bathed in the waters even when they knew piranhas were swimming about their bodies.

Roosevelt was experiencing the hardships of the field in a new way. This was nothing like Africa, where game was abundant and he could keep the whole caravan in meat with his rifle. In this neotropical forest, he did occasionally catch a glimpse of tapirs in the river downstream, but the animals were too far away to warrant a chase. Far from the speed he could achieve over an open plain on horseback, every step in this forest was laborious, and the game was simply much faster than Roosevelt and his men. They could of course stop for several days, to attempt to hunt and kill a large animal, but there was no way to avoid the cost incurred by any time spent hunting. As Roosevelt turned to the unforgiving river, he realized that this trip was unlike his previous hunts and travels. Here he was not chasing animals; instead he was pursuing the water. History was a powerful reminder of the perils of this kind of chase: the first expedition to try mapping one of the unknown rivers of the Brazilian highlands had ended in starvation and death.[60] And Roosevelt was again living out elements of the frontier adventures he had consumed as a youth, stories of danger, ferocious animals, mishaps, and unrelenting conditions in which human lives could go awry.

Roosevelt's own life began to veer toward a perilous end on March 27. Several of the men were working two canoes through a narrow channel in the river when they lost their grip on the boats, which were whisked toward the rocky riverbank. "In the twinkling of an eye," the dugouts became pinned against the rocks just below the surface.[61] The men called for help and all available hands, including Roosevelt, waded into the water in the hope of salvaging the craft. As Roosevelt stood with his men, "straining and lifting to their uttermost," he briefly slipped and gashed his right leg on a rock.[62] Unbeknownst to most of the men, Roosevelt had injured his left leg years earlier in a collision with a trolley car, and it had never properly healed.[63] Roosevelt described this injury—which had left both of his legs compromised—as the result of his "own clumsiness," and as being "somewhat bothersome" over the next several days.[64] Cherrie recalled the gravity of the event differently: "From that time on he was a very sick man." [65] On the twenty-ninth, Roosevelt never left camp. During the next three days the men moved the canoes around another falls, and it became clear that Roosevelt was experiencing coronary stress. Roosevelt walked slowly to the new camp, and as he arrived Cherrie observed: "He lay flat down on the damp earth for some time before recovering."[66] On the same day, Kermit recorded in his diary that he was very worried about his father's heart.[67]

The loss of another boat was only a backdrop for the events of April 3. The men carried the heavy loads along a crude portage trail and dropped them when they arrived at the new site just above the "sinister rapids of the chasm" through which they were traveling.[68] At a waypoint of bags along the trail, Roosevelt looked on as one hardworking sergeant, called Paishon, dropped his bag and rifle and headed back for more gear. Shortly after that, another man—a brute with European blood named Julio—laid his bag down, picked up Paishon's rifle, and headed back down the trail mumbling to himself. Although Roosevelt felt Julio was "utterly worthless, being an inborn, lazy shirk with the heart of a ferocious cur in the body of a bullock," it wasn't uncommon for any of the men to carry a rifle to hunt monkeys or birds for food.[69] But in this arduous moment, the "evil in men's natures," often concealed, boiled to the surface in Julio.[70] And it was no surprise to Roosevelt that Julio had plenty of evil lurking below his hardened surface. He had avoided work throughout the expedition, periodically feigning illness to avoid the harsh toil. He had been caught stealing food on more than one occasion, and on this morning he had been caught again. Chafed by this type of slacking, Paishon had chided him for his slow work earlier that day.

Barely sixty seconds after Julio picked up the rifle, a single shot rang out in the forest from the direction where he had headed. Then, running footsteps could be heard, pounding the soggy earth in Roosevelt's direction. Three men appeared and told Roosevelt that Paishon was dead, shot through the heart by Julio. Even in his weakened condition, Roosevelt joined several others who methodically searched the trail leading to Paishon's body, their rifles trained on any potential movement in the lush foliage. When they reached their previous camp, they saw no sign of Julio, and learned that the gun he had used was found.

They did not attempt to track Julio any further. They still had several days more of work to get the expedition over the rocky cliffs and through the rapids of the small gorge. It was a perilous point in the journey: the men's internal organs were taxed by fever, and dysentery, and lack of food; their muscles were damaged by overuse and repeated contusions; their skin was blistered, burned, chafed, stung, bitten, and scraped into swollen and itchy shrouds. Roosevelt harbored no illusions about the kind of price that pursuing justice could extract in the wilderness. In the back of his mind were memories of the long days and even longer nights he had spent on the Little Missouri while bringing the boat thieves to justice. Now, on the Duvida, Roosevelt's legs were already blistered and he had a festering wound; he could hardly walk. In this shape neither he nor any other men on the expedition could afford to add anything like the blisters he had sustained when he marched the boat thieves back to Dickinson. The success of this expedition, and the lives of all the men, were on a precarious perch above the rocky boulders of the chasm. The men pushed on with watchful eyes.

After the murder, the men of the Roosevelt-Rondon Scientific Expedition continued to drag themselves through the early days of April. On the fourth, Roosevelt suffered an attack of malaria and his fever spiked to 104 °F.[71] The next day he was somewhat better, but Kermit had a fever and Cherrie was sick to his stomach.[72] Meat had been scarce, with a rare monkey providing a few bites of meat for each man. But the distinction that Roosevelt had once made between strength and hardihood was only an academic one now; he possessed neither as his condition worsened.[73] One evening, he asked to be left behind: "Cherrie, I want you and Kermit to go ahead. We have reached the point where some of us must stop. I feel I am only a burden to the party."[74] In a rare exception to the norm, no one followed the Colonel's orders.

On the third day after the murder, the expedition finally passed the rapids and the boats eased out of the gorge and back onto the river. As they did so, Julio appeared on the bank, calling out to each boat as it glided by, hoping to be rescued from the unforgiving forest. Rondon passed him first, without acknowledging him. All the others followed his lead. Once past Julio, Rondon pulled off to the side of the river to consult Roosevelt, but a full discussion had to wait until they made camp for the night, miles down the river.[75] Given his official status in the Brazilian military, Rondon felt that it was his duty to capture Julio and have him face justice. Although Roosevelt would have preferred to leave him to meet his fate in the woods, he respected Rondon's authority. A search party went back to look for Julio the next day, but they found no further trace.

The ups and downs continued when on the fourteenth the men found a delicious crop of nuts, which they ravenously devoured. The next day, however, half the men were so sick from the meal that they could not work.[76] Despite the illness, that day also marked a turning point. Roosevelt recorded it as a "red-letter day": after running a smooth twenty-five kilometers of river they saw the initials "J. A." carved into a post, a sign of a rubberman's claim.[77] A

(NEXT SPREAD) Roosevelt had cut his leg on a rock when he and several other men were attempting to free two canoes that had become pinned against the rocks in a narrow channel in the river. Although Roosevelt downplayed the injury, it compounded his health issues, and Cherrie attested: "From that point on he was a very sick man." Kermit, Cherrie, Rondon, and the other men on the expedition were frequently sick with dysentery and fevers, but the elder Roosevelt suffered from this injury as well as from pulmonary stress and malaria. Kermit recorded in his diary that he was "much worried" about his father. Kermit and Belle Roosevelt Papers, Library of Congress.

Much more cheerful than on
Xmas day for I have got 3½ and
a half cost of that dreary with
stretching between B & myself—
Am reading Quentin Durward
thought our way slowly along by
rapids, making two portages
& nearly losing our canoe.

13 Easter MONDAY [103-262]
Bank Holiday

We fought our way along slowly
at first; nearly lost the Balse
& Koncho's canoe; had to stop
for 3 hrs. To make paddles; at
2.30 we finished a portage
& started off expecting to soon
have to stop again; but the rapids
proved suddenly passable
& on we went till five; things
steadily improving. We
camped in silence with the
noise of cachoeiras for
the first time in a month.
Father not well;— much worried

it asleep by my inflamed; arm
very worried! We made a
fine marcc at first; struck
rapids; once the canoes went thru
while extra men walked, & once
we had to portage everything; ran
several rapids & camped at last
in the quiet. Saw much keys. found
year old signs of rubber explorers.
Men ate nuts which made
them sick. Rain part of time.

The men still sick, so Souza & I
paddled the Balsa; my arms
are sore from the number of
injections of quinine I had.
First found a rubber man's boundary
stake J.A.; later on found his new
hut; later an old hut & miserable
negro Raymundo who told us
that we were in the Castanho.
Lower down met another hut with
3 men, a woman, & child (the two latter
thought we were Indians & fled; but
found the men & all came) Bath; the
Jews talked; first full feed for
over a month. I better but not well.

short run later, they came to the "clean, cool, picturesque house of palm thatch" of one of the rubbermen.[78]

With these signs of civilization, Roosevelt knew "it was time to get out."[79] The men felt a palpable sense of relief. No longer was the entire expedition in danger. Still, it was not clear that everyone would make it. And here, in the final days of the expedition, Theodore Roosevelt was succumbing to the ravages of nature. His leg, heart, and immune system were the front lines of the struggle. The men draped a makeshift tent over his canoe, and Cherrie snapped a photograph as it went by.[80] Roosevelt lay still in the bottom of the boat, dredging old verse from the back of his delirious brain and reciting it aloud as he floated down the river.

There were still twelve days left on the Duvida. But now, amid traces of civilization, they were able to buy food and supplies from the rubbermen and hire guides to help them more easily navigate the rapids. The men's health slowly returned, and on April 26 they spent a last night under the meager cover of their canvas. After a final brief run of rapids on the twenty-seventh, they boarded a river steamboat bound for Manaus. Now out of danger, Roosevelt began a slow recovery. As he did so, he reflected on the accomplishments of the expedition, such as the scientific value of the roughly 2,500 birds and 500 mammals that Cherrie and Miller had collected. Still bedridden, he pointed to some of the elements that had driven him on the river—the human challenges of exploration—as he began to hone the telling of his last epic adventure for a letter he would write to Lauro Müller once he reached Manaus:

> We have had a hard and somewhat dangerous but very successful trip. No less than six weeks were spent in slowly [*sic*] and with peril and exhausting labor forcing our way down through what seemed a literally endless succession of rapids and cataracts. For forty-eight days we saw no human being. In passing these rapids we lost five of the seven canoes with which we started and had to build others. One of our best men lost his life in the rapids. Under the strain one of the men went completely bad, shirked all his work, stole his comrades' food and when punished by the sergeant he with cold-blooded deliberation murdered the sergeant and fled into the wilderness. Col. Rondon's dog, running ahead of

him while hunting, was shot by two Indians; by his death he
in all probability saved the life of his master. We have put
on the map a river about 1500 kilometers in length running from just south of the 13th degree to north of the 5th
degree and the biggest affluent of the Madeira.[81]

Roosevelt ended the letter with a characteristic flourish: "My dear
Sir, I thank you from my heart for the chance to take part in this
great work of exploration."

Upon his safe emergence from the Amazon, Roosevelt had now added exploration to his already sizeable resume of field credentials.
He had joined with a foreign contingent and undergone a grueling
expedition which had mapped a previously unknown river that
was, as he repeatedly pointed out, as long as the "Rhine or Elbe,"
and rendered it his own extended book.[82] Now a seasoned explorer
himself, Roosevelt could identify with the forces that drove people
through the extreme cycle of geographical exploration. Along
with the rest of the world he could watch over the next several
years as Shackleton's Imperial Transantarctic Exploring Expedition confronted the kind of intense trials he himself had faced.[83]
Only a short way into the trip, the *Endurance* became icebound and
was crushed to splinters by the incredible forces of the expanding
ice. Shackleton and his men retrofitted their lifeboats—wholly unsuited for travel in the open Antarctic Ocean—to be their means
of transport. Food was often scarce, with seals, penguins, and sled
dogs augmenting their rations. Then, Shackleton took part of the
crew on a harrowing trip over hundreds of miles of open ocean
to South Georgia Island. Incredibly, they arrived intact. It was,
however, more than three months before they could get back to
Elephant Island for the other twenty-two men Shackleton had left
there under the command of Frank Wild.

All who survived the Roosevelt-Rondon expedition understood
something of what Shackleton and his men had endured, having
dedicated themselves to the goals of exploration. Like the goal
of Roosevelt's expedition, which had shifted from natural history
collecting to geographical exploration, Shackleton's exploring
goals evolved over time. After making two unsuccessful attempts
to reach the South Pole and then learning of Roald Amundsen's

26ᵗʰ Oct 1915   16 TUESDAY [47—318]
Shrove Tuesday.

The ship's destruction was primarily caused by her inability to rise during the severe pressure on the 26ᵗʰ Dec 1915. Her unfortunate position in relation to the circum-jacent floes & the direction of the assailing pressure are ~~obviously~~ the reasons ascribed & are obvious. The ship was subjected to terrific strains by the pressure exerting its force against the starboard quarter aft So great was this force that the ship was forced

C   D   B   A

BIRDSEYE OF FLOE DURING CRUSHING OF SHIP 26–27TH OCTR 1915 LAT 69.85 LONG 51.38 W arrival there, Shackleton shifted his sights to a trans-Antarctic crossing. Both Roosevelt's and Shackleton's explorations reveal that the stated goals of such expeditions weren't primary. Rather, the underlying intention of heading to the field for strenuous challenge and adventure was their driving force. Roosevelt, now among the weathered cast of geographical explorers, had confronted the most basal aspects of animal life, the struggle for survival against the most extreme challenges that nature could offer. And he had come out hobbling, but still very much alive.

(FACING) The Transantarctic Exploring Expedition, led by Ernest Shackleton, began its planning at the same time as Roosevelt's South American expedition. Although Shackleton's was a much longer adventure that sought to cross the entire Antarctic continent, the men of these two expeditions experienced similar trials, such as broken boats. Before Shackleton's boat, the *Endurance*, ever reached Antarctica, it became stuck in an ice floe and was crushed to pieces by the forces of the expanding ice. Their expedition photographer, Frank Hurley, captured the "broken" moment in his diary. Library of New South Wales.

The Democracy of the Field

Roosevelt's return from South America in May of 1914 was nothing like his seemingly cosmic arrival in New York after his African safari. There were no resounding salutes from battleships; instead, a few boats blew their horns in recognition.[1] And he certainly didn't bound up to the pilothouse—he was still only in shape to limp.

Those who saw him quietly assessed his figure. Despite his dark tan, the deep lines on his face had multiplied. His neck was thin. His body was thinner—was it thirty-five pounds he had lost? Was it fifty-five? Seventy? Estimates ranged.[2] Roosevelt made some simple remarks on his adventures, always keeping one eye on the black case he jealously guarded, which contained his manuscript. Given how dearly he had paid on the Duvida for his stories, he was determined that *Scribner's* would get its account. Despite his frail body, he still exhibited good humor, and even joked about how the cane he was carrying represented his dedication to the use of the "big stick."[3] But here, in this relatively peaceful scene in New York Harbor, after fifty-five years of life, Theodore Roosevelt was officially old.

The type of sober appraisal of age that Roosevelt so often applied to the animals he hunted—as when he ran his fingers over the worn teeth of a cougar or the frayed plumage of a bird—was now turned back on him. Upon his return, *The New York Times* published a telling pair of photographs, one taken before and one after the South American adventure. In the first photo, Roosevelt appeared thick, muscular, and confident. In the second, his wan face and squinting eyes bolstered the argument that he had sustained physical damage on his trip. Roosevelt had joked in Africa about his feelings of old age, but after his harrowing adventure in Amazonia the evidence began to show.[4] Less than five months before these photographs were published, he had impressed the

Brazilians on a jaguar hunt with his characteristic "physical resistance and endurance."[5] But that was to be the last of the displays of his almost unbelievable vigor.

Roosevelt's health did gradually improve, and he settled into a methodical progression of appearances throughout Europe and the United States in the summer of 1914. He spent much of July and August in Oyster Bay, and in September he departed for a Midwestern swing, not returning to Sagamore Hill until the start of November. He campaigned fiercely for Progressive Party candidates, always touching on America's importance in the world, especially because Germany had declared war on Russia, France, and Belgium in early August. Although he also gave lectures about his Brazilian trip, and although his published accounts began to appear in newspapers and magazines, Roosevelt's vigorous outdoor exploits were now largely in the past.[6] Even when he returned to natural areas in his remaining years, there were signs that his field life was nearing the end of a long sequence of events: the Broadway seal and the early days at Loantaka; Europe and the Adirondacks; the Mattawamkeag in Maine with Sewall and Dow; Midwest tramping with Elliott; the Badlands as a rancher; Cuba as a soldier and colonel; Yellowstone and Yosemite as president and conservationist; exploring and collecting in Africa and the Amazon. Roosevelt was tired and triumphant, and now his place in the field was more that of an onlooker and observer than that of a participant. His underlying motivation remained, but what he did in the field had changed.

When a German submarine sent a torpedo into the hull of the *Lusitania* on May 7, 1915 killing more than a thousand passengers, Roosevelt's long-standing criticism of the Wilson administration intensified. The scale of this piracy was worse than anything the "old-time" pirates had ever committed, and Roosevelt railed at the supporters of Wilson and Secretary of State William Jennings Bryan, those who he felt constituted the "flubdub and pacificist vote," the group made up of "every soft creature, every coward and weakling, every man who can't look more than six inches ahead."[7]

Having made his feelings known, Roosevelt turned, as he so often did, directly from politics to nature. He escaped in early June to the barrier islands on the Gulf Coast of Louisiana, finally paying a visit to the habitat he had saved from the ravages of bird

One of Roosevelt's last trips to the field was to Breton National Wildlife Refuge, a series of barrier islands he had set aside in one of his many works of conservation. Roosevelt toured the islands, making observations of pelicans, black skimmers, and the many other birds that were saved by his efforts. TRC.

plumers by making it Breton National Wildlife Refuge in 1904.[8] Now, more than a decade later, Roosevelt was returning to visit the reserve, to again thump on the book of conservation through an article in *Scribner's*.[9]

After a restful train ride with Edith to New Orleans, Roosevelt arrived in Pass Christian, Mississippi. There he met his old friend John Parker, a businessman and emerging leader in the Progressive Party. That afternoon, Roosevelt took in the lush nature of the coast surrounding Parker's home, marveling at the beautiful mimosas and oleanders and the long stretches of "fragrant pine forest."[10] Bird life surrounded him, with thrashers, mockingbirds, kingbirds, and grackles dipping and diving through trees and underbrush. Before setting off to see the coastal bird life on the barrier islands the next day, Roosevelt paused to entertain a group of children who had gathered in the gallery of Parker's home.[11] In the role of storyteller-naturalist, Roosevelt delighted the young crowd with an account of an African lion hunt, recreating the entertainment Selous had provided to his own children in the White House years before. The subtle physical clues of Roosevelt's advancing age were lost on the children, but his gesticulations were somewhat constrained as he was still recovering from a fall he had taken from his horse less than two weeks earlier, in which he had broken two ribs. He himself had described the scene: "I struck the ground a good deal as if I had been a walrus."[12] More than ever, Roosevelt's narratives were now of the past, his presence only echoing the dashing and physical bravado that had accompanied his stories as a younger man. Roosevelt, Parker, and an entourage that included the naturalist and photographer Herbert Job left the port at Pass Christian at 4 a.m. the next morning. By noon they were on the islands.

Through his viewfinder, Job captured the scene on film. Job was a "camera-hunter," like Frank Chapman, whose influence encouraged Roosevelt to at least consider tapering his use of the gun and replacing it with more peaceful implements for nature study.[13] Roosevelt walked over the sand and observed the eggs of royal terns and black skimmers in nests that were not much more than indentations in the sand. With his once again rounded belly, Roosevelt had a slight waddle as he walked barefoot over the sand to observe the birds. He sat cross-legged, and then lay down on his side. His mind turned to how he would convey his feelings about the plume hunters and eggers who harmed these types of natal refuges: "The illegal business of killing breeding birds, of leaving nestlings to starve wholesale, and of general ruthless extermination, more and more tends to attract men of the same moral category as those who sell whiskey to Indians and combine the running of 'blind pigs' with highway robbery and murder for hire."[14] At another point during his visits to the islands, Roosevelt plunged his knees into the sand and scooped up a handful of green sea turtle eggs for closer examination, while Job released his shutter and created another iconic photograph of Roosevelt, which revealed his new place in the context of fieldwork. In his images, Job captured an element of awkwardness, an aged version of the fumbling Roosevelt had done with his pocket rule when he had first entertained natural history study with the Broadway seal. At that childhood moment, he had not been doing any real natural history; he was just wading into the craft. Now, despite his celebrity and significant contributions, he was a visitor at Breton. He was no longer in the middle of the action.

After another jaunt to the islands on June 10, Roosevelt received news that invigorated his hope that the United States would soon enter the war: Bryan had finally resigned. Roosevelt's first question upon receiving a stack of newspapers at Brattledore Island was, "Has war broken out?"[15] Although the answer was no, Roosevelt—no fan of Wilson—penned a note to him the next day expressing his support and willingness to do anything he could to further the aims of the nation.[16] In this remote coastal habitat, the old Rough Rider ached to mount his horse and take to the battlefield again. Unfortunately for Roosevelt, Wilson's reluctance to wage war continued, even with a new secretary of state.

Once Roosevelt was back in New York, he looked to the needs of the country and how he could serve once the United States finally did enter the war. As he had done in his preparations for the fight in Cuba, he conferred with Leonard Wood. Roosevelt and a group of others lobbied for Wood to extend the student training camps he had previously run at Plattsburg Barracks in upstate New York, only this time to include professionals as well.[17] That summer, Wood began the camp with more than 1,200 promising young officers. As the summer progressed, Roosevelt stewed about Germany, feeling that if he were president, he and all four of his sons would have already been mobilized to fight in the war with Germany.[18] He visited Plattsburg on August 25 to review the troops with Wood. On the evening of his visit, and before boarding the train back to New York City, Roosevelt made a comment that, despite Wood's best efforts, caused a flap.[19] He told reporters: "I wish to make one comment on the statement so frequently made that we must stand by the President. I heartily subscribe to this on condition, and only on condition, that it is followed by the statement 'So long as the President stands by the country.'"[20] Roosevelt's words redoubled his criticism that the United States had not stood up to fight in Europe. With these stinging words still reverberating in the papers, and the White House furious in reply, Roosevelt escaped for several weeks of voyageur-like travel in the North Woods of Quebec during September.

In September of 1915, Roosevelt traveled to the North Woods of Quebec to hunt moose. In what he described as a "pas mal curieux," Roosevelt was stalked by an angry moose. Roosevelt eventually shot the moose, his second of the trip. Roosevelt published this image from the trip in *A Book-Lover's Holidays in the Open*.

Roosevelt marveled at the strapping physiques of his two French Canadian guides as he followed them over the rocky trail toward a patchwork system of glacial lakes. The group, laden with canoes and supplies, tramped to the relative comfort of the cabins kept by the Tourilli Club, a private group that owned 250 square miles of wilderness in southern Quebec. The conditions Roosevelt encountered there lay comfortably between those of his boat cruise at Breton earlier in the summer and his dugout-canoe travel in Brazil. It was, however, still wilderness travel, and Roosevelt hopped in and out of canoes, rambled over slick boulders, and followed his guides—their foreheads strained by tumplines—over rickety bridges. But the cabins were neat and clean, and the canoes floated with their gunwales well above the water's surface.

On his second day out, Roosevelt met up with his old friend and hunting companion Alexander Lambert. Halfway down a portage trail, he hailed Lambert, who hoisted a canoe onto his own back, and together they trudged down the trail, catching up and looking forward to adding this trip to their long resume of hunting adventures. After several days in camp, Roosevelt broke off from the group, patrolling the lakes in search of interesting wildlife. At one point he quietly took refuge on a bank, watched a family of beavers frolic around their lodge, and observed how a female moose and her two calves drove their heads into the mucky waters and came up with tender meals of aquatic plants. His hours of watching and cataloguing behaviors raised questions in his mind about the distribution and abundance of species; the absence of porcupines piqued his curiosity. Once his need for solitude was quenched, and with a recognition that meat supplies were dwindling, Roosevelt joined the others to begin hunting the animals that his permit allowed him: one moose and two caribou.

The men struck out after breakfast on the first day of their hunt, and less than half an hour passed before Roosevelt obtained his "wished-for fresh meat."[21] He shot a yearling caribou that he had sighted fifty yards off. With his first prize secured, he paddled the rest of the day, searching for game. But he only saw one other cow caribou, which was swimming across a lake. The water reflected starlight by the time they returned to camp, the shore being no more than a dark outline against the twinkling sky. Comfortably fed, the men were lulled to sleep by the plaintive wail of loons echoing off the lake.

The next day, Roosevelt got his bull moose. He caught sight of the animal from his canoe. The waves on the lake caused the boat to rock as he raised his gun and his first shot veered well from his mark. But his second "slew the mighty bull."[22] The familiar and bloody process of dressing the animal ensued, and once the canoe was filled to capacity with meat and the trophy head, they set off to return to camp. Unbeknownst to them, the real story of the moose hunt had just begun.

With the canoe approaching the portage trail, Roosevelt caught sight of another bull moose. It was even more impressive in size and antlers than the one they had just shot. As they approached the shore, the moose briefly gazed at the canoe but then ambled along, giving the men the impression that it had taken no notice of them. The moose tracked their canoe down the shoreline, and soon enough Roosevelt realized that the "big, black, evil-looking beast" clearly "meant mischief."[23] Not wanting a confrontation, the men reversed their course and paddled back in the opposite direction. The moose turned to follow. After a hundred yards the men turned again, and the moose turned with them. For more than an hour the moose stalked them, smashing its large antlers on trees, stomping the ground, and licking its lips with its gangly tongue. Eventually, the animal trotted away, giving the men an opening to slip out of the water and start down the portage trail. They had hardly taken their equipment and meat from the boats when they heard a crashing noise. Out of the forest, the angry moose charged toward them "like a locomotive," with the "hair on his withers bristling."[24] Roosevelt grabbed his rifle and took a warning shot above the animal's head in hopes of scaring it off, but as it continued to charge he lowered the gun and placed a shot directly into its chest. The bullet stopped the moose not thirty feet away. Roosevelt then pumped several more bullets into the animal to make sure the party was out of danger. It was immediately clear to Roosevelt that such aggression, even in a male moose, was an uncommonly curious experience—a "*pas mal curieux*"—that generated a perfect title to intrigue his readers in *Scribner's*.[25]

Even with such material, Roosevelt left the North Woods a bit shaken. He knew that his body wasn't up for many more of these dramatic encounters. He left his readers with a somber note on fall in the North Woods: "The weather had grown colder. The loons had begun to gather on the larger lakes in preparation for their southward flight. . . . Birch and maple were donning the bravery with which they greet the oncoming north—crimson and gold their banners flaunted in the eyes of the dying year."[26] Even though he described the moose hunt as "extraordinary an experience as I have ever had in the hunting field," he realized that his days in that field were waning.[27] Upon his return to Oyster Bay he wrote to Kermit, saying, "I shot atrociously, and saw and walked so badly that I shall never again make an exhibition of myself by going on a hunting trip. I'm past it!"[28] He realized that his physical condition did not compete as favorably with huge beasts as it once had. He confided to his friend Charles Washburn that "he didn't want to be 'taken care of'" in any future encounters.[29] He planned to stick to finishing his last hunting book, and then turn to some historical projects.

For the remainder of the fall of 1915, Roosevelt gave speeches in the New York area and met with colleagues at his office at the *Metropolitan* magazine, building on the ideas on national presence that he had developed in his *America and the World War*, published earlier that year. As the icy winter began to wear on, Roosevelt and Edith set off for a tropical holiday, with a bit of natural history travel included, in British Guiana and Trinidad.

None of the hardships of Roosevelt's previous trips to Brazil and Cuba followed him on his vacation with Edith. Instead, they "revelled in the mountains and warm blue seas, and the rich tropical vegetation, and the trade winds, and its queer tropical life."[30] The majority of their stops provided a combination of recreation and diplomacy, as they island hopped throughout the Lesser Antilles, calling on islands like St. Thomas, Guadeloupe, Dominica, and Martinique. The warm sun and the groves teeming with fruits of the tropics—lime, banana, coffee, cacao, and coconut—soothed Roosevelt's skin, eyes, and belly. He took in the people and the architecture of colonization, and wove it together in "Where the Steady Trade-Winds Blow," one of two articles he was writing for *Scribner's* about the trip.[31]

Although he was largely a tourist, Roosevelt's stop in British Guiana provided him with an opportunity to spend three days at the New York Zoological Society's tropical field station. There he met his old friend, the baldheaded and brooding William Beebe, who was in the midst of setting up his station for scientific research on tropical forests. Roosevelt installed Edith and himself in the airy tropical hut of a nearby rubber planter, which provided "about as much privacy as a gold fish" had in its bowl.[32] This open life of the tropics was enjoyable even for Edith, as she and Roosevelt laughed over meals with Beebe, who even paused to collect spiders while they ate.[33]

Roosevelt and Beebe took long walks together in the forest, Beebe pointing out furtive bird life, and Roosevelt reacquainting himself with some of the "old friends," such as the cotingas, that he knew from his previous trip to the Amazon. With so much work looming for Beebe in getting his research agenda going, even Roosevelt realized that he was diverting Beebe's attention with his constant stream of questions on the wildlife, Beebe always being generous with thorough answers. Roosevelt did pick up some natural history tidbits, and of course he had a chance to share some of his own stories, but his main impact on the field station was to raise its standing through his own celebrity and the article he was preparing. Roosevelt's visit provided a much-needed injection of outside support, both personal and professional, to Beebe and his station.[34]

After finishing their swing through Trinidad, the Roosevelts returned home content and rested, having put together a satisfying combination of sightseeing, natural history tourism, and politicking. Back home, Roosevelt spent much of the next year in his now-normal Oyster Bay life, writing and speaking, trumpeting his ideas through the *Metropolitan* and though his new relationship with the *Kansas City Star*.[35]

By the spring of 1917, America's direct involvement in the war was imminent. Plans were already forming in Roosevelt's head to lead a division into battle. He sent a telegram to Secretary of War Newton Baker that requested authorization for him to personally form "three regiment brigades of infantry, one brigade of cavalry, one brigade of artillery, one regiment of engineers, one motorcycle machine-gun regiment, one aero squadron, and of course the supply branches, and so forth."[36] Despite such enthusiastic plans, Baker refused on the grounds that a much larger force would be assembled by an act of Congress, and officers would be chosen from the regular army.

With Baker's refusal to permit him to raise his own contingent, Roosevelt pounded his fist and trumpeted his credentials, pleading his case in a letter to Henry Cabot Lodge: "I shall answer respectfully pointing out that I am the retired Commander-in-Chief of the whole Army, and that towards the close of the Santiago expedition I actually commanded a brigade—I am a retired volunteer officer also. Will you tell some of my friends in the Senate and House about the matter . . . ?"[37] Roosevelt had at least convinced the *Boston Daily Globe* that he was about to be placed in command of an army of one hundred thousand men.[38] The press, however, held no sway with Baker, and for Roosevelt there would be no direct engagement in the war or new post, no Rough Riders adventure for the twentieth century.[39] Instead, his service would have to be lived out through his voice, and the only drops of Roosevelt's blood that would be spilled on the battlefield would be those that surged in the veins of his sons.

After his exchanges with Baker, Roosevelt felt there was no reason for him to further delay a trip he had planned to hunt devilfish in Florida. Given that Congress wouldn't reconvene until April 2, there was still time for a quick trip to the Gulf Coast for some hunting before any decisions would be made on the war. Before he left, Roosevelt made a final hedge against unforeseen developments, writing to Lodge: "I can return within forty-eight hours; if there is need to, wire me."[40] With that, he headed south to the warm sands of Florida's Gulf Coast, near Sanibel and Captiva Islands.

Given a life so focused on human interaction, it is no surprise that Roosevelt's last major hunting trip brought him back into contact with a previous connection. Consuming a new issue of *The American Museum Journal* the previous fall, he had become intrigued by an article entitled "My Fight with the Devilfish."[41] The author, Russell J. Coles, was a tobacco dealer by trade, but was also a keen naturalist and fisherman who had carefully studied the sharks and rays that inhabit the coastal waters of the southeastern

Roosevelt's final trip to the field took place on water, to hunt giant manta rays near the islands of Sanibel and Captiva, off the western coast of Florida. Roosevelt posed for a photograph with Russell J. Coles, his companion on the trip, who had refined a technique for hunting these animals using a harpoon, a spade lance, and a wooden "drogue." One of the manta rays Roosevelt killed was the second-largest known at the time. TRC.

United States.[42] Fascinated by their natural history and daunted by their size, Coles described his challenge of developing the hunting techniques necessary to acquire a prime specimen of the manta ray, *Manta birostris,* for the AMNH in New York. Coles's story was filled with material that exhilarated Roosevelt: hunting, danger, large beasts, and discovery of new natural history. The manta rays, or devilfish, that Coles described were huge animals that could reach sizes of more than twenty feet across. On the last page of the article, the final illustration encapsulated the adventure of hunting devilfish, an account much more exciting than the ones Roosevelt had read about as a child.[43] In the drawing, Coles and five other men perched in a small boat that was riding the back of a huge devilfish. Coles stood in the bow with a lance, ready to sever the main nerve of the massive leviathan. Roosevelt had never been much for fishing, but what he saw in this article was different:

it was hunting on the sea. Without hesitation, he wrote to Coles to find out more.

Not every single name that Roosevelt had encountered during his presidency stuck in his prodigious memory, and he did not remember that he had actually been in contact with Coles when he was president years before. Coles had written Roosevelt to express his concerns about the shabby equipment in the lifesaving station at Cape Lookout, North Carolina. Coles had been near that station in 1908 when a severe storm put several boats in danger, and had bravely assembled a band of volunteers to join the ill-equipped lifesaving crew in rescuing the crew of one vessel. After hearing Coles's tale, Roosevelt had used his power to make sure that the lifesaving equipment was improved. Now, back in contact for a different reason, Coles and Roosevelt talked over the details of hunting devilfish, and made plans for a trip together the following spring.

The preparations for the devilfish hunt were not unlike the advance work Roosevelt had undertaken for his African safari. Coles visited Roosevelt at home in November of 1916, and in December sent him a package with a regular whale harpoon and a "dummy" harpoon for practice.[44] He continued to send Roosevelt instructions on harpoon throwing in words and sketches, as well as advising him on clothing and firearms.[45] As the start of the hunt approached in March, Coles literally counted down the days in his letters.[46]

In the end, the trip was shorter than Roosevelt had hoped, but he still had a chance to experience the full spectrum of the devilfish hunt. Once he and Coles had set themselves up in the modest houseboat that would serve as their base of operations, Coles gave him a tutorial in the use of his specially designed implements. First, the eight-foot harpoon, or "iron," would be thrown from the boat in the hope that it would penetrate deep into the manta's body. If that was successful, a wooden drogue—a large set of wooden plates—would be attached to the harpoon rope and thrown into the water to slow down the manta. Finally, on close approach, the hunter would wield the spade-shaped lance and attempt to hack into the ray and sever its spinal nerve—the best way to render the giant beast still. The lesson was short, as Roosevelt took to the sport "like a duck to water," with Coles generously suggesting that "the Colonel could spear a whale if necessary."[47]

As the hunters cruised through the waters off Captiva Island, their small motorboat came upon a school of mantas. Wasting no time, Roosevelt hurled the iron. It struck one animal directly, plunging two feet deep into the body of a male with fins spanning more than thirteen feet. Although the other fishermen would have used both hands on the iron, Roosevelt steadied his fifty-eight-year-old frame at the front of the boat by grasping a cord with one hand and flinging the harpoon with his other. The physical limitations revealed on his moose hunt were still in the back of his mind; a new caution was present even in his bold actions. He and Coles threw out the drogue, and after only eleven minutes of fight the boat approached the animal. Roosevelt brought the spade lance to bear, and finished off his first fish.

Only ten minutes after they had finished hauling their first manta ashore, the men were in sight of another devilfish, this time a "real monster."[48] They immediately gave chase. Once in range, Roosevelt again took his perch at the front of the boat and harpooned the manta in the same spot where he had hit the first one. After a short struggle, he sent another harpoon into its body. The angered animal swept waves of water into the boat with its winglike fins, drenching the men. It proceeded to swim under the thirty-foot launch, surfacing and jolting the bow into the air. Then, pointing its nose toward the deep, it pulled the boat several feet into the sea. Not giving up, the fish took off over the surface of the ocean in an exhilarating chase. With Roosevelt's hands firmly on the rope, the manta dragged the boat, bouncing through the open ocean for two miles before it slowed enough for the men to approach. The animal was finally finished off with the spade lance. Exhausted, the men dragged it to the beach and pulled it up next to their first specimen. Measurements revealed that the fish was sixteen feet, eight inches across—a size second only to that of the one Coles had previously collected for the AMNH.

The devilfish hunt provided an exciting story for Roosevelt to tell, but it was not without its somber aspects. The reassurance that Roosevelt had taken in most of his hunts, that specimens should provide mounts for museums or meat for the table, could not be applied here. Devilfish are inedible, and he had not been able to convince the AMNH to send a naturalist along to prepare the specimens for the museum. After making measurements, taking photographs, and then dissecting the animals' stomachs to determine whether their dietary preferences could be discovered—they couldn't—a tired Roosevelt left the specimens behind for lower forms of life to consume.

Any lingering misgivings that Roosevelt may have had about leaving his devilfish behind were quickly forgotten as he barreled up the seaboard on April 2. He stopped in Washington as Congress began its deliberations on entering the World War. He hovered there as several days of machinations commenced, and by April 6 President Wilson signed the official declaration of war.[49]

Already back in Oyster Bay once the official announcement came, the Roosevelt household readied their men for their commissions on the battlefield. As they all prepared to travel to Boston for Archie's wedding to his "war bride," Grace Lockwood, Roosevelt continued to press the issue of his own participation in the war.[50] Despite his extensive pleas and his passionate argument that he could raise scores of troops—indeed, thousands of applications to serve were piling up on his desk each day—Baker would not enlist Roosevelt's services.[51] Frustrated, Roosevelt was left only to fight with his pen and to work to secure posts for his sons.[52] Largely due to Roosevelt's efforts, by midsummer Ted and Archie had sailed to join General John J. Pershing's ground forces in France. Kermit left to begin serving in Mesopotamia with the British forces there. And Quentin was off to join the air squadron in France.

As 1917 progressed, the democracy of the field drew nearer to Roosevelt. His old lion hunter friend, Frederick Selous, had—amazingly, given his age—been serving as a captain in England's Twenty-Fifth Royal Fusiliers. Unlike Roosevelt, Selous was in strapping health, his heart especially strong, which allowed him to spend almost two years in east Africa pushing back the German forces.[53] On January 4, 1917, however, Selous was leading the charge of his Fusiliers in the foothills of German East Africa when a shot struck him in the head.[54] As it had done for so many others, the equality of a savage war confronted the old hunter. His now sixty-five-year-old, still muscular body could do nothing to prevent his fate. Upon learning of Selous's death, Roosevelt responded by remarking on how many people had thought he would die on the hunt, and that "the death he actually met was better still."[55] Roosevelt wondered: "Who could wish a better life, or a better death, or desire to leave a more honorable heritage to his family and his nation?" Selous was buried in the cool cover of a tamarind tree, and the war went on without him.

There was a hint of envy in Roosevelt's tone when he wrote his memorial of Selous in *The Outlook*. He himself would never meet such a fate. For one thing, his body was too frail to lead a contingent in actual battle, even if Baker had allowed him to assume a command. With four of Roosevelt's offspring out in the fighting, though, it was only a matter of time until the chilling fairness of the war came even closer. In March of 1918, news arrived in Oyster Bay that Archie had been injured, his kneecap shattered and arm paralyzed by shrapnel. Ted Jr. had also suffered in a gas attack. And although Roosevelt had prepared himself for the ultimate sacrifice of all his sons, he was crushed when news arrived that Quentin, just a decade after his snake-charming antics in the White House, had been shot down and killed in a dogfight with a German plane near Marne, France. Hermann Hagedorn, Roosevelt's friend and eventual biographer, recalled how Quentin's death drained life from Roosevelt: "The old side of him was gone, that old exuberance . . . the boy in him had died."[56]

Though Roosevelt had sometimes given the impression that he simply couldn't be killed, the most fundamental equality of nature applied to him too.[57] Despite efforts, he could not escape aging and death. After the rib-breaking walrus flop from his horse in 1915, *The New York Times* placed the event in the context of his life's previous injuries and narrow escapes:

> The accident is merely the latest of many, for the Colonel's life has been one of more accidents met and dangers faced than usually falls to the lot of an ordinary citizen. On Oct. 14, 1912, he was shot and seriously wounded by an assassin in Milwaukee. It was the most serious injury that ever befell him but there had been many lesser ones before. . . . As a ranchman and hunter he had risked his life herding cattle, hunting wild beasts, joining posses to hunt down outlaws, and as Police Commissioner, soldier in the Spanish War, President and African huntsman he has faced beasts

and men who would have injured him if they could. . . .
At Pittsfield, Mass., in 1902 his carriage was run down by
an electric car and the Colonel was hurled out, cut and
bruised. . . . He has been in train wrecks and automobile
accidents, but luck has been with him.[58]

This published litany only brushed the surface of Roosevelt's
scrapes. He had avoided the charges of buffalo, grizzlies, rhinos,
lions, elephants, and moose. Countless bullets had miraculously
avoided his flesh in Cuba. He had fended off injuries and near
starvation on the River of Doubt, and a lifetime of pathogens,
not the least of which was malaria, had invaded his body and tor-
mented his organs.

For those who had accepted that Roosevelt would actually suc-
cumb to the mortal forces of nature, the end that came wasn't the
type of death they might have expected. He would not be shot on
the battlefield, nor would he lie down next to his wagon to expire
after an epic battle with a ferocious animal.[59] Luck had helped him
avoid a dramatic fate, but after Quentin's death the blunt edge of
Roosevelt's mortality began to press in more rapidly.

Given the number of times that Roosevelt had witnessed and
described how the cycle of nature played out in the field, he was
no stranger to this cold march:

> Death by violence, death by cold, death by starvation—
> these are the normal endings of the stately and beautiful
> creatures of the wilderness. The sentimentalists who prattle
> about the peaceful life of nature do not realize its utter
> mercilessness; although all they would have to do would
> be to look at the birds in the winter woods, or even at the
> insects on a cold morning or cold evening. Life is hard and
> cruel for all the lower creatures, and for man also. . . .[60]

Now, in 1918, life's sometimes painful circle began to close for
Roosevelt too.[61] He had already spent February in the hospital,
being treated for abscesses near his intestines and in his ear ca-
nals. In late October, just after his sixtieth birthday, he was again
consulting his physicians about a painful swelling in his legs that
was consistent with rheumatism. On the day the war finally came

to an end and the armistice was signed—November 11—Roosevelt was back in the hospital, a stay that lasted until Christmas Eve.[62]

Back at home in Oyster Bay, Roosevelt looked gray and tired as Christmas passed and New Year's Day approached. He watched the children play with their new toys, and hobbled about the house as best he could. Edith telephoned Roosevelt's old valet, James Amos:[63] Might he be able to get free from his job at the detective agency to look after Theodore? Amos did not hesitate. Roosevelt continued his activity, dictating new articles for the *Metropolitan* and the *Kansas City Star* in the first days of January. Part of his mind was still in the field; he wrote William Beebe with corrections to a manuscript on pheasants, and corresponded with Russell Coles about a second devilfish hunt they were planning.[64] Despite describing himself as "utterly worthless" in his letter to Coles on New Year's Day, he still felt it was likely that he and Archie would be able to hunt devilfish in early March. On the night of January 5, Amos helped Roosevelt into bed and turned down the light. He sat in the darkness and listened to Roosevelt's peaceful breathing. Roosevelt's quiet comforted him after seeing the pain and anguish he had experienced over the previous days. Edith checked back after midnight, and then returned to bed. Shortly before 4:15 a.m., Amos heard Roosevelt's breathing become irregular. It stopped, and then started again. Amos leaned closer, putting his ear close to Roosevelt's mouth. Then, only silence remained. The Colonel was no longer with him. Roosevelt's great heart had finally given out to the most inevitable reality of nature.

The news of Roosevelt's death reduced John Burroughs to tears the following evening. Burroughs wasn't inclined to flock to Sagamore Hill to watch wreaths being dropped from noisy low-flying aircraft in tribute. As he often did, he instead found comfort in natural sounds as he scratched his thoughts in his journal. The day after the news had come, he wrote: "Heard of Roosevelt's death last night and have had a lump in my throat ever since. I love him more than I thought I did."[65] Over the next days he began the difficult work of writing a memoriam for *Natural History*, to be published that month. He admitted to himself: "I think I must have unconsciously felt that his power to live was unconquerable . . . . He always seemed to have an unlimited reserve of health and power."[66] Burroughs sat considering his warm memories of Roosevelt: tramping with him in Yellowstone, rambling with him in Rock Creek Park, and trading visits with him at their respective retreats at Slabsides, Sagamore Hill, and Pine Knot. Burroughs remembered how when Roosevelt arrived, his aura preceded him like a strong wind that would blow open the door; "You felt his radiant energy before he got halfway up the stairs."[67]

Even with only a few days of distance from his death, Burroughs's keen eye drilled down on what had made Roosevelt so unique: "Roosevelt was a many-sided man and every side was like an electric battery."[68] He had been a true world leader; he had written stacks of books; he had ranched, hunted, conserved, and fought. But these many sides were not isolated from each other. To Burroughs, these facets were like the independent cells of a large battery working together to feed a common charge. Burroughs summed up Roosevelt's presence in two words: "live wire."[69] Roosevelt couldn't have assembled such a massive string of conservation if he had not undertaken his adventures as a hunter, naturalist, and a rancher. He could not have wielded the big stick in so many situations without the persona of strength derived from so many outdoor pursuits. It was how these seemingly disparate parts, some of which seemed at times to be contradictory, came together that took Roosevelt's life from impressive to unique. As many historians have noted, he truly was a "marvel of many-sidedness."[70]

Later in January, once Roosevelt's funeral and burial had taken place, Burroughs drove to the gravesite near Sagamore Hill and stood in front of the mounds of flowers and wreaths that obscured the ground under which Roosevelt lay. Again tears streamed down his face and into his long white beard, and he accepted reassurances from the attending guard: When former President Taft was there, he had "wept profusely" too.[71] Staring at the mounded monument, his gaze wandering beyond leafless woods into the cold clear bay, Burroughs considered not only who Roosevelt had been, but where he fit in the history of the United States. He settled on the idea that he had been the "most potent force for pure Americanism, in the best sense, in our history."[72]

Burroughs was not alone in considering the question of where Roosevelt fit in US history. It already had been broached well before his death, as the journalist Julian Street published a set of his impressions of Roosevelt, entitled *The Most Interesting American*.[73] And by October 27—the date when Roosevelt would have turned sixty-one—people gathered in different forums around the country to remember him. From coast to coast, admirers of Roosevelt inevitably picked up on these themes of Street and Burroughs.

One group of politicians and diplomats gathered amidst the lush accommodations of the Waldorf Astoria in New York for a birthday remembrance of Roosevelt. The president of the Rocky Mountain Club, John Hammond, hosted the event and suggested, as had many others, that Roosevelt was "worthy to be named with Washington and Lincoln."[74] Jean Jusserand used his post as French ambassador to add Benjamin Franklin to Hammond's list.[75] But a veteran of New York politics, Job Elmer Hedges, begged to disagree with Hammond. To Hedges it added nothing to compare Roosevelt to Washington or Lincoln, as he felt that Roosevelt had been like neither: "Washington created; Lincoln preserved; Roosevelt vitalized." For Hedges, Roosevelt's achievements rested on his ability to achieve "official and human contact with a large number of people."[76] As the night wore on and the lamps glowed warmer, the collective consideration of Roosevelt widened its horizons.

Elihu Root raised Roosevelt's stature by comparing him to the Greek mythological half-giant Antaeus.[77] Secretary of the Interior Franklin Lane predicted the rise of a Roosevelt legend with his observation that "the Idylls and Sagas and the Iliads have been woven about men of this mold."[78] In his view, authors would tell Roosevelt's story in the fashion that Homer had done for Achilles and Tennyson had done for King Arthur.

We can imagine that, were he there in the flesh, Roosevelt's thoughts on his placement as a historical figure would be similar to his reaction to Charles Eliot's list for his five feet of books. Books, like humans, are each so unique—how would one choose the most interesting and valuable ones? But Roosevelt had after all become engulfed in Eliot's discussion, and he too was fond of superlatives: in Africa he had ranked the most interesting and dangerous animals a hunter could encounter.[79] In just such a fashion, the men at the Waldorf that night raised up for consideration Roosevelt's achievements, the astounding number of intriguing stories he had generated, and the simple impact of his life. Not only had he affected people, though; he had touched them. Many, like Elihu Root, publicly expressed their love for him.[80]

No one put Roosevelt's contributions forward as the work of a singular genius, like the portraiture of John Singer Sargent or the science of Albert Einstein. The collected pursuits of Renaissance men like Da Vinci and Benjamin Franklin would not hit the mark as comparisons either. But Burroughs had earlier pointed to the fact that what had made Roosevelt unique had to do with integration and unity: such a set of character traits had "rarely been united in one man."[81] Roosevelt's achievements had not simply grown from independent areas of mastery. Rather, his was a synthetic persona that had been nourished by his underlying motivation to take to the field for adventure—as natural historian, writer, rancher, soldier, explorer, conservationist, and world leader—with elements that flowed like independent streams, rivulets, and gushing tributaries into one common and charging river. This force of nature had grown from Roosevelt's robust, forceful, naturalistic, bombastic, teeth-clapping, animal-skinning, keen-eyed, avalanche-like persona, which had been born and bred in the field.

The tender reminiscences of the men who gathered at the Waldorf may have started them down a road of nostalgic folly. There is also the possibility, much considered since then, that they identified some truth about the uniqueness of Roosevelt's life, achievements, and humanity, and that the legacy of Theodore Roosevelt—a man who was guided by adventure—stands alone.

Acknowledgments

This book would not have become a reality without the support of my beautiful wife, Jen. At every point along the way she has given me encouragement and positive energy. She has my limitless love and thanks.

I have dedicated this book to my sons, Mitchell and Riley. Each day, their enthusiasm, humor, curiosity, and love is a source of inspiration for me. It has been a true joy to talk with them about so many Roosevelt stories: the boat thieves, the swim with sharks in Cuba, the walrus-flop from a horse, the River of Doubt mishaps, the tracking of grizzlies, and Roosevelt's college life on Winthrop Street, a place we pass by each day.

My parents, Charles and Dorothea Canfield, have nurtured my education and provided me with wise guidance over four decades. When I became interested in Theodore Roosevelt, they supported me and even sent reports from the Badlands on what they were able to discover there. I could not ask for more loving and supportive parents. My siblings Lori Peiffer, Greg Canfield, and David Canfield, have also been incredibly supportive. Thanks also to Ken and Sam Johnston, especially for providing levity at critical times. I would also like to warmly recognize Holly Johnston for lending her academic ear and support, for reading drafts, and also for providing considerable logistical support.

I have had the incredible fortune of being a part of the communities at Eliot House and Harvard University for more than a decade. The people with whom I have had the pleasure of working are too numerous to mention here, but their positive effects on my life have been significant. I would like to thank Sue Weltman, Francisco Medeiros, Gail O'Keefe, and Doug Melton for all they have done to support me as close colleagues and friends over many years. More recently, I have come to depend on the meticulous and steadfast support of my close teammate Craig Carey. His positive presence makes each day a more joyful enterprise. For the past fifteen years I have been incredibly lucky to learn from and work with Naomi E. Pierce. I would not be where I am today if she had not invested in me, and for that I am truly thankful.

It is an act of kindness for a person to provide feedback on a developing manuscript, especially in the rough going of early drafts. I am tremendously fortunate to have had the investment of many as I prepared this book. Along with anonymous reviewers, I would especially like to thank those who reviewed parts of the manuscript: Andrew Berry, David Canfield, Grant Calder, Paul Farber, Brett Flehinger, Sydelle Kramer, Stephen Lassonde, Betsy Lerner, Ralph Lutts, Jennifer Mills, Ryan Rippel, Brandon Tilley, Bari Walsh, and Mary Winsor. Kevin Van Anglen deserves particular thanks for his thorough review and detailed comments on the entire manuscript. I would also like to thank those who have provided support, feedback, and advice while I have navigated all aspects of this project, especially Glenn Adelson, Sidney Bland, Martin Christiansen, Howard Ehrlich, James Engell, Kelly Fuhrmann, Anne Greene, Paul Grossman, John Gruber, Kathy Horton, Joseph MacDougald, Pamelia Markwood, Candice Millard, Robert Moore, Edmund Morris, Philip Morse, Craig Neff, Lisa New, John Park, Shauna Potocky, Tweed Roosevelt, and David Weininger.

Given the wide range of Theodore Roosevelt's interests, I have consulted a similarly diverse set of experts in preparing this manuscript about him, and am grateful for their input and comments on the manuscript: Greta Binford, Bernd Blossey, Terry Bowyer, Leslie Boyer, Janet Browne, Victoria Cain, Bryan Connolly, Kathleen Dalton, Charles Davis, Philip Droege, Sam Droege, John Francis, Steve Goodman, Michael Heithaus, Edward Kohn, Karen Kramer, Donald Kroodsma, Zarin Machanda, Peter Der Manuelian, Julie Meachen, Melinda Peters, Robert Raguso, Alon Rosen, Lynette Roth, Mark Siddell, and Stephan Wolohojian. I would especially like to recognize the efforts of my friends and colleagues Stefan Cover, Gary Alpert and Karsten Hartel at the Museum of Comparative Zoology.

This project could not have been completed without the guidance of highly skilled individuals at a host of libraries and museums. Despite often receiving much less support than they deserve, these people are among the most helpful and intellectually generous I have met. They include Ellen Alers (Smithsonian Institution Archives), William Allman (curator, the White House), Bonnie Coles (Library of Congress), Lisa Long Feldmann (Isabella Stuart Gardner Museum), Laura Foster (Frederic Remington Museum), Randall Forston (Navy Department Library), Alfred Fry (Falvey Memorial Library, Villanova University), John Haynes (Library of Congress), Joan Hunt (Tioga County Historical Society), Bassey Irele (Widener Library, Harvard University), Patrick Kerwin (Library of Congress), Bruce Kirby (Library of Congress), Lynn Laffey (Morris County Park Commission), Alexandra Lane (White House Historical Association), Marlo Mallery, (Theodore Roosevelt Center, Dickinson State University), Eric Olsen (Morristown National Historic Park), Chamisa Redmond (Library of Congress), Mai Reitmeyer (American Museum of Natural History), Trish Richard (University of Pacific Library), Bailey Romaine (Newberry Library), Paul Sweet (American Museum of Natural History), Julie Tripp (Boone and Crockett Club), Michele Tucker (Saranac Lake Free Library), Amy Verone (Sagamore Hill National Historic Site) Becky Whidden (Falvey Memorial Library, Villanova University), Naomi Woodburn (Cambridge University Library), Kelly Wooten (Rubenstein Library of Duke University).

I owe a special thanks to the many members of the Harvard University Libraries who have provided support that has far exceeded what one could reasonably expect. At the Ernst Mayr Library of the Museum of Comparative Zoology, I would like to thank Dorothy Barr, Ronnie Broadfoot, Dana Fisher, Connie Rinaldo, Mary Sears, and Robert Young. At Widener Library, I would like to thank Bassey Irele. I owe a debt of gratitude to the sage counsel of Fred Burchsted, who has provided me with specific feedback on this work as well as a wealth of references and potential avenues to explore in my research.

Part of the inspiration for this project came from my access to the 1909 diary from Roosevelt's African safari that is held in the Theodore Roosevelt Collection at Houghton Library. Since my first glimpses of that document, I have benefited not only from the stunning collection there but, more importantly, from the knowledge and expertise of those who work there. I had the great fortune of meeting Wallace Dailey during the last months of his tenure as curator, and his generosity in sharing his knowledge of the collection was a great gift. I only wish that I had been able to take notes more quickly during our conversations. Even more significantly, this work was enhanced by the patient and guiding hand of Heather Cole. Even in my moments of desperation in trying to locate appropriate sources and documents, Heather calmly led me to the gems of the collection. I deeply appreciate her advice and direction.

It has been a great pleasure to benefit from the expert advice and support of many members of the University of Chicago Press. The text of this book was greatly improved by the highly skilled editing of Renaldo Migaldi; I truly appreciate his patience and incredible attention to detail. I would like to thank Logan Ryan Smith for his help in preparing the manuscript, and Jill Shimabukuro for her outstanding work in creating the book's design. I give my particular gratitude to Christie Henry for her unwavering belief in the project, and for her guidance and good humor.

Selected
Field Notes and Writings
of Theodore Roosevelt

During his wide-ranging travels, Theodore Roosevelt created a diverse body of field notes. The majority of his accounts were made in bound diaries, journals, and notebooks, but other writings, such as letters, manuscripts, and drawings, also contain relevant documentation he made while in the field.

This appendix identifies forty-three documents that demonstrate the breadth of the observations and records that relate to Roosevelt's trips to the field. Although it contains the majority of his journals and diaries, it is not meant to be exhaustive. The descriptions presented here are arranged in a set of loose categories. *Journals* are chronological accounts of events, are made in bound books with blank or lined pages. *Diaries* are bound books with pre-printed dates produced for that purpose, such as the Standard and Excelsior brand diaries. *Notebooks* are bound books that contain notes and descriptions which are not organized chronologically, such as Roosevelt's many detailed accounts of birds and mammals. Finally, *manuscripts* include short papers that Roosevelt wrote as a child in anticipation of reading to his family or members of the Roosevelt Museum, unbound sketches and drawings of natural history, and actual manuscript drafts that Roosevelt wrote while on safari in Africa. This taxonomy of Roosevelt's field notes is meant simply as a general guide, given that not every document fits neatly into a category (e.g., Notes on Natural History [TRC MS Am 1454.32] begins with undated notes, and then compiles journal accounts).

The majority of the material described here is held in the Theodore Roosevelt Collection (TRC) at Harvard's Houghton Library and in the Theodore Roosevelt Papers (TRP) at the Library of Congress. The relevant material in the TRC is catalogued in finding aids such as "MS Am 1540: Roosevelt, Theodore, 1858–1919, Theodore Roosevelt correspondence and compositions," "MS Am 1834: Roosevelt, Theodore, 1858–1919, additional correspondence and compositions," and "MS Am 1454: Roosevelt, Theodore, 1858–1919, diaries and notebooks." Links to scanned images of many of the original manuscripts are available in these finding aids. Roosevelt's diaries from 1878 to 1884 are held in the TRP and can be located using the finding aid "Theodore Roosevelt Papers: A Finding Aid to the Collection in the Library of Congress."

Although letters are not covered in this appendix, Roosevelt's correspondence often either was written "in the field" or was related to his field pursuits. Along with the selection published in Morison et al.'s *The Letters of Theodore Roosevelt*, a huge repository of Roosevelt's letters exist in the TRP, and can be searched using the three-volume *Index to the Theodore Roosevelt Papers* (Washington: Library of Congress, 1969). An electronic copy of this index is available on the LOC website. Letters also exist at other locations. In the TRC, relevant letters can be found using several different finding aids, including "MS Am 1454.48: Roosevelt, Theodore, 1858–1919, childhood correspondence," "MS Am 1834: Roosevelt, Theodore, 1858–1919, additional correspondence and compositions," "MS Am 1541 (in part): Roosevelt, Theodore, 1858–1919, letters to Kermit Roosevelt," "MS Am 1541.2: Roosevelt, Theodore, 1858–1919, letters to Ethel Roosevelt Derby." The Theodore Roosevelt Center at Dickinson State University also has a growing collection of digitized letters from these and other collections.

Some of the material covered in this appendix was published in *Theodore Roosevelt's Diaries of Boyhood and Youth* (New York: Scribner's, 1928). Although this volume has enabled many researchers to access Roosevelt's early writings without having to access the manuscripts, it should be used with caution. The actual source manuscripts of the material are not indicated, and in several places the transcription switches between manuscripts without indication. Most notably, there are two documents that detail the beginning of Roosevelt's "grand tour" on May 12, 1869, and *Diaries of*

Boyhood begins with a transcription of one (TRC MS Am 1454.55 [3]) and then switches to the other (TRC MS Am 1454.55 [2]) when the first ends. This is significant because it shows that Roosevelt recopied at least some of his diaries and journals after they were initially made. For example, Roosevelt's entry for May 12, 1869 is widely quoted as the text from *Diaries of Boyhood* and the entry in grand tour journal 1 (TRC MS Am 1454.55 [3]): "We go to Europe to day. We sail in the English Steamship, Scotia. It was very hard parting from our friend."[1] However, this is clearly an edited version of the May 12, 1869, entry from his 1869 diary, grand tour (TRC MS Am 1454.55 [2]): "A clear and warm day. We sailed for urope today. We sailed on the 'Scoitia.'" Other such accounts of corrections of misspellings, capitalization, and grammar suggest that the diary was written first (e.g., May 13, "mononous" to "monatonous"; May 15, "dolfins" to "dolphins"; May 18, "west indies" to "West Indies").

These examples reveal how Roosevelt followed in the traditions of the great naturalists, returning to his written accounts and re-writing and revising his entries in different journals and note-books. Although dated accounts in journals imply that the entries were written on the dates indicated, a review of Roosevelt's manu-scripts suggest that one should be careful about that assumption. A thorough examination of what can be determined about when and where these individual documents were created is important and may raise fundamental questions about Roosevelt's writing process, but it is outside the scope of this book.

Roosevelt's diaries from 1877 to 1886 are the subject of a forth-coming book by Edward P. Kohn, *A Most Glorious Ride: The Diaries of Theodore Roosevelt 1877–1886* (Albany: State University of New York Press, 2015). Unfortunately, the publication schedule for this volume has prevented Kohn's work from being referenced here, but the book is sure to become the authoritative work on these manu-scripts. It will also include one diary fragment not listed here: in 1882 Roosevelt kept a diary entitled "Diary of 5 Months in the New York Legislature," which is also transcribed in Morison et al., *Let-ters II*, 1469–73. The original of this document is held at the TRB.

1. "THREE WEEKS OF MY LIFE AGE NINE YEARS." TRC MS AM 1454.55 (1). *Jour-nal.* The first surviving journal of Theodore Roosevelt begins on August 10, 1868, when its author was nine years old, and concludes on September 5, 1868. The entries describe Roosevelt's rambles

around the home his family had rented at Barrytown, New York, in the Catskill Mountains. It is transcribed in *Diaries of Boyhood*, 1–9.

2. "RECORD OF THE ROOSEVELT MUSEUM." TRC MS AM 1541 (277). *Manuscript.* This document records the museum Roosevelt established in his home with his cousins James West Roosevelt and William Emlen Roosevelt. Its members kept collections and met periodically from about 1867 to 1874.

3. "MY EXPEDITION AND ADVENTURES." TRC MS AM 1454.35. *Manuscript.* This short essay with a watercolor cover was written in approximately 1868. Roosevelt describes adventures with his siblings and cousins, including rowing to a waterfall and being chased by dogs.

4. "ABOUT INSECTS AND FISHES." TRC MS AM 1541 (286). *Manuscript.* At the age of nine years, Roosevelt wrote this treatise on butterflies, dragonflies, fireflies, beetles, spiders, ticks, fish, crayfish, and other animals in a formal scientific format. He was careful to record that all of the "stories were gained by observation" and that "most of the insects are not in other books."

5. "THE WAR OF THE WOODS." TRC MS AM 1541 (287). *Manuscript.* This set of stories, in code and pictures, is housed in a notebook on the cover of which Roosevelt had originally written "1869 Natural history of Animals." The manuscript contains a story written in code, partially translated in the document, entitled "The War of the Woods," followed by two pages illustrated with stick figures.

6. 1869 DIARY, GRAND TOUR. TRC MS AM 1454.55 (2). *Diary.* In this Excelsior brand diary, with dates pre-printed three to a page, Roosevelt's accounts of his family's "grand tour" of Europe begin on May 12 and continue until September 14. Several pages later, Roosevelt began using this diary as a miniature plant press, placing flowers and foliage between the pages to dry. After his last plant specimen, beginning on the date reserved in the diary for November 21, Roosevelt began lists and notes about his and his father's money, the countries he went to in Europe, pieces of money saved for his collection, foreign languages, places he stayed, photographs he collected, a note on a visit to the doctor that states "nothing radically the matter with me but that I had a tendency to Bronkitius and some asmer," a floor plan of the boat that traveled on Loch Lomond in Scotland, and a list of the animals he rode upon during the trip. On the page dated December 24, Roosevelt returned to writing diary entries for Christmas Eve and Christmas Day. At

some point during the trip, Roosevelt returned to the front of the diary, beginning on the page dated January 1, where he wrote additional lists such as "the names of the friends I made in Europe," and then on the page dated January 31 he wrote: "As a great deal of my book we could not write in because we [could] not [call] may 12ᵗʰ Jan 1ˢᵗ I will write some accounts of the excursion we went and make it much longer than I could in my diary." He then writes these descriptions on the pages reserved in the diary for January 31 to March 13. These remarks are transcribed in *Diaries of Boyhood*, 49–55. The entries from August 8 to September 9 are also transcribed in *Diaries of Boyhood*, 40–49.

7. GRAND TOUR JOURNAL 1. TRC MS AM 1454.55 (3). *Journal.* This blank journal begins with an entry Roosevelt made for May 12, 1869, and continues until the last full entry, for August 7, 1869. These entries are transcribed in *Diaries of Boyhood, 10–39*. This journal then ends with a partial entry: "1869. August 8. Sun. Cham." There are six blank pages at the end of this journal.

This journal provides entries for May 12, 1869, to August 7, 1869, a range also covered in the first Excelsior diary (TRC MS Am 1454.55 2]). The entries in this journal appear to be edited versions of the accounts that appear in the Excelsior diary. The handwriting in this journal is less juvenile than that in the Excelsior diary: errors of spelling and capitalization have been corrected, and the flow of sentences has obviously been improved.

8. GRAND TOUR JOURNAL 2. TRC MS AM 1454.55 (4). *Journal.* This document begins with the title "My Journal of Northern Italy," and covers the dates ranging from September 9, 1869 to December 2, 1869. It also includes sections entitled "My Journal in Austria," "My Journal in Saxony," "My Journal in Prussia," "My Journal in Belgiem," and "My Journal in France." Roosevelt created a geographic index at the end. This journal is transcribed in *Diaries of Boyhood*, 59–106. The entry for September 9 that appears on page 59 in *Diaries of Boyhood* is from this journal, but a second transcription of the same day from the Excelsior diary appears on page 49 of *Diaries of Boyhood*, thus providing a point of direct comparison.

In this journal, Roosevelt made a revealing footnote in his entry for September 15. The entry reads: "Let the aniverserry of the morning of the day as one of the greatest humiliations and losses of my life. I lost my watch today." The passage later continues: "I then bought this book and we aslso a pencil." Roosevelt placed an asterisk next to the strikethrough of "this," and a note at the bottom of the page that says: "I mean a book." Presumably Roosevelt was copying an earlier set of diary or journal entries, as he had done with his first accounts of the journey beginning on May 12, and when he came to the entry that said "this book," he felt the need to change it because this recopied version of the journal entry was being written in a book different from the one he had described purchasing. The term "a book" refers to the original diary or journal, which is not part of any known collection.

9. GRAND TOUR JOURNAL 3. TRC MS AM 1454.55 (5). *Journal.* This journal contains entries from December 3, 1869, to January 8, 1870. It contains sections entitled "The Continuation of my Journal in France," "My Journal in Italy," and "My Journal in the Papel States." The entries are transcribed in *Diaries of Boyhood*, 107–58. The entries from December 24 and 25 are more extensive than those made for those dates in the first Excelsior diary (MS Am 1454.55 [2]). This journal ends with notes on accounts, and has floor plans of hotels in which Roosevelt and his family stayed.

10. GRAND TOUR JOURNAL 4. TRC MS AM 1454.55 (6). *Journal.* This document begins on January 9, 1870, with "My Journal in the Papel States," and it continues to September 10, 1870. It documents Roosevelt's travels through such European cities as Rome, Florence, Paris, and London. A continuing section entitled "Now My Journal in the United States" covers his return to New York and his late summer rambles. A note after the entry for August 4 states: "I lost my Journal till September 10th (we were at Oyster Bay and Sarato Richfield)." There are various notes on his accounts at the back of this volume, and the journal entries are transcribed in *Diaries of Boyhood*, 159–238.

11. "STARTED FOR THE ADIRONDACKS." TRC MS AM 1454.55 (7). *Journal.* This document covers Roosevelt's travels from August 1 to 31, 1871, in the Adirondacks with his uncle Cornelius Roosevelt and his wife Laura, his uncle Hilborne West, his wife Susy and their son James West, his mother and father and siblings Anna, Corinne, and Elliott. Their travels took them to Lake George, Plattsburg, Paul Smiths, Lake Placid, and White River Junction in New York State, and to Mount Washington, North Conway, and Lake Win-

nipesuakee in New Hampshire. In his daily accounts, Roosevelt records natural history observations and describes species using Latin names. Roosevelt's father and uncle West struck out with the three boys, along with guides, in boats into "the bush" on August 8. Along the way they saw tracks of deer, wolves, and bears and fished, fought off blackflies, and camped in tents. Roosevelt fell asleep as his father read from *The Last of the Mohicans*. This journal is transcribed in *Diaries of Boyhood*, 239–60.

12. "NOTES ON THE FAUNA OF THE ADIRONDAC MTS." TRC MS AM 1454.31. *Notebook*. Roosevelt's own description of this document in his "preface" to this notebook describes it best: "The following notes were made during the last two weeks of July, 1871, the last two weeks of August 1874, the first two weeks of August 1875, and the last week of June and first week of July 1877, in Franklin Co., New York, chiefly by Lake St Regis and in the woods north and west for a distance of some twenty miles, but also by the Sarranac Lakes, and on the roads from Malone and Plattsburg." Roosevelt crossed out the last paragraph of his preface and added a sentence which suggests that when he returned to create this document, presumably sometime in late 1877 or early 1878, as an undergraduate, he was feeling that the observations and natural history he had accumulated did not match the rigor of his current work: "In my expeditions into the woods I went much more as a hunter and fisherman than as an ornithologist; and so in my notes I can only pretend to give a few remarks on the common summer residents of the region." He divided the accounts in the document into taxonomic groups: "Mammals," "Birds," and "Fishes."

13. ANIMAL DRAWINGS AND SKETCHES. TRC MS AM 1541 (288). *Manuscript*. This set of sixteen drawings and sketches is presumably from the 1870s, and it includes renderings of mice, shrews, weasels, a Spanish sparrow, African wildlife, and sailboats. Two of the sketches feature anatomical details such as bone structures, heads, and paws. In Dresden in 1873 after his trip to Egypt and the Holy Lands, Roosevelt studied with a painter named Wegener, "a man of considerable talent, a specialist in the painting of prairie scenes and author of several books on animal life."[2] It seems likely that Roosevelt was able to study with Johann Friedrich Wilhelm Wegener (1812–79), a Dresden-born painter, etcher, and lithographer

who had traveled widely and painted many landscapes, including some in the United States.[3]

14. "NOTES ON NATURAL HISTORY." TRC MS AM 1454.32, TRB. *Journal.* Although this document begins with accounts of species and natural history anecdotes related to Roosevelt by others, such as the taxidermist "Mr. J. G. Bell," the majority of it contains journal entries. Roosevelt records dates beginning in the late summer of 1872, and makes a marginal note part way into the document: "Animals of Dobbs Ferry N. Y. Observations made in the summer of 1872." Roosevelt continues to add observations for different locations, moving on to "Notes on Mammals of Garrisons N. T. made in 1875 by Mr. W. Osborn," and then "Orange New Jersey Sept 16th 1872," and "Mt. Washington N. H." The notebook then continues with "Field Book for 1874 and 1875 Chiefly Ornithology," with accounts ranging from 1874 to 1875 at Oyster Bay and Saint Regis Lake in New York state; Seabright, New Jersey; Mount Mansfield and Burlington in Vermont; and Garrisons, New York. The last part of the book includes a table of the number of skins Roosevelt collected in 1875, a "game record" for 1874 and 1875, indexes to mammals and birds, a page of bird sketches, and a page with a map and notes of his accounts.

15. JOURNAL IN EGYPT AND THE HOLY LANDS. TRC MS AM 1454.55 (8). *Journal.* Roosevelt began this journal on October 16, 1872 as he "sailed in the Russia," and finished it on May 12, 1873, at the Great Exposition in Vienna. The journal is a chronological record of Roosevelt's explorations at such sites as the Great Pyramids, the Ramesseum, and Jerusalem, and of the shots he took at many birds and also at jackals. The end of the bound journal is filled with doodles, sketches, accounts, and names, one of the most notable being a very legible "Edith Carow." After the accounts from the Old World, there are two pages that describe a "Diary in the North Eastern States in August of 1872." This account details travels which Roosevelt started in New York on August 19, continued to Boston (where he saw the Bunker Hill Monument) and Moosehead Lake in Maine, and then completed back in New York on August 30.

16. "ZOOLOGICAL RECORD" OF EGYPT AND THE HOLY LANDS. TRC MS AM 1454.37. *Notebook.* The first page of this document outlines its dates of coverage as being "from Oct 1872 to September 1873," and its author as "T. Roosevelt Jr." This notebook compiles nonchrono-

logical facts, observations, and collecting records from Roosevelt's travels in Egypt and the Holy Lands in sections including "Zoölogical Record"; "Ornithological Record"; "Ornithological Observations"; "Catalogue of Birds"; "Reptilia, Classified by Brehm"; "Batrachia, Classified according to Brehm"; and "Game Record." These accounts build on the journal entries Roosevelt kept for this trip, and compile the natural history information and specimens he gathered in the style of Elliott Coues and John James Audubon.

17. "REMARKS ON BIRDS 1874," 2 VOLS. TRC MS AM 1454.33. *Notebooks.* Containing species accounts of birds, mostly those Roosevelt collected on his 1872–73 trip to Egypt and the Holy Lands, this two-volume document sets out the physical measurements and descriptions of a range of largely Old World birds, along with accounts of their behavior.

18. "ARDEA RUSSATA." TRC MS AM 1541 (290). *Manuscript.* This four-page description of the "buff fronted cow heron" was informed by a specimen Roosevelt collected in Egypt on December 23, 1872. He provides ample measurements and estimations of the bird's plumage, as well as perspectives on its behavior, such as how he had "occasionally seen it fishing for small fish in the pools left by the retiring waters of the Nile" and how the "Naturalist Brehm says that he has seen as many as twenty of these birds on the back of a single elephant." A marginal note on the last page of the manuscript suggests that it was "presented by Mr. T. Roosevelt Jr. April 7th 1874," presumably to the gathered members of his natural history society in the service of the Roosevelt Museum.

19. "ORNITHOLOGY OF EGYPT BETWEEN CAIRO AND ASSOUAN." TRC MS AM 1541 (291). *Manuscript.* In this four-page paper, Roosevelt first describes the physical geography of the region, and then details the birds to be found there, such as vultures, sand grouse, sand larks, chats, and "trumpeter Bullfinch, or rosy or desert sparrow (as it is indifferently termed)." The paper was "read. Dec. 22 1874 by T. Roosevelt Jr.," likely at a meeting of his childhood natural history society.

20. "REMARKS ON THE COLOURATION OF BIRDS." TRC MS AM 1541 (289). *Manuscript.* In a four-page presentation format similar to his "Ardea russata" (TRC MS Am 1541 [290]) and "Ornithology of Egypt between Cairo and Assouan" (TRC MS Am 1541 [291]), Roosevelt suggests that he will "do nothing more than give a few observations

on the colouration of various birds," and goes on to discuss the general variation seen in primaries, secondaries, teriaries, wing coverts, and tail feathers. Given that the manuscript is undated, one assumes that it was presented to the natural history society sometime around 1874.

21. 1875 DIARY, "T. R. JR. SPORTING & COLLECTING." TRC MS AM 1454.55 (9). *Diary.* In this Pocket Diary, Roosevelt makes entries from January 16 to November 6, and records his observations of birds and collections of "skins." He records his time in Oyster Bay and Saint Regis Lake, New York. At the end of the diary, he includes in the "memoranda" pages a summary of collections and game record from 1874 and 1875. Roosevelt kept two Pocket Diary books for 1875, and in the other (TRC MS Am 1454.55 [10]) he recorded his athletic accomplishments. Although some dates, like August 25, have entries in both journals, the content does not overlap, with natural history records in one and athletic information in the other.

22. 1875 DIARY, "ROOSEVELT SPORTING CALENDAR." TRC MS AM 1454.55 (10). *Diary.* In a Pocket Diary for 1875, Roosevelt recorded his exploits on the playing field, in explicit comparison to his relatives. Entries are scattered over dates from August 21 to December 11. Events include racing, the standing jump, the running jump, the standing high jump, the running high jump, vaulting, boxing, and wrestling. In the section at the end reserved for "memoranda," Roosevelt recorded his records, and his bodily measurements on November 1, 1875.

23. "REMARKS ON THE ZOOLOGY OF OYSTER BAY." TRC MS AM 1454.34. *Notebook.* Roosevelt indicated on the title page of this notebook that he commenced this work in October of 1875, but the specimens it records indicate that he continued to add collection records at least into 1877. His "preface" describes how he adopted the "classification of Coues, in his Key to North American Birds." In "Part I. Ornithology," Roosevelt presents species accounts of 115 birds, starting with "Turdus migratorius" (the American robin) and ending with "Empidonax acadicus" (Acadian flycatcher, now *Empidonax virescens*). Each species account records information such as the numbers of the specimens Roosevelt collected, the collection dates, the contents of the crops, and the birds' physical measurements. He continues with thirteen accounts, some incomplete,

in "Part 2^d Mammals," following the classification of "Baird" and "Allen." He completes his notebook with one-page lists of species in "Part 3^d Reptiles," "Part 4th Amphibia," and "Part 5th Fishes," all according to "Dekay."

24. "FIELD BOOK OF ZOOLOGY. 1876 & 1877 & 1878 & 1879." TRC MS AM 1454.38. *Journal.* Roosevelt packed this volume with journal accounts on natural history, arranged by locality. The first account details his natural history study in Oyster Bay, in separate chronological sections for the years 1876–79. The notes on this location are by far the most numerous, filling 166 of the 271 pages used in this bound volume. After his journal for Oyster Bay, Roosevelt continues with short accounts for "Forest Hill (near Boston)" in 1877, "Island Falls Aroostook Co. Maine" for 1878 and 1879, and "Garrisons New York" for 1876 and 1877. He then adds two pages of journal material for a trip "made in Long Island Sound," July 12–15, 1876, and follows it with a two-page account of a trip to Red Bank, New Jersey, July 4–8, 1876. The placement of these two accounts in reverse chronological order highlights a feature of the entire manuscript: these journals were written or copied from other journals or diaries, and from memory, some time after they were written. Roosevelt completes his "Field Book of Zoology" with accounts from Cambridge, Massachusetts, starting shortly after his arrival at Harvard in 1876, and provides additional accounts for the years 1877, 1878, and 1879. The amount of material covered in each of those years roughly tracks the waxing and waning of his dedication to pursuing a career as a scientist. There are two journal pages devoted to 1876, twenty-two to 1877, and one each for 1878 and 1879.

25. 1877 DIARY. TRC MS AM 1454.55 (11). *Diary.* Roosevelt began writing in this Standard Diary as he returned to Harvard on January 7 to continue his first-year studies, and it continues into the fall of his sophomore year. The first months of this journal have a few brief entries. Short accounts on four days in April (April 1, 10, 15, and 16) from Forest Hill, Massachusetts, contain lists of species that appear in much more detailed form in the accounts for Forest Hill in Roosevelt's "Field Book of Zoology" (TRC MS Am 1454.38) for those same dates. It seems likely that this is an example of how Roosevelt first made brief notes in a pocket diary

and then significantly expanded them in subsequent accounts, a practice he later used extensively in his African safari. In June, Roosevelt records his travel to the "Adirondacs" with Harry Minot, his sporadic rambles in Oyster Bay in July and August, and his return to Harvard on September 27. Roosevelt's observations with Minot helped fuel their publication "The Summer Birds of the Adirondacks." He makes short accounts on some dates in the fall of 1877 about his studies and sporting exploits, and ends the year with several poignant entries about his father's illness. In the "memoranda" section at the end of the diary, he notes his "Collections for year" and "Game bag."

26. 1878 DIARY. TRP. *Diary*. Shortly after Roosevelt returned to Harvard for the spring of his sophomore year, his father died. Many of the accounts in this Excelsior Diary made during that spring are of grief and soul-searching. He spent much of the summer of 1878 in Oyster Bay, and then in September went to hunt in Maine, where he met Bill Sewall and Wilmot Dow—two locals who would become longtime companions—before returning to Harvard for the fall of his junior year. On Friday, October 18, he went with his friend Dick Saltonstall to Chestnut Hill, where he met Alice Lee. The next day, he described Alice as "a very sweet pretty girl," and on Sunday, after church, he recorded that he "went chestnutting with Miss Alice Lee." Not much more than a month later, he recorded a vow to marry her, but later tore the pages for November 29–30 from the binding.

27. 1879 DIARY. TRP. *Diary*. Roosevelt recorded in his Standard Diary for 1879 how he returned to Island Falls, Maine, in late February to snowshoe and hunt with Sewall and Dow. After he returned to Cambridge in March, many of his entries are consumed with Alice. He spent the summer of 1879 living the outdoor life at Oyster Bay, becoming "brown from the waist up" (July 9) and returned to Harvard after another trip to Maine in late August and early September. At the end of the diary he recorded his accounts for 1877–79, and a "game bag" tally for the years 1874 to 1879.

28. 1880 DIARY. TRP. Diary. As he began his last term at Harvard, Roosevelt's accounts in his Excelsior Diary reveal that he was looking to the future. He recorded choosing a diamond ring for Alice on February 2, and reported paying less attention to his studies as he reflected on the joy of his college years and his optimism

for his future life with Alice. He wrote a glowing assessment of his time in college after commencement on June 30. Starting in mid-August, Roosevelt recorded the adventures he and his brother Elliott had had on their "Midwest tramp" in Illinois, Minnesota, and Iowa. He continued to keep diary entries for his marriage to Alice Lee on his twenty-second birthday (October 27). His account on New Year's Eve describes his enchantment with his "Darling Wifie": "Thus ends by far the happiest year I have ever spent." In subsequent pages he summarized his expenses for 1878–80 and tallied an extensive "game bag" for the years 1873–80.

29. 1881. DIARY. TRP. *Diary.* Roosevelt made short but regular accounts throughout his Excelsior Diary for 1881. Many of the accounts for January and February recount sleigh rides and parties, and by March 21 Roosevelt admits to himself that he has "been rather loafing lately" but is "now working very hard at my law." He worked on his law studies and his "Naval History" at the Astor Library in May, then left that month for a honeymoon in Europe. He did not arrive back in the United States until October 2. Upon his return, he worked at his law studies and at his book, and made a successful run for New York assemblyman. Although Roosevelt did document a few outdoor experiences in Europe—he climbed the Matterhorn on August 4—the notes at the end of this diary only document expenses; there is no game bag tally for 1881.

30. 1882 DIARY. TRP. *Diary.* The Daily Memorandum Book, made by Francis & Loutrel in New York, that Roosevelt selected to document 1882 remains largely empty. There are twenty-four days that contain entries, with the majority of those including short phrases that indicate the opening and adjournment of the legislature and Roosevelt's movements between Albany, New York, and Boston. The end of the book has only one additional note: "Cash for 1882, On Hand, Jan 1st 300.00."

31. 1883 DIARY. TRP. *Diary.* Although it was printed with the dates for 1883, Roosevelt used this Daily Memorandum Book for 1883 to record events from both that year and 1884. He filled the pages for January 1 to January 10 with accounts for those days in 1883, describing his activities in the New York Assembly. He also recorded a game bag for his "sporting trip on Little Missouri, Dakota, Sept 10th—26th, 1883" in the section at the end of the book marked "Miscellaneous." This is when Roosevelt shot his buffalo. He also

documented accounts for 1883 in the section for "cash." In the pages reserved for August of 1883, Roosevelt later recorded his "Trip from Little Missouri to the Bighorn Mts." from August 16 to October 4, 1884. Presumably, when Roosevelt began his trip to the Bighorn Mountains, he had this largely empty diary from 1883 with him, but not his diary for 1884 (1884 diary, TRP).

Given that calendar dates and days of the week change from year to year, Roosevelt needed to compensate for entering diary entries for 1884 in a diary with preprinted dates for 1883. On the preprinted page for August 18, 1883, a Saturday, in this diary, Roosevelt recorded the events for Saturday, August 16, 1884. He crossed out the printed "18" and wrote in "16" and "1884." He did a similar thing for the following two days; on the page for Sunday he crossed out "19" and wrote in "17"; on the page for Monday he crossed out "20" and wrote in "18." Roosevelt made a daily diary account on Tuesday, August 19, 1884, but he left the preprinted "21 Tuesday" on the page. Roosevelt then continued to follow the day of the week for his accounts, but did not correct the calendar dates until the page with the preprinted "September" and "1 Saturday." On this page he crossed out "September" and wrote in "Aug 30th." He corrected the pages for the next three days, but then followed a similar pattern throughout much of September, entering his accounts on the correct day of the week (leaving the calendar dates uncorrected). At the transition from September to October, he made a set of corrections similar to those he had done for the previous month.

32. 1884 DIARY. TRP. *Diary.* The entries in this Excelsior Diary for 1884 begin with a large "X" directly under the February 14 date, followed by: "The light has gone out of my life." Roosevelt fills the space allotted to February 16 and 17 with a description of how on the 14th his first child, Alice Lee Roosevelt, was born, and then his wife died in his arms. He continues the tragic narrative with: "My mother had died in the same house, on the same day, but a few hours previously." Although he returned to Albany that spring, the next entry in his diary is not until June 9, marking his arrival at his ranch in the Badlands. He made several additional entries in June, and then the diary is blank until the appearance of additional entries from the Badlands in November and Decem-

ber. Roosevelt documented his trip to the Bighorn Mountains in August, September, and early October in his diary for 1883 (1883 diary, TRP).

33. 1886 DIARY, BADLANDS. TRC MS AM 1454.55 (12). *Diary*. Unlike many of Roosevelt's other diaries, the pages of this Excelsior diary contain entries that are rarely more than a few words or a sentence in length. Despite being spartan, the entry on March 24—"Thieves stole boat; started to build another to go after them"—is part of an early telling of one of Roosevelt's best stories.

34. ACCOUNT BOOK OF THE MALTESE CROSS RANCH. TRC MS AM 1454.39. *Notebook*. Starting with an ink sketch of the Maltese Cross brand, Roosevelt used this notebook to record contracts, accounts, receipts, and information about his ranch and cattle herd.

35. 1898 DIARY, CUBA. TRC MS AM 1454.39. *Diary*. The first entry Roosevelt made in this Standard Diary on April 16 is a caustic assessment of President McKinley's reluctance to go to war, describing how McKinley's "weakness and vacillation are even more ludicrous than painful." Roosevelt documented his frustrations with the War Department in the days that led up to the Spanish American War, and also kept brief notes on the battles and activities of the Rough Riders.

36. 1901 DIARY, COUGAR HUNT. TRC MS AM 1454.55 (13). *Diary*. Roosevelt made entries in this Standard Diary only during the trip he took in 1901 to hunt cougar and bobcat with Philip Stewart, Gerald Webb, and John Goff. In the sections at the end of the diary reserved for "memoranda" and "cash account," Roosevelt included information on cougars that he had gathered on his hunting trip.

37. 1905 DIARY, HUNTING IN OKLAHOMA AND COLORADO. TRC MS AM 1454.55 (14). *Diary*. In this Excelsior Diary for 1905, Roosevelt recorded his Western hunting trip during April and May. On this trip, he hunted coyotes with "Catch 'Em Alive" Jack Abernathy in Oklahoma, and black bear with John Goff, Alexander Lambert, and Philip Stewart in Colorado.

38. CANEBRAKE NOTEBOOK. TRC MS AM 1454.56. *Notebook*. This document includes undated notes on the trip Roosevelt took to Stamboul, Louisiana, in 1907 to hunt for bear. Roosevelt records observations of diverse wildlife, including ivory-billed woodpeckers, and documents his long-anticipated killing of a Louisiana black

TITLE	1870s	1880s	1890s	1900s
1 "Three weeks of my life"	J			
2 Roosevelt Museum	M M M M M M			
3 "Expedition & Adventures"	M M			
4 "About insects and fishes"	M			
5 "The War of the Woods"	M			
6 1869 diary, grand tour	D			
7 Grand tour journal 1	J			
8 Grand tour journal 2	J			
9 Grand tour journal 3	J			
10 Grand tour journal 4	J			
11 "Started for the Adirondacks"	J			
12 "Fauna of the Adirondac Mts."	N N N			
13 Drawings and sketches	M M M M M M M M M M M M M M			
14 "Notes on Natural History"	J J J J			
15 Egypt & Holy Lands journal	J J			
16 "Zoological Record"	N N N N			
17 "Remarks on birds" (2 vols.)	N			
18 "Ardea russata"	M			
19 "Ornithology of Egypt"	M			
20 "Colouration of Birds"	M			
21 1875 diary	D			
22 1875 diary	D			
23 "Zoology of Oyster Bay"	N N N			
24 "Field Book of Zoology"	J J J			
25 1877 diary	D			
26 1878 diary	D			

#	Document	Markings
27	1879 diary	D
28	1880 diary	D
29	1881 diary	D
30	1882 diary	D
31	1883 diary	D D
32	1884 diary	D
33	1886 diary, Badlands	D
34	Maltese Cross Ranch	N N N
35	1898 diary, Cuba	D
36	1901 diary, cougar hunt	D
37	1905 diary, Okla. and Colo.	D
38	Canebrake notebook	N
39	1909 diary, Africa 1	D
40	1910 diary, Africa 2	D
41	"African Game Trails"	M M
42	African life history	N N
43	Game book	N N N N N N N N N N N N N N N

Roosevelt created a large body of written work over the course of his life that related to his trips to the field, including journals (J), diaries (D), notebooks (N), and manuscripts (M). The chronological accounts (journals and diaries) are charted here relative to their dates of coverage. The nonchronological accounts are charted according to the estimated dates of their creation (in the case of manuscripts) and the dates their content covers (in the case notebooks). Documents that can fit into more than one category have been placed in the section that best describes the majority of their material.

bear (*Ursus americanus luteolus*). Roosevelt notes that upon investigation, the bear was found to have beetles, acorns, and palmetto berries in its stomach.

39. 1909 DIARY, AFRICA 1. TRC MS AM 1454.55 (15). *Diary.* Although Roosevelt's first entries in this Excelsior Diary are sparse—mostly documenting his voyage from New York to Mombasa, starting on March 23—the records start to become expansive on April 24 with descriptions of his hunts. Roosevelt records his collection of diverse game, including lions, zebras, gazelles, dik diks, rhinoceros, giraffes, hyenas, pythons, and whydah birds. He includes measurements of height and weight, notes on stomach contents, and sketches of the animals and the placement of his bullets.

40. 1910 DIARY, AFRICA 2. TRC MS AM 1454.55 (16), TRB. *Diary.* Roosevelt recorded the 1910 part of his safari in a T. J. & J. Smith's Pocket Diary. New Year's Day found him trekking up the White Nile to find the white rhinoceros. Although the diary contains some sketches and notes on game, he made far fewer notes than he had in his 1909 diary.

41. "AFRICAN GAME TRAILS" MANUSCRIPT. TRC MS AM 1454.28. *Manuscript.* Along with keeping extensive field notes in his diaries while on safari, Roosevelt wrote a series of articles for *Scribner's Magazine,* which later would be published in book form. Although they were a different form of "field notes," Roosevelt wrote the text of these articles and sent multiple copies—sometimes one copy through Nairobi and the other through Cairo—to his editor in New York. The original manuscript is now housed in the TRC.

42. AFRICAN LIFE HISTORY NOTEBOOKS. TRC MS AM 1834 (1089). *Notebooks.* These three notebooks contain manuscript notes for Roosevelt's book *Life-Histories of African Game Animals,* which he published in 1914 with Edmund Heller. These undated notebooks were presumably filled well after he returned from Africa, and contained information assimilated from his memory and other notes.

43. GAME BOOK. TRC MS AM 1454.29. *Notebook.* This document begins with the title "Trophies at Sagamore Hill, Theodore Roosevelt," and provides taxonomically arranged information on the species of big game that Roosevelt collected. The dates, localities, and other details are included, along with references to where the collection of those specimens is described in Roosevelt's published hunting accounts.

Selected
Theodore Roosevelt
Bibliography

Along with Roosevelt's significant body of written work in his diaries, notebooks, journals, and letters, he placed a torrent of writing in print. Unfortunately, a comprehensive bibliography of Roosevelt's work has never been published. One of the most extensive treatments of Roosevelt's writings is John Hall Wheelock's alphabetically arranged *A Bibliography of Theodore Roosevelt* (New York: Charles Scribner's Sons, 1920). Additional lists and resources on Roosevelt's bibliography are held in the TRC, including the most comprehensive unpublished resource, which is a set of several thousand index cards detailing Roosevelt's published writings.

As outlined in Wheelock, an overlapping and sometimes bewildering set of "collected works" of Roosevelt have been published, beginning in 1901. Just as Roosevelt returned to his diary and journal accounts to make fuller descriptions of natural history in his notebooks, his published writings were also layered. Many of his writings first appeared in serial publications like *Century Magazine* and *Scribner's Magazine* and then became chapters in his books. Two examples of this are the articles Roosevelt wrote for *Scribner's Magazine* on his trips to Africa and the River of Doubt, which later became *African Game Trails* and *Through the Brazilian Wilderness.*

The following is a chronological selection of Roosevelt's books. It largely follows Wheelock and other unpublished sources.

The Naval War of 1812: Or the History of the United States Navy during the Last War With Great Britain. New York: G. P. Putnam's Sons, 1882.

Hunting Trips of a Ranchman: Sketches of Sport on the Northern Cattle Plains. New York: G. P. Putnam's Sons, 1885.

Thomas Hart Benton. Boston: Houghton Mifflin, 1886.

Essays on the Practical Politics (Questions of the Day, No. 49). New York: G. P. Putnam's Sons, 1888.

Ranch Life and the Hunting Trail. New York: Century, 1888.

The Winning of the West, Vols. I and II. New York: G. P. Putnam's Sons, 1889. Contains "From the Alleghanies to the Mississippi, 1769–1776," and "From the Alleghanies to the Mississippi, 1777–1783."

New York. New York: Longmans, Green & Company, 1891.

The Wilderness Hunter: An Account of the Big Game of the United States, and its Chase With Horse, Hound, and Rifle. New York: G. P. Putnam's Sons, 1893.

Gouverneur Morris. Boston: Houghton Mifflin, 1888.

American Big Game Hunting: Book of the Boone and Crockett Club. Edited by Roosevelt and G. B. Grinnell. New York: Forest and Stream, 1893.

The Winning of the West, Vol. III. New York: G. P. Putnam's Sons, 1894. Contains "Founding of the Trans-Alleghany Commonwealths, 1784–1790."

Hunting in Many Lands: Book of the Boone and Crockett Club. Edited by Roosevelt and G. B. Grinnell. New York: Forest and Stream, 1895.

The Winning of the West, Vol. IV. New York: G. P. Putnam's Sons, 1896. Contains "Louisiana and the Northwest, 1791–1807."

American Ideals and Other Essays, Social and Political. New York: G. P. Putnam's Sons, 1897.

Trail and Camp Fire: Book of the Boone and Crockett Club. Edited by Roosevelt and G. B. Grinnell. New York: Forest and Stream, 1897.

Hero Tales from American History. With H. C. Lodge. New York: Century, 1898.

Big Game Hunting in the Rockies and in the Great Plains. New York: G. P. Putnam's Sons, 1899.

The Rough Riders. New York: Charles Scribner's Sons, 1899.

Hunting the Grisly and Other Sketches: An Account of the Big Game of the United States, and its Chase With Horse, Hound, and Rifle. New York: G. P. Putnam's Sons, 1900. Wheelock notes: "This is a reprint of Part II of the 'Wilderness Hunter,' originally published in 1893."

Hunting Trips on the Prairie and in the Mountains. New York: G. P. Putnam's Sons, 1900. The title page of the book includes the note: "'Hunting Trips of a Ranchman' Part II."

Oliver Cromwell. New York: Charles Scribner's Sons, 1900.

The Strenuous Life: Essays and Addresses. New York: Century, 1900.

The Deer Family. With T. S. Van Dyke, D. G. Eliot, and A. J. Stone. New York: Macmillan, 1902.

Outdoor Pastimes of an American Hunter. New York: Charles Scribner's Sons, 1905.

Good Hunting in Pursuit of Big Game in the West. New York: Harper & Bros., 1907.

Stories of the Great West. New York: Century, 1909.

African and European Addresses. New York: G. P. Putnam's Sons, 1910.

African Game Trails: An Account of the African Wanderings of an American Hunter Naturalist. New York: Charles Scribner's Sons, 1910.

Biological Analogies in History: Delivered before the University of Oxford, June 7, 1910.
    London: Henry Frowde, 1910.

The New Nationalism. New York: Outlook, 1910.

Applied Ethics; Being One of the William Belden Noble Lectures for 1910. Cambridge,
    MA: Harvard University Press, 1911.

Conservation of Womanhood and Childhood. New York: Funk & Wagnalls, 1912.

Chapters of a Possible Autobiography. New York: Outlook, 1913.

History as Literature, and Other Essays. New York: Charles Scribner's Sons, 1913.

Theodore Roosevelt: An Autobiography. New York: Macmillan., 1913.

Life-Histories of African Game Animals. New York: Charles Scribner's Sons, 1914.

Through the Brazilian Wilderness. New York: Charles Scribner's Sons, 1914.

America and the World War. New York: Charles Scribner's Sons, 1915.

Americanism: An Address. New York: National Americanization Committee, 1916.

A Book-Lover's Holidays in the Open. New York: Charles Scribner's Sons, 1916.

Fear God and Take Your Own Part. New York: George H. Doran, 1916.

The Foes of Our Own Household. New York: George H. Doran, 1917.

National Strength and International Duty. Princeton, NJ: Princeton University Press,
    1917.

The Great Adventure: Present-Day Studies In American Nationalism. New York: Charles
    Scribner's Sons, 1918.

Notes

The sources consulted are listed in full in this work, with the exception of the following, which are abbreviated:

TRB Theodore Roosevelt Birthplace National Historic Site
TRC Theodore Roosevelt Collection, Harvard University
TRCDS Theodore Roosevelt Center, Dickinson State University
TRP Theodore Roosevelt Papers, Library of Congress

INTRODUCTION

1. "President Gives Welcome to 6,800," *Chicago Daily Tribune*, January 2, 1903. Roosevelt's New Year's Day open houses have become legendary. For a thorough description of a later event, see E. Morris, *The Rise of Theodore Roosevelt* (New York: Random House, 1979), xi–xxxiv. For a description of the White House renovations see: C. Moore, "The Restoration of the White House," *Century Magazine* 65 (1903): 807–31; G. Brown, "The New White House," *Harper's Weekly* 50 (1906): 989–93, 1003; M. Schuyler, "The New White House," *Architectural Record* 13 (1903): 359–88.

2. "White House Ball," *Washington Post*, January 4, 1902; "Dined at White House," *Washington Post*, January 17, 1902; "In the New East Room," *Washington Post*, December 19, 1902; "Speech in East Room," *Washington Post*, November 20, 1903; "Jackies at White House," *Washington Post*, November 3, 1903; "A Bride at the White House," *New York Tribune*, February 18, 1906. Roosevelt hosted numerous wrestling matches in the White House; see "Jiu Jitsu Beats Grant," *Sun*, March 2, 1905; "Mighty Japanese Amuses Roosevelt," *New York Times*, November 12, 1907; L. B. Johnson, *A White House Diary* (New York: Holt, Rinehart and Winston, 1970), 65.

3. See E. Looker, *The White House Gang* (New York: Fleming H. Revell, 1929), which was also published as a series of articles written by Earle Looker that appeared in *Good Housekeeping* between August 1929 and January 1930; I. H. Hooker, *Forty-Two Years in the White House* (Boston: Houghton Mifflin, 1934), 28–29.

4. TRP, letter from Roosevelt to Theodore Roosevelt, Jr., January 3, 1909.

5. Looker, *The White House Gang*, 16.

6. "Roosevelt Led 60 on a Bully Tramp," *New York Times*, November 8, 1908; "Led by President," *Washington Post*, November 8, 1908; Theodore Roosevelt, *An Autobiography* (New York: Macmillan, 1913), 52; C. Depew, *My Memories of Eighty Years* (New York: Scribner's, 1922), 170.

7. Theodore Roosevelt, the subject of this book, is now generally referred to as

"Theodore Roosevelt." His father is Theodore Roosevelt Sr. His son, technically Theodore Roosevelt III, is known as Theodore Roosevelt Jr. Confusion can arise when the young Theodore Roosevelt refers to himself as "Theodore Roosevelt Jr." in his notebooks.

8. *The Letters of Theodore Roosevelt* is an eight-volume selection of Roosevelt's letters that was published by Harvard University Press between 1951 and 1954, under the direction of lead editor E. E. Morison. Other editors who contributed to the project were J. M. Blum, J. J. Buckley, H. W. Wigglesworth, S. Rice, and A. D. Chandler. Even-numbered volumes contain appendixes that include timelines of Roosevelt's life as well as indexes to the letters. Here, this work is referred to as "Morison et al.," with the volume number and pages indicated. Morison et al., *Letters III* (Cambridge, MA: Harvard University Press, 1951), 422–23, letter from Roosevelt to Theodore Roosevelt, Jr., February 9, 1903; "Roosevelt Boys to Hunt," *New York Times*, February 24, 1903.

9. W. W. Sewall, *Bill Sewall's Story of T. R.* (New York: Harper and Bros., 1919), 111.

10. Quotation from Morison et al., *Letters III*, 422, letter from Roosevelt to Kermit Roosevelt, February 8, 1903; H. Hagedorn, *Roosevelt in the Bad Lands* (Boston: Houghton Mifflin, 1921), 468.

11. Morison et al., *Letters III*, 422–23, letter from Roosevelt to Theodore Roosevelt Jr., February 9, 1903.

12. H. Hagedorn, *The Boys' Life of Theodore Roosevelt* (New York: Harper & Brothers, 1918), 63–64.

13. D. Sinclair, "The Monarchical Manners of the White House," *Harper's Weekly* 6 (1908): 14–15.

14. The author's grandfather, B. L. Canfield, recounted stories to his family of how, as a child sitting on a hill, he witnessed Roosevelt giving a speech in Battle Creek, Michigan, from the back of a train. The thing he remembered most was that Roosevelt's face turned bright red as he delivered his speech.

15. "Sargent, the Artist, Arrives," *Boston Daily Globe*, January 19, 1903.

16. "John S. Sargent," *New York Times*, January 20, 1903.

17. Quotation from Morison et al, *Letters III*, 264, letter from Roosevelt to Henry White, May 15, 1902. For Roosevelt's solicitation of Sargent's services, and accounts of his subsequent interactions during his visit, see TRP, letter from Roosevelt to John Singer Sargent, May 13, 1902; TRP, letter from Robert Collier to Theodore Roosevelt, December 6, 1902; TRP, letter from Roosevelt to John Singer Sargent, January 29, 1903; TRP, letter from Roosevelt to John Singer Sargent, February 3, 1903; TRP, Roosevelt diary entry, February 1, 1903; TRC MS Am 1541(50), letter from Roosevelt to Kermit Roosevelt, February 15, 1903; TRC MS Am 1541(51), letter from Roosevelt to Kermit Roosevelt, February 19, 1903; W. Kloss, *Art in the White House: A Nation's Pride* (Washington: White House Historical Association, 1992), 225.

18. "Chartran Will Paint Roosevelt," *San Francisco Chronicle*, January 4, 1903; "Portraits of Mrs. Roosevelt and the President's Daughter," *Boston Daily Globe*, February 9, 1903; TRC MS Am 1541 (48), letter from Roosevelt to Kermit Roosevelt, February 1, 1903.

19. L. F. Abbott, ed., *The Letters of Archie Butt* (New York: Doubleday, Page & Co., 1924), 329. A print of Chartran's portrait is housed in the New York Public Library's Miriam and Ira D. Wallach Division of Art, record 1940324. For Roosevelt's assessment of the portrait—"Chartran has been painting my picture. I do not particularly like it"—see TRC MS Am 1541 (48), letter from Roosevelt to Kermit Roosevelt, February 1, 1903.

20. R. Ormond and E. Kilmurray, *John Singer Sargent: Complete Paintings Vols. 1–3* (New Haven: Yale University Press, 1998–2003).
21. N. M. Butler, *Across the Busy Years, Vol. II* (New York: Scribner's, 1940), 328–29.
22. TRC MS Am 1541 (50), letter from Roosevelt to Kermit Roosevelt, February 15, 1903.
23. H. Rood, ed., *Memories of the White House: The Home Life of Our Presidents from Lincoln to Roosevelt* (Boston: Little, Brown, 1911), 272–73.
24. For a description of the "hero cycle," see J. Campbell, *The Hero with a Thousand Faces, 3rd Edition* (Novato, CA: New World Library, 2008), 23–31; D. M. Mac-Neil, *The Emergence of the American Frontier Hero 1682–1826* (New York: Palgrave MacMillan, 2009), 15–16. For the emergence of the hero in frontier literature, see R. Slotkin, *Regeneration through Violence* (Norman: University of Oklahoma Press, 1973), 268–69. Roosevelt recounted "hero tales" in H. C. Lodge and T. Roosevelt, *Hero Tales from American History* (New York: Century, 1895).
25. For an overview of world exploration and many examples of this "cycle," see *Atlas of Exploration* (Oxford, Oxford University Press, 2008); Fleming, F., *Off the Map* (New York: Atlantic Monthly Press, 2004).
26. TRC MS Am 1541 (50), letter from Roosevelt to Kermit Roosevelt, February 15, 1903.
27. "Society in Washington," *New York Times*, February 14, 1903.
28. TRC MS Am 1541 (50), letter from Roosevelt to Kermit Roosevelt, February 15, 1903.
29. Quotation from letter from John Singer Sargent to Isabella Stewart Gardner [determined February 1903]. See also letter from John Singer Sargent to Isabella Stewart Gardner, February 10, 1903. John Singer Sargent letters from the Isabella Stewart Gardner Correspondence, Museum Archives, Isabella Stewart Gardner Museum, Boston.
30. Letter from John Singer Sargent to James Ford Rhodes, April 19, 1920. James Ford Rhodes Papers, Massachusetts Historical Society.
31. *Selections from the Correspondence of Theodore Roosevelt and Henry Cabot Lodge, 1884–1918, Volume II* (New York: Scribner's, 1925), 1–2. See also T. McCulloch, "Theodore Roosevelt and Canada: Alaska, the 'Big Stick,' and the North Atlantic Triangle, 1901–1909," in S. Ricard, ed., *A Companion to Theodore Roosevelt* (Malden, MA: Wiley-Blackwell, 2011), 293–313.
32. TRC MS Am 1541 (51), letter from Roosevelt to Kermit Roosevelt, February 19, 1903.
33. TRC MS Am 1541 (51), letter from Roosevelt to Kermit Roosevelt, February 19, 1903.
34. TRC MS Am 1541 (48), letter from Roosevelt to Kermit Roosevelt, February 1, 1903.
35. TRC MS Am 1541 (51), letter from Roosevelt to Kermit Roosevelt, February 19, 1903.
36. Although "Native Americans" is the preferred term, Roosevelt used "Indians" in his writings. Both terms appear in this book.
37. TRC MS Am 1541 (50), letter from Roosevelt to Kermit Roosevelt, February 15, 1903.
38. Morison et al., *Letters III*, 429–30, letter from Roosevelt to John Pitcher, February 18, 1903.
39. "Mrs. Roosevelt at the Play," *New York Times*, February 20, 1903.
40. "About People and Social Incidents," *New York Tribune*, March 19, 1903.
41. TRP, letter from Robert Collier to Theodore Roosevelt, December 6, 1902.

42. Quotation from "Roosevelt's New Portrait," *New York Times*, March 23, 1903. See also: "At the White House," *New York Tribune*, March 19, 1903.

43. "Roosevelt's New Portrait," *New York Times*, March 23, 1903.

44. Letter from Henry Adams to Elizabeth Cameron, March 8, 1903. Quoted in W. C. Ford, ed., *Letters of Henry Adams* (Boston: Houghton Mifflin, 1938), 398.

45. Letter from Henry Adams to Elizabeth Cameron, March 8, 1903. Quoted in Ford, ed., *Letters of Henry Adams*, 398.

46. Roosevelt, *Autobiography*.

47. "Art Topics," *Washington Post*, March 29, 1903.

CHAPTER ONE

1. Roosevelt describes the seal incident in *An Autobiography* (New York: Macmillan, 1913), 17–18; also recounted in C. Putnam, *Theodore Roosevelt: The Formative Years* (New York: Scribner's, 1958), 29; E. Morris, *The Rise of Theodore Roosevelt* (New York: Random House, 1979), 17–18; D. McCullough, *Mornings on Horseback* (New York: Simon and Schuster, 1981), 118; P. R. Cutright, *Theodore Roosevelt: The Making of a Conservationist* (Urbana: University of Illinois Press, 1985), 1–2; D. Brinkley, *The Wilderness Warrior* (New York: Harper Collins, 2009), 29–30. The likely natural history of Manhattan was reconstructed in E. W. Sanderson, *Mannahatta* (New York: Abrams, 2009). The home at 28 East 20th Street in Manhattan is now the Theodore Roosevelt Birthplace National Historic Site, but it is not original. The original home was demolished in 1916 and was later rebuilt in the style of the original as a memorial to Roosevelt.

2. T. Roosevelt, *New York* (London: Longmans, Green, 1891), 201.

3. The area near Morristown, New Jersey, was at first a summer escape for wealthy New Yorkers, but over the late nineteenth and early twentieth century it became the location of vast mansions of the Gilded Age. See J. W. Rae and J. W. Rae, Jr., *Morristown's Forgotten Past:"The Gilded Age"* (Morristown, NJ: J. Rae, 1979), v–3. See also Putnam, *Formative*, 31.

4. B. Hoskins, *Morris Township, New Jersey: A Glimpse into the Past* (Morristown, NJ: Joint Free Library of Morristown and Morris Township, 1987), 105–7.

5. Corinne Roosevelt Robinson, *My Brother Theodore Roosevelt* (New York: Scribner's, 1921), 36.

6. Robinson, *My Brother*, 36; also cited in Morris, *Rise*, 17.

7. Roosevelt, *Autobiography*, 18; also cited in P. R. Cutright, *Theodore Roosevelt: The Naturalist* (New York: Harper and Bros., 1956), 3; Putnam, *Formative*, 30; Morris, *Rise*, 19; Cutright, *Conservationist*, 8.

8. TRC MS Am 1541 (277), "Record of the Roosevelt Museum." Also cited in Cutright, *Naturalist*, 3; Cutright, *Conservationist*, 8; Brinkley, *Warrior*, 30.

9. L. Hansen, ed., *The Linnaeus Apostles: Global Science & Adventure, Vol. I.* (London: IK Foundation, 2010)

10. TRC MS Am 1454.48 (18), "Roosevelt letter to Martha Bulloch Roosevelt, April 28, 1868"; also quoted in Morris, *Rise*, 19–20; Cutright, *Conservationist*, 9; Brinkley, *Warrior*, 32.

11. TRC MS Am 1454.48 (18), Roosevelt letter to Theodore Roosevelt, Sr., April 30, 1868. Also quoted in Cutright, *Conservationist*, 9; Brinkley, *Warrior*, 32–33.

12. Putnam, *Formative*, 30. Cited in Morris, *Rise*, 19.

13. Roosevelt, *Autobiography*, 15; also cited in Morris, *Rise*, 14; Cutright, *Conservationist*, 7. Roosevelt was heavily influenced by strong women throughout his life, see McCullough, *Horseback*, 44–47, and Dalton, *Strenuous*.

14. John S. C. Abbott, *David Crockett* (New York: Dodd, Mead, 1902), 259.
15. Roosevelt, *Hunting Trips of a Ranchman*, 27–28. See also McCullough, *Horseback*, 47.
16. Robinson, *My Brother*, 2.
17. Robinson, *My Brother*, 2.
18. Robinson, *My Brother*, 35; also cited in Putnam, *Formative*, 31.
19. Rev. J. G. Wood, *Homes Without Hands* (London: Longman's Green, 1866); Roosevelt recalls the influence of this book in *Autobiography*, 21; also mentioned in Cutright, *Naturalist*, 2; Putnam, *Formative*, 27; Morris, *Rise*, 16; McCullough, *Horseback*, 119; Cutright, *Conservationist*, 6; Brinkley, *Warrior*, 29.
20. Roosevelt's sister Anna describes her memory of Roosevelt as a boy, before he could read, dragging "Life of Livingston" around the family library, see A. R. Cowles, "Each Room Has Many Memories," *Woman's Roosevelt Memorial Bulletin* 1, no. 3 (1920): 2–3. Given that Anna describes Roosevelt as not being able to read, her description suggests that this took place sometime in the early 1860s. David Livingstone's *Missionary Travels and Researches in South Africa* was first published in 1857 (London: John Murray). A similar volume, *Livingstone's Travels and Researches in South Africa* (Philadelphia: J. W. Bradley, 1858) also appeared in 1858. This memory suggests that the young Roosevelt had looked at one of these early volumes, given that titles similar to "Life of Livingstone" appeared later, including H. G. Adams, *The Life and Adventures of Dr. Livingstone in the Interior of South Africa* (London: J. Blackwood, 1870); J. S. Roberts, *The Life and Explorations of David Livingstone* (London: Adam, 1874); J. E. Ritchie, *The Life and Discoveries of David Livingstone* (London: A. Fullarton, 1876). Roosevelt possessed a copy of G. W. Blaikie's *The Personal Life of David Livingstone* that had been inscribed "To TR Bwana Makeeba," obviously sometime after his African safari. See volume SAHI 5629 in the library collection at the Sagamore Hill National Historic Site. See related references to Livingstone in Cutright, *Naturalist*, 2; Putnam, *Formative*, 27; Morris, *Rise*, 15; McCullough, *Horseback*, 118; Cutright, *Conservationist*, 5; Brinkley, *Warrior*, 24–25.
21. Quotation from Roosevelt, *Autobiography*, 17. For *The Boy Hunters* as a likely influence on Roosevelt, see Cutright, *Conservationist*, 11; Brinkley, *Warrior* 26. For discussions of Reid's influence on Roosevelt, see Roosevelt, *Autobiography*, 19; McCullough, *Horseback*, 118–19; G. Bederman, *Manliness and Civilization* (Chicago: University of Chicago Press, 1995), 172–75; Brinkley, *Warrior*, 25–28.
22. A wide literature considers how frontier and adventure stories influenced ideas of empire, manliness, hunting, and violence. See M. Green, *Dreams of Adventure, Deeds of Empire* (New York: Basic Books, 1979); J. Richards, *Imperialism and Juvenile Literature* (Manchester, UK: Manchester University Press, 1989); J. Bristow, *Empire Boys* (London: Harper Collins, 1991); M. D. Kutzer, *Empire's Children* (New York: Garland Publishing, 2000); Bederman, *Manliness and Civilization*, 172–75.
23. M. Reid, *The Boy Hunters; or, Adventures in Search of a White Buffalo* (Boston: Ticknor and Fields, 1868), 9.
24. Reid, *Boy Hunters*, 16–17.
25. Reid, *Boy Hunters*, 17.
26. Reid, *Boy Hunters*, 11.
27. Reid, *Boy Hunters*, 11, 12.
28. Reid, *Boy Hunters*, 71; see Brinkley, *Warrior*, 733, for reference to Roosevelt's disdain for crocodiles.
29. Reid, *Boy Hunters*, 12.

30. TRC MS Am 1454.55 (1), "Three weeks of my life Age nine Years," August 10, 1868. See also *Theodore Roosevelt's Diaries of Boyhood and Youth* (New York: Scribner's, 1928), 3. Roosevelt sometimes returned to his journals and diaries and recopied accounts (see appendix 1). Given no other evidence, here the assumption is made that this is his original account.

31. TRC MS Am 1454.55 (1), "Three weeks of my life Age nine Years," August 10, 1868. See also *Diaries of Boyhood*, 3.

32. TRC MS Am 1454.55 (1), "Three weeks of my life Age nine Years," August 17, 1868. See also *Diaries of Boyhood*, 5.

33. TRC MS Am 1454.55 (1), "Three weeks of my life Age nine Years," August 17 and 21, 1868. See also *Diaries of Boyhood*, 5, 7. However, note differences in recorded dates between manuscript and book.

34. TRC MS Am 1454.55 (1), "Three weeks of my life Age nine Years," August 21, 1868. See also *Diaries of Boyhood*, 7.

35. TRC MS Am 1454.55 (1), "Three weeks of my life Age nine Years," August 19, 1868. See also *Diaries of Boyhood*, 6. Also cited in Cutright, *Conservationist*, 11.

36. TRC MS Am 1454.55 (1), "Three weeks of my life Age nine Years," August 17, 1868. See also *Diaries of Boyhood*, 5–6.

37. Roosevelt's notebook TRC MS Am 1541 (286), "About insects and fishes," does not indicate a specific locality. Given that he records his age as "nine years" and that he spent the summer of 1868 in the Catskills, it is assumed that these observations were taken there.

38. T. Roosevelt, "My Life as a Naturalist," *American Museum Journal* 18 (1918): 321–22.

39. TRC MS Am 1541(286), "About Insects and Fishes."

40. The quotes from Roosevelt's work in the following paragraphs are taken from TRC MS Am 1541(286), "About Insects and Fishes." Also quoted in Cutright, *Conservationist*, 12–13.

41. In *My Brother*, 2, Roosevelt's sister Corinne remembers that Roosevelt presented an essay called "The Foregoing Ant" to the family when he was seven. This essay does not survive, and the title word "foregoing" is of some question. Corinne suggests that Roosevelt's use of "foregoing" was derived from a passage he had read in J. G. Wood's *The Illustrated Natural History* (London: Routledge, Warne, and Routledge, 1863), in three volumes. However, in Wood's section on ants, the word "foregoing" does not appear, and it is possible that Roosevelt mistakenly used "foregoing" for "foraging," as Brinkley's discussion suggests (Brinkley, *Warrior*, 28–29). Though many of Roosevelt's observations were correct, not all ants have castes like his "officer" and "soilder."

42. Roosevelt is likely describing the carpenter ant, *Camponotus pennsylvanicus*, which is one of the relatively small number of Nearctic ant species that have castes with distinct sizes and behaviors. See A. Ellison, N. Gotelli, E. Farnsworth, and G. Alpert, *A Field Guide to the Ants of New England* (New Haven: Yale University Press, 2012), 14. For those reading further in the original manuscript, Roosevelt's "doubble ant" may well be *Formica obscuriventris* or *F. exsectoides*, given that they frequently forage on shrubs and trees (this is not arboreal nesting, which is largely a tropical phenomenon in ants). *F. exsectoides* also makes hills in this area, and could also account for some of the hills Roosevelt was investigating near his "brown path ant." Many thanks to Stefan Cover and Gary Alpert in the Entomology Department at the Museum of Comparative Zoology, Harvard University, for helping with identifications.

43. Quotations from TRC MS Am 1541(286), "About Insects and Fishes." For back-

ground and identifications, L. Smith, *The Inland Fishes of New York State* (Albany: New York State Department of Environmental Conservation, 1985); Karsten Hartel, Ichthyology Department, Museum of Comparative Zoology, personal communication.

44. TRC MS Am 1541(286), "About Insects and Fishes."

45. Roosevelt's observation taps into the rich natural history associated with the bioluminescent signals of "fireflies" (insects in the beetle family Lampyridae). Although the most apparent and widely studied aspects of firefly biolumines-cence are nocturnal mating signals, some firefly species are day-flying and do not produce light, and other nocturnal light-producing species will occasionally produce light during the day in response to predators. See S. M. Long, S. Lewis, L. Jean-Louis, G. Ramos, J. Richmond, and E. M. Jakob, "Firefly Flashing and Jumping Spider Predation," *Animal Behaviour* 83 (2012): 81–86, and references therein.

46. TRC MS Am 1454.35, "My Expeditions and Adventures."

47. TRC MS Am 1454.35, "My Expeditions and Adventures."

48. TRC MS Am 1541 (287), "War of the Woods." N.B.: A note with this manuscript suggests that this is "American Indian Sign Language," but this is likely not a code from Native American cultures, but instead a code Roosevelt cobbled together or picked up from a publication; also cited in K. Dalton, *Theodore Roosevelt: A Strenuous Life* (New York: Knopf, 2002), 44.

49. See: R. L. Nichols, "Theodore Roosevelt and the Indians," in S. Ricard, ed., *A Companion to Theodore Roosevelt* (Malden, MA: Wiley-Blackwell, 2011), 186–97.

50. Quoted from Bickmore's "unpublished memoir" in: G. Hellman, *Bankers, Bones & Beetles: The First Century of the American Museum of Natural History* (Garden City, NY: AMNH Press, 1969), 14.

51. Bickmore had been referred to Theodore Sr. and had won his backing and sup-port. At the time of his interactions with the senior Roosevelt, Bickmore had just published his own account of his travels: A. S. Bickmore, *Travels in the East Indian Archipelago* (New York: D. Appleton, 1869).

52. Bickmore had organized a massive expedition throughout southeast Asia to recollect the trove of shells of the seventeenth-century naturalist Georgius Rumphius that had been lost. See Bickmore, *Travels*, 13.

53. Bickmore, *Travels*, 230.

54. Bickmore, *Travels*, 538.

55. Bickmore, *Travels*, 541.

56. Bickmore, *Travels*, 537–42.

57. J. A. Gable, "Theodore Roosevelt and the American Museum of Natural His-tory," *Theodore Roosevelt Association Journal* 8 (1982): 2–6; H. F. Osborn, *The American Museum of Natural History: Its Origin, Its History The Growth of Its Depart-ments* (New York: Irving Press, 1911); see also Brinkley, *Warrior*, 43.

58. A. Bickmore, 1908. Unpublished manuscript: "An Autobiography, with a Histor-ical Sketch of the Founding and Early Development of the American Museum of Natural History," American Museum of Natural History Research Library. For a discussion of Agassiz's creationist views, see E. Mayr, *Evolution and the Diversity of Life* (Cambridge, MA: Belknap Press of Harvard University Press, 1976), 251–76.

59. L. Agassiz, "Fifth Annual Report," in *Annual Report of the Trustees of the Museum of Comparative Zoölogy* (Boston: Wright & Potter, 1864), 7.

60. By a Former Pupil [Samual Scudder], "In the Laboratory with Agassiz," *Every Saturday* 1 (14) (1874): 369–70.

61. See Dalton, *Strenuous*, 18–19, 40.

62. T. Roosevelt, *The Strenuous Life: Essays and Addresses* (New York: Century, 1911), 1.

CHAPTER TWO

1. L. Withey, *Grand Tours and Cook's Tours* (New York: William Morrow, 1997); E. Chaney, *The Evolution of the Grand Tour* (London: Frank Cass, 1998); J. Black, *Italy and the Grand Tour* (New Haven: Yale University Press, 2003).

2. McCullough, *Horseback*, 27–29.

3. Roosevelt, *Autobiography*, 17; see Putnam, *Formative*, 59, for similar claim of Roosevelt's underestimation of the importance of the grand tour, and Cutright, *Conservationist*, 20, for a claim that agrees with Roosevelt's assessment; also cited in Morris, *Rise*, 22.

4. Bickmore, *Travels*, 5–6.

5. Twin accounts of the date range from May 12 to September 14, 1869, exist in Roosevelt's writings, in TRC MS Am 1454.55 (2) and TRC MS Am 1454.55 (3). This account (May 12, 1869) and the subsequent renderings from this range follow the second of the two accounts, taken from TRC MS Am 1454.55 (3), grand tour journal 1; see also *Diaries of Boyhood*, 13. Also cited in Putnam, *Formative*, 59; and Cutright, *Conservationist*, 15. See also appendix 1 for discussion of the manuscript sources.

6. For an explanation of the contents of the grand tour notes, see appendix 1. In the Galapagos Islands, Charles Darwin kept his initial field notes in small red leather notebooks, and then used them to make fuller accounts in his notebooks while on board the HMS *Beagle*. See G. Chancellor and J. Van Wyhe, *Charles Darwin's Notebooks from the Voyage of the* Beagle, (Cambridge: Cambridge University Press, 2009), xvii; M. R. Canfield, ed., *Field Notes on Science and Nature* (Cambridge, MA: Harvard University Press, 2011), 2–3.

7. TRC MS Am 1454.55 (3), grand tour journal 1, June 12, 1869; see also *Diaries of Boyhood*, 21.

8. TRC MS Am 1454.55 (3), grand tour journal 1, June 8, 1869; see also *Diaries of Boyhood*, 20–21.

9. TRC MS Am 1454.55 (3), grand tour journal 1, June 24, 1869; see also *Diaries of Boyhood*, 24–25.

10. TRC MS Am 1454.55 (3), grand tour journal 1, July 5, 1869; see also *Diaries of Boyhood*, 28.

11. TRC MS Am 1454.55 (4), grand tour journal 2, September 4, 1869; see also *Diaries of Boyhood*, 66–67. Also cited in Putnam, *Formative*, 63; Morris, *Rise*, 25.

12. TRC MS Am 1454.55 (4), grand tour journal 2, September 26, 1869; see also *Diaries of Boyhood*, 67. TRC MS Am 1454.55 (6), grand tour journal 4, January 21, 1870; see also *Diaries of Boyhood*, 166. Also cited in Putnam, *Formative*, 63; Morris, *Rise*, 25; McCullough, *Horseback*, 98; Cutright, *Conservationist*, 17, 24.

13. TRC MS Am 1454.55 (4), grand tour journal 2, October 10, 1869; see also *Diaries of Boyhood*, 74–75.

14. An extended discussion of Roosevelt's asthma symptoms and their possible underlying causes appears in McCullough, *Horseback*, 93–111. For specific reference to the role of the "out of doors," see 111.

15. TRC MS Am 1454.55 (4), grand tour journal 2, October 15, 1869; see also *Diaries of Boyhood*, 77. Also cited in Morris, *Rise*, 26; McCullough, *Horseback*, 99; Cutright, *Conservationist*, 17.

16. TRC MS Am 1454.55 (4), grand tour journal 2, October 26, 1869; see also *Diaries*

of Boyhood, 85. Also cite in McCullough, *Horseback*, 104; Cutright, *Conservationist*, 19; Brinkley, *Warrior*, 37.

17. TRC MS Am 1454.55 (4), grand tour journal 2, October 26, 1869; see also *Diaries of Boyhood*, 84.

18. TRC MS Am 1454.55 (6), grand tour journal 4, March 25, 1870; see also *Diaries of Boyhood*, 205. Also cited in McCullough, *Horseback*, 90.

19. TRC MS Am 1454.55 (3), grand tour journal 1, June 22, 1869; see also *Diaries of Boyhood*, 24. Also cited in Morris, *Rise*, 23; Cutright, *Conservationist*, 16.

20. TRC MS Am 1454.55 (3), grand tour journal 1, June 30, 1869; see also *Diaries of Boyhood*, 26. Also cited in Putnam, *Formative*, 62.

21. TRC MS Am 1454.55 (4), grand tour journal 2, October 20, 1869; see also *Diaries of Boyhood*, 79.

22. TRC MS Am 1454.55 (6), grand tour journal 4, April 17, 1870; see also *Diaries of Boyhood*, 212–13; also cited in Putnam, *Formative*, 70; Morris, *Rise*, 29; McCullough, *Horseback*, 106–7.

23. TRC MS Am 1454.55 (6), grand tour journal 4, April 24, 1870; see also *Diaries of Boyhood*, 214–15.

24. TRC MS Am 1454.55 (6), grand tour journal 4, January 23, 1870; see also *Diaries of Boyhood*, 168–69.

25. TRC MS Am 1454.55 (6), grand tour journal 4, May 24, 1870; see also *Diaries of Boyhood*, 224; also cited in Brinkley, *Warrior*, 38.

26. TRC MS Am 1454.55 (6), grand tour journal 4, March 30, 1870; see also *Diaries of Boyhood*, 206.

27. Roosevelt, *Autobiography*, 22.

28. Roosevelt, *Autobiography*, 22.

29. TRC MS Am 1454.55 (6), grand tour journal 4, June 27, 1870; see also *Diaries of Boyhood*, 231–32.

30. Roosevelt, *Autobiography*, 22. Roosevelt's association with Bell is also cited in Hagedorn, *Boys' Life*, 38; Cutright, *Naturalist*, 7; Putnam, *Formative*, 74; McCullough, *Horseback*, 121; Cutright, *Conservationist*, 31–32; Brinkley, *Warrior*, 54.

31. J. J. Audubon, *John James Audubon: Writings and Drawings* (New York: Library of America, 1999), 553.

32. Audubon, *Writings and Drawings*, 639.

33. Audubon, *Writings and Drawings*, 646.

34. Audubon, *Writings and Drawings*, 733.

35. Audubon, *Writings and Drawings*, 622.

36. C. Darwin, *The Autobiography of Charles Darwin 1809–1882* (New York: W. W. Norton, 1958), 64.

37. Darwin, *Autobiography*, 68.

38. Roosevelt, "My Life as a Naturalist," 84

39. TRC MS Am 1454.32, "Notes on Natural History." See also Cutright, *Conservationist*, 32.

40. Roosevelt, *Autobiography*, 28.

41. Audubon, *Writings and Drawings*, 3.

42. Audubon, *Writings and Drawings*, 25–27.

43. Audubon, *Writings and Drawings*, 52.

44. TRC MS Am 1454.55 (7), "Started for the Adirondacks," August 12, 1871; see also *Diaries of Boyhood*, 251.

45. D. Hart-Davis, *Audubon's Elephant: America's Greatest Naturalist and the Making of The Birds of America* (New York: Henry Holt, 2004); Audubon, *Writings and Drawings*; R. Rhodes, *John James Audubon: The Making of an American* (New York: Knopf, 2004).

46. L. Vedder, *John James Audubon and the Birds of America: A Visionary Achievement in Ornithological Illustration* (San Marino, CA: Huntington Library, 2006), 32–34.

47. J. J. Audubon, *Ornithological biography; or, An account of the habits of the birds of the United States of America: accompanied by descriptions of the objects represented in the work entitled The birds of America: And interspersed with delineations of American scenery and manners* (Edinburgh: A. Black, 1839).

48. Audubon, *Writings and Drawings*, 756.

49. TRC MS Am 1454.32, "Notes on Natural History"; also cited in Cutright, *Conservationist*, 27–29.

50. Along with the sketches contained in TRC MS Am 1454.32, "Notes on Natural History," the TRC holds a separate set of drawings from the 1870s; TRC MS Am 1541 (288).

51. J. J. Audubon and J. Bachman, *The Viviparous Quadrupeds of North America* (New York: J. J. Audubon, 1846–54).

52. TRC MS Am 1541(288), animal drawings and sketches.

53. TRC MS Am 1541(288), animal drawings and sketches. Roosevelt erroneously spells the genus "Scalops."

54. John James Audubon Letters and Drawings (MS Am 21, MS Am 21.5). Houghton Library, Harvard University. Box 8. Belted kingfisher, Chute de l'Ohio, 1808 Jul. 15. Pastel, graphite, and ink on paper.

55. C. Linnaeus, *Instructions for Naturalists on Voyages of Exploration*, reprinted in L. Hansen, ed., *The Linnaeus Apostles: Global Science & Adventure, Vol. I.* (London: IK Foundation, 2010), 204.

56. Darwin, *Autobiography*, 53.

57. TRC MS Am 1454.55 (7), "Started for the Adirondacks," August 3, 1871; see also *Diaries of Boyhood*, 243. Also cited in Cutright, *Naturalist*, 5; Cutright, *Conservationist*, 34.

58. In his Mississippi River journal, Audubon refers to the "white headed eagle" by Linnaeus's original name, *Falco leucocephalus*. Audubon, *Writings and Drawings*, 25.

59. American Ornithologists' Union, *Check-List of North American Birds, 7th Edition* (Lawrence, KS: Allen Press, 1998), 91.

60. *P. roosevelti* was originally described in W. M. Mann, "The Ants of the Fiji Islands," *Bulletin of the Museum of Comparative Zoology* 64 (1921): 401–99; revised in E. Sarnat, "A Taxonomic Revision of the *Pheidole roosevelti*-group (Hymenoptera: Formicidae) in Fiji," *Zootaxa* 1767 (2008): 1–36. D. Borror, *Dictionary of Word Roots and Combining Forms* (Mountain View, CA: Mayfield, 1988).

61. TRC MS Am 1454.55 (7), "Started for the Adirondacks," August 8, 1871; see also *Diaries of Boyhood*, 247.

62. The influence of Linnaeus on Roosevelt is discussed in Cutright, *Conservationist*, 35; Morris, *Rise*, 33; Brinkley, *Warrior*, 65–66.

63. Linnaeus, *Instructions*, 204.

64. Linnaeus, *Instructions*, 204.

65. E. C. Agassiz, ed., *Louis Agassiz: His Life and Correspondence* (Boston: Houghton Mifflin, 1885), 145.

66. Linnaeus, *Instructions*, 204.

67. TRC MS Am 1454.55 (7), "Started for the Adirondacks," August 16, 1871; see also *Diaries of Boyhood*, 254.

68. TRC MS Am 1454.32, "Notes on Natural History," "Hylodes pickeringi."

69. TRC MS Am 1454.32, "Notes on Natural History," "Passer domesticus."

70. Letter from A. Cutler to V. Pyle, September 18, 1901; contained in reminis-

cences of Arthur Cutler on Theodore Roosevelt, TRC R 310 C97s.

71. Morison et al., *Letters I*, 6, letter from Roosevelt to Theodore Roosevelt Sr., September 18, 1872; also cited in Putnam, *The Formative Years*, 79; McCullough, *Horseback*, 119; Cutright, *Conservationist*, 32.

72. Cutright, *Conservationist*, 34.

73. Brinkley, *Warrior*, 77–92; Hagedorn, *Boys' Life*, 38; Putnam, *Formative*, 78; Robinson, *My Brother*, 52; quoted in Cutright, *Conservationist*, 32.

74. TRC MS Am 1454.40 (1), record of the Roosevelt Museum; cited also in Cutright, *Conservationist*, 30.

75. TRC MS Am 1454.40 (1), record of the Roosevelt Museum.

76. TRC MS Am 1454.40 (1), record of the Roosevelt Museum.

77. Childhood museums were common in the nineteenth century, and other naturalists such as Louis Agassiz and William Beebe described having kept them.

78. Cutright, *Conservationist*, 34. Among other things, Roosevelt's father gave him a shotgun for Christmas in 1872, and also in 1877.

79. J. Burroughs, *The Writings of John Burroughs: XV Leaf and Tendril* (Boston: Houghton Mifflin, 1908), 2. See also: C. Z. Walker, *The Art of Seeing Things: Essays by John Burroughs* (Syracuse, NY: Syracuse University Press, 2001), 3.

80. TRC MS Am 1454.55 (7), "Started for the Adirondacks," August 8, 1871; see also *Diaries of Boyhood*, 247; also cited in McCullough, *Horseback*, 120; Brinkley, *Warrior*, 41. For the placement of this story in the literature of adventure, see M. Green, *Seven Types of Adventure Tale* (University Park, PA: Pennsylvania State University Press, 1991), 95–120.

81. American Museum of Natural History, *Third and Fourth Annual Reports of the American Museum of Natural History* (New York, AMNH Publication), 26. Also quoted in McCullough, *Horseback*, 121; Cutright, *Conservationist*, 37; Brinkley, *Warrior*, 45.

82. For descriptions of Roosevelt's hunting implements, including his Tiffany's Bowie knife, see R. L. Wilson, *Theodore Roosevelt, Hunter-Conservationist* (Missoula, MT: Boone and Crockett Club, 2009).

83. J. Burroughs, "Theodore Roosevelt: His Americanism Reached into the Marrow of His Bones," *Natural History* 19 (1919): 4–7.

84. Although current usage of the word "woodcraft" generally refers to woodworking, use of the term in Roosevelt's time often was often in the context of natural history.

1. A recipe for arsenical soap is given in the book on birds that Roosevelt used on his trip: A. C. Smith, *The Nile and Its Banks: A Journal of Travels in Egypt and Nubia*, 2 Vols. (London: John Murray, 1868), 282.

2. TRC MS Am 1454.55 (8), Egypt and Holy Lands journal, October 26, 1872; see also *Diaries of Boyhood*, 264; Morris, *Rise*, 37; Putnam, *Formative*, 82; Brinkley, *Warrior*, 54.

3. Roosevelt, *Autobiography*, 24.

4. TRC MS Am 1454.55 (8), Egypt and Holy Lands journal, October 28, 1872; see also *Diaries of Boyhood*, 265. Also cited in Cutright, *Conservationist*, 41.

5. TRC MS Am 1454.55 (8), Egypt and Holy Lands journal, November 20, 1872; see also *Diaries of Boyhood*, 272.

6. TRC MS Am 1454.55 (8), Egypt and Holy Lands journal, October 28, 1872; see also *Diaries of Boyhood*, 265.

7. TRC MS Am 1454.55 (8), Egypt and Holy Lands journal, November 28, 1872; see also *Diaries of Boyhood*, 276. Also quoted in Morris, *Rise*, 37; Cutright, *Conservationist*, 42; Putnam, *Formative*; 85; Brinkley, *Warrior*, 55.

8. TRC MS Am 1454.55 (8), Egypt and Holy Lands journal, November 28, 1872; see also *Diaries of Boyhood*, 277. Also cited in Cutright, *Conservationist*, 43.

9. TRC MS Am 1454.55 (8), Egypt and the Holy Lands journal, December 3, 1872; see also *Diaries of Boyhood*, 282.

10. TRC MS Am 1454.55 (8), Egypt and Holy Lands journal, December 3, 1872; see also *Diaries of Boyhood*, 283; also cited in Putnam, *Formative*, 87.

11. Descriptions of Waynman Dixon's discovery of the "air shafts" appear in H.W.C., "Recent Discoveries in the Great Pyramid of Egypt: Ancient Egyptian Weight." *Nature* 7 (1872): 146–49; and P. Smyth, *Our Inheritance in the Great Pyramid* (London: Isbister, 1874), 363–64.

12. See R. Bauval and A. Gilbert, *The Orion Mystery: Unlocking the Secrets of the Pyramids* (London: Heinemann, 1994), 231.

13. H.W.C., "Recent Discoveries in the Great Pyramid of Egypt: Ancient Egyptian Weight." *Nature* 7 (1872): 146–49.

14. Bauval and Gilbert, *The Orion Mystery*, 231.

15. H.W.C., "Recent Discoveries in the Great Pyramid of Egypt: Ancient Egyptian Weight." *Nature* 7 (1872): 146–49.

16. "Progress in Science: Geology" (no author), *Journal of Science* 10 (1873): 273; M. Drower, ed., *Letters from the Desert: The Correspondence of Flinders and Hilda Petrie* (Oxford: Aris & Phillips, 2004), 14.

17. TRC MS Am 1454.55 (8), Egypt and Holy Lands journal, December 3, 1872; see also *Diaries of Boyhood*, 283–84.

18. Roosevelt does not mention Dixon by name. Waynman Dixon was one of the early Egyptologists to take up residence in the tombs at Giza, and was living there when Roosevelt visited. Roosevelt's description of an Englishman who discovered two shafts suggests that he met Waynman Dixon. Thanks to Peter Der Manuelian, Philip J. King Professor of Egyptology, Harvard University, for assistance in confirming this determination.

19. TRC MS Am 1454.55 (8), Egypt and Holy Lands journal, December 3, 1872; see also *Diaries of Boyhood*, 285.

20. TRC MS Am 1454.55 (8), Egypt and Holy Lands journal, December 3, 1872; see also *Diaries of Boyhood*, 285–86. Also cited in Putnam, *Formative*, 86.

21. TRC MS Am 1454.55 (8), Egypt and Holy Lands journal, December 3, 1872; see also *Diaries of Boyhood*, 286.

22. TRC MS Am 1454.37. "Zoological record" of Egypt and the Holy Lands.

23. TRC MS Am 1454.55 (8), Egypt and Holy Lands journal, December 3, 1872; see also *Diaries of Boyhood*, 286.

24. TRC MS Am 1454.55 (8), Egypt and Holy Lands journal, November 28, 1872; see also *Diaries of Boyhood*, 277.

25. TRC MS Am 1454.55 (8), Egypt and Holy Lands journal, December 6, 1872; see also *Diaries of Boyhood*, 288.

26. TRC MS Am 1454.55 (8), Egypt and Holy Lands journal, February 27, 1873; see also *Diaries of Boyhood*, 315.

27. TRC MS Am 1454.55 (8), Egypt and Holy Lands journal, December 6, 1872; see also *Diaries of Boyhood*, 288. Also cited in Cutright, *Conservationist*, 42–43.

28. S. Mayes, *The Great Belzoni: Archaeologist Extraordinary* (New York: Walker and Co., 1961).

29. G. Belzoni, *Narrative of the Operations and Recent Discoveries within the Pyramids,*

Temples, Tombs, and Excavations in Egypt and Nubia (London: John Murray, 1820), 230–49.

30. TRC MS Am 1454.55 (8), Egypt and Holy Lands journal, January 13, 1873; see also *Diaries of Boyhood*, 305.

31. TRC MS Am 1454.55 (8), Egypt and Holy Lands journal, January 13, 1873; see also *Diaries of Boyhood*, 305.

32. TRC MS Am 1454.55 (8), Egypt and Holy Lands journal, December 13, 1872; see also *Diaries of Boyhood*, 290. Also cited in Cutright, *Conservationist*, 45; McCullough, *Horseback*, 122.

33. TRC MS Am 1454.55 (8), Egypt and Holy Lands journal, December 13, 1872; see also *Diaries of Boyhood*, 290. Also cited in Morris, *Rise*, 39.

34. TRC MS Am 1454.55 (8), Egypt and Holy Lands journal, December 13, 1872; see also *Diaries of Boyhood*, 290–91.

35. R. U. Johnson, *Remembered Yesterdays* (Boston: Little, Brown, 1923), 388; P. Schullery, "Theodore Roosevelt: The Scandal of the Hunter as Nature Lover," in N. A. Naylor, D. Brinkley, J. A. Gable, eds., *Theodore Roosevelt: Many-Sided American* (Interlaken, NY: Heart of the Lakes Publishing, 1992), 221–30; M. Cartmill, *A View to a Death in the Morning* (Cambridge, MA: Harvard University Press, 1993); D. J. Herman, *Hunting and the American Imagination* (Washington: Smithsonian Institution Press, 2001); R. L. Wilson, *Theodore Roosevelt: Hunter-Conservationist* (Missoula, MT: Boone and Crockett Club, 2009); E. D. Thomas, *How Sportsmen Saved the World* (Guilford, CT: Lyons Press, 2010); P. O'Toole, "Roosevelt in Africa," in S. Ricard, ed., *A Companion to Theodore Roosevelt* (Malden, MA: Wiley-Blackwell, 2011), 435–51.

36. TRC MS Am 1454.55 (8), Egypt and Holy Lands journal, December 25, 1872; see also *Diaries of Boyhood*, 296. Also cited in Morris, *Rise*, 39.

37. TRC MS Am 1454.33, "Remarks on Birds," vol. 1.

38. TRC MS Am 1454.33, "Remarks on Birds," vol. 1. See related discussion and similar description of the event by Roosevelt in a different notebook quoted in Cutright, *Conservationist*, 50.

39. TRC MS Am 1454.55 (8), Egypt and Holy Lands journal entry on January 11, 1872; see also *Diaries of Boyhood*, 304.

40. Belzoni, *Narrative of the Operations and Recent Discoveries within the Pyramids*, 45.

41. The taxonomic placement of this bird during Roosevelt's time would have been *Charadrius spinosus*. It is currently referred to as the spur-winged lapwing, *Vanellus spinosus* (Charadriidae). With kind thanks to Steven Goodman for advice and information on the ornithology of Egypt.

42. TRC MS Am 1454.33, "Remarks on Birds," vol. 1.

43. G. Rawlinson, *History of Herodotus*, Vol. II (London: John Murray, 1862), 98. Interestingly, the title page of this book describes that it was "assisted by J. G. Wilkinson."

44. C. E. Raven, *English Naturalists from Neckam to Ray* (Cambridge: Cambridge University Press, 1947), 18–19.

45. J. G. Wilkinson, *The Manners and Customs of the Ancient Egyptians*, Vol. II (London: John Murray, 1878), 133.

46. Wilkinson, *Manners and Customs*, 134.

47. Smith, *The Nile and Its Banks*, 255–56. Cited in Cutright, *Conservationist*, 44.

48. TRC MS Am 1454.33, "Remarks on Birds," vol. 1.

49. TRC MS Am 1454.33, "Remarks on Birds," vol. 1.

50. Thanks to Mark Siddall, curator at the Division of Invertebrate Zoology, American Museum of Natural History, for confirming that leeches in the genus *Placob-*

delloides abound in the Nile River. For references on leeches feeding in the dental sockets of crocodiles, see H. B. Cott, "Scientific Results of an Inquiry into the Ecology and Economic Status of the Nile Crocodile (*Crocodilus niloticus*) in Uganda and Northern Rhodesia," *Transactions of the Zoological Society of London* 29, vol. 4 (1961): 211–56.

51.   T. Howell, "Breeding Biology of the Egyptian Plover, *Pluvianus aegyptius* (Aves: Glareolidae)." *University of California Publications in Zoology* 133 (1979): 1–77.

52.   TRC MS Am 1454.33, "Remarks on Birds," vol. 1. Also cited in Cutright, *Conservationist*, 64.

53.   TRC MS Am 1454.55 (8), Egypt and Holy Lands journal, March 17, 1873; see also *Diaries*, 321–23. Various accounts of Roosevelt's jackal hunt appear in Cutright, *Conservationist*, 56–57; Putnam, *Formative*, 94; Morris, *Rise*, 42; Brinkley, *Warrior*, 58.

54.   See Putnam, *Formative*, 102–15, for a discussion of Roosevelt's time in Dresden.

55.   Morison et al., *Letters I*, 11, Roosevelt letter to Theodore Roosevelt Sr., June 29, 1873.

56.   Quotation from TRC MS Am 1454.48 (19), Roosevelt letter to Martha Roosevelt, May 29, 1873. See also Morison et al., *Letters I*, 11, Roosevelt letter to Theodore Roosevelt Sr., June 29, 1873.

57.   Morison et al., *Letters I*, 8, Roosevelt letter to Theodore Roosevelt Sr., June 15, 1873.

58.   TRC MS Am 1454.57, Dresden Literary American Club, June 1 to July 11, 1873.

59.   Morison et al., *Letters I*, 10, Roosevelt letter to Theodore Roosevelt Sr., June 22, 1873; Morison et al., *Letters I*, 11, Roosevelt letter to Theodore Roosevelt Sr., June 29, 1873; TRC MS Am 1454.48 (6), Roosevelt letter to Anna Bulloch Gracie, June 15, 1873.

60.   Morison et al., *Letters I*, 8, Roosevelt letter to Theodore Roosevelt Sr., June 15, 1873.

61.   Morison et al., *Letters I*, 11, Roosevelt letter to Theodore Roosevelt Sr., June 29, 1873.

62.   L. Viereck, "Roosevelt's German Days," *Success Magazine* 8 (1905): 672B–672D. Viereck describes Roosevelt's studies with Wegener, "a man of considerable talent, a specialist in the painting of prairie scenes and author of several books on animal life." The assumption is made that this is Johann Friedrich Wilhelm Wegener (1812–79), a Dresden-born painter, etcher, and lithographer who had traveled widely and painted many landscapes, including those of the United States. See P. C. Merrill, *German Immigrant Artists in America: A Biographical Dictionary* (Lanham, MD: Scarecrow Press, 1997), 283.

63.   TRC MS Am 1454.48 (6), Roosevelt letter to Anna Bulloch Gracie, June 15, 1873. Also quoted in Morris, *Rise*, 45; Putnam, *Formative*, 105;

64.   TRC MS Am 1454.48 (2), Roosevelt letter to Anna Roosevelt, September 21, 1873.

65.   TRC MS Am 1454.48 (20), Roosevelt letter to Martha Roosevelt, October 5, 1873. For description of Roosevelt's reading stance, see Hagedorn, *Boys' Life*, 39.

66.   TRC MS Am 1454.48 (2), Roosevelt letter to Anna Roosevelt, September 21, 1873.

67.   C. Darwin and A. R. Wallace, "On the Tendency of Species to Form Varieties; and on the Perpetuation of Varieties and Species by Means of Natural Selection," *Journal of the Proceedings of the Linnean Society of London, Zoology*, 3 (1858): 46–50.

68.   See similar discussion in Brinkley, *Warrior*, 63–64.

69. T. H. Huxley, *Evidence as to Man's Place in Nature* (New York: D. Appleton, 1863). The many fossil human ancestors that are known today were mostly discovered after Huxley's book was published, so he did not have those available to him.

70. J. Browne, "Darwin in Caricature: A Study in the Popularization and Dissemination of Evolutionary Theory," in B. Larson and F. Brauer, eds., *The Art of Evolution: Darwin, Darwinisms, and Visual Culture* (Hanover, NH: Dartmouth College Press, 2009), 18–39.

71. For examples of caricatures of Roosevelt, see J. D. Valaik, *Theodore Roosevelt: An American Hero in Caricature* (Buffalo, NY: Western New York Heritage Institute of Canisius College, 1993).

72. T. Roosevelt, "Kidd's 'Social Evolution.'" 1895. *North American Review* 61: 94–109.

73. D. H. Burton, "Theodore Roosevelt's Social Darwinism and Views on Imperialism," *Journal of the History of Ideas* 26, vol. 1 (1965): 103–18; T. G. Dyer, *Theodore Roosevelt and the Idea of Race* (Baton Rouge: Louisiana State University Press, 1980), 52; Bederman, *Manliness and Civilization*, 172–88; C. Chin, "Uplifting the Barbarian," in S. Ricard, ed., *A Companion to Theodore Roosevelt* (Malden, MA: Wiley-Blackwell, 2011), 417–34. A. M. Johnston, "Sex and Gender in Roosevelt's America," in S. Ricard, ed., *A Companion to Theodore Roosevelt* (Malden, MA: Wiley-Blackwell, 2011), 112–34.

74. Vierick, "Roosevelt's German Days."

CHAPTER FOUR

1. Reminiscences of Arthur Cutler on Theodore Roosevelt, TRC R 310 C97s.

2. For Roosevelt's travels and observations between 1873 and 1876, see TRC MS Am 1454.32, "Notes on Natural History"; TRC MS Am 1454.34, "Remarks on the Zoology of Oyster Bay"; TRC MS Am 1454.55 (9), 1875 Diary, "T. R. Jr. Sporting and collecting"; and TRC MS Am 1454.31, "Notes on the Fauna of the Adirondac Mts." See also Cutright, *Conservationist*, 70–96; M. P. Griffin, *The Amazing Bird Collection of Young Mr. Roosevelt*, (Xlibiris, 2014) .

3. J. E. Hammond, *Oyster Bay* (Charleston, SC: Arcadia Publishing, 2009), 57.

4. TRC MS Am 1454.55 (9), 1875 diary, "T. R. Jr. Sporting and Collecting."

5. The surname Coues is pronounced "cows." See W. J. Kolodnicki, "Theodore Roosevelt's Boyhood Hero," *Theodore Roosevelt Association Journal* 8 (1982): 9–10.

6. TRC MS Am 1454.34, "Remarks on the Zoology of Oyster Bay."

7. E. Coues, *Key to North American Birds* (Salem, MA: Naturalists' Agency, 1872); E. Coues, *Field Ornithology* (Salem, MA: Naturalists' Agency, 1874); see related discussion of Coues in P. R. Cutright and M. J. Brodhead, *Elliott Coues: Naturalist and Frontier Historian* (Urbana: University of Illinois Press, 1981), 127–29; Brinkley, *Warrior*, 95–96.

8. Coues, *Field Ornithology*, 4.

9. Coues, *Field Ornithology*, 44–45; also cited in J. Perrine and J. Patton, "Letters to the Future," in Canfield, *Field Notes on Science and Nature*, 211–50.

10. For a description of Roosevelt's notebooks, see appendix 1; P. R. Cutright, "The boyhood natural history notebooks of Theodore Roosevelt," *Theodore Roosevelt Association Journal* 8 (1982): 2–15; Cutright, *Conservationist*, 91–95. For his early publications, see P. R. Cutright, "Twin Literary Rarities of T. R.," *Theodore Roosevelt Association Journal* 11 (1982): 5–12.

11. TRC MS Am 1454.32, "Notes on Natural History."

12. TRC MS Am 1454.55 (9), 1875 diary, "T. R. Jr. Sporting and collecting," August 6, 1875.

13. TRC MS Am 1454.34, "Remarks on the Zoology of Oyster Bay." See related quotes in Brinkley, *Warrior*, 97.

14. TRC MS Am 1454.31, "Notes on the Fauna of the Adirondac Mts." Also cited in Cutright, *Conservationist*, 91; Brinkley, *Warrior*, 97.

15. A wealth of literature exists on songs and song sharing in species that Roosevelt observed, including the house wren, winter wren, and marsh wren. Roosevelt's notes were more abundant on the house wren (*Troglodytes aedon*); see TRC MS Am 1454.34, "Remarks on the Zoology of Oyster Bay." For studies on this topic, see D. Kroodsma, "Vocal Dueling among Male Marsh Wrens: Evidence for Ritualized Expressions of Dominance/Subordinance," *Auk* 96 (1979): 506–15; S. Camacho-Schlenker, H. Courvoisier, and T. Aubin, "Song Sharing and Singing Strategies in the Winter Wren *Troglodytes troglodytes*," *Behavioural Processes* 87 (2011): 260–67; D. Rendall and C. D. Kaluthota, "Song Organization and Variability in Northern House Wrens (*Troglodytes aedon parkmanii*) in Western Canada," *Auk* 130 (2013): 617–28.

16. See TRC MS Am 1454.34, "Remarks on the Zoology of Oyster Bay," and C. N. Templeton, E. Greene, and K. Davis, "Allometry of Alarm Calls: Black-Capped Chickadees Encode Information about Predator Size," *Science* 308 (2005): 1934–37.

17. See TRC MS Am 1454.34, "Remarks on the Zoology of Oyster Bay," and D. Kroodsma, P. Houlihan, P. Fallon, and J. Wells, "Song Development by Grey Catbirds," *Animal Behaviour* 54 (1997): 457–64.

18. One example appears in N. Davies, R. Kilner, and D. Noble, "Nestling Cuckoos, *Cuculus canorus*, Exploit Hosts with Begging Calls that Mimic a Brood," *Proceedings of the Royal Society of London B* 265 (1998): 673–78.

19. TRC MS Am 1454.34, "Remarks on the Zoology of Oyster Bay."

20. Roosevelt's special attention to birdsong has been noted in Cutright, *Naturalist*, 17; Morris, *Rise*, 65–66; Cutright, *Conservationist*, 81–83. For an overview of the history of birdsong notation, see T. Hold, "Notation of Bird-Song: A Review and a Recommendation," *Ibis* 112 (1970): 151–72.

21. TRC MS Am 1454.38, "FieldBook of Zoology," May 27, 1876.

22. TRC MS Am 1454.38, "Field Book of Zoology," June 17, 1876. Roosevelt also includes a long line, roughly over the "ero" in "whero" in this passage.

23. TRC MS Am 1454.38, "Field Book of Zoology," July 17, 1876. Additional examples of approximations of songs can be found in TRC MS Am 1454.34, "Remarks on the Zoology of Oyster Bay," and in Cutright, "The Boyhood Natural History Notebooks," 2–15; Cutright, *Conservationist*, 82.

24. Gardner Wilkinson used Kircher's work in trying to decipher the hieroglyphs he encountered in Egypt. See J. Thompson, *Sir Gardner Wilkinson and His Circle* (Austin: University of Texas Press, 1992), 31. For an overview of Kircher's interests and contributions, see P. Findlen, ed., *Athanasius Kircher: The Last Man Who Knew Everything* (New York: Routledge, 2004).

25. P. Mauriès, *Cabinets of Curiosities* (London: Thames and Hudson, 2002), 160–63.

26. A. Kircher, *Musurgia universalis, sive ars magna consoni et dissoni* (Romae: Ex typographia haeredum Francisci Corbelletti, 1650), plate between pages 30 and 31.

27. Hold, "Notation of Bird-Song,", 151–72.

28. Kircher, *Musurgia*, cited in Hold, "Notation of Bird-Song," 151–72; E. A. Armstrong, *A Study in Bird Song*, 2nd Ed. (New York: Dover Publications, 1973), 232.

29. See TRC MS Am 1454.31, "Notes on the Fauna of the Adirondac Mts.," and TRC MS Am 1454.32, "Notes on Natural History."

30. J. Burton, "Master of Nature's Music: Ludwig Koch, 1881–1974," *Country Life* 157 (1975): 390–91.

31. W. H. Thorpe, *Bird-Song: The Biology of Vocal Communication and Expression in Birds* (Cambridge: Cambridge University Press, 1961), xii; A. A. Saunders, *Bird Song: New York State Museum Handbook 7* (Albany: University of the State of New York, 1929).

32. For an extensive list of Coues's publications, see Cutright and Brodhead, *Coues*, 445–69.

33. TRC MS Am 1454.32, "Notes on Natural History."

34. Quotation from TRC MS Am 1834 (120), letter from Roosevelt to Anna Roosevelt, August 6, 1876. Also quoted in Morris, *Rise*, 51; Dalton, *Strenuous*, 58. Reminiscences of Arthur Cutler on Theodore Roosevelt, TRC R 310 C97s. See also Putnam, *Formative*, 126; McCullough, *Horseback*, 140; Cutright, *Conservationist*, 73; Dalton, *Strenuous*, 58; Brinkley, *Warrior*, 68.

35. M. Sullivan, "Roosevelt at Harvard," *Boston Evening Transcript*, July 11, 1900. See also Cutright, *Naturalist*, 9, 13; Putnam, *Formative*, 134–35; Morris, *Rise*, 60; Cutright, *Conservationist*, 97; Brinkley, *Warrior*, 100–101.

36. Morison et al., *Letters I*, 16, letter from Roosevelt to Martha Bulloch Roosevelt, September 29, 1876; Cutright, *Conservationist*, 98.

37. Putnam, *Formative*, 132; Cutright, *Conservationist*, 99.

38. Cutright, *Conservationist*, 99.

39. D. Wilhelm, *Theodore Roosevelt as an Undergraduate* (Boston: John W. Luce, 1910), 63. Also quoted in Morris, *Rise*, 58. For Roosevelt in social context at Harvard, see Morris, *Rise*, 56–58.

40. T. Roosevelt, "Summer Birds of the Adirondacks in Franklin County, N.Y." Privately printed, four pages; also cited in Cutright, *Naturalist*, 18; Morris, *Rise*, 65; Cutright, *Conservationist*, 102; P. R. Cutright, "Twin Literary Rarities of TR," *Theodore Roosevelt Association Journal* 9 (1985): 5–12; Dalton, *Strenuous*, 65; Brinkley, *Warrior*, 106–7.

41. W. E. Davis, *History of the Nuttall Ornithological Club 1873–1986* (Cambridge, MA: Nuttall Ornithological Club, 1987).

42. J. A. Allen, "Summer Birds of the Adirondacks," *Bulletin of the Nuttall Ornithological Club* 3 (1878): 36. Roosevelt and Minot's paper was reviewed first in the *Bulletin* by J. A. Allen, and then in the next issue was more fully covered by C. H. Merriam; cited in Cutright, "Twin Literary Rarities," 8, 15–50.

43. See Cutright and Brodhead, *Coues*, 15–50, for details of Coues's early life.

44. Cutright and Brodhead, *Coues*, 31.

45. Cutright and Brodhead, *Coues*, 105–37.

46. E. Coues, *Key to North American Birds* (Boston: Estes and Lauriat, 1894), 2.

47. Coues, *Field Ornithology*, 5.

48. Coues, *Field Ornithology*, 27.

49. Coues, *Field Ornithology*, 30.

50. TRP, letter from Roosevelt to Philip Stewart, July 16, 1901. Also cited in Brinkley, *Warrior*, 836.

51. E. Coues, *Birds of the Colorado Valley: A Repository of Scientific and Popular Information concerning North American Ornithology. Part First. Passeres to Laniidae. U.S. Geological Survery of the Territories, Miscellaneous Publications, No. 11* (Washington: US Government Printing Office, 1878), 115; also cited in Cutright and Brodhead, *Coues*, 77.

52. TRC MS Am 1454.55 (11), 1877 diary, September 22, 1877.

53. T. Roosevelt, "Notes on Some of the Birds of Oyster Bay, Long Island," privately printed; see Cutright, "Twin Literary Rarities," 8; also cited in Cutright, *Naturalist*, 25; Morris, *Rise*, 66.

54. Roosevelt's coursework is compiled in Wilhelm, Donald, *Theodore Roosevelt as an Undergraduate* (Boston: John W. Luce, 1910), 107–11.

55. TRC MS Am 1454.55 (11), 1877 diary, October 8.

56. TRC MS Am 1454.55 (11), 1877 diary, December 15.

57. Morris, *Rise*, 69; quotation in TRC MS Am 1454.55 (11), 1877 diary, December 21.

58. TRC MS Am 1454.55 (11), 1877 diary, December 25. Also cited in Putnam, *Formative*, 147.

59. TRP 1878 diary, February 9. Also cited in Putnam, *Formative*, 148.
    Roosevelt's use of the night train is described in Morris, *Rise*, 70, although Roosevelt describes taking the "night boat" on many of his subsequent trips to New York.

60. TRP 1878 diary, February 12.

61. Roosevelt, *Autobiography*, 8; also cited in Brinkley, *Warrior*, 43.

62. Roosevelt, *Autobiography*, 10.

63. Roosevelt, *Autobiography*, 10.

64. Roosevelt, *Autobiography*, 12.

65. TRP 1878 diary, February 22; McCullough, *Horseback*, 192.

66. TRP 1878 diary, March 3 and March 5; cited in McCullough, *Horseback*, 192.

67. TRP 1878 diary, March 19; McCullough, *Horseback*, 193.

68. TRP 1878 diary, April 11. Also cited in Putnam, *Formative*, 152.

69. Roosevelt, *Autobiography*, 28–29; quoted in part in Brinkley, *Warrior*, 67.

70. Roosevelt, *Autobiography*, 29,

71. TRP 1878 diary, February 23; also cited in Morris, *Rise*, 72; McCullough, *Horseback*, 211.

72. TRP 1878 diary, March 7.

73. J. L. Laughlin, "Roosevelt's College Days," *American Review of Reviews*, October, 1924. A document including an advance copy of this article, a draft of the article annotated before publication, and a copy of a letter written to Laughlin from Delmar Leighton is held in the TRC, R 320 L36r.

74. TRP 1878 diary, March 7; McCullough, *Horseback*, 196.

75. E. Mayr, *The Growth of Biological Thought* (Cambridge, MA: Belknap Press of Harvard University Press, 1982), 113.

76. M. Winsor, *Reading the Shape of Nature* (Chicago: University of Chicago Press, 1991), 173–74. See also Cutright, *Naturalist*, 30, for a description of Mark's recollection of Roosevelt.

77. Roosevelt, *Autobiography*, 29.

78. Roosevelt, *Autobiography*, 29; also cited in Brinkley, *Warrior*, 110.

79. The department eventually split into two, which now exist as the Department of Molecular and Cellular Biology and the Department of Organismic and Evolutionary Biology. For overview of this conflict at Harvard, see "The Molecular Wars," in E. O. Wilson, *Naturalist* (Washington: Island Press, 1994), 218–37. Interestingly, these modern departments have become much more intertwined in faculty research and teaching, and Wilson and Watson have returned to collegial activities after a mutual recognition that they study the same fundamental subject, simply at different levels. Kind thanks to Andrew J. Berry for his perspective on comments.

80. Roosevelt's report to Harvard Overseers, June 21, 1893, quoted in Cutright, *Conservationist*, 189.

81. A. Agassiz, *Three Cruises of the United States Coast and Geodetic Survey Steamer* Blake, 2 Volumes (Cambridge, MA: Museum of Comparative Zoology Bulletin, 1888); A. Agassiz and S. W. Garman, *Exploration of Lake Titicaca*, Volume 3 (Cambridge, MA: Museum of Comparative Zoology Bulletin, 1879–80).

82. TRP 1878 diary, January 8; TRP 1878 diary, October 14.

83. W. James, *The Will to Believe and Other Essays in Popular Philosophy* (New York: Longmans Green, 1897); W. James, *Essays in Radical Empiricism* (New York: Longmans Green, 1912).

84. Houghton Library, Harvard University, bMS Am 1556.41.1, William James Brazil diary.

85. Houghton Library, Harvard University, bMS Am 1092.9 (2517), letter to Henry James, Sr. and Mary Robertson Walsh James, October 21, 1865. Also quoted in M. H. Machado, *Brazil through the Eyes of William James* (Cambridge: DRCLAS, 2006), 80.

86. Quotation from F. J. Ranlett, "Theodore Roosevelt's College Rank and Studies," *Harvard Graduates' Magazine* 15 (1907): 578–83. See also TRP, letter from Roosevelt to F. J. Ranlett, June 24, 1907; Cutright, *Naturalist*, 20, and McCullough, *Horseback*, 207, 220, for a description of student-professor interactions at the time.

87. TRC MS Am 1454.38, "Field Book of Zoology," May 6, 1878. Also cited in Cutright, *Conservationist*, 109–10.

88. TRP 1878 diary, January 14.

89. Sewall, *Sewall's Story*, 2; also cited in Morris, *Rise*, 75; Cutright, *Conservationist*, 111;

90. Sewall, *Sewall's Story*, 2–3; also cited in Putnam, *Formative*, 157.

91. Sewall, *Sewall's Story*, 3; also cited in A. Vietze, *Becoming Teddy Roosevelt* (Rockport, ME: Down East, 2010), 19.

92. For the ubiquity of the "old guide" in the frontier literature and in Defoe's *The Pioneers*, see M. Green, *Seven Types of Adventure Tale* (University Park, PA: Pennsylvania State University Press, 1991), 100.

93. Sewall, *Sewall's Story*, 5

94. TRP 1878 diary, September 14; also cited in Putnam, *Formative*, 173; Brinkley, *Warrior*, 113.

95. See Morris, *Rise*, 89.

96. For example, see photograph in Putnam, *Formative*, 147 (facing plate); Brinkley, *Warrior*, 114; Vietze, *Becoming*, 118.

97. TRP 1879 diary, March 26; also cited in Putnam, *Formative*, 173.

98. TRP 1879 diary, August 26–27.

99. TRP 1878 diary, April 20–22; see also McCullough, *Horseback*, 197.

100. See twin accounts of May 12, 1869, in TRC MS Am 1454.55 (2), Roosevelt's grand tour 1869 diary, and TRC MS 1454.55 (3), grand tour journal 1. See also *Diaries of Boyhood*, 13; Putnam, *Formative*, 59–60; and appendix 1 for a discussion of the manuscripts.

101. TRC MS Am 1454.55 (4), Roosevelt grand tour journal 2; see also *Diaries of Boyhood*, 103. Also cited in Putnam, *Formative*, 69–70; Morris, *Rise*, 27; Cutright, *Conservationist*, 18; Dalton, *Strenuous*, 47.

102. Putnam, *Formative*, 170; Morris, *Rise*, 74.

103. TRP 1878 diary, August 22; also cited in Robinson, *My Brother*, 102; Morris, *Rise*, 74.

104. For similar interpretation, see Morris, *Rise*, 74; Dalton, *Strenuous*, 70.
105. TRP 1878 diary, October 19; Dalton, *Strenuous*, 70,
106. Quotation from Morris, *Rise*, 82. Descriptions of Alice Lee in Putnam, *Formative*, 167–68; McCullough, *Horseback*, 226.
107. Descriptions of Roosevelt's courtship with Alice Lee appear in Putnam, *Formative*, 170–75; Morris, *Rise*, 80–113. see TRP 1878 diary, November 28 and December 1.
108. A subset of these quotations were also used in Putnam, *Formative*, 177–79, to describe this time.
109. TRP 1878 diary, September 1; also quoted in Morris, *Rise*, 75.
110. TRP 1878 diary, December 26; also quoted in Putnam, *Formative*, 177; Morris, *Rise*, 87; Cutright, *Conservationist*, 127.
111. TRP 1879 diary, August 18; also cited in Putnam, *Formative*, 178.
112. Morison et al., *Letters I*, 43, letter from Roosevelt to Henry D. Minot, February 13, 1880. Also quoted in Putnam, *Formative*, 178; Morris, *Rise*, 87; Dalton, *Strenuous*, 72.
113. TRP 1880 diary, March 25; cited in Putnam, *Formative*, 179; Morris, *Rise*, 106.
114. J. L. Laughlin, "Roosevelt's College Days," *American Review of Reviews*, October, 1924. Also cited in Cutright, *Naturalist*, 27.
115. TRP 1880 diary, June 29; also cited in Putnam, *Formative*, 197; Morris, *Rise*, 108.
116. TRP 1880 diary, July 1; cited in slightly altered form in Morris, *Rise*, 109.
117. Alice's death, which would happen four years after Rooosevelt's graduation, clearly contributed to his subsequent recollections of his time at Harvard. He would not talk of Alice in his later years, and in his *Autobiography* he would make no mention of the enormous influence she had on him during his college years. See also Morris, *Rise*, 232–33.
118. Roosevelt, *Autobiography*, 30.
119. TRP 1879 diary, August 11.

CHAPTER FIVE

1. C. F. Hoffman, *Wild Scenes in the Forest and Prairie with Sketches of American Life, Vol. I* (New York: William H. Colyer, 1843), 18. Cited as early use of the term "buckboard"; see *Oxford English Dictionary*, Third Edition (online). Accessed February 2012.
2. Hoffman, *Wild Scenes*, 19.
3. TRP 1880 diary, September 10.
4. TRP 1880 diary, September 10.
5. TRP 1880 diary, September 23.
6. TRC MS Am (1454.55 (4), grand tour journal 4, October 26, 1869; see also *Diaries of Boyhood*, 85; McCullough, *Horseback*, 104; Cutright, *Conservationist*, 19; Brinkley, *Warrior*, 37.
7. TRP 1880 diary, August 18.
8. TRP 1880 diary, August 19.
9. TRP 1880 diary, August 19.
10. TRP 1880 diary, August 22.
11. TRP 1880 diary, August 9.
12. TRP 1880 diary, July 30; TRP 1880 diary, June 27.
13. TRP 1880 diary, August 24.
14. TRP 1880 diary, August 26.
15. D. L. Jackson and L. J. Jackson, *The Farm as Natural Habitat: Reconnecting Food*

Systems with Ecosystems (Washington: Island Press, 2002), 138. Cited in C. F. Mutel, *The Emerald Horizon: The History of Nature in Iowa* (Iowa City: University of Iowa Press, 2008), 114.

16.　TRP 1880 diary, September 12.

17.　TRP 1880 diary, September 19.

18.　TRP 1880 diary, September 19.

19.　TRP 1880 diary, September 19.

20.　TRP 1880 diary, September 20.

21.　TRP 1880 diary, September 22. Also quoted in Putnam, *Formative*, 208.

22.　TRP 1880 diary, September 25.

23.　M. Drower, ed., *Letters from the Desert: The Correspondence of Flinders and Hilda Petrie* (Oxford: Aris and Phillips, 2004), 26.

24.　TRP 1880 diary, August 22, 1880; TRP 1880 diary, September 15.

25.　M. Drower, ed., *Letters from the Desert*, 16–17.

26.　TRP 1880 diary, August 31.

27.　C. W. Eliot, *Educatonal Reform: Essays and Addresses* (New York: Century, 1901), 22.

28.　See K. Townsend, *Manhood at Harvard: William James and Others* (Cambridge, MA: Harvard University Press, 1996).

29.　Cited in Dalton, *Strenuous*, 75.

30.　For quotation and discussion, see Bederman, *Manliness and Civilization*, 172. See also A. M. Johnston, "Sex and Gender in Roosevelt's America," in S. Ricard, ed., *A Companion to Theodore Roosevelt* (Malden, MA: Wiley-Blackwell, 2011), 112–34.

31.　TRP 1880 diary, August 23.

32.　TRP 1880 diary, September 5.

33.　TRP 1880 diary, September 24. Also cited in Putnam, *Formative*, 208; Morris, *Rise*, 112; Brinkley, *Warrior*, 135.

34.　TRP 1880 diary, August 17. Also quoted in Brinkley, *Warrior*, 128.

35.　McCullough, *Horseback*, 249.

36.　Morison et al., *Letters I*, 46, letter from Roosevelt to Anna Roosevelt, August 22, 1880. Also quoted in Putnam, *Formative*, 203; Morris, *Rise*, 111, Brinkley, *Warrior*, 130.

37.　TRC MS Am 1834 (1000), Roosevelt letter to Martha Bulloch Roosevelt, August 25, 1880. Also quoted in Putnam, *Formative*, 203; Brinkley, *Warrior*, 131.

38.　Green, *Seven Types of Adventure Tale*, 97.

39.　TRC MS Am 1834 (178), letter from Roosevelt to Anna Roosevelt, September 2, 1880. Also quoted in Morris, *Rise*, 111.

40.　TRP 1880 diary, August 25. Also quoted in Putnam, *Formative*, 203.

41.　Morison et al., *Letters I*, 74, letter from Roosevelt to Anna Roosevelt, August 22, 1880. Also quoted in Putnam, *Formative*, 203; Brinkley, *Warrior*, 130.

42.　National Park Service Public Use Statistics Office, http://www.nature.nps.gov/ stats/park.cfm. Accessed February 2012.

43.　T. Roosevelt, *Presidential Addresses and State Papers, Volume I* (New York: Review of Reviews Company, 1910), 370.

44.　Estimate of Roosevelt's appearance in C. Depew, *My Memories of Eighty Years* (New York: Scribner's, 1922), 159. For an overview of Roosevelt's early professional career, see E. P. Kohn, "Theodore Roosevelt's Early Political Career: The Making of an Independent Republican and Urban Progressive," in S. Ricard, ed., *A Companion to Theodore Roosevelt* (Malden, MA: Wiley-Blackwell, 2011), 27–44, and references therein.

45.　M. Sullivan, *Our Times: The United States 1900–1925, Vol. II, America Finding*

Herself (New York: Scribner's, 1927), 213, 215–35. See also Morris, *Rise*, 144; S. L. Watts, *Rough Rider in the White House* (Chicago: University of Chicago Press, 2003), 126; Dalton, *Strenuous*, 98.

46. Many of the quotations that emphasize Roosevelt's naturalistic qualities are also quoted in Morris, *Rise*, and other biographies. This quotation appears in Morris, *Rise*, 162, taken from an interview with Isaac Hunt on September 23, 1923, in a "supplementary statement" at the Theodore Roosevelt Birthplace. At the time of this writing, the collections at the Birthplace were not open for examination.

47. TRC MS Am 1540 (6), letter from Roosevelt to Martha Bulloch Roosevelt, September 4, 1883; also cited in Morris, *Rise*, 174; TRP 1879 diary, September 24.

48. R. S. Baker, *American Chronicle: The Autobiography of Ray Stannard Baker* (New York: Scribner's, 1945), 171. Also cited in D. K. Goodwin, *The Bully Pulpit* (New York: Simon and Schuster, 2013), 361. L. Lang, *Ranching with Roosevelt* (Philadelphia: J. B. Lippincott, 1926), 114; also quoted in Morris, *Rise*, 204.

49. Sullivan, *Our Times*, 218; O. Wister, Roosevelt: *The Story of a Friendship* (New York: Macmillan, 1930), 6.

50. Cited in Morris, *Rise*, 158; Morison et al., *Letters III*, 635, letter from Roosevelt to Theodore Roosevelt Jr. Also cited in Morris, *Rise*, 168.

51. Cited in Morris, *Rise*, 160, from Isaac Hunt interview at TRB; the original was not available for examination at the time of this writing.

52. J. Burroughs, "Theodore Roosevelt: His Americanism Reached into the Marrow of His Bones," *Natural History* 19 (1919): 5–7.

53. For descriptions of this meeting, see Putnam, *Formative*, 308; Morris, *Rise*, 182.

54. See Morris, *Rise*, 183.

55. *The Wonderland of the World* (Chicago: Rand McNally, 1884), 3.

56. *The Wonderland of the World* (Chicago: Rand McNally, 1884), 19.

57. Putnam, *Formative*, 313; Morris, *Rise*, 190

58. Roosevelt, *Autobiography*, 104.

59. Roosevelt, *Autobiography*, 110.

60. Roosevelt, *Autobiography*, 110.

61. The account of Roosevelt's meeting with Frank Vine and Joe Ferris follows Hagedorn, *Bad Lands*, 9–12.

62. Hagedorn, *Bad Lands*, 10.

63. Lang, *Ranching*, 100; Morris, *Rise*, 191.

64. Lang, *Ranching*, 60. Also quoted in Putnam, *Formative*, 321.

65. Hagedorn, *Bad Lands*, 15.

66. Roosevelt, *Autobiography*, 106. Also cited in Hagedorn, *Bad Lands*, 14; Putnam, *Formative*, 326; Morris, *Rise*, 199.

67. Hagedorn, *Bad Lands*, 17. Also quoted in R. L. Di Silvestro, *Theodore Roosevelt in the Badlands* (New York: Walker and Co., 2011), 47.

68. For a similar point on Roosevelt's first "hold" in the Badlands, see: Hagedorn, *Bad Lands*, 17.

69. See Lang, *Ranching*, 33 ("cling like gumbo mud"), 112 ("waded through wet gumbo for days").

70. Lang, *Ranching*, 113.

71. Lang, *Ranching*, 113. Also quoted in Putnam, *Formative*, 330; Morris, *Rise*, 203.

72. Putnam, *Formative*, 317.

73. This description of the buffalo hunt follows T. Roosevelt, *Hunting Trips of a Ranchman* (New York: G. P. Putnam's Sons, 1886), 276–88. See also Hagedorn, *Bad Lands*, 18–45.

74. Roosevelt, *Hunting Trips*, 281.
75. Roosevelt, *Hunting Trips*, 282.
76. Roosevelt, *Hunting Trips*, 285. Also quoted in Hagedorn, *Bad Lands*, 37; Morris, *Rise*, 207–8; Di Silvestro, *Badlands*, 54.
77. Roosevelt, *Hunting Trips*, 287. Also quoted in Putnam, *Formative*, 345.
78. TRD MS Am 1454.29, "Game Book"; TRC MS Am 1541.9 (103), letter from Roosevelt to Alice Lee Roosevelt, September 20, 1883.
79. TRC MS Am 1541.9 (103), letter from Roosevelt to Alice Lee Roosevelt, September 20, 1883. For a description of the ball, see TRP 1883 diary, "Miscellaneous."
80. Hagedorn, *Bad Lands*, 45. Also cited in Putnam, *Formative*, 345; Morris, *Rise*, 212; Cutright, *Conservationist*, 148;
81. Bederman, *Manliness and Civilization*, 176.
82. Quotation from Hagedorn, *Bad Lands*, 9. For the buffalo hunt in the context of conservation, see A. C. Isenberg, *The Destruction of the Bison* (Cambridge: Cambridge University Press, 2000); W. T. Hornaday, *The Extermination of the American Bison* (Washington: Smithsonian Institution Press, 2002); C. T. Rubin, *Conservation Reconsidered: Nature, Virtue, and American Liberal Democracy* (Lanham, MD: Rowman and Littlefield, 2000).
83. A buffalo hunt does not appear in Roosevelt's 1883 diary (TRP), but the animals he killed are indicated in the section at the end of the diary marked "Miscellaneous." The buffalo also is indicated in his "Game Book," TRC MS Am 1454.29.
84. Lang, *Ranching*, 119. Also quoted in Cutright, *Naturalist*, 42; Putnam, *Formative*, 346; Morris, *Rise*, 212; Cutright, *Conservationist*, 148; Di Silvestro, *Badlands*, 57.
85. TRC MS Am 1541.9 (103), letter from Roosevelt to Alice Lee Roosevelt, September 20, 1883. "Darling Wifie, Hurrah! The luck has turned at last. I will bring you home the head of a great buffalo bull." Three days later he wrote to Alice: "The heads of the buffalo and stags will look grandly in our hall." See TRC MS am (104), letter from Roosevelt to Alice Lee Roosevelt, September 23, 1880.
86. Morris, *Rise*, 209.
87. See Putnam, *Formative*, 337.
88. TRC MS Am 1541.9 (104), letter from Roosevelt to Alice Lee Roosevelt, September 23, 1883.
89. TRC MS Am 1541.9 (104), letter from Roosevelt to Alice Lee Roosevelt, September 23, 1883.
90. Morison et al., *Letters I*, 65, letter from Roosevelt to Alice Lee Roosevelt, February 6, 1884.
91. Morison et al., *Letters I*, 65, telegram from Roosevelt to Dora Watkins, February 13, 1884. Also quoted in Morris, *Rise*, 228; Dalton, *Strenuous*, 88.
92. Versions of this quote and scene appear in various sources, including Putnam, *Formative*, 386; Morris, *Rise*, 229; Brinkley, *Warrior*, 166; Di Silvestro, *Badlands*, 54. The origin of the quote is described in Putnam, *Formative*, 386 (note 12); and Morris, *Rise*, 816 (note 69), with the original documents in the TRC R110 P93r.
93. TRP 1878 diary, November 2. Also cited in Morris, *Rise*, 79.
94. Roosevelt's diary entry for February 14 in his 1884 diary (TRP) contains a large "X" followed by: "The light has gone out of my life."

CHAPTER SIX

1. T. Roosevelt, *The Wilderness Hunter* (New York: G. P. Putnam's Sons, 1893), xv.
2. Quotations from T. Roosevelt, "What 'Americanism' Means," *The Forum* (1894): 196–206. See also A. M. Johnston, "Sex and Gender in Roosevelt's America," in

S. Ricard, ed., *A Companion to Theodore Roosevelt* (Malden, MA: Wiley-Blackwell, 2011), 112–34; L. G. Dorsey, "'We Want Americans Pure and Simple': Theodore Roosevelt and the Myth of Americanism," *Rhetoric and Public Affairs* 6, no. 1 (2003): 55–78.

3. Roosevelt, *Autobiography*, 119. Also quoted in Hagedorn, *Bad Lands*, 387; Di Silvestro, *Badlands*, 169.

4. Roosevelt, *Autobiography*, 117.

5. Roosevelt, *Autobiography*, 117. Also quoted in W. D. Lewis, *The Life of Theodore Roosevelt* (Philadelphia: John C. Winston, 1919), 73–74.

6. TRP 1884 diary, June 16.

7. Morison et al., *Letters I*, 73–74, letter from Roosevelt to Anna Roosevelt, June 17, 1884. Also quoted in Di Silvestro, *Badlands*, 94.

8. The description of Roosevelt's trip follows chapter 6, "A Trip on the Prairie," in Roosevelt, *Hunting Trips*, 191–233.

9. Roosevelt, *Hunting Trips*, 209.

10. Roosevelt, *Hunting Trips*, 211.

11. Roosevelt, *Hunting Trips*, chapter 6. See also TRP 1884, diary, June 18.

12. Roosevelt later recalled how Sewall and Dow compared his woodcutting to that of a beaver. See Roosevelt, *Autobiography*, 108. See also Morris, *Rise*, 287.

13. TRP 1883 diary, August 16, 1884. See appendix 1 for a description of how Roosevelt entered events of 1884 in his 1883 diary. Note that in some places, printed dates in the diary are offset from the actual dates of events. For reference, the dates in these notes follow the dates actually printed or indicated on each page of the diary.

14. For an overview, see M. E. Snodgrass, *Encyclopedia of Frontier Literature* (Santa Barbara, CA: ABC-CLIO, 1997).

15. This account of Roosevelt's grizzly hunt is adapted from his diary accounts and Roosevelt, *Hunting Trips*, 331–41.

16. TRP 1883 diary, August 16–17, 1884.

17. TRP 1883 diary, August 17, 1884.

18. TRP 1883 diary, August 16, 1884.

19. TRP 1883 diary, September 15.

20. TRP 1879 diary, August 26–27.

21. TRP 1883 diary, September 15.

22. TRP 1883 diary, September 18: "Away it started and, running at top speed in my light moccasins I got another shot and broke his back."

23. TRP 1883 diary, September 12.

24. TRP 1883 diary, September 15.

25. TRP 1883 diary, September 15.

26. Morison et al., *Letters I*, 82, letter from Roosevelt to Anna Roosevelt, September 20, 1884.

27. Morison et al., *Letters I*, 82, letter from Roosevelt to Anna Roosevelt, September 20, 1884.

28. Morison et al., *Letters I*, 82, letter from Roosevelt to Anna Roosevelt, September 20, 1884.

29. Roosevelt, *Hunting Trips*, 318.

30. Roosevelt, *Hunting Trips*, 319–20.

31. Roosevelt, *Hunting Trips*, 324.

32. Roosevelt, *Hunting Trips*, 330; Di Silvestro, *Badlands*, 132.

33. Roosevelt, *Hunting Trips*, 336.

34. Roosevelt, *Hunting Trips*, 335–36.

35. Roosevelt, *Hunting Trips,* 336.
36. Roosevelt, *Hunting Trips,* 338.
37. See Roosevelt, *Wilderness Hunter,* chapter 14, "Old Ephraim, the Grisly Bear," and chapter 15, "Hunting the Grisly."
38. T. Roosevelt, "The Boone and Crockett Club," *Harper's Weekly* 37 (1893): 267.
39. Roosevelt, *Wilderness Hunter,* xv.
40. Roosevelt, *Autobiography,* 135–36. Also described in Hagedorn, *Bad Lands,* 242–45; Morris, *Rise,* 275–76; Di Silvestro, *Badlands,* 114.
41. Roosevelt, *Autobiography,* 136.
42. Roosevelt, *Autobiography,* 136.
43. Roosevelt, *Autobiography,* 136. Roosevelt documented his aptitude for boxing long before his time in the Badlands. In a letter to his father from Dresden in 1873, he wrote:

> The boxing gloves are a source of great amusement to us. When ever Johnie comes to see us we have an hours boxing or so. Each round takes one to two minutes. The best round yet was one yesterday between Johnie and I. I shall describe it briefly. After some striking and warding, I got Johnie into a corner, when he sprung out. We each warded off a right hand blow and brough in a left hander. His took effect behind my ear, and for a minute I saw stars and reeled back to the centre of the room, while Johnie had had his nose and upper lip mashed together and been driven back against the door. I was so weak however that I was driven across the room, simply warding off blows, but then I almost disabled his left arm, and drove him back to the middle where some sharp boxing occurred. I got in one on his forehead which raised a bump, but my eye was made black and blue. At this minute 'Up' was called and we had to separate. Elliott can box better than either of us as he was a winter at a boxing school If you offered rewards for bloody noses you would spend a fortune on me alone.

Quotation from Morison et al., *Letters I,* 8–9, letter from Roosevelt to Theodore Roosevelt, Sr., June 15, 1873.
44. T. Roosevelt, *Ranch Life and the Hunting-Trail* (New York: Century, 1896). See chapter 6, "Frontier Types," for Frederic Remington's illustrations of these scenes.
45. Sewall, *Sewall's Story,* 21; Hagedorn, *Bad Lands,* 207–8; Di Silvestro, *Badlands,* 140. See also Di Silvestro, *Badlands,* 305n9, for identification of Paddock.
46. Roosevelt, *Ranch Life,* 102.
47. Roosevelt, *Ranch Life,* 103; Roosevelt, *Autobiography,* 125. For Roosevelt and Native Americans, see T. G. Dyer, *Theodore Roosevelt and the Idea of Race* (Baton Rouge: Louisiana State University Press, 1980), 69–88; W. T. Hagan, *Theodore Roosevelt and Six Friends of the Indian* (Norman: University of Oklahoma Press, 1997); R. L. Nichols, "Theodore Roosevelt and the Indians," in S. Ricard, ed., *A Companion to Theodore Roosevelt* (Malden, MA: Wiley-Blackwell, 2011), 186–97.
48. Roosevelt, *Wilderness Hunter,* xv.
49. Roosevelt, *Hunting Trips,* 73.
50. Roosevelt, *Hunting Trips,* 73.
51. Roosevelt, *Hunting Trips,* 73.
52. Roosevelt, *Hunting Trips,* 295.
53. Roosevelt, *Hunting Trips,* 13.
54. "Hunting Trips of a Ranchman," *Overland Monthly and Out West Magazine,* 8, no. 44, (1886): 223.

55. G. B. Grinnell, *Audubon Park: The History of the Site of the Hispanic Society of America and Neighbouring Institutions* (New York: Printed by Order of the Trustees, 1927).

56. For the background of Grinnell's early life at Audubon Park and the Marsh Expedition, see M. Punke, *Last Stand: George Bird Grinnell, the Battle to Save the Buffalo and the Birth of the New West* (New York: HarperCollins, 2007).

57. C. Parsons, *George Bird Grinnell: A Biographical Sketch* (Lanham, MD: University Press of America), 60.

58. G. B. Grinnell, "New Publications: Hunting Trips of a Ranchman," *Forest and Stream* 23 (1885): 451. Also cited in J. F. Reiger, *American Sportsmen and the Origins of Conservation*, 3rd ed. (Corvallis: Oregon State University Press, 2001), 146. See also Brinkley, *Warrior*, 184–89, for an account of Roosevelt's relationship with Grinnell.

59. G. B. Grinnell's introduction in T. Roosevelt, *The Works of Theodore Roosevelt, Volume I, National Edition* (New York: Scribner's, 1926), xv–xvi.

60. W. G. Sheldon, "A History of the Boone and Crockett Club," an unpublished manuscript at the Boone and Crocket Club archives.

61. "Mr. Roosevelt's Americanism: The Wilderness Hunter," *New York Times*, August 6, 1893.

62. "The Wilderness Hunter" *Forest and Stream*, 4 (1893): 76.

63. For overview of Roosevelt's guns, see R. L. Wilson, *Theodore Roosevelt. Outdoorsman* (New York: Winchester Press, 1971), also cited in T. Roosevelt, "Theodore Roosevelt's African Safari," in N. A. Naylor, D. Brinkley, J. A. Gable, eds., *Theodore Roosevelt: Many-Sided American* (Interlaken, NY: Heart of the Lakes Publishing, 1992), 413–32; R. L. Wilson, *Theodore Roosevelt: Hunter-Conservationist* (Missoula, MT: Boone and Crockett Club, 2009).

64. Roosevelt, *Hunting Trips*, 69.

65. This account of the "boat thieves" story follows Roosevelt's own account in "Sheriff's Work on a Ranch" in Roosevelt, *Ranch Life*, 111–29; Roosevelt's diary entries; and Sewall, *Sewall's Story*, 58–75.

66. TRC MS Am 1454.55(12), 1886 diary, March 24–30.

67. Roosevelt, *Ranch Life*, 118.

68. Roosevelt, *Ranch Life*, 120.

69. Sewall, *Sewall's Story*, 68.

70. Roosevelt, *Ranch Life*, 123.

71. Roosevelt wrote to his sister Corinne and described reading *Anna Karenina* (Morison et al., *Letters I*, 96, letter from Roosevelt to Corinne Roosevelt Robinson, April 12, 1886). Although the book had been translated into English that year, Roosevelt seems to have taken the French version, as he refers to it as "Anna Karénine."

72. "A Cowboy Episode: Fatal Fighting at Arm's Length with Forty-Five Caliber Revolvers," *National Police Gazette*, January 30, 1886.

73. In *Ranch Life*, 126, Roosevelt describes the men's reading material: "They had quite a stock of books. . . . Dime novels and the inevitable 'History of the James Brothers'—a book that, together with the 'Police Gazette,' is to be found in the hands of every professed or putative ruffian in the West." The *Police Gazette* was both a magazine and a book series, "Police Gazette Library of Sensation," which included *Lives of the Poisoners: How They Killed and What They Killed With* (New York: R. K. Fox, 1882) and *Billy LeRoy: The Colorado Bandit* ((New York, R. K. Fox, 1881). Roosevelt's reference to the "History of the James Brothers" may refer to one of several titles released in the years before the boat thieves incident, including J. Donald, *Outlaws of the Border: A Complete and Authentic History of the*

Lives of Frank and Jesse James, the Younger Brothers, and Their Robber Companions (Chicago: Coburn & Newman, 1882); J. W. Buel, *The Border Outlaws: An Authentic and Thrilling History of the Most Noted Bandits of Ancient or Modern Times, The Younger Brothers, Jesse and Frank James, and their Comrades in Crime* (Saint Louis: Historical Publishing, 1881); *The Outlaw Brothers, Frank and Jesse James: Lives and Adventures of the Scourges of the Plains* (R. K. Fox, 1881).

74. D. Cline, *Alias Billy the Kid: The Man behind the Legend* (Santa Fe, NM: Sunstone Press, 1986), 123. See also: F. Nolan, ed., *The Billy the Kid Reader* (Norman: University of Oklahoma Press, 2007); J. D. Boggs, *Billy the Kid on Film, 1911–2012* (Jeffferson, NC: McFarland, 2013), 19.

75. Roosevelt, *Autobiography*, 131–32: "Such a man was Billy the Kid, the notorious man-killer and desperado of New Mexico, who was himself finally slain by a friend of mine, Pat Garrett."

76. Sewall, *Sewall's Story*, 71–72.

77. Sewall, *Sewall's Story*, 74.

78. Roosevelt, *Ranch Life*, 128.

79. See Hagedorn's *Bad Lands* notes, TRC 332 H12P; Morris, *Rise*, 325.

80. Morison et al., *Letters I*, 95–96, letter from Roosevelt to Corinne Roosevelt Robinson, April 12, 1886; Morison et al., *Letters I*, 97–98, letter from Roosevelt to Henry Cabot Lodge, April 16, 1886.

81. Roosevelt, *Autobiography*, 15; Bold, *Frontier Club*, 100.

82. TRC MS Am 1834 (208), letter from Roosevelt to his sister Anna Roosevelt Cowles, April 12, 1884.

83. Slotkin, *Gunfighter Nation*, 125; quotation in R. W. Etulain, *Telling Western Stories* (Albuquerque: University of New Mexico Press, 1999), 3.

84. Morison et al., *Letters I*, 101–2, letter from Roosevelt to Henry Cabot Lodge, May 20, 1886.

85. Roosevelt had published a six-part series, "Ranch Life and Game Shooting in the West," with *Outing* in 1886, the last part of which was T. Roosevelt, "Water Fowl and Prairie Fowl," *Outing* 8 (1886): 522–25. Remington's illustrations appeared with articles in the next volume (9).

86. Cited in B. W. Dippie, *The Frederic Remington Art Museum Collection* (Ogdensburg, NY: Frederic Remington Art Museum), 60.

87. T. Roosevelt, "Sheriff's Work on a Ranch," *Century Magazine* 1 (1888): 39–51.

88. P. Samuels and H. Samuels, *Frederic Remington: A Biography* (New York: Doubleday, 1982), 92. Remington eventually wrote many articles of his own, but his illustrations were his longest-lasting contribution; he was never fully embraced by the Boone and Crockett Club, and never became a member. See R. L. Buckland, *Frederic Remington: The Writer* (New York: Twayne Publishers, 2000); C. Bold, *The Frontier Club* (Oxford: Oxford University Press, 2013), 35.

89. Roosevelt, *Autobiography*, 128.

90. A selection of publications recount the "boat thieves" story: R. C. V. Meyers, *Theodore Roosevelt, Patriot and Statesman* (Philadelphia: P. W. Ziegler, 1902), 89–96; G. W. Douglas, *The Many-Sided Roosevelt: An Anecdotal Biography* (New York: Dodd, Mead, 1907), 65–71; D. Henderson, *"Great-Heart": The Life Story of Theodore Roosevelt* (New York: Knopf, 1919), 26–29; T. H. Russell, *Theodore Roosevelt, Typical American* (n.p.: L. H. Walter, 1919), 120–21; W. R. Thayer, *Theodore Roosevelt: An Intimate Biography* (Boston: Houghton Mifflin, 1919), 65–66; Sewall, *Sewall's Story*, 58–75; E. L. Pearson, *Theodore Roosevelt* (New York: Macmillan, 1920), 33–36; Hagedorn, *Bad Lands*, 367–86; N. Whitelaw, *Theodore Roosevelt Takes Charge* (Morton Grove, IL: A. Whitman, 1992), 55; S. B. Bopp, "From the

Bunkhouse to the White House," *American Cowboy*, March/April 2000, 74–75; H. P. Jeffers, *Roosevelt the Explorer* (Lanham, MD: Taylor Trade, 2003), 63–64; J. Benge and G. Benge, *Theodore Roosevelt: An American Original* (Lynnwood, WA: Emerald Books, 2005), 103–6; P. Grondahl, *I Rose Like a Rocket: The Political Education of Theodore Roosevelt* (Lincoln: University of Nebraska Press, 2007), 162–64; R. Di Silvestro, *Theodore Roosevelt in the Badlands* (New York: Walker & Co., 2011), 198–217.

91. T. Roosevelt, *The Winning of the West* (New York: G. P. Putnam's Sons, 1889–96). See R. Slotkin, *Gunfighter Nation* (New York: Atheneum, 1992), 29–62; S. McVeigh, *The American Western* (Edinburgh: Edinburgh University Press, 2007), 13–21; K. M. Dalton, "Theodore Roosevelt's Contradictory Legacies: From Imperialist Nationalism to Advocacy of a Progressive Welfare State," in Ricard, *A Companion to Theodore Roosevelt*, 485–501; G. Scharnhorst, "'All Hat and No Cattle': Romance, Realism, and Late Nineteenth Century Western American Fiction," in N. S. Witschi, ed., *The Literature and Culture of the American West* (Oxford: Wiley-Blackwell, 2011), 281–96.

92. For the founding and history of the Boone and Crockett Club, see "Boone and Crockett Club, Founded January 1888," Boone and Crockett Club Records, MSS 738; "The Boone and Crockett Club," *Forest and Stream* 30 (1888): 124; J. F. Reiger, *American Sportsmen and the Origins of Conservation, 3rd Edition* (Corvallis: Oregon State University Press, 2001), 146–74. Roosevelt and Grinnell's co-edited books include T. Roosevelt and G. B. Grinnell, *American Big-Game Hunting* (New York: Forest and Stream, 1893); T. Roosevelt and G. B. Grinnell, *Hunting in Many Lands* (New York: Forest and Stream, 1895); G. B. Grinnell and T. Roosevelt, *Trail and Camp-Fire* (New York: Forest and Stream, 1897).

93. L. Budner, "Hunting, Ranching, and Writing: Did Theodore Roosevelt's Western Experiences Significantly Influence His Later Career and Political Thought?" in Naylor et al., *Many-Sided American*, 161–68; Bold, *Frontier Club*, 37–54.

94. O. Wister, *Roosevelt: The Story of a Friendship*; J. Tuska and V. Piekarski, eds., *Encyclopedia of Frontier and Western Fiction* (New York: McGraw-Hill, 1983), 297–98; McVeigh, *The American Western*, 38–57.

95. O. Wister, *Roosevelt: The Story of a Friendship* (New York: MacMillan, 1930), 37.

96. For other perspectives on women, Native Americans, and African Americans in the West and Western literature, see M. L. Billington and R. D. Hardaway, eds., *African Americans on the Western Frontier* (Niwot: University Press of Colorado, 1998); N. Baym, *Women Writers of the American West, 1833–1927* (Urbana: University of Illinois Press, 2011); M. K. Johnson, "African American Literature and Culture and the American West," in: Witschi, *The Literature and Culture of the American West*, 161–76; K. Washburn, "Writing the Indigenous West," in Witschi, *The Literature and Culture of the American West*, 191–212; C. Halverson, "Housing the American West: Western Women's Literature, Early Twentieth Century and Beyond," in Witschi, *The Literature and Culture of the American West*, 353–66.

97. Roosevelt, *Wilderness Hunter*, xv.

98. Morison et al., *Letters I*, 104–5, letter from Roosevelt to Anna Roosevelt, June 28, 1886.

99. Morison et al., *Letters I*, 100–101, letter from Roosevelt to Anna Roosevelt, May 15, 1886.

100. Morison et al., *Letters I*, 108–9, letter from Roosevelt to Henry Cabot Lodge, August 20, 1886.

101. Roosevelt had originally planned to call the house "Leeholm," but after Alice's death he changed it to "Sagamore Hill."

102. Morison et al., *Letters I*, 110–11, letter from Roosevelt to Elihu Root and William Bellamy, October 16, 1886.
103. Morison et al., *Letters I*, 115, letter from Roosevelt to Henry Cabot Lodge, November 1, 1886.
104. Morris, *Edith Kermit Roosevelt*, 79–83.
105. 1886. Diary, TRC MS Am 1454.55 (12).
106. Lang, *Ranching*, 241.
107. Lang, *Ranching*, 242.
108. Lang, *Ranching*, 250–51.
109. See Morris, *Rise*, 363–67.
110. See appendix 1.
111. TRC MS Am 1454.32, "Notes on Natural History," entry on "Passer domesticus."
112. Lang, *Ranching*, 224.
113. Lang, *Ranching*, 224.
114. For an exhaustive treatment of Roosevelt's conservation agenda, see Brinkley, *Warrior*.
115. T. Roosevelt, *Outdoor Pastimes of an American Hunter* (New York: Charles Scribner's Sons, 1905), 317.
116. Morison et al., *Letters I*, 233–34, letter from Roosevelt to Gertrude Carow, October 18, 1890.
117. Morison et al., *Letters I*, 233–34, letter from Roosevelt to Gertrude Carow, October 18, 1890.
118. Robinson, *My Brother*, 139, 147; see also Hagedorn, *Bad Lands*, 113–16, for Bill Jones and his relationship with Roosevelt.
119. Morison et al., *Letters I*, 233–34, letter from Roosevelt to Gertrude Carow, October 18, 1890.
120. Kohn, "Theodore Roosevelt's Early Political Career: The Making of an Independent Republican and Urban Progressive"; E. P. Kohn, *Heir to the Empire City* (New York: Basic Books, 2014).

CHAPTER SEVEN

1. A description of Roosevelt's desk appears in "Washington Gets Excited," *New York Times*, May 2, 1897. A similar potrayal appeared in Morris, *Rise*, 588–90.
2. Roosevelt, *Autobiography*, 144–45.
3. T. Roosevelt, *Gouverneur Morris* (Boston: Houghton Mifflin, 1888). In this biography, Roosevelt attributes Morris's peg leg to an accident while riding in a horse-drawn carriage (see Roosevelt, *Morris*, 109). It is at least possible that Morris's leg injury and subsequent amputation resulted from a jump from a window in one of his philandering escapades. For this latter interpretation, see R. Brookhiser, *Gentleman Revolutionary: Gouverneur Morris, the Rake Who Wrote the Constitution* (New York: Free Press, 2003), 61–62.
4. H. C. Lodge and T. Roosevelt, *Hero Tales from American History* (New York: Century, 1985); T. Roosevelt and G. B. Grinnell, eds., *American Big-Game Hunting: The Book of the Boone and Crockett Club* (New York: Forest and Stream, 1893); Roosevelt and G. B. Grinnell, eds., *Hunting in Many Lands: The Book of the Boone and Crockett Club* (New York: Forest and Stream Publishing, 1895); Roosevelt and G. B. Grinnell, eds., *Trail and Camp-fire: The Book of the Boone and Crockett Club* (New York: Forest and Stream Publishing, 1893).
5. Roosevelt, *Autobiography*, 189.
6. Quotation from L. Steffens, *The Autobiography of Lincoln Steffens* (New York: Harcourt, Brace, and Co., 1931), 263. For Roosevelt's nighttime patrols, see J. A.

Riis, *The Making of an American* (New York: Macmillan, 1904), 330; Goodwin, *Bully Pulpit*, 208.

7. See: J. Smith, "The Assistant Secretary of the Navy and the Spanish American War Hero," in Ricard, *A Companion to Theodore Roosevelt*, 45–58.

8. Roosevelt, *Autobiography*, 227.

9. Morison et al., *Letters I*, 672–73, letter from Roosevelt to Henry Cabot Lodge, September 11, 1897.

10. See *New York Herald* and *New York Sun*, Sept. 9, 1897. Also cited in Morris, *Rise*, 610.

11. See M. Long, ed., *The Journal of John D. Long* (Rindge, NH: Richard Smith, 1956), 216. Diary entries of February 25–26 include: "In the evening, Roosevelt, whom I left as Acting-Secretary during the afternoon, came around. He is so enthusiastic and loyal that he is, in certain aspects, invaluable, yet I lack confidence in his good judgment and discretion." He continues: "I find that Roosevelt, in his precipitate way, has come very near causing more of an explosion than happened to the *Maine*."

12. Long, *The Journal of John D. Long*, 223. For an account of Roosevelt's push for war, see E. Thomas, *The War Lovers* (New York: Little, Brown, 2010).

13. Conflicting explanations for the sinking of the *Maine* were debated directly after it occurred. The *Atlanta Constitution* ran the headline "'Twas the Deed of a Designing Dastard that Submerged the Battleship Maine" on February 17, 1898. Others reported that it was likely an accident; see "Views of Naval Experts: Prof. Alger, an Authority on High Explosives, Says No Torpedo Wrecked the Maine," *New York Times*, February 19, 1898; "Administration is Mystified, But Strongly of the Opinion that the Disaster Was Accidental," *Washington Post*, February 17, 1898. After the government's investigation report was issued, newspapers reported thus: "Mine Wrecked the Maine: A High Government Official Gives This as the Conclusion of the Inquiry," *New York Times*, March 26, 1898. Much debate since has ensued on the cause of the wreck, with many concluding that it resulted from spontaneous combustion of coal that caused ordnance on board to explode. See D. Wegner, "New Interpretations of How the USS *Maine* Was Lost," in E. J. Marolda, *Theodore Roosevelt, The U.S. Navy, and the Spanish-American War* (New York: Palgrave, 2001), 7–17.

14. TRC MS Am 1454.55 (12a), Cuba diary, April 16, 1898.

15. Roosevelt, *Wilderness Hunter*, 305–6; *Selections from the Correspondence of Theodore Roosevelt and Henry Cabot Lodge, 1884–1918* (New York: Scribner's, 1925), 34.

16. M. Chanler, *Roman Spring: Memoirs* (Boston: Little, Brown, 1934), 285. Similar quotation in Morris, *Rise*, 641.

17. Quotations from Long's journal in Long, *The Journal of John D. Long*, 223–24.

18. Roosevelt, *Autobiography*, 237.

19. Roosevelt's father was a Lincoln Republican, but his wife Martha and her family supported the confederacy, and this contributed to his unwillingness to fight. See Morris, *Rise*, 8–9.

20. K. M. Dalton, "Theodore Roosevelt's Contradictory Legacies: From Imperialist Nationalism to Advocacy of a Progressive Welfare State," in Ricard, *A Companion to Theodore Roosevelt*, 485–501. The role of gender in Roosevelt's drive to go to war is discussed in Bederman, *Manliness and Civilzation*, 190–91.

21. See K. Dalton, "Theodore Roosevelt and the Idea of War," *Theodore Roosevelt Association Journal* 7, no. 4 (1981): 6–12.

22. Sewall, *Sewall's Story*, 103.

23. "Mr. Roosevelt's War Ambition," *New York Times*, April 19, 1898.

24. "Will Mr. Roosevelt Resign?" *New York Times*, April 22, 1898.

25. "Mr. Roosevelt's Intentions," *New York Times*, April 26, 1898.

26. "Roosevelt Leaves Office," *New York Times*, April 30, 1898.

27. Letter by Roosevelt to Edith, June 18, 1897, quoted in H. Hagedorn, *Leonard Wood: A Biography, Vol. I* (New York: Harper & Brothers, 1931), 138; J. MacCallum, *Leonard Wood: Rough Rider, Surgeon, Architect of American Imperialism* (New York: New York University Press, 2006), 53. Wood also recalled meeting Roosevelt that night; see Wood, *Roosevelt As We Knew Him*, 46–47.

28. J. L. Lane, ed., *Chasing Geronimo: The Journal of Leonard Wood, May–September 1886* (Lincoln: University of Nebraska Press, 1970; Bison Books Edition, 2009), 74. It is unlikely that Wood's wound resulted from a tarantula bite. Rather, he may have been bitten by a centipede (*Scolopendra* sp.), the Arizona brown spider, or the desert brown spider (*Loxosceles* sp.), which would have caused the wound and resulting fever and chills. The extreme heat likely exacerbated the situation and led to him falling down, as well as his delirium and fever. However, it is also possible that this was an infection and not the effect from a bite; there is even a remote possibility that it was a rattlesnake bite he could have gotten in the brush. Rattlesnake bites are the most common cause of the symptoms Wood describes. With kind thanks to Prof. Greta Binford, Lewis and Clark College, and Dr. Leslie Boyer, University of Arizona Medical Center, for consultation.

29. See Lane, *Geronimo*, 90.

30. Morison et al., *Letters I*, 689–91, letter from Roosevelt to Bellamy Storer, September 26, 1897.

31. Roosevelt, *The Rough Riders* (New York: Scribner's, 1899), 5.

32. Roosevelt, *Autobiography*, 237.

33. Quotation attributed to a letter from Roosevelt to Winthrop Chanler on March 15, 1898; quoted in H. F. Pringle, *Theodore Roosevelt: A Biography* (New York: Harcourt, Brace and Co., 1931), 182.

34. Roosevelt, *Rough Riders*, 6.

35. For quotation and a description of Roosevelt's attempts to obtain an Army post, see Roosevelt, *Rough Riders*, 5–6.

36. TRC MS Am 1454.55 (12a), Cuba diary, May 6, 1898.

37. Kohn, *Empire City*, 75.

38. H. La Monte, "With the 'Rough Riders,'" *St. Nicholas*, 26 (1899): 832–40.

39. TRC MS Am 1454.55 (12a), Cuba diary, May 6, 1898. The assumption is made that Roosevelt used his office for his official business. Roosevelt wrote a letter that same day to Secretary Long from the "Navy Department," which refers to an enclosed letter to the president, presumably his official resignation. See G. W. Allen, ed., *Papers of John Davis Long: 1897–1904* (Norwood, MA: Plimpton Press for the Massachusetts Historical Society, 1939), 115.

40. E. Marshall, *The Story of the Rough Riders: 1st U. S. Volunteer Cavalry* (New York: G. W. Dillingham, 1899), 27; Hagedorn, *Wood*, 146, estimates that Roosevelt received twenty-three thousand applications.

41. Roosevelt, *Rough Riders*, 11.

42. Roosevelt, *Rough Riders*, 20.

43. M. L. Billington, "Buffalo Soldiers in the American West, 1865–1900," in Billington and Hardaway, eds., *African Americans on the Western Frontier*, 54–71; K. W. Porter, Black Cowboys in the American West," in: Billington and Hardaway, eds., *African Americans on the Western Frontier*, 110–27.

44. Roosevelt, *Rough Riders*, 27.

45. Morison et al., *Letters I*, 108, letter from Roosevelt to Henry Cabot Lodge, August

10, 1886. For the origin of the "Rough Riders" name, see P. Samuels and H. Samuels, *Teddy Roosevelt at San Juan: The Making of a President* (College Station: Texas A&M University Press, 1997), 16–17.

46. V. C. Jones, "Before the Colors Fade: The Last of the Rough Riders," *American Heritage* 20 (1969): 42–44, 93–95.

47. TRC MS Am 1454.55 (12a), Cuba diary, May 7, 1898.

48. For discussion of the underlying causes of the organizational aspects that frustrated Roosevelt, see G. A. Cosmas, *An Army for Empire* (Columbia: University of Missouri Press, 1971), 139–76.

49. In a letter to his daughter Ethel from San Antonio on May 20, 1898, Roosevelt wrote, "You never saw such dust." TRC MS Am 1541.2 (5).

50. TRC MS Am 1454.55 (12a), Cuba diary, May 19, 1898.

51. Roosevelt, *Rough Riders*, 19.

52. TRC MS Am 1454.55 (12a), Cuba diary, May 20, 1898. Also quoted in Samuels and Samuels, *Teddy Roosevelt at San Juan*, 42.

53. Roosevelt, *Rough Riders*, 221–22.

54. TRC MS Am 1454.55 (12a), Cuba diary, May 21, 1898.

55. TRC MS Am 1454.55 (12a), Cuba diary, May 21, 1898.

56. TRC MS Am 1454.55 (12a), Cuba diary, June 2, 1898.

57. TRC MS Am 1454.55 (12a), Cuba diary, June 5, 1898.

58. This account of acquiring the transport adapted from Morison et al., *Letters II*, 840–41, letter from Roosevelt to Henry Cabot Lodge, June 12, 1898.

59. TRC MS Am 1454.55 (12a), Cuba diary, June 8, 1898.

60. Although Roosevelt's first wife, Alice Lee, appeared in many accounts in his earlier diaries, Edith was only occasionally mentioned in his later notebooks and diaries.

61. M. T. Chanler, *Winthrop Chanler's Letters* (privately printed, 1951), 65.

62. Morison et al., *Letters II*, 843–44, letter from Roosevelt to Corinne Roosevelt Robinson, June 15, 1898. This letter is the basis of the textual account of the sea trip to Cuba. Also quoted in Robinson, *My Brother*, 170; H. W. Brands, *T. R.: The Last Romantic* (New York: Basic Books, 1997), 346. See also TRC MS Am 1454.55(12a), Roosevelt's Cuba diary, June 18, 1898, for a diary account of the schooner incident.

63. TRC MS Am 1454.55 (12a), Cuba diary, June 18, 1898.

64. Morison et al., *Letters II*, 843–45, letter from Roosevelt to Corinne Roosevelt Robinson, June 15, 1898.

65. Roosevelt, *Rough Riders*, 87. Some of the birdcalls Roosevelt heard were likely the sounds of Spanish soldiers communicating to each other. See Morris, *Rise*, 674, and references in note 56.

66. R. H. Davis, *The Cuban and Porto Rican Campaigns* (New York: Charles Scribner's Sons, 1898), 140.

67. Roosevelt, *Rough Riders*, 80. Also quoted in Morris, *Rise*, 670.

68. As is often the case, the historical accounts of this battle do not entirely agree with one another. This account of the battle at Las Guasimas is derived from Davis, *The Cuban and Porto Rican Campaigns*, 120–72; E. Marshall, *The Story of the Rough Riders* (New York: G. W. Dillingham, 1899), 101–36; Roosevelt, *Rough Riders*, 73–109; Pringle, *Theodore Roosevelt*, 190–92; Morris, *Rise*, 670–76; Samuels and Samuels, *Teddy Roosevelt*, 138–63.

69. Morison et al., *Letters II*, 844, letter from Roosevelt to Corinne Roosevelt Robinson, June 15, 1898.

70. These sounds of the Mauser bullets were described in J. G. Winter, "The Fight

of the Rough Riders," *Outlook*, September 3, 1898. An article in *The New York Times* on August 16, 1898, entitled "The Krag-Jogensen Gun: It Is Inferior in Many Respects to the Mauser used by the Spaniards," described how the Mauser was faster, more humane, and penetrated wood a full ten inches deeper than the bullets used by the Americans. Reports from physicians who were treating the wounded from the Cuban campaign confirmed the merciful nature of the Mauser. See "The Mauser Bullet Not So Deadly as Had Been Expected," *New York Tribune*, July 31, 1898; "In the Thick of Battle: Dodging a Shell and the Work of the Wonderful Mauser Bullet," *Washington Post*, December 25, 1898. When Leonard Wood returned to the battle site at Las Guasimas he "found the field for more than half a mile literally covered with empty Mauser cartridges" and "thousands of bullets [. . .] found imbedded in trees, many of the latter being so riddled that they are now decaying." Quotations from "Rough Riders Battleground: Gen. Wood to Place Crosses Where Capron and Fish Fell," *New York Times*, October 24, 1898.

71. V. C. Jones, "Before the Colors Fade: The Last of the Rough Riders," *American Heritage* 20 (1969): 42–44, 93–95.

72. F. A. McCurdy and J. K. McCurdy, *Two Rough Riders* (New York: F. Tennyson Neely, 1902), 10.

73. TRC MS Am 1454.55 (12a), Cuba diary, June 24, 1898.

74. Morison et al., *Letters II*, 845, letter from Roosevelt to Corinne Roosevelt Robinson, June 15, 1898.

75. Morris, *Rise*, 678.

76. TRC MS Am 1454.55 (12a) Cuba diary, June 29, 1898.

77. McCurdy and McCurdy, *Two Rough Riders*, 12.

78. Quotation in Roosevelt, *Autobiography*, 256.

79. Roosevelt, *Autobiography*, 261.

80. F. Remington, "With the Fifth Corps," *Harper's New Monthly Magazine*, 97 (1898): 962–65. For Kipling's poem, see R. Kipling, *Departmental Ditties, Barrack-Room Ballads and Other Verses* (New York: United States Book Company, 1890), 86–87: "An' a goatskin water-bag / Was all the field-equipment 'e could find. / In a sidin' through the day, / Where the 'eat would make your bloomin' eyebrows crawl."

81. P. Samuels and H. Samuels, *Frederic Remington: A Biography* (Garden City, NY: Doubleday, 1982), 280–82; B. W. Dippie, *The Frederic Remington Art Museum Collection* (Ogdensburg, NY: Frederic Remington Art Museum, 2001), 120–21.

82. The rendering of the siege of Kettle Hill and San Juan Hill is adapted from TRC MS Am 1454.55 (12a), Roosevelt's Cuba diary; Davis, *The Cuban and Porto Rican Campaigns*, 120–72; E. Marshall, *The Story of the Rough Riders* (New York: G. W. Dillingham, 1899), 101–36; Roosevelt, *Rough Riders*, 73–159; Pringle, *Theodore Roosevelt*, 190–92; Morris, *Rise*, 670–76; Samuels and Samuels, *Teddy Roosevelt*, 138–63.

83. Roosevelt, *Rough Riders*, 127. Strangely, the man to whom Roosevelt addressed this question was shot dead in the grass just as Roosevelt was speaking to him.

84. Roosevelt, *Rough Riders*, 130.

85. The interpretation that Roosevelt killed the Spaniard on Kettle Hill follows Morris, *Rise*, 686, and related endnote.

86. V. C. Jones, "Before the Colors Fade: The Last of the Rough Riders," *American Heritage* 20 (1969): 42–44, 93–95.

87. Quoted in Morris, *Rise*, 687.

88. Letter from R. H. Ferguson to Edith Roosevelt, July 5, 1898, quoted in Morris,

Rise, 687. A similar quotation appears in S. J. Morris, *Edith Kermit Roosevelt* (New York: Coward, McCann & Geoghegan, 1980), 181.

89. Morris, *Rise*, 690. The source manuscript at the TRB was not available for study at the time of this writing.

90. See J. R. Pierce and J. Writer, *Yellow Jack: How Yellow Fever Ravaged America and Walter Reed Discovered Its Deadly Secrets* (Hoboken, NJ: Wiley, 2005), 121–22. The myth that yellow fever was transmitted by fetid sheets and materials was debunked just a few years later, on that very island of Cuba.

91. Morison et al., *Letters II*, 863, letter from Roosevelt to Henry Cabot Lodge, July 31, 1898.

92. Morison et al., *Letters II*, 865, letter from Roosevelt and other officers to William Shafter, August 3, 1898.

93. Pringle, *Theodore Roosevelt*, 196–97; Morris, *Rise*, 693.

94. Scene described in "Hugged Col. Roosevelt," *Sun*, August 16, 1898.

95. "The Rough Riders Land at Montauk," *New York Times*, August 16, 1898.

96. V. C. Jones, "Before the Colors Fade: The Last of the Rough Riders," *American Heritage* 20 (1969): 42–44, 93–95.

97. J. P. Kerr, *A Bully Father* (New York: Random House, 1995), 128; quotation in this text is from a letter from Roosevelt to his son Theodore Jr., dated October 4, 1903; see also Morison, *Letters III*, 614–15.

98. "The Cowboy Regiments." *New York Times*, April 28, 1898.

99. Roosevelt, *Rough Riders*.

100. Bold, *Frontier Club*, 142–52.

101. "The Rough Riders Land at Montauk," *New York Times*, August 16, 1898.

102. "The Return of Roosevelt," *New York Times*, August 16, 1898.

103. Depew, *My Memories of Eighty Years*, 162.

104. Depew, *My Memories of Eighty Years*, 162.

105. "'Teddy Shut Out,'" *Boston Daily Globe*, January 3, 1899; "Gov. Roosevelt Shut Out," *New York Times*, January 3, 1899; "Roosevelt a Housebreaker," *New York Tribune*, January 3, 1899; F. T. Parsons, *Perchance Some Day* (privately printed, 1951), 124.

106. For overview of Roosevelt's transition from a Rough Rider to governor, see S. Doherty, "The Rough Rider as Super-Politician: Theodore Roosevelt's Ascendancy on the National Political Stage," in S. Ricard, ed., *A Companion to Theodore Roosevelt* (Malden, MA: Wiley-Blackwell, 2011), 59–77.

107. TRP, letter from Roosevelt to Henry L. Sprague, January 26, 1900. See also Morison, et al., *Letters II*, 1141.

108. This and subsequent quotations from the 1900 Annual Message are taken from the excerpt in Roosevelt, *Autobiography*, 337–39.

109. "Protecting Song Birds," *New York Tribune*, May 4, 1900; G. W. Chessman, *Governor Theodore Roosevelt* (Cambridge, MA: Harvard University Press, 1965), 249–53. See also Brinkley, *Warrior*, 342–367.

110. "Roosevelt as King of North Dakota," *Atlanta Constitution*, September 6, 1910. See other references to this day in Putman, *Formative*, 310. See J. Burroughs, *Camping & Tramping with Roosevelt* (Boston: Houghton, Mifflin, and Co., 1907), 14–15, for a description of Roosevelt's earlier suggestion of this link.

111. Long, *The Journal of John D. Long*, 224.

112. Morison et al., *Letters II*, 1154, letter from Roosevelt to Henry Cabot Lodge, January 30, 1900; Morison et al., *Letters II*, 1157, letter from Roosevelt to Thomas Collier Platt, February 1, 1900.

113. Morison et al., *Letters II*, 1159, letter from Roosevelt to Anna Roosevelt Cowles, February 2, 1900.

114. In February, Roosevelt began to understand that Platt was under pressure from the insurance industry to move Roosevelt out, given that he had just ousted Payn. See Morison et al., *Letters II*, 1166, letter from Roosevelt to Henry Cabot Lodge, February 3, 1900. Quotations from Thomas Collier Platt, and Louis J. Lang, eds., *The Autobiography of Thomas Collier Platt* (New York: B. W. Dodge, 1910), 397.

115. Platt and Lang, eds., *The Autobiography of Thomas Collier Platt*, 396–97. Also cited in Goodwin, *Bully Pulpit*, 273.

116. Morison et al., *Letters II*, 1509.

117. "Roosevelt Faces Michigan Voters," *Atlanta Constitution*, September 8, 1900; "Rough Riders And Bands of Indians," *Cincinnati Enquirer*, September 13, 1900; "Toughs Attack Gov. Roosevelt," *Chicago Daily Tribune*, September 27, 1900.

118. Morison et al., *Letters I*, 108, letter from Roosevelt to Henry Cabot Lodge, August 10, 1886; Roosevelt, *Autobiography*, 138.

CHAPTER EIGHT

1. This recounting of the cougar hunt is adapted from Roosevelt's 1901 diary, cougar hunt entries (TRC MS Am 1454.55(13)); the first chapter, "With the Cougar Hounds," in T. Roosevelt, *Outdoor Pastimes*, which was originally published in two parts in *Scribner's Magazine* 30 (1901): 417–35, 545–64. See also J. A. McGuire, "The Roosevelt Lion Hunt," *Outdoor Life*, March 1901.

2. The following account of Roosevelt's cougar hunt follows his description in *Outdoor Pastimes* and his diary, TRC MS Am 1454.55(13), 1901 diary, cougar hunt. His extensive description of Goff's pack appears in Roosevelt, *Outdoor Pastimes*, 4–11.

3. For this and subsequent quotations in this paragraph, see Roosevelt, *Outdoor Pastimes*, 6–8.

4. Morison et al., *Letters III*, 437, letter from Roosevelt to John Pitcher, March 2, 1903. Roosevelt writes: "But without a good pack it is a waste of time to go after mountain lions."

5. Roosevelt, *Outdoor Pastimes*, 35.

6. Roosevelt, *Outdoor Pastimes*, 36.

7. TRP letter from Roosevelt to F. Selous, March 8, 1901.

8. TRC MS Am 1454.55 (13), 1901 diary, cougar hunt, January 14.

9. Roosevelt, *Outdoor Pastimes*, 6. Roosevelt kept tabs on the status of the dogs, and Goff wrote to Roosevelt just before Christmas with an update on the pack, relating that "Old Boxer still 'packs' but always ready for a chase." TRP letter from Goff to Roosevelt, December 23, 1901.

10. This and subsequent quotation from T. Roosevelt, "The Need of Trained Observation," *Outing* 37 (1901): 631–33.

11. For a discussion of the cougar's predation biology and diet, see K. Murphy and T. K. Ruth, "Diet and Prey Selection of a Perfect Predator," in M. Hornocker and S. Negri, *Cougar: Ecology and Conservation* (Chicago: University of Chicago Press, 2010), 118–37. Roosevelt recorded that all of the cougars that he collected had only fed on deer, given the contents of their stomachs; see Roosevelt, *Outdoor Pastimes*, 29.

12. "The cougar is a very singular beast, shy and elusive to an extraordinary degree, very cowardly and yet blood thirsty and ferocious." Roosevelt, *Outdoor Pastimes*, 17. "The cougar is as large, as powerful, and as formidably armed as the Indian panther." Roosevelt, *Outdoor Pastimes*, 22.

13. TRP letter to C. H. Merriam, May 14, 1901.

14. TRP letter to C. H. Merriam, May 14, 1901.

15. TRC MS Am 1454.55 (13), 1901 diary, cougar hunt, addenda and cash account. Although Roosevelt refers to this animal as a "lynx," it was a bobcat, *Lynx rufus*, like the ones he shot on the trip. See Smithsonian Institution collection #USNH 119987.

16. Roosevelt, *Autobiography*, 46.

17. Morison et al., *Letters III*, 9, letter from Roosevelt to John Goff, March 8, 1901.

18. For Roosevelt's peregrinations in late spring and summer 1901, see "Roosevelt Put to Severe Test," *Chicago Daily Tribune*, March 6, 1901; "Boston Guest," *Boston Daily Globe*, April 30, 1901; "Vice-President's Collections of Skins," *New York Tribune*, April 21, 1901; "Roosevelt Lays a Cornerstone," *New York Tribune*, May 19, 1901; "Formally Open Buffalo's Fair," *Chicago Daily Tribune*, May 21, 1901; "Vice President to Go to Harvard," *New York Times*, June 25, 1901; "Col. Roosevelt on a Fishing Trip," *New York Times*, July 23, 1901; "Roosevelt Pays West a Tribute," *Chicago Daily Tribune*, August 3, 1901; "Roosevelt Going on a Coyote Chase," *Detroit Free Press*, August 6, 1901.

19. Quotation from "National Duties: Address at Minnesota State Fair, September 2, 1901" in T. Roosevelt, *Strenuous Life*, 288. For an account of Roosevelt's speech at the fair, see "Col. Roosevelt Talks to the Minnesotans," *New York Times*, September 3, 1901.

20. "Hunting Cougars with Roosevelt," *The Vermonter* 7 (1901): 373.

21. This account of how Roosevelt learned the news of the assassination attempt follows "Vice President's Sorrow," *New York Times*, September 8, 1901; C. S. Forbes, "President Roosevelt," *The Vermonter* 7 (1901): 363–72. A slightly different version appears in R. B. Williams, "TR Receives His Summons to the Presidency," *Bell Telephone Magazine* 30, no. 3 (1951): 196–204.

22. "Vice President's Sorrow," *New York Times*, September 8, 1901.

23. "Mr. Roosevelt Gets Reassuring News," *New York Times*, September 8, 1901.

24. The story of Roosevelt's return from Mount Marcy has been retold in many sources. This account follows H. Radford, "President Roosevelt's Ascent of Mt. Marcy," *Forest Leaves: A Quarterly Magazine* 2, no. 1 (1904): 4–8; "TR Receives His Summons to the Presidency," *Bell Telephone Magazine* 30, no. 3 (1951): 196–204; E. C. Murphy, *Theodore Roosevelt's Night Ride to the Presidency* (Blue Mountain Lake, NY: Adirondack Museum, 1977).

25. "President Roosevelt's Ascent of Mt. Marcy," *Forest Leaves: A Quarterly Magazine* 2, no. 1 (1904): 4–8.

26. "President Roosevelt's Ascent of Mt. Marcy," *Forest Leaves: A Quarterly Magazine* 2, no. 1 (1904): 4–8.

27. "Roosevelt's Response to Duty's Call: Wild Nocturnal Ride of the Vice-President," *Los Angeles Times*, September 15, 1901.

28. The exact content of the paper Roosevelt received is dubious. This account follows the assumption in Murphy, *Night Ride*, 34.

29. Roosevelt's trip from the Tahawus Club to Buffalo is reconstructed from Roosevelt, *Autobiography*, 379; "Roosevelt's Response to Duty's Call: Wild Nocturnal Ride of the Vice-President," *Los Angeles Times*, September 15, 1901; "Roosevelt's Long Night Ride Over the Rough Roads of the Mountains," *San Francisco Chronicle*, September 15, 1901; "Roosevelt at Albany," *Los Angeles Times*, September 15, 1901.

30. Murphy, *Night Ride*, 26.

31. See "Roosevelt Takes Oath," *Boston Daily Globe*, September 15, 1901; "Roosevelt Takes Oath of Office," *San Francisco Chronicle*, September 15, 1901; "Roosevelt

Is Now President; Takes the Oath," *Chicago Daily Tribune*, September 15, 1901.

32. "Roosevelt Takes Oath," *Boston Daily Globe*, September 15, 1901.

33. E. Morris, "'A Few Pregnant Days': Theodore Roosevelt and the Venezuelan Crisis of 1902," *Theodore Roosevelt Association Journal* 15 (1989): 2–13; E. Morris, *Theodore Rex* (New York: Random House, 2001), 181–92; C. C. Hodge, "The Global Strategist: The Navy as the Nation's Big Stick," in S. Ricard, ed., *A Companion to Theodore Roosevelt* (Malden, MA: Wiley-Blackwell, 2011), 257–73; W. N. Tilchin, "Anglo-American Partnership: The Foundation of Theodore Roosevelt's Foreign Policy," in S. Ricard, ed., *A Companion to Theodore Roosevelt* (Malden, MA: Wiley-Blackwell, 2011), 314–28.

34. R. Gros, ed., *T. R. in Cartoon* (New York: Saalfield, 1910).

35. Roosevelt's developing idea of the "big stick" can be seen in his articulation of George Washington's philosophy of how preparations for war and a strong military are the best way to achieve peace. See "Washington's Forgotten Maxim," in T. Roosevelt, *The Works of Theodore Roosevelt, National Edition* (New York: Scribner's Sons, 1926), 182–99.

36. Morison et al., *Letters III*, 389, letter from Roosevelt to Kermit Roosevelt, December 2, 1902. See also Morris, *Rex*, 631; Leonard Wood diary, TRP.

37. "Roosevelt Whacks Dr. Long Once More," *New York Times*, August 21, 1907. This newspaper article refers back to Roosevelt's earlier "whacks," which began in private correspondence with John Burroughs and led to his eventual publication of a rebuke of William J. Long in 1907, referenced below. Also cited in R. H. Lutts, *The Nature Fakers* (Golden, CO: Fulcrum, 1990), 128. For a thorough account of the "nature fakers," see Lutts, *Nature Fakers*.

38. Morison et al., *Letters III*, 441–43, letter from Roosevelt to John Burroughs, March 7, 1903. Burroughs's article appears in the March 1903 issue of the *Atlantic Monthly*, 298–309.

39. Letter from Roosevelt to Frederick Selous, February 15, 1898, National Archives of Zimbabwe.

40. Quotation from letter from Roosevelt to Frederick Selous, February 15, 1898, National Archives of Zimbabwe. In his letter, Roosevelt referred to Henry Astbury Leveson, who, under the pen name "The Old Shekarry," was the author of books such as *The Forest and the Field* (London: Saunders, Otley, and Co., 1867) and *The Hunting Grounds of the Old World* (London: Saunders, Otley, and Co., 1860). Roosevelt also referred to the gorilla story told by Fitz William Thomas Pollok, under the pen name "Colonel Pollok," in his *Incidents of Foreign Sport and Travel* (London: Chapman and Hall, 1894), 378–86.

41. C. Johnson, *John Burroughs Talks* (Boston: Houghton Mifflin, 1922), 284.

42. J. Burroughs, *Winter Sunshine* (New York: Houghton Mifflin, 1886), 34.

43. J. Burroughs, *The Writings of John Burroughs: XV Leaf and Tendril* (Boston: Houghton Mifflin, 1908), 2. See also C. Z. Walker, *The Art of Seeing Things: Essays by John Burroughs* (Syracuse, NY: Syracuse University Press, 2001), 3.

44. J. Burroughs, "Real and Sham Natural History," *Atlantic Monthly* 309 (1903): 298–309.

45. W. J. Long, *School of the Woods: Some Life Studies of Animal Instincts and Animal Training* (Boston: Ginn, 1902).

46. See Lutts, *Nature Fakers*, 55, for Long's educational background.

47. Burroughs, "Real and Sham Natural History," 298–309.

48. Burroughs, "Real and Sham Natural History," 298–309.

49. Quotation from W. J. Long, "The Modern School of Nature-Study and Its Critics," *North American Review* 176 (1903): 688–98. See also "Wm. J. Long in De-

fence: The Young Naturalist Responds," *Boston Evening Transcript*, March 14, 1903. See also Chapman, *Bird-Lover*, 182–83.

50. Hermit, "The Intelligence of Wild Things," *Forest and Stream* 60, no. 5 (1903): 83–84.

51. Hermit, "The Intelligence of Wild Things," 83–84.

52. Morison et al., *Letters III*, 468, letter from Roosevelt to George Bird Grinnell, April 24, 1903.

53. Morison et al., *Letters III*, 468, letter from Roosevelt to George Bird Grinnell, April 24, 1903.

54. E. B. Clark, "Roosevelt on the Nature Fakirs," *Everybody's Magazine* 16 (1907): 770–74; T. Roosevelt, "Nature Fakers," *Everybody's Magazine* 17 (1907): 427–30.

55. Clark, "Roosevelt on the Nature Fakirs," 770–74.

56. Clark, "Roosevelt on the Nature Fakirs," 770–74.

57. Rudyard Kipling developed fictional explanations of how animal characteristics came to be, including his description of how tigers got their stripes in *The Second Jungle Book* (New York: Century, 1895), 20–21. Kipling also published a more extensive set of these descriptions for children as *Just So Stories* (New York: Doubleday, Page, and Co., 1902). Human cultures have long developed explanations for how animal features originated, and these fall under what anthropologists call "etiological myths." See F. Lentricchia and T. McLaughlin, eds., *Critical Terms for Literary Study, Second Edition* (Chicago: University of Chicago Press, 1995), 72.

58. Quotation from Roosevelt, "Nature Fakers," 427–30. Roosevelt's reference to *Jungle Book* characters appears in Clark, "Roosevelt on the Nature Fakirs," 770–74.

59. W. J. Long, *Northern Trails: Some Studies of Animal Life in the Far North* (Boston: Ginn, 1905), 162.

60. Long, *Northern Trails*, xv; also quoted in Clark, "Roosevelt on the Nature Fakirs," 770–74.

61. Roosevelt, "Nature Fakers," 427–30.

62. W. J. Long, "The Modern School of Nature-Study and Its Critics," *North American Review* 176 (1903): 688–98.

63. W. J. Long, *A Little Brother to the Bear* (Boston: Ginn, 1903), 101–6, 226–30.

64. N. White, *Abbott H. Thayer: Painter and Naturalist* (Hartford: Connecticut Printers, 1951). For other considerations of the "concealing coloration controversy," see F. Chapman, *Autobiography of a Bird-Lover* (D. Appleton, 1933) 78–80; Cutright, *Naturalist*, 225–40; S. J. Gould, *Bully for Brontosaurus* (New York: Norton, 1991), 209–28.

65. A. H. Thayer, "The Law Which Underlies Protective Coloration," *Auk* 13 (1896): 124–29; E. B. Poulton, "The Meaning of the White Under Sides of Animals," *Nature* 65 (1902): 596; A. H. Thayer, "The Law Which Underlies Protective Coloration," *Nature* 65 (1902): 597. For general discussion of Thayer and countershading, see S. Kingsland, "Abbott Thayer and the Protective Coloration Debate," *Journal of the History of Biology* 11 (1978): 223–44; G. Ruxton, M. P. Speed, and D. J. Kelly, "What, If Anything, Is the Adaptive Value of Countershading?" *Animal Behaviour* 68 (2004): 445–51; R. R. Behrens, "Nature's Artistry: Abbott H. Thayer's Assertions about Camouflage in Art, War and Nature," in M. Stevens and S. Merilaita, *Animal Camouflage: Mechanisms and Function* (Cambridge: Cambridge University Press, 2011), 87–100; H. R. Shell, *Hide and Seek: Camouflage, Animal Skin and the Media of Reconnaissance, 1859–1945* (New York: Zone Books, 2012).

66. G. H. Thayer, *Concealing-Coloration in the Animal Kingdom* (New York: Macmillan, 1909).

67. T. Roosevelt, "Revealing and Concealing Coloration in Birds and Mammals," *Bulletin of the American Museum of Natural History* 30 (1911): 119–231.

68. F. C. Selous, *African Nature Notes and Reminiscences* (London: MacMillan, 1908).

69. T. Roosevelt, "Revealing and Concealing Coloration in Birds and Mammals," *Bulletin of the American Museum of Natural History* 30 (1911): 119–231. See also Appendix E in T. Roosevelt, *African Game Trails: An Account of the African Wanderings of an American Hunter-Naturalist* (New York: Scribner's, 1910), 491–512.

70. Roosevelt, "Revealing and Concealing Coloration in Birds and Mammals," 119–231.

71. Roosevelt, "Revealing and Concealing Coloration in Birds and Mammals."

72. S. J. Gould and R. C. Lewontin, "The Spandrels of San Marco and the Panglossian Paradigm: A Critique of the Adaptationist Programme," *Proceedings of the Royal Society B* 205 (1979): 581–98.

73. The "Spandrels" paper has generated a small literature of its own, with even the exact meaning of "spandrels" being questioned. It seems that "pendentive" may be more accurate for this particular aspect of architecture. See R. Mark, "Architecture and Evolution," *American Scientist* 84 (1996): 383–89. Also cited in M. Pigliucci and J. Kaplan, "The Fall and Rise of Dr. Pangloss: Adaptationism and the Spandrels Paper 20 Years Later," *Trends in Ecology and Evolution* 15(2): 66–69. Discussion on the paper has been so fruitful partly because it covered a range of interrelated issues, only touched on here, including the current use of structures versus their evolutionary origins, "constraints" in evolution, and evolutionary change in the absence of natural selection (e.g., genetic drift).

74. Roosevelt, "Revealing and Concealing Coloration in Birds and Mammals," 119–231.

75. F. H. Allen, "Remarks on the Case of Roosevelt vs. Thayer, with a Few Independent Suggestions on the Concealing Coloration Question," *Auk* 29 (1912): 489–507. Also quoted in Gould, *Bully for Brontosaurus*, 209.

CHAPTER NINE

1. Morison et al., *Letters III*, 441–43, letter from Roosevelt to John Burroughs, March 7, 1903.

2. Morison et al., *Letters III*, 441–43, letter from Roosevelt to John Burroughs, March 7, 1903.

3. "How Roosevelt Will Spend Trip," *Chicago Daily Tribune*, March 15, 1903.

4. Morison et al., *Letters III*, 429–30, letter from Roosevelt to John Pitcher, February 18, 1903.

5. Morison et al., *Letters III*, 437–38, letter from Roosevelt to John Pitcher, March 2, 1903.

6. Morison et al., *Letters* III, 441, letter from Roosevelt to Frederick Weyerhaeuser, March 5, 1903. Also quoted in Brinkley, *Warrior*, 503.

7. "Speak Softly; Carry Big Stick; Says Roosevelt," *Chicago Daily Tribune*, April 3, 1903.

8. Quotation from Burroughs, *Camping & Tramping*, 10.

9. Burroughs, *Camping & Tramping*, 16.

10. "Roosevelt Leaves Park," *Chicago Daily Tribune*, April 24, 1903.

11. Roosevelt, *Outdoor Pastimes*, 293–94; Burroughs, *Camping & Tramping*, 23.

12. Burroughs, *Camping & Tramping*, 29.

13. Burroughs, *Camping & Tramping*, 6.
14. Burroughs, *Camping & Tramping*, 47.
15. Descriptions of wildlife in this paragraph follow Roosevelt, *Outdoor Pastimes*, 293–301. Quotation from Burroughs, *Camping & Tramping*, 48.
16. Burroughs, *Camping & Tramping*, 64–65.
17. Burroughs, *Camping & Tramping*, 33–35; Roosevelt, *Outdoor Pastimes*, 309.
18. Roosevelt, *Outdoor Pastimes*, 303–4, 308; Burroughs, *Camping & Tramping*, 39–40; Roosevelt, *Autobiography*, 346–47.
19. "Adventure in Park," *Washington Post*, April 24, 1903; Burroughs, *Camping & Tramping*, 73–74.
20. Burroughs, *Camping & Tramping*, 43–44.
21. In Roosevelt's March 7, 1903, letter to Burroughs (Morison et al., *Letters III*, 441) he addresses Burroughs as "My dear Mr. Burroughs," but in a letter shortly after their return from Yellowstone he addresses him as "Dear Oom John" (Morison et al., *Letters III*, 486). Roosevelt refers to this transition: "There could be no pleasanter or more interesting companion than John Burroughs—'Oom John,' as we soon grew to call him." See Roosevelt, *Outdoor Pastimes*, 300, for quotation. According to the *Oxford English Dictionary*, "oom" is a word with Dutch roots that is "used as a respectful form of address to an older or elderly man." *OED*, online edition, accessed June 19, 2012. See related discussion in Brinkley, *Warrior*, 370–71.
22. The skin and skull of Roosevelt's montane vole specimen is still lodged in the Mammals Division of the National Museum of Natural History, Smithsonian Institution, number 126419, as *Microtus montanus nanus*. Incident described in Burroughs, *Camping & Tramping*, 66; Roosevelt, *Outdoor Pastimes*, 308; Morison et al., *Letters III*, 463, letter from Roosevelt to C. H. Merriam, April 22, 1903.
23. Account and quotations in this paragraph drawn from Burroughs, *Camping & Tramping*, 51–59.
24. Roosevelt's speech at the Yellowstone gate was published as "The President Helps Lay a Cornerstone," *New York Times*, April 25, 1903. It was also reprinted as "The President in the Park," *Forest and Stream* 18 (1903): 346–47.
25. "The President in the Park," *Forest and Stream* 18 (1903): 346–47.
26. Pinchot's philosophy was used in many of his writings, including G. Pinchot, *The Fight for Conservation* (New York: Doubleday, Page & Co., 1910), 48. For Roosevelt's conflicted position in balancing the interests of conservation and preservation, see S. P. Hays, *Conservation and the Gospel of Efficiency* (Cambridge, MA: Harvard University Press, 1959), 122–46; S. Fox, *John Muir and His Legacy* (Boston: Little, Brown, 1981), 103–47; C. Miller, *Gifford Pinchot and the Making of Modern Environmentalism* (Washington: Island Press, 2001), 147–76; C. Miller, "When Elephants Were Green: Gifford Pinchot, the GOP, and the Conservation Movement," *Theodore Roosevelt Association Journal* 28, no. 4 (2007): 12–22.
27. Burroughs, *Camping & Tramping*, 6–7.
28. For discussion of the perspective of sportsmen as "participants" in nature, see J. F. Reiger, *American Sportsmen and the Origins of Conservation, 3rd Edition* (Corvallis: Oregon State University Press, 2001), 55.
29. "President Visits an Awful Place," *Los Angeles Times*, May 7, 1903. Full quotation appears: "The President has seen the Grand Cañon of Arizona. 'The only word I can use for it,' said Mr. Roosevelt, with impressive emphasis, 'is awful. It filled me with awe such as I have never before known. It is beyond comparison; it is beyond description.'"
30. "Visits Grand Canyon," *Washington Post*, May 7, 1903.

31. L. M. Dilsaver, *America's National Park System: The Critical Documents* (Lanham, MD: Rowman & Littlefield, 1994), 40–41.

32. T. Roosevelt, "A Cougar Hunt on the Rim of the Grand Canyon" in *A Book-Lover's Holidays in the Open* (New York: Scribner's, 1916), chapter 1.

33. "Woman with 36 Children Cooks Roosevelt's Beans," *Atlanta Constitution*, May 12, 1903. The reporting of Mrs. Gesetterest's offspring is self-contradictory, the *Constitution* claiming thirty-six children in its headline and thirty-four in its text.

34. See Dyer, *Theodore Roosevelt and the Idea of Race*, 143–67.

35. "Roosevelt Likes Play," *Chicago Daily Tribune*, May 8, 1903; "San Francisco Greets President Roosevelt, *New York Times*, May 13, 1903; "President Roosevelt Bids Farewell to San Francisco and the People and Leaves for Yosemite," *San Francisco Chronicle*, May 15, 1903.

36. J. Butler and E. Butler, "Kindred Spirits: The Relationship between John Burroughs and John Muir," in: C. Z. Walker, *Sharp Eyes: John Burroughs and American Nature Writing* (Syracuse, NY: Syracuse University Press, 2000), 80–92.

37. See B. J. Gisel, *Nature's Beloved Son* (Berkeley, CA: Heyday Books, 2008), 55–76, for Muir's collections, notebook excerpts, and a description of his trip.

38. For an overview of Muir's approach to conservation, see B. G. Norton, *Toward Unity among Environmentalists* (New York: Oxford University Press, 1991), 17–38.

39. Quotation and account of Muir's reluctance from W. F. Kimes, "With Theodore Roosevelt and John Muir in Yosemite," *Brand Book of the Los Angeles Westerners* 14 (1974): 189–204.

40. Letter to John Muir on March 14, 1903. John Muir Papers, Holt-Atherton Special Collections, University of the Pacific.

41. This account of Roosevelt's trip in Yosemite relies mostly on "Charlie Leidig's Report of President Roosevelt's Visit in May, 1903," an unpublished report in the Yosemite National Park Library, and W. F. Kimes, "With Theodore Roosevelt and John Muir in Yosemite," 189–204. Other accounts consulted include "President Roosevelt Rests among the Giant Sequoias of Mariposa," *San Francisco Chronicle*, May 16, 1903; "Roosevelt Pitches His Camp Near Bleak Sentinel Dome in Snow Storm," *San Francisco Chronicle*, May 17, 1903; "Roosevelt Has Supper in Camp," *Chicago Daily Tribune*, May 18, 1903; "Roosevelt Enthusiastic over the Wonders of the Yosemite," *San Francisco Chronicle*, May 18, 1903; Morison et al., *Letters III*, 476, letter from Roosevelt to John Muir on May 19, 1903; W. F. Badé, *The Life and Letters of John Muir, Volume II* (Boston: Houghton Mifflin Co., 1924), 408–13; T. Kerasote, "Roosevelt and Muir," *The Bugle: The Quarterly Journal of the Rocky Mountain Elk Foundation*, Winter 1997, 77–89; Morris, *Rex*, 230–31; D. Worster, *A Passion for Nature: The Life of John Muir* (Oxford: Oxford University Press, 2008), 366–68; Brinkley, *Warrior*, 536–47.

42. Muir wrote extensively about the evidence of effects of glaciers in Yosemite. See T. Gifford, ed., *John Muir: His Life and Letters and Other Writings* (London: Baton Wicks, 1996), 393–488.

43. "Charlie Leidig's Report of President Roosevelt's Visit in May, 1903."

44. "Charlie Leidig's Report of President Roosevelt's Visit in May, 1903."

45. "Charlie Leidig's Report of President Roosevelt's Visit in May, 1903."

46. Letter quoted in W. F. Kimes, "With Theodore Roosevelt and John Muir in Yosemite," 189–204.

47. Morison et al., *Letters III*, 475, letter from Roosevelt to Ethan Hitchcock, May 19, 1903.

48. White House "Zoo" Possible, *New York Times*, May 19, 1903.

49. "Pets at the White House," *Washington Post*, January 22, 1907.

50. "Pets at the White House," *Washington Post*, January 22, 1907; "Young America in the White House," *New York Times*, March 17, 1907.

51. "Banished from the White House: Man-Eating Bulldog in Exile," *San Francisco Chronicle*, July 24, 1907.

52. "Pony in the White House," *New York Times*, April 27, 1903. "Young America in the White House," *New York Times*, March 17, 1907.

53. This account and exchange was adapted from "Took Three Snakes into White House," *New York Times*, September 27, 1907. See also "The White House Snakes," *Washington Post*, September 28, 1907. Roosevelt made an account of the incident in a letter to Archie on September 28, 1907, reprinted in Morison et al., *Letters V*, 810–11; Z. M. Jack, *The Green Roosevelt* (New York: Cambria Press, 2010), 32–33.

54. TRC MS Am 1541 (79), letter from Roosevelt to Kermit Roosevelt, May 28, 1904. Also quoted in J. B. Bishop, *Theodore Roosevelt's Letters to His Children* (New York: Scribner's, 1919), 96–98.

55. Sagamore Historic Site, letter from Roosevelt to Quentin Roosevelt, June 12, 1904. Also printed in Bishop, *Letters to His Children*, 98–99; Jack, *Green Roosevelt*, 30–31.

56. Bishop, *Letters to His Children*, 99–100.

57. Bishop, *Letters to His Children*, 32–34.

58. Wood, *As We Knew Him*, 295.

59. Wood, *As We Knew Him*, 296.

60. Roosevelt, *Autobiography*, 52. J. J. Jusserand, "Personal Memories of Theodore Roosevelt," *Journal of American History* 13 (1919): 330–25. Roosevelt also took his children for "rambles down Rock Creek." See TRP letter from Roosevelt to Kermit Roosevelt, March 1, 1903.

61. Burroughs, *Camping & Tramping*, 83.

62. TRC MS Am 1454.43, "Birds seen around Washington." For the history and published version of Roosevelt's Washington bird list, see L. Maynard, *Birds of Washington and Vicinity* (Washington: Woodward and Lothrop, 1909); L. Maynard, "President Roosevelt's List of Birds," *Bird Lore* 7 (1910): 53–55.

63. See Brinkley, *Warrior*, 472, for a breakdown of these reserves.

64. B. W. Daynes and G. Sussman, *White House Politics and the Environment* (College Station: Texas A&M University Press, 2010), 16–17.

65. This is now the Pelican Island National Wildlife Refuge. For quotation, see F. Chapman, *Autobiography of a Bird Lover* (New York: D. Appleton-Century Co., 1933), 181–82. Also quoted in Cutright, *Naturalist*, 177–78; Morris, *Rex*, 519; Brinkley, *Warrior*, 1; Daynes and Sussman, *White House Politics and the Environment*, 16. For a detailed list of Roosevelt's conservation legislation, see Brinkley, *Warrior*, appendix and references therein.

66. Sullys Hill was later changed to Sullys Hill National Game Preserve.

67. After his hunts in Colorado in February and August of 1901 while vice president, Roosevelt had hunted bear in Mississippi in November of 1902; but the trip to Oklahoma and Colorado during April and May of 1905 was his next major hunting trip.

68. Roosevelt's involvement in negotiations between Japan and Russia while he was in the field is discussed in T. Dennett, *Roosevelt and the Russo-Japanese War* (Gloucester, MA: Peter Smith, 1959), 170–88.

69. This account of Roosevelt's wolf and bear hunting trip in 1905 was distilled from the records in his personal diary (TRC MS Am 1454.55 [14], 1905 diary,

Hunting in OK and CO), on the two articles he wrote on it for *Scribner's Magazine* that were eventually reprinted in *Outdoor Pastimes* (T. Roosevelt, "A Colorado Bear Hunt," *Scribner's Magazine* 38, no. 4 [1905]: 386–408; T. Roosevelt, "A Wolf Hunt in Oklahoma," *Scribner's Magazine* 38, no. 5 [1905]: 513–32), and on the accounts in Brinkley, *Warrior*, 599–608.

70. "The President's Vacation," *The Independent* 58 (1905): 745.

71. Although Roosevelt referred to his hunt as "wolf-coursing," he primarily hunted coyotes, which were also known as "wolves," in Oklahoma. The "wolf" specimens from Roosevelt's Oklahoma hunt that are lodged in the Division of Mammals, National Museum of Natural History (NMNH) are predominantly coyotes, *Canis latrans*. See specimen 136983 in NMNH catalog. He did collect one "red wolf," *Canis rufus*, specimen 136879. In earlier hunts in North Dakota and Montana, Roosevelt collected the larger gray wolves, *Canis lupus*, that are also in the NMNH collection.

72. See J. Abernathy, *"Catch 'Em Alive Jack": The Life and Adventures of an American Pioneer* (New York: Association Press, 1936); R. J. Ward, *The Greatest Wolf Hunter That Ever Lived: The Story of Catch 'Em Alive Jack Abernathy* (Amarillo, TX: Custom Printing Co., 2005).

73. Abernathy, *"Catch 'Em Alive Jack,"* 101. Also quoted in Ward, *The Greatest Wolf Hunter*, 95; Brinkley, *Warrior*, 601.

74. T. Roosevelt, "A Wolf Hunt in Oklahoma," *Scribner's Magazine* 38, no. 5 (1905): 513–32. Similar quotation in Brinkley, *Warrior*, 607.

75. TRC MS Am 1454.55 (14), 1905 diary, hunting in Oklahoma and Colorado, April 11.

76. TRC MS Am 1454.55 (14), 1905 diary, hunting in Olahoma and Colorado, April 11.

77. TRC MS Am 1454.55 (14), 1905 diary, hunting in Oklahoma and Colorado, April 12; Roosevelt, "A Wolf Hunt in Oklahoma."

78. Roosevelt, "A Wolf Hunt in Oklahoma."

79. The Louisiana black bear, *Usus americanus luteolus*, is one of many subspecies of black bear in North America. See J. Warrillow, M. Culver, E. Hallerman, and M. Vaughan, "Subspecific Affinity of Black Bears in the White River National Wildlife Refuge," *Journal of Heredity* 92 (2001): 226–33. For a thorough account of Roosevelt's 1902 bear hunt and the "Teddy bear," see M. F. Buchanan, *Holt Collier: His Life, His Roosevelt Hunts, and the Origin of the Teddy Bear* (Jackson, MS: Centennial Press, 2002); Brinkley, *Warrior*, 431–45.

80. "Bear Hunting in the Canebrakes and Swamps of Mississippi," *Atlanta Constitution*, November 20, 1902.

81. T. Roosevelt, "In the Louisiana Canebrakes," *Scribner's Magazine*, 43 (1908): 47–60. Collier's complicated and intriguing life story is carefully told in Buchanan, *Collier*.

82. TRP letter from Roosevelt to P. Stewart, November 24, 1902. Also quoted in Buchanan, *Collier*, 177–78.

83. "Drawing the Line in Mississippi," *Washington Post*, November 16, 1902. Cited in Buchanan, *Collier*, 178–79.

84. Buchanan, *Collier*, 179. For a similar interpretation, see Brinkley, *Warrior*, 442.

85. See Kimes, "With Roosevelt," 201, for an account of when Roosevelt was in Yosemite. A young boy called out, "Hi Teddy," and the president stopped his horse and reprimanded the boy. This is an example of Roosevelt's sensitivity to the nickname and the respect he demanded. For additional discussion, see Brinkley, *Warrior*, 445.

86. "More 'Teddy' Pets," *Washington Post*, May 4, 1907.
87. Roosevelt, *Outdoor Pastimes*, 70.
88. TRC MS Am 1454.55 (14), 1905 diary, hunting in Oklahoma and Colorado, April 18. Roosevelt brought Skip home with him from Colorado, and he became a beloved pet in the White House.
89. For these and following quotes on the "fossil" horse, see Roosevelt, *Outdoor Pastimes*, 69–70.
90. TRC MS Am 1454.55 (14), 1905 diary, hunting in Oklahoma and Colorado, April 17.
91. TRC MS Am 1454.55 (14), 1905 diary, hunting in Oklahoma and Colorado, April 18.
92. This and previous quotation from TRC MS Am 1454.55 (14), 1905 diary, hunting in Oklahoma and Colorado, April 24.
93. Roosevelt, "A Colorado Bear Hunt."
94. TRC MS Am 1454.56, canebrake notebook.
95. TRC MS Am 1454.56, canebrake notebook; Roosevelt, "In the Louisiana Canebrakes," 51–52.
96. TRC MS Am 1454.56, canebrake notebook; Roosevelt, "In the Louisiana Canebrakes," 48.
97. TRC MS Am 1541.2 (29), letter from Roosevelt to Ethel Roosevelt, October 6, 1907.
98. TRC MS Am 1454.56, canebrake notebook.
99. Roosevelt jotted, "Swamp rabbit swims / Marsh rabbit [misnomer?]" in his notebook to remind himself to confirm the identity between the two related species, TRC MS Am 1454.56, canebrake notebook. These two rabbits have non-overlapping ranges, with the swamp rabbit (*Sylvilagus aquaticus*) found in Louisiana. The swamp rabbit was also the subject of a much later encounter with another president, Jimmy Carter. See "Bunny Goes Bugs: Rabbit Attacks President," *Washington Post*, August 30, 1979.
100. TRC MS Am 1454.56, canebrake notebook.
101. TRC MS Am 1541.2 (45), letter from Roosevelt to Edith Roosevelt, October 10, 1907.
102. TRC MS Am 1454.56, canebrake notebook.
103. "Roosevelt Tells of Hunting Trip," *New York Times*, October 21, 1907. See also Roosevelt, "In the Louisiana Canebrakes," 47–60.
104. B. DeVoto, ed., *Mark Twain in Eruption* (New York: Harper & Brothers, 1940), 12. The month before this entry, Twain declined an invitation to pilot Roosevelt down the Mississippi, even publishing a poem about his refusal. See "Twain Not to Pilot," *Washington Post*, September 11, 1907; "Mark Twain to the President," *Washington Post*, September 14, 1907.
105. R. U. Johnson, *Remembered Yesterdays* (Boston: Little, Brown, 1923), 388. Also quoted in Nash, *Wilderness*, 139.
106. H. Herdman, "The Day Strenuous," *Pacific Monthly* 8 (1905): 430. Places where material was omitted are indicated by ellipses.
107. D. Harmon, F. P. McMannon, and D. T. Pitcaithley, "The Importance of the Antiquities Act," in D. Harmon, F. P. McMannon, and D. T. Pitcaithley, *The Antiquities Act: A Century of American Archaeology, Historic Preservation, and Nature Conservation* (Tucson: University of Arizona Press, 2006), 1–12. The quotations from the Antiquities Act in this paragraph are taken from the transcription and facsimile that appear in this reference.
108. See Cutright, *Conservationist*, 225–26; also Brinkely, *Warrior*, appendix, for a compiled list.

109. See "Address of President Roosevelt at the Opening of the Conference on the Conservation of Natural Resources, at the White House Wednesday Morning, May 13 1908, at 10:30 o'clock," (Washington: Government Printing Office, 1908); Cutright, *Conservationist*, 227–29; Morris, *Rex*, 514–19; Brinkley, *Warrior*, 769–74.

110. Quotation and Roosevelt's perspective hunting from TRP letter from Roosevelt to Hamlin Garland, April 4, 1901.

111. TRP letter from Roosevelt to Philip Stewart, July 16, 1901.

112. B. Bull, *Safari: A Chronicle of Adventure* (London: Viking, 1988), 179–80; P. O'Toole, "Roosevelt in Africa," in S. Ricard, ed., *A Companion to Theodore Roosevelt* (Malden, MA: Wiley-Blackwell, 2011), 435–51.

113. For examples, see A. J. Lane, *The Brownsville Affair: National Crisis and Black Reaction* (Port Washington, NY: Kennikat Press, 1971); D. J. Pasani, *Water and American Government* (Berkeley: University of California Press, 2002; J. W. Simpson, *Dam!: Water, Power, Politics, and Preservation in Hetch Hetchy and Yosemite National Park* (New York: Pantheon, 2005).

114. T. Roosevelt, *The Works of Theodore Roosevelt, National Edition, Vol. XV* (New York: Scribner's, 1926), 517–18.

115. Roosevelt, *Works XV*, 526.

116. Various tallies of Roosevelt's total contributions exist. This account follows Brinkley, *Warrior*, 406, 825–30.

117. For Roosevelt's complicated conservation legacy, see C. Miller, "Keeper of His Conscience? Pinchot, Roosevelt, and the Politics of Conservation," in Naylor, et al., *Theodore Roosevelt: Many-Sided American*, 231–44; J. Salmon, "'With Utter Disregard of Pain and Woe': Theodore Roosevelt on Conservation and Nature," in C. T. Rubin, ed., *Conservation Reconsidered* (Lanham, MD: Rowman & Littlefield, 2000), 33–65; D. J. Philippon, *Conserving Words: How American Nature Writers Shaped the Environmental Movement* (Athens: University of Georgia Press, 2004), 33–71; L. E. Baier, "The Cradle of Conservation: Theodore Roosevelt's Elkhorn Ranch, an Icon of America's National Identity," *Theodore Roosevelt Association Journal* 28 (2007): 12–24; E. Fishman, "The Quality of Theodore Roosevelt's Environmentalism," in Ricard, ed., *A Companion to Theodore Roosevelt*, 173–85.

CHAPTER TEN

1. Roosevelt, *Game Trails*, 15. In *Game Trails*, Roosevelt established the train ride from Mombasa to Kapiti literally as the first chapter in the story of the safari, with his ride on the cowcatcher as the iconic image. See similar portrayals in *Game Trails*, chapter 1; and Warrington Dawson's account in his British East Africa log. E. Morris, *Colonel Roosevelt* (New York: Random House, 2010), 3–4.

2. H. Johnston, "Where Roosevelt Will Hunt," *National Geographic Magazine*, 20 (1909): 207–56.

3. British East Africa log, box 36, page 79. Francis Warrington Dawson Family Papers, David M. Rubenstein Rare Book and Manuscript Library, Duke University.

4. Roosevelt, *Game Trails*, 13.

5. A range of large cats lived at the same time as our human ancestors, including during the late Pleistocene, and there was mutual antagonism with at least some species. With thanks to Julie Meachen, Des Moines University, for consultation and perspective. See also A. Tuner, *The Big Cats and Their Fossil Relatives* (New York: Columbia University Press, 1997), 185.

6. Roosevelt believed in a hierarchy of races, ranging from savages and barbarians to the civilized societies like those of the United States and Britain. He

believed that with time and influence, societies could move up this hierarchy to become more civilized. See T. G. Dyer, *Theodore Roosevelt and the Idea of Race* (Baton Rouge: Louisiana State University Press, 1980); C. Chin, "Uplifting the Barbarian," in S. Ricard, ed., *A Companion to Theodore Roosevelt* (Malden, MA: Wiley-Blackwell, 2011), 417–34 and references therein. Quotation from Morison et al., *Letters VI*, 1089, letter from Roosevelt to George Trevelyan, June 19, 1908. Roosevelt discussed the importance of these animals in chapter 8, "Primitive Man; and the Horse, the Lion, and the Elephant," in T. Roosevelt, *A Book-Lover's Holiday in the Open* (New York: Charles Scribner's Sons, 1916).

7. Roosevelt's sister Anna describes her memory of him as a boy, before he could read, dragging "Life of Livingston" around the family library; see A. R. Cowles, "Each Room Has Many Memories," *Woman's Roosevelt Memorial Bulletin* 1, no. 3 (1920): 2–3.

8. Selous called Roosevelt's assessment of him as the "greatest of the world's big game hunters" as "bunkum"; quoted in J. G. Millais, *Life of Frederick Courtenay Selous, D.S.O.* (New York: Longmans, Green, 1919), 355. See B. Herne, *White Hunters* (New York: Henry Holt, 1999) for an overview of the game hunters in Africa during the time of Roosevelt's safari.

9. Millais, *Selous*, 13. Also cited in S. Taylor, *The Mighty Nimrod: A Life of Frederick Courteney Selous* (London: Collins, 1989), 12.

10. F. C. Selous, *Travel and Adventure in South-East Africa* (London: Rowland Ward, 1893); F. C. Selous, *A Hunter's Wanderings in Africa* (London: R. Bentley and Son, 1895).

11. TRP letter from Roosevelt to Frederick Selous, February 15, 1898. Copies of this and other correspondence between Roosevelt and Selous are held in TRP and the National Archives of Zimbabwe. With thanks to Bassey Irele, librarian for Sub-Saharan Africa, Widener Library, Harvard University, for arranging access to these collections. Also cited in E. Hahn, "My dear Selous . . . ," *American Heritage Magazine* 14 (1963): 40–42, 92–99.

12. TRP letter from Roosevelt to Frederick Selous, February 15, 1898.

13. T. Roosevelt, "Frederick Courteney Selous," *Outlook*, March 17, 1917: 410–11.

14. TRC MS Am 1541 (130), letter from Roosevelt to Kermit Roosevelt, November 19, 1905.

15. In F. Selous's introduction in J. H. Patterson, *The Man-Eaters of Tsavo* (London: MacMillan, 1908), x. Patterson later visited the White House himself, in November of 1908, to aid Roosevelt in preparations for the safari. See Morison et al., *Letters VI*, 1375–76, letter from Roosevelt to Kermit Roosevelt, November 22, 1908.

16. With thanks to K. Van Anglen for consultation and perspective.

17. For a general account of the construction of the Uganda Railway, see W. R. Foran, *A Cuckoo in Kenya* (London: Hutchinson, 1936), 58–60; C. Miller, *The Lunatic Express* (New York: Macmillan, 1971).

18. The following rendering of the man-eaters follows the accounts in Patterson, *Man-Eaters*, 61–106; 282–88; B. D. Patterson, *The Lions of Tsavo* (New York: McGraw-Hill, 2004). See also R. B. Foran, *The Kenya Police 1887–1960* (London: Robert Hale, 1962), 10–14.

19. Patterson, *Man-Eaters*, 69.

20. "Man-Eating Lions in Uganda," *The Youth's Companion*, April 10, 1902.

21. Patterson, *Man-Eaters*, 284. Other accounts suggest that the men thought that these were reflections from the eyes of rats. See Foran, *The Kenya Police*, 11.

22. TRC MS Am 1541 (130), letter from Roosevelt to Kermit Roosevelt, November 19, 1905.

23. Roosevelt states that Selous told the children stories of lions and hyena during his visit. TRC MS Am 1541 (130), letter from Roosevelt to Kermit Roosevelt, November 19, 1905. In his 1907 foreword to Patterson's *Man-Eaters*, Selous later wrote of his interaction with Roosevelt: "It was some years after I read the first account published of the Tsavo man-eaters that I made the acquaintance of President Roosevelt. I told him all I remembered about it, and he was so deeply interested in the story—as he is in all true stories of the nature and characteristics of wild animals—that he begged me to send him the short printed account as published in *The Field*. This I did; and it was only in the last letter I received from him that, referring to this story, President Roosevelt wrote: 'I think that the incident of the Uganda man-eating lions, described in those two articles you sent me, is the most remarkable account of which we have any record'" (Patterson, *Man-Eaters*, x–xi). Several weeks after Selous's visit to the White House, Roosevelt wrote him: "I have been delighted with all the pieces you sent me and have read and reread them all. Do go on with your lion article" (Morison et al., *Letters V*, 115, letter from Roosevelt to Frederick Selous, December 18, 1905). Selous actually sent Roosevelt copies of the articles that had been printed in *The Wide World Magazine*, those being "more easily obtainable" than back issues of *The Field*; see TRP letter from Frederick Selous to Theodore Roosevelt, November 29, 1905. The two original articles in question are J. H. Patterson, "The Tsavo Man-Eating Lions.—I," *The Field, The Country Gentleman's Newspaper* 95, no. 2460 (February 17, 1900): 205; J. H. Patterson, "The Tsavo Man-Eating Lions.—II," *The Field, The Country Gentleman's Newspaper* 95, no. 2461 (February 24, 1900): 232–33. Patterson later sent Roosevelt his book on the subject (letter from Roosevelt to John H. Patterson, March 20, 1908, Morison et al., *Letters V*, 824) and visited the White House in 1908 as Roosevelt began to plan his African safari (letter from Roosevelt to Kermit Roosevelt, November 22, 1908, Morison et al., *Letters VI*, 1375).

24. F. C. Selous, *African Nature Notes and Reminiscences* (London: MacMillan, 1908).

25. Roosevelt's idea of a safari had percolated throughout his presidency. Along with Selous, he corresponded with and was visited by Patterson and by the naturalist and taxidermist Carl Akeley. See C. Akeley, *In Brightest Africa* (Garden City, NY: Garden City Publishing, 1923), 158–59; Morison et al., *Letters VI*, 978–79, letter from Roosevelt to John Patterson, March 20,1908; Morison et al., *Letters VI*, 1375–76, letter from Roosevelt to Kermit Roosevelt, November 22, 1908.

26. TRP letter from Roosevelt to F. Selous, March 20, 1908. Hahn, "My dear Selous . . . ," 40–42, 92–99.

27. TRP letter from Roosevelt to A. Pease, August 22, 1908; TRP letter from Roosevelt to A. Pease, September 5, 1908.

28. TRP letter from Roosevelt to F. Selous, April 29, 1908.

29. TRP letter from Roosevelt to F. Selous, November 7, 1908; Bronson, *In Closed Territory*, 184.

30. Quotation from Hahn, "My dear Selous . . ." *American Heritage Magazine* 14, vol. 3 (1963): 40–42, 92–99. Extensive consideration of Roosevelt's food preferences appear in TRP letter from Roosevelt to F. Selous, October 12, 1908.

31. TRP letter from Roosevelt to F. Selous, July 21, 1908.

32. Quotation in TRP letter from Roosevelt to J. Patterson, November 2, 1908.

33. TRP letter from Roosevelt to F. Jackson, November 2, 1908.

34. TRP letter from Roosevelt to R. Bridges, January 4, 1909.

35. Roosevelt's letters in the TRP during the year before his safari exhibit extensive correspondence regarding his developing plans for equipment and his itinerary; see also Cutright, *Naturalist*, 186–97. His letters to F. Selous and E.

Buxton are the most abundant. Letters contributing to the descriptions in this paragraphs are TRP letter from Roosevelt to E. Buxton, June 25, 1908; TRP letter from Roosevelt to H. Osborn, July 23, 1908; TRP letter from Roosevelt to F. Selous, July 21, 1908; TRP letter from Roosevelt to A. Pease, August 22, 1908; TRP letter from Roosevelt to E. Buxton, September 25, 1908; TRP letter from Roosevelt to J. Patterson, October 12, 1908; TRP letter to E. Mearns, November 6, 1908; TRP letter from Roosevelt to H. Osborn, November 11, 1908; TRP letter from Roosevelt to K. Roosevelt, November 22, 1908; TRP letter from Roosevelt to C. Akeley, February 27, 1909; TRP letter from Roosevelt to C. Akeley, February 28, 1909.

36. Robinson, *My Brother*, 251.

37. A list of the contents of Roosevelt's "pigskin library" appears in Roosevelt, *Game Trails*, appendix F, and a description of the library is made in Roosevelt, *Game Trails*, 23–24; K. Roosevelt, *Happy Hunting Grounds*, 29–30. Throughout the trip, additions were made to the library, including "Alice's Adventures" and "Dumas's 'Louves de Machecoul'" (Roosevelt, *Game Trails*, 162) and "Goethe's 'Faust,'" "Darwin's 'Voyage of the Beagle,' and Huxley's 'Essays'" (Roosevelt, *Game Trails*, 368). The pigskin library was a source of pride throughout the trip; see J. McCutcheon, *In Africa* (Indianapolis: Bobbs-Merrill, 1910), 160–61.

38. Morison et al., *Letters VI*, 1060, letter from Roosevelt to Kermit Roosevelt, June 6, 1908.

39. Morison et al., *Letters VI*, 1061, letter from Roosevelt to Frank Chapman, June 7, 1908.

40. TRC MS Am 1541 (227), letter from Roosevelt to Kermit Roosevelt, May 17, 1908.

41. Quotation in Morison et al., *Letters VI*, 1241, letter from Roosevelt to Cecil Spring Rice, September 17, 1908. See also TRP, letter from Roosevelt to Kermit Roosevelt, September 14, 1908. Roosevelt refers to an article in the "Philadelphia Ledger," which appears under the subheading "A Tragic Finale?" in "What Roosevelt May Encounter in Africa," *Public Ledger*, September 6, 1908.

42. "Taxidermist Says Roosevelt Will Be Safe in East Africa," *Washington Post*, March 8, 1909.

43. J. T. McCutcheon, *Drawn from Memory* (Indianapolis: Bobbs-Merrill, 1950), 236.

44. TRP letter from Roosevelt to J. Patterson, July 6, 1908.

45. TRP letter from Roosevelt to T. Roosevelt, Jr., November 16, 1908.

46. TRP letter from Roosevelt to A. Pease, December 12, 1908.

47. TRP letter from Roosevelt to F. Selous, September 12, 1908; TRP letter from Roosevelt to A. Pease, October 12, 1908. Roosevelt's use of the term "Cook's tourist" refers to a series of popular guides for tourism published by Thomas Cook, e.g. *Cook's American Traveller's Gazette* and *Cook's Tourist's Handbook for Northern Italy* (London: T. Cook and Son, 1875).

48. TRP letter from Roosevelt to K. Roosevelt, September 27, 1908.

49. Morison et al., *Letters VI*, 1060, letter from Roosevelt to Kermit Roosevelt, June 6, 1908.

50. Morison et al., *Letters VI*, 1060, letter from Roosevelt to Kermit Roosevelt, June 6, 1908.

51. Quotation in TRP letter from Roosevelt to the Winchester Repeating Arms Company, December 5, 1908; see also TRP letter from Roosevelt to the Winchester Repeating Arms Company, December 31, 1908.

52. TRP letter from Roosevelt to Kermit Roosevelt, January 23, 1909. Roosevelt suggested to Kermit: "We have a first class target-practice rifle arrangement, such as they use in the Navy, in the top hall, in the attic, where I shall soon begin to

practice." The author was not able to find evidence that this shooting range ever came into use. Special thanks to William Allman, curator, the White House, for consultation on this topic.

53. Morison et al., *Letters VI*, 1093–94, letter from Roosevelt to Charles Doolittle Walcott, June 20, 1908.

54. Morison et al., *Letters VI*, 1093–94, letter from Roosevelt to Charles Doolittle Walcott, June 20, 1908.

55. Morison et al., *Letters VI*, 1093–94, letter from Roosevelt to Charles Doolittle Walcott, June 20, 1908.

56. For photograph of crates in New York with "TR" labels, see frontispiece to F. W. Unger, *Roosevelt's Africa Trip*, publisher unknown, c. 1909.

57. Quotations from Kermit Roosevelt, *The Happy Hunting-Grounds* (New York: Scribner's, 1920), 25. Additional description of Mearns can be found in C. W. Richmond, "In Memoriam: Edgar Alexander Mearns," *Auk* 35, vol. 1 (1918): 1–18.

58. TRP letter from Roosevelt to Edgar Mearns, January 3, 1909.

59. Edgar A. Mearns Papers, Smithsonian Institution, collection 7083, box 1, folder 4. Letter from E. Mearns to Ella Mearns, June 22, 1909.

60. H. W. Grinnell, "Edmund Heller: 1875–1939," *Journal of Mammalogy* 28 (1947): 209–18.

61. A. Loring, *African Adventure Stories* (New York: Scribner's, 1914), 47. For an overview of the names given to the Americans on the expedition by the native Africans, see P. O'Toole, *When Trumpets Call* (New York: Simon and Schuster, 2005), 47. Heller's sense of humor is described in McCutcheon, *In Africa*, 152.

62. W. O. Lay, *J. Alden Loring: A Naturalist Afield* (Oswego, NY: Tioga County Historical Society, 1999); Edgar A. Mearns Papers, Smithsonian Institution, collection 7083, box 1, folder 4. Letter from E. Mearns to Ella Mearns, June 22, 1909.

63. J. A. Loring, "Interesting Observations of Prairie-Dogs," *St. Nicholas Magazine* 34 (1907): 552–52.

64. J. A. Loring, *Young Folks' Nature Field Book* (Boston: Dana Estes, 1906).

65. Quotation from TRP letter from Roosevelt to E. Buxton, October 23, 1908. See also TRP letter from Roosevelt to E. Heller, October 24, 1908; TRP letter from Roosevelt to J. Loring, January 2, 1909.

66. Quotation in previous sentence from TRP letter from Roosevelt to E. Mearns, January 3, 1909. See also TRP letter from Roosevelt to C. Walcott, January 3, 1909.

67. Quotations from TRP letter from Roosevelt to R. Bridges, August 14, 1908; TRP letter from Roosevelt to F. Selous, November 25, 1908. See also TRP letter from Roosevelt to E. Buxton, September 10, 1908.

68. TRP letter from Roosevelt to E. Heller, November 8, 1908.

69. Morison et al., *Letters VII*, 6–7, letter from Roosevelt to Corinne Roosevelt Robinson, April 14, 1909.

70. Roosevelt wrote to Corinne from aboard the *Admiral*, saying: "Neither Kermit nor I like sea voyages, and this is a sea voyage of 30 days; but we are both of us philosophers, and there is much about the voyage, inasmuch as we *had* to make it, which is pleasant . . . . He leads his own life, but continually turns up in my cabin, solemnly kisses me, and then solemnly strums his mandolin or talks" (Morison et al., *Letters VII*, 6, letter from Roosevelt to Corinne Roosevelt Robinson, April 14, 1909).

71. Edgar A. Mearns Papers, Smithsonian Institution, collection 7083, box 1, folder 4. Letter from E. Mearns to his mother, April 1, 1909.

72. Edgar A. Mearns Papers, Smithsonian Institution, collection 7083, box 1, folder 4. Letter from E. Mearns to Ella and Lillian Mearns, April 21, 1909. Roosevelt, *Game Trails*, 6–7.

73. British East Africa log, box 36, pp. 64–65. Francis Warrington Dawson Family Papers, David M. Rubenstein Rare Book and Manuscript Library, Duke University. Roosevelt, *Game Trails*, 6–7.

74. The quotation in the previous sentence and Roosevelt's recounting of his meeting with Huebner appears in Roosevelt, *Game Trails*, 9–10. The account of Huebner also appears in Patterson, *Man-Eaters*, 286.

75. Quotation from British East Africa log, box 36, page 74. Francis Warrington Dawson Family Papers, David M. Rubenstein Rare Book and Manuscript Library, Duke University. Dawson recorded in his log how Roosevelt made an agreement with the newspapermen that he would "do what he could" for them in Mombasa if they did not follow him inland on safari. Same reference, page 81.

76. Descriptions from: British East Africa log, box 36, pp. 74, 79. Francis Warrington Dawson Family Papers, David M. Rubenstein Rare Book and Manuscript Library, Duke University.

77. British East Africa log, box 36, page 99. Francis Warrington Dawson Family Papers, David M. Rubenstein Rare Book and Manuscript Library, Duke University.

78. Roosevelt, *Game Trails*, 19, for quotations in this and the previous sentence.

79. British East Africa log, box 36, page 84. Francis Warrington Dawson Family Papers, David M. Rubenstein Rare Book and Manuscript Library, Duke University. See also Roosevelt, *Game Trails*, 216. Various spellings and translations of this moniker appear throughout Roosevelt's works and the accounts of other members of the safari. See also McCutcheon, *In Africa*, 157; H. H. Johnston, "The Roosevelts in Africa," *Outlook* 96 (1910): 864–69.

80. The members of the expedition used the word "boys" to refer to the native attendants. This is a term laden with racial prejudice, and many of these assistants were in fact not young boys. In a letter to his mother on May 16, 1909, Loring described his porters as "like children," and on May 30, 1909, he described how the "boys sing and shout all night. Like children, have childrens voices and are easily amused." J. A. Loring Papers, Tioga County Historical Society.

81. The native African porters were frequently abused. See E. B. Bronson, *In Closed Territory* (Chicago: A. C. McClurg, 1910), 182–83. Dawson also reports that they were accustomed to "being sworn at by enraged white masters." See British East Africa log, box 36, page 82. Francis Warrington Dawson Family Papers, David M. Rubenstein Rare Book and Manuscript Library, Duke University.

82. Roosevelt, *Game Trails*, 17.

83. Roosevelt regularly referred to the equipment for the expedition as "impedimenta."

84. Loring letter May 16, 1909, J. A. Loring Papers, Tioga County Historical Society.

85. The numbers and composition of porters and attendants varied over the course of the safari. In the early part of the trip in the Sotik, Roosevelt counted 196 porters alone, "in addition to the askaris, tent boys, gun-bearers, and saises" (Roosevelt, *Game Trails*, 150). Morison et al. estimate that there were 260 native Africans on safari, of which 200 were porters (Morison et al., *Letters VII*, 13, note 1). Loring estimates 250; Loring letter May 16, 1909, J. A. Loring Papers, Tioga County Historical Society.

86. Loring letter May 16, 1909, J. A. Loring Papers, Tioga County Historical Society.

87. Quotation from Roosevelt, *Game Trails*, 84–85. This description of the safari closely follows Roosevelt's in that same section of *Game Trails*.

88. Dawson recorded the scene as Roosevelt eyed the distant hills. British East Africa log, box 36, page 81. Francis Warrington Dawson Family Papers, David M. Rubenstein Rare Book and Manuscript Library, Duke University. Roosevelt's description in *Game Trails* of the fez and its use reinforces the hierarchical relationship of the British Empire and the Ottoman Empire, and again highlights Roosevelt's hierarchical idea of race.

89. TRC MS Am 1454.55(15), 1909 diary, Africa, April 24.

90. Roosevelt, *Game Trails*, 27.

91. Roosevelt, *Game Trails*, 45.

92. "Alleged Plot to Kill Roosevelt," *Atlanta Constitution*, May 16, 1903; "Arrested During Roosevelt Visit," *Chicago Daily Tribune*, May 20, 1903; "Fear a Shot at Roosevelt," *Chicago Daily Tribune*, May 27, 1903.

93. TRC MS Am 1454.55 (15), 1909 diary, Africa, April 28.

94. J. G. Pease, *A Wealth of Happiness and Many Bitter Trials: The Journals of Sir Alfred Edward Pease, a Restless Man* (York, UK: Ebnor Press, 1992), 282–83.

95. Roosevelt, *Game Trails*, 73.

96. Roosevelt, *Game Trails*, 73.

97. Loring letter May 2, 1909, J. A. Loring Papers, Tioga County Historical Society.

98. TRP letter from Roosevelt to Robert Bridges, June 30, 1908.

99. As Morris notes (*Colonel*, 15), Roosevelt rendered his experiences only shortly after they happened. In effect, both his diaries and his *Scribner's* articles became a form of "field notes." See appendix 1 for further discussion.

100. Roosevelt, *Game Trails*, 1–2.

101. Morison et al., *Letters VII*, 8–9, letters from Roosevelt to Robert Bridges, May 12 and 23, 1909.

102. See Roosevelt, *Game Trails*, 206.

103. Roosevelt, *Game Trails*, 69.

104. This photograph does not appear in the Scribner's 1910 edition of *African Game Trails*, but was published on page 172 of the Syndicate Publishing edition of *African Game Trails* (1910), which contained many additional photographs.

105. Edgar A. Mearns Papers, Smithsonian Institution, collection 7083, box 1, folder 4. Letter from E. Mearns to Ella Mearns, June 22, 1909.

106. See "Appendix IV: Chronology," in Morison et al., *Letters VIII*, 1466–69, for a detailed description of Roosevelt's travels in Africa.

107. Morison et al., *Letters VII*, 11–12, letter from Roosevelt to Anna Roosevelt Cowles, May 19, 1909.

108. Morison et al., *Letters VII*, 17–18, letter from Roosevelt to Anna Roosevelt Cowles, June 21, 1909.

109. Morison et al., *Letters VII*, 17–18, letter from Roosevelt to Anna Roosevelt Cowles, June 21, 1909.

110. Morison et al., *Letters VII*, 16, letter from Roosevelt to Corinne Roosevelt Robinson, June 21, 1909.

111. Edgar A. Mearns Papers, Smithsonian Institution, collection 7083, box 1, folder 4. Letter from Edgar Mearns to Ella Mearns, June 22, 1909.

112. Morison et al., *Letters VII*, 16–17, letter from Roosevelt to Corinne Roosevelt Robinson, June 21, 1909.

113. Morison et al., *Letters VII*, 26, letter from Roosevelt to Corinne Roosevelt Robinson, July 27, 1909.

114. Morison et al., *Letters VII*, 16–17, letter from Roosevelt to Corinne Roosevelt Robinson, June 21, 1909.

115. Morison et al., *Letters VII*, 19–20, letter from Roosevelt to Robert Bridges, July 17, 1909.

116. Morison et al., *Letters VII*, 24, letter from Roosevelt to Henry Cabot Lodge, July 26, 1909.

117. Livingstone, *Missionary Travels*, 498.

118. British East Africa log, box 36, pp. 127–28. Francis Warrington Dawson Family Papers, David M. Rubenstein Rare Book and Manuscript Library, Duke University.

119. Roosevelt, *Game Trails*, 215.

120. British East Africa Log, box 36, pp. 128–29. Francis Warrington Dawson Family Papers, David M. Rubenstein Rare Book and Manuscript Library, Duke University.

121. W. Dawson, *Opportunity and TR* (Chicago, 1924), 103.

122. Dawson's description appears in British East Africa log, box 36, page 138. Francis Warrington Dawson Family Papers, David M. Rubenstein Rare Book and Manuscript Library, Duke University. The following account and quotations on Dawson's interaction with Roosevelt on the hippo hunt follow *Opportunity and TR* 102–11, as well as Dawson's British East Africa log, page 139, and his "scribble diary," both in the Dawson Family Papers. The unpublished documents reveal nothing of the story about Roosevelt being upset that is contained in Dawson's later published work, and instead describe the experience as "wonderful luck— and thrilling adventures." See also Morris, *Colonel*, 17–18, for another account.

123. TRC MS Am 1454.26 (o), letter from Roosevelt to John C. O'Laughlin, July 16, 1909.

124. TRC MS Am1454.55 (15), 1909 diary, Africa 1, July 20.

125. Foran, *A Cuckoo in Kenya*, 151.

126. Quotation from TRC MS Am 1834 (827), letter from Roosevelt to Ethel Roosevelt. Roosevelt's diary entries while in Nairobi were extremely short, and he documented the events of race week only as "races" (TRC MS Am 1454.55 [15], 1909 diary, Africa 1, July 29, Roosevelt provides a more substantial rendering in *Game Trails*, 273. For an overall description of race week, see Foran, *A Cuckoo in Kenya*, 151–57.

127. Morison et al., *Letters VII*, 19–20, letter from Roosevelt to Robert Bridges, July 17, 1909.

128. Roosevelt, *Game Trails*, 237. The account of the elephant hunt presented here closely follows Roosevelt's own account in *Game Trails*.

129. Roosevelt, *Game Trails*, 251.

130. Roosevelt, *Game Trails*, 253.

131. Roosevelt, *Game Trails*, 253.

132. Roosevelt, *Game Trails*, 253–54.

133. J. T. McCutcheon, *In Africa* (Indianapolis: Bobbs-Merrill, 1910), 137.

134. Diary of John T. McCutcheon, November 14, 1909. John T. McCutcheon Papers, box 34, Newberry Library, Chicago. Accounts of Akeley's meeting of Roosevelt's safari appear in Roosevelt, *Game Trails*, 346–50; Akeley, *In Brightest Africa*, 160–63.

135. Roosevelt, *Game Trails*, 383.

136. TRP letter from Roosevelt to Robert Peary, November 7, 1908.

137. Quotation from Roosevelt, *Game Trails*, 292. Roosevelt quickly shot down Frederick A. Cook's claim that he had discovered the pole first; see Morison et al., *Letters VII*, 31–32, letter from Roosevelt to William Foran, September 12, 1909, and related footnote; Morison et al., *Letters VII*, 38, letter from Roosevelt to William Loeb, Jr., November 12, 1909.

138. Morison et al., *Letters VII*, 29–30, letter from Roosevelt to Henry Cabot Lodge and Anna Cabot Mills Lodge, September 10, 1909.

139. Morison et al., *Letters VII*, 23, letter from Roosevelt to Henry Cabot Lodge, July 26, 1909.

140. Morison et al., *Letters VII*, 21, letter from Roosevelt to Henry White, July 21, 1909.

141. Roosevelt, *Game Trails*, 397.

142. Roosevelt, *Game Trails*, 188. Roosevelt begins chapter 14 of *Game Trails* with a quote from Poe's *Tales*.

143. Roosevelt, *Game Trails*, 394, 397.

144. Roosevelt, *Game Trails*, 400.

145. Morison et al., *Letters VII*, 22, letter from Roosevelt to Robert Bridges, July 17, 1909.

146. Quotation in TRP Roosevelt letter to E. N. Buxton, July 21, 1908. Roosevelt was keen to get the same access to Lado as Winston Churchill had obtained, and he even corresponded with Churchill, thanking him for sending along a copy of his recent book on his travels. Roosevelt had followed the earlier publication of Churchill's African travels in the *Strand Magazine* starting in May 1908, and was particularly interested in Churchill's section on the white rhino. See Winston Churchill, *My African Journey* (New York: Hodder and Stoughton, n.d.), 168–87; TRP letter from Roosevelt to R. Wingate, November 27, 1908; TRP letter from Roosevelt to W. Churchill, January 6, 1909; G. Beare, *Index to the Strand Magazine, 1891–1950* (Westport, CT: Greenwood Press, 1982), 55–56.

147. Roosevelt, *Game Trails*, 401.

148. Bull, *Safari*, 179–80.

149. Roosevelt, *Game Trails*, 412. Roosevelt admitted: "Too little is known of these northern square-mouthed rhino for us to be sure that they are not lingering slowly toward extinction; and, lest this should be the case, we were not willing to kill any for trophies; while, on the other hand, we deemed it really important to get good groups for the National Museum in Washington and the American Museum in New York, and a head for the National Collection of Heads and Horns which was started by Mr. Hornaday, the director of the Bronx Zoological Park" (Roosevelt, *Game Trails*, 412).

150. Roosevelt, *Game Trails*, 403.

151. TRC MS Am 1454.55 (16), 1910 diary, Africa 2, January 22.

152. For overviews of African safaris and the stories that they generated, see Bull, *Safari*; Herne, *White Hunters*.

153. P. O'Toole, "Roosevelt in Africa," in S. Ricard, ed., *A Companion to Theodore Roosevelt* (Malden, MA: Wiley-Blackwell, 2011), 435–51.

154. Roosevelt tried to distinguish himself from game butchers in many of the letters he sent to fellow naturalists in the year before the safari. For examples, see TRP letter from Roosevelt to E. Buxton, May 23, 1908; TRP letter from Roosevelt to F. Selous, June 25, 1908; TRP letter from Roosevelt to R. J. Cuninghame, December 26, 1908; TRP letter from Roosevelt to J. Burroughs, January 12, 1909.

155. "Called Game Butcher: Mr. Roosevelt's Hunting Denounced by Dr. Long," *Washington Post*, May 27, 1909.

156. Quotation from TRP letter from Roosevelt to F. Jackson, November 2, 1908. See also TRP letter from Roosevelt to F. Selous, June 25, 1908; TRP letter from Roosevelt to J. Patterson, July 6, 1908; McCutcheon, *In Africa*, 152.

157. TRP letter from Roosevelt to F. Selous, June 25, 1908; TRP letter from Roosevelt to E. Buxton, June 25, 1908.

158. Roosevelt, *Game Trails*, vii.
159. Quotations from the subtitles in A. Lundeberg and F. Seymour, *The Great Roosevelt African Hunt* (Chicago: D. B. McCurdy, 1910); J. H. Mowbray, *Roosevelt's Marvelous Exploits in the Wilds of Africa* (s.n., 1910).
160. H. H. Johnston, "The Roosevelts in Africa," *Outlook* 96 (1910): 864–69; P. B. Bicknell, "Mr. Roosevelt's Jungle Book," *Dial* 49 (1910),173–75; S. E. White, "Nine Books of the Month: I. Colonel Roosevelt's 'Game Trails,'" *Bookman*, 32 (1910): 170–71.
161. A. Guiterman, "Rhymed Reviews: African Game Trails," *Life* 55 (1910): 693–94.
162. See Dalton, *Strenuous*, 358, and notes therein.
163. Roosevelt wrote his speeches for the Sorbonne and Oxford before he left the United States. See: TRP letter to Kermit Roosevelt, November 22, 1908. Quotation from "Citizenship in a Republic," delivered at the Sorbonne on April 23, 1909, in T. Roosevelt, *Presidential Addresses and State Papers and European Addresses, December 8, 1908 to June 7, 1910* (New York: Review of Reviews, 1910), 2186.
164. J. L. Thompson, *Theodore Roosevelt Abroad* (New York: Palgrave MacMillan, 2010), x.
165. O'Toole, *When Trumpets Call*, 73–92; Thompson, *Theodore Roosevelt Abroad*, 101–49.
166. British East Africa log, box 36, page 119. Francis Warrington Dawson Family Papers, David M. Rubenstein Rare Book and Manuscript Library, Duke University.
167. Quotation from "Roosevelt Greeted by Cheers of Thousands," *Washington Post*, June 19, 1910. Description of Roosevelt's return to New York from this and also from "Million Join in Welcome to Roosevelt," *New York Times*, June 19, 1910; "Roosevelt in New York is Greeted Like a King," *Detroit Free Press*, June 19, 1910; "Give Roosevelt Record Breaking Welcome to U.S.," *Chicago Daily Tribune*, June 19, 1910; "Roosevelt Gets Grandest Welcome Ever Given Returning American on Arrival in New York," *Boston Daily Globe*, June 19, 1910.
168. Quotations from "Roosevelt in New York is Greeted like a King," *Detroit Free Press*, June 19, 1910; "Give Roosevelt Record Breaking Welcome to U.S.," *Chicago Daily Tribune*, June 19, 1910; "Roosevelt Greeted by Cheers of Thousands," *Washington Post*, June 19, 1910. Estimates of attendance varied, with the *New York Times* suggesting at least a million ("Million Join in Welcome to Roosevelt," *New York Times*, June 19, 1910). The New York *World* estimated 1.5 million; see Morris, *Colonel*, 608.
169. The Abernathy boys generated plenty of copy of their own in June 1910, including "Abernathy Boys Ride Here Today," *New York Times*, June 11, 1910; "Abernathy Boys Put Ban on Kissing," *New York Times*, June 12, 1910; "Children Finish 2,300 Mile Ride," *Detroit Free Press*, June 12, 1910; "Game Youths End Long Ride," *Los Angeles Times*, June 12, 1910. See also M. Abernathy, *The Ride of the Abernathy Boys* (New York: Doubleday, Page, 1911); A. Abernathy, *Bud & Me: The True Adventures of the Abernathy Boys* (Irving, TX: Dove Creek Press, 1998).
170. For an overview of this election, see B. Flehinger, *The 1912 Election and the Power of Progressivism: A Brief History with Documents* (Boston: Bedford/St. Martin's, 2003); C. Delahaye, "The New Nationalism and Progressive Issues: The Break with Taft and the 1912 Campaign," in S. Ricard, ed., *A Companion to Theodore Roosevelt* (Malden, MA: Wiley-Blackwell, 2011), 452–67.
171. Quotation from Morison et al., *Letters VII*, 705, letter from Roosevelt to William Bigelow, February 5, 1913. Numerous other accounts exist of what Roosevelt said at that moment. Account of the assassination follows P. J. Roosevelt, "Poli-

tics of the Year 1912: An Intimate Progressive View (TRC MS Am 1454.25; this source also contains a sketch of Roosevelt's position in the automobile relative to Schrank's gunshot); O. Remey, H. Cochems, and W. Bloodgood, *The Attempted Assassination of Ex-President Theodore Roosevelt* (Milwaukee: Progressive Publishing, 1912); S. Gores, "The Attempted Assassination of Teddy Roosevelt," 1970, *Wisconsin Magazine of History* 53, no. 4: 269–77.

172. This and the subsequent quotation taken from Remey et al., *The Attempted Assassination*, 25–26, 29. The speech and glasses case that evidence the effects of the bullet are housed in the TRC MS Am 1454.58.

173. "Roosevelt Shot in Right Breast by Fanatic at Milwaukee," *Hartford Courant*, October 15, 1912.

174. In a letter to Cecil Spring Rice, Roosevelt described his feelings on how a Rough Rider should act: "For eleven years I have been prepared any day to be shot; and if any one of the officers of my regiment had abandoned the battle merely because he received a wound that did nothing worse than break a rib, I should never have trusted that officer again. I would have expected him to keep on in the fight as long as he could stand; and what I expect lieutenants to do I expect, a fortiori, a leader to do" (see Morison et al., *Letters VII*, 680, letter from Roosevelt to Cecil Spring Rice, December 31, 1912).

175. Letter from Roosevelt to Frederick Selous, November 1, 1912. National Archives of Zimbabwe. Also quoted in Hahn, "My Dear Selous . . . ," 40–42, 92–99.

CHAPTER ELEVEN

1. "Roosevelt Meets Defeat Buoyantly," *New York Times*, November 6, 1912.

2. For Roosevelt's editorial relationship with *The Outlook*, see "Mr. Roosevelt and the Outlook," *Outlook*, November 7, 1908; "Mr. Roosevelt and the Outlook," *Outlook*, April 2, 1910; "Mr. Roosevelt Resigns from the Editorial Staff of the Outlook," *Outlook*, July 11, 1914.

3. T. Roosevelt, "Chapters of a Possible Autobiography: First Chapter: Boyhood and Youth," *Outlook*, February 22, 1913. This series of chapters concluded at the end of 1913 in *The Outlook*. See "Mr. Roosevelt's Autobiography," *Outlook*, December 27, 1913.

4. T. Roosevelt and E. Heller, *Life-Histories of African Game Animals*, 2 Vols. (New York: Scribner's, 1914).

5. Roosevelt began the three-part series of articles on his Arizona trip with "A Cougar Hunt on the Rim of the Grand Canyon," *Outlook*, October 4, 1913. This and the other two *Outlook* articles, "Across the Navajo Desert" and "The Hopi Snake Dance," were eventually reprinted in his *A Book-Lover's Holiday in the Open*. See also Morris, *Colonel*, 285–94.

6. Morison et al., *Letters VII*, 741, letter from Roosevelt to Arthur Hamilton Lee, July 7, 1913. Also cited in Morris, *Colonel*, 284.

7. The most extensive and thorough treatment of Roosevelt's Brazilian expedition appears in C. Millard, *The River of Doubt* (New York: Doubleday, 2005). For this specific reference, see: T. Roosevelt, *Through the Brazilian Wilderness* (New York: Scribner's, 1914), 2; Millard, *Doubt*, 26–32 and references therein.

8. "Shackleton's Daring Transantarctic Trip Will Be Boldest Ever Attempted by Man," *Washington Post*, February 1, 1914.

9. F. Hurley, *South with Endurance: Shackleton's Antarctic Expedition 1914–1917: The Photographs of Frank Hurley* (New York: Simon & Schuster, 2001), 46. The source of this widely reproduced quotation, or "advertisement," has not been tied to a

primary source. It is likely that it never ran but was introduced into the lore of Shackleton's expedition sometime after they returned.

10. See Morison et al., *Letters VI*, 1375, letter from Roosevelt to Kermit Roosevelt, November 22, 1908.

11. For Zahm's account of meeting Fiala, including quotations in this paragraph, see J. A. Zahm, *Through South America's Southland* (New York: D. Appleton, 1916), 11–12. Also quoted in part in Millard, *Doubt*, 32.

12. See Milliard, *Doubt*, 31–32.

13. L. E. Miller, *In the Wilds of South America* (New York: Scribner's, 1918), 194; Cherrie, private journal, October 1, 1913. AMNH.

14. Rondon, *Lectures*, 11.

15. Rondon, *Lectures*, 12. Also quoted in Millard, *Doubt*, 58. See also Morison et al., *Letters VII*, 754, letter from Roosevelt to Frank Chapman, November 4, 1913.

16. See Milliard, *Doubt*, 77–78 and citation therein.

17. Roosevelt, *Brazilian Wilderness*, 9.

18. Cherrie, private journal, October 23, 1913. AMNH; Miller, *Wilds*, 198.

19. H. F. Osborn, *Impressions of Great Naturalists* (New York: Scribner's, 1924), 179–80. Also quoted in J. R. Ornig, *My Last Chance to Be a Boy* (Baton Rouge: Louisiana State University Press, 1994), 52; P. O'Toole, *When Trumpets Call: Theodore Roosevelt after the White House* (New York: Simon & Schuster, 2005), 253; Millard, *Doubt*, 62.

20. Morison et al., *Letters VII*, 756, letter from Roosevelt to Henry Cabot Lodge, December 12, 1913, also quoted in Ornig, *Boy*, 73; Morison et al., *Letters VII*, 754, letter from Roosevelt to Frank Chapman, November 4, 1913.

21. Cherrie, private journal, October 23, 1913. AMNH.

22. Morison et al., *Letters VII*, 757, letter from Roosevelt to Henry Cabot Lodge, December 12, 1913. Also quoted in Ornig, *Boy*, 73.

23. T. Roosevelt, "American Internationalism," *Outlook*, November 1, 1913; T. Roosevelt, "Democratic Ideals," *Outlook*, November 15, 1913.

24. Miller, *In the Wilds*, 198. See also Millard, *Doubt*, 63.

25. Cherrie, private journal, November 8, 1913. AMNH.

26. Miller, *In the Wilds*, 201.

27. Miller, *In the Wilds*, 201–2.

28. Miller, *In the Wilds*, 206.

29. Cherrie, private journal, November 17, 1913. AMNH.

30. Cherrie, private journal, November 25, 1913. AMNH. Also quoted in Ornig, *Boy*, 82; Millard, *Doubt*, 110.

31. Cherrie, private journal, December 24, 1913. AMNH.

32. Cherrie, private journal, December 24, 1913. AMNH.

33. Rondon, *Lectures*, 36.

34. Rondon, *Lectures*, 37.

35. Roosevelt, *Brazilian Wilderness*, 179–80; Miller, *Into the Wilds*, 231. For Cherrie's thoughts and purported experiences with the supernatural, see G. Cherrie, *Dark Trails*, (New York: G. P. Putnam, 1930).

36. For two quotations, see Roosevelt, *Brazilian Wilderness*, 182–83; Rondon, *Lectures*, 40–41.

37. Morison et al., *Letters VIII*, 904–5, letter from Roosevelt to John Keltie, February 25, 1915. Quotation and Roosevelt's perspective in the following paragraph is based on the text of this letter.

38. Roosevelt, *Brazilian Wilderness*, 202.

39. Cherrie, private journal, February 3, 1914. AMNH. Also quoted in Ornig, *Boy*, 114.

40. Rondon, *Lectures*, 46.
41. KBRP, family correspondence series, February 1, 1914. Also quoted in Ornig, *Boy*, 112; H. P. Jeffers, *Roosevelt the Explorer* (Lanham, MD: Taylor Trade Publishing, 2003), 235; Millard, *Doubt*, 107; Morris, *Colonel*, 321.
42. Rondon, *Lectures*, 49;
43. Cherrie, private journal, February 4, 1914. AMNH. Also quoted in Ornig, *Boy*, 116.
44. Cherrie describes Fiala leaving the others "almost in tears." Cherrie, private journal, February 4, 1914. AMNH.
45. "To Accompany Shackleton," *New York Times*, February 6, 1914.
46. Cherrie, private journal, February 13, 1914. AMNH.
47. Cherrie, private journal, February 25, 1914. AMNH. Roosevelt, *Brazilian Wilderness*, 240–41; Miller, *In the Wilds*, 240.
48. Miller's photograph appears between pages 244 and 245 in Roosevelt, *Brazilian Wilderness*.
49. Roosevelt, *Brazilian Wilderness*, 243. Also quoted in Ornig, *Boy*, 132; Millard, *Doubt*, 134.
50. Cherrie, private journal, February 27, 1914. AMNH. Kermit and Belle Papers, Library of Congress, Kermit Roosevelt diary, February 27, 1914. Roosevelt, *Brazilian Wilderness*, 243–45.
51. Roosevelt, *Brazilian Wilderness*, 181.
52. Roosevelt, *Brazilian Wilderness*, 253.
53. Cherrie, private journal, March 4, 1914. AMNH.
54. Cherrie, private journal, March 11, 1914. AMNH.
55. Various accounts exist of the events that led to Simplicio's death on March 15, 1914: Roosevelt, *Brazilian Wilderness*, 268–71; Rondon, *Lectures*, 80–81; Ornig, *Boy*, 147–48; Dalton, *Strenuous*, 433–34; Millard, *Doubt*, 199–211; Morris, *Colonel*, 323–33. See also Cherrie, private journal, March 15, 1914, AMNH; KBRP LOC, Kermit Roosevelt diary, March 15–17, 1914.
56. Rondon, *Lectures*, 81. Also quoted in Millard, *Doubt*, 210; Morris, *Colonel*, 333.
57. Roosevelt, *Brazilian Wilderness*, 271.
58. Quotation from Roosevelt, *Brazilian Wilderness*, 271. Other descriptions of the loss of Lobo include Cherrie, private journal, March 16, 1914, AMNH; Ornig, *Boy*, 149; Millard, *Doubt*, 218; Morris, *Colonel*, 334.
59. Roosevelt, *Brazilian Wilderness*, 298.
60. Roosevelt, *Brazilian Wilderness*, 301.
61. Cherrie, private journal, March 27, 1914. AMNH.
62. Quotation from Cherrie, private journal, March 27, 1914. AMNH. See also K. Roosevelt, *The Long Trail* (New York: Review of Reviews, 1921),
63. Morris, *Rex*, 141–43.
64. Roosevelt, *Brazilian Wilderness*, 309.
65. G. Cherrie account in Explorer's Club, *Theodore Roosevelt: Memorial Meeting at the Explorer's Club, March 1, 1919* (New York: Explorer's Club, 1919) . 20–28. Also quoted in Millard, *Doubt*, 262.
66. Cherrie, private journal, April 2, 1914. AMNH. For insight on Roosevelt's heart condition, see a biographical note in Morris, *Colonel*, 676.
67. KBRP LOC, Kermit Roosevelt diary, April 2, 1914.
68. Quotation from Roosevelt, *Brazilian Wilderness*, 300.
69. Quotation from Roosevelt, *Brazilian Wilderness*, 290. Also quoted in Millard, *Doubt*, 195; Morris, *Colonel Roosevelt*, 331. This account of Paishon's murder is adapted from Cherrie, private journal, April 3, 1914, AMNH; KBRP Kermit Roosevelt diary, April 3, 1914; Roosevelt, *Brazilian Wilderness* 304–7; Rondon,

Lectures, 104–8; Ornig, *Boy*, 173–74; Millard, *Doubt*, 289–92; Morris, *Colonel*, 338–39.

70. Roosevelt, *Brazilian Wilderness*, 302.

71. Roosevelt and other members of the party were treated by a Brazilian medic, one Dr. Cajazeira, with shots of quinine. See Millard, *Doubt*, 295–96. Other references to Roosevelt's malarial fever include KBRP Kermit Roosevelt diary, April 4, 1914; "Col. Roosevelt as His Guide Remembers Him," *New York Times*, January 6, 1929; Rondon, *Lectures*, 108–9; Morris, *Colonel*, 339–40.

72. Kermit was also receiving treatment for malaria, and his arms were sore from the "number of injections of quinine." KBRP Kermit Roosevelt diary, April 15, 1914.

73. Morison et al., *Letters VII*, 17, letter from Roosevelt to Corinne Roosevelt Robinson, June 21, 1909.

74. Explorers Club, *Theodore Roosevelt: Memorial Meeting at the Explorers Club, March 1, 1919* (New York: Explorers Club, 1919), 26. For Rondon's account of Roosevelt asking to be left behind, see "Col. Roosevelt as His Guide Remembers Him," *New York Times*, January 6, 1929.

75. Millard, *Doubt*, 302.

76. KBRP Kermit Roosevelt diary, April 14, 1914.

77. KBRP Kermit Roosevelt diary, April 15, 1914; Cherrie, private journal, April 15, 1914, AMNH; Roosevelt, *Brazilian Wilderness*, 316.

78. Roosevelt, *Brazilian Wilderness*, 316.

79. Roosevelt, *Brazilian Wilderness*, 319.

80. The photograph appears in Roosevelt, *Brazilian Wilderness*, facing page 324.

81. Morison et al., *Letters VII*, 759–60, letter from Roosevelt to Lauro Müller, April 30, 1914.

82. Roosevelt, *Brazilian Wilderness*, 317.

83. Account's of Shackleton's expedition appear in Hurley, *South with Endurance*; A. Lansing, *Endurance: Shackleton's Incredible Voyage* (London: Weidenfeld & Nicolson, 1959); E. Shackleton, *South: The Story of Shackleton's Last Expedition 1914–1917* (London: Century, 1991). Roosevelt did not publicly comment on Shackleton's expedition, but he visited J. S. Keltie at the British Geographical Society in June of 1914. The *Roosevelt*, the boat used in Peary's expedition, was also considered for Shackleton's trip; see "To Accompany Shackleton," *New York Times*, February 6, 1914.

CHAPTER TWELVE

1. "Roosevelt Back, Is Silent on 1916," *Washington Post*, May 20, 1914. After he made his way to Oyster Bay, Roosevelt did receive a significant welcome party.

2. "Roosevelt Returns 35 Pounds Lighter," *New York Times*, May 20, 1914; "Roosevelt Back, Is Silent on 1916," *Washington Post*, May 20, 1914 (subheadlines include "Looks Well, But Is Thin, Lost 55 Pounds in Jungle"); F. Wood, *Roosevelt As We Knew Him*, 394 (this includes an account from Charles Washburn, who suggests that Roosevelt had in 1915 "regained the 70 pounds he lost in Brazil").

3. For accounts of Roosevelt's guarding of his manuscript, and his jokes regarding the "big stick," see "Roosevelt Returns 35 Pounds Lighter," *New York Times*, May 20, 1914; "Roosevelt Back, Is Silent on 1916," *Washington Post*, May 20, 1914; "Using Cane and Very Thin But Oozing the Old 'Pep' T. Roosevelt Has Returned," *Atlanta Constitution*, May 20, 1914.

4. Morison et al., *Letters VII*, 26–27, letter from Roosevelt to George Trevelyan,

September 10, 1909: "I always take in my saddle pocket some volume (I am too old now to be satisfied merely with a hunter's life)"; Morison et al., *Letters VII*, 32–33, letter from Roosevelt to Arthur Lee, October 6, 1909: "My trip has been a great success. I am now an elderly man, not fit for very hard exertion, & only a fair shot."

5. Rondon, *Lectures*, 33.
6. "Through the Brazilian Wilderness, by Theodore Roosevelt," *Washington Post*, September 20, 1914; "Through the Brazilian Wilderness: Up the River of Tapirs," *Atlanta Constitution*, September 20, 1914; "Through the Brazilian Wilderness: Up the River of Tapirs," *Detroit Free Press*, September 20, 1914.
7. "'Pure Piracy' Says Roosevelt," *Atlanta Constitution*, May 8, 1915; Morison et al., *Letters VIII*, 922, letter from Roosevelt to Archibald Roosevelt, May 19, 1915. Also quoted in Brands, *Last Romantic*, 756.
8. See Brinkley, *Warrior*, 570–71, for description of the Breton Island Federal Bird Reservation.
9. T. Roosevelt, "The Bird Refuges of Louisiana," *Scribner's Magazine* 59 (1916): 261–80.
10. Roosevelt, "The Bird Refuges of Louisiana."
11. Account of Roosevelt's lion story at Parker's home appears in Wood, *As We Knew Him*, 229–32.
12. Quotation in Morison et al., *Letters VIII*, 941, letter from Roosevelt to Arthur Lee, June 17, 1915. See also "Roosevelt Has a Broken Rib," *Washington Post*, May 28, 1915; "Roosevelt Breaks Rib in Fall from a Horse," *New York Times*, May 28, 1915.
13. H. K. Job, *Wild Wings: Adventures of a Camera-Hunter among the Larger Wild Birds of North America on Sea and Land* (Boston: Houghton, Mifflin, 1905). See TRP letter from Roosevelt to H. K. Job, September 29, 1905, which is also reprinted in the introductory material to *Wild Wings*. See also F. Chapman, *Bird Studies with a Camera* (New York: D. Appleton, 1900), viii; T. Roosevelt et al., *The Deer Family* (New York: Macmillan, 1902), 26.
14. Roosevelt, "The Bird Refuges of Louisiana." Also quoted in Brinkley, *Warrior*, 571.
15. "Col Roosevelt Upholds Wilson," *Boston Daily Globe*, June 12, 1915.
16. Morris, *Colonel*, 428–29. Roosevelt's statement was printed in "Roosevelt Upholds Wilson against Bryan; Pledges His 'Heartiest Support' to President," *New York Times*, June 12, 1915. His praise of Wilson was reported widely in the press (e.g., in "Col Roosevelt Upholds Wilson," *Boston Daily Globe*, June 12 1915; "Roosevelt Backs Wilson in Split with Commoner," *Detroit Free Press*, June 12, 1915).
17. R. B. Perry, *The Plattsburg Movement* (New York: E. P. Dutton, 1921), 28–29; J. G. Clifford, *The Citizen Soldiers: The Plattsburg Training Camp Movement, 1913–1920* (Lexington: University of Kentucky Press, 1972), 54–58; J. C. Lane, *Armed Progressive: General Leonard Wood* (Lincoln: University of Nebraska Press, 1978), 193–95.
18. Morison et al., *Letters VIII*, 937, letter from Roosevelt to Arthur Lee, June 17, 1915.
19. Roosevelt gave Wood an advance copy of his speech, which Wood edited heavily. See H. Hagedorn, *Leonard Wood: A Biography, Volume II* (New York: Harper & Brothers, 1931), 163. News reports appeared over the next several days explaining the incredulity of the Wilson administration: "Big Stick. Roosevelt Talk Stirs Garrison," *Los Angeles Times*, August 27, 1915; "Colonel Roosevelt Chased by Some Washington Hornets," *Wall Street Journal*, August 27, 1915.

20. "Stand by President Only So Long as President Stands by Country, Says Col. Roosevelt at Plattsburg," *Washington Post*, August 26, 1915. Similar quotation in Perry, *Plattsburg Movement*, 44.

21. Quotation and rendering of Roosevelt's Quebec trip based on T. Roosevelt, "A Curious Experience," *Scribner's Magazine* 59, no. 2 (1916): 155–67.

22. Roosevelt, "A Curious Experience," 164.

23. Roosevelt, "A Curious Experience," 165–66.

24. TRC MS Am 1541(259), letter from Roosevelt to Kermit Roosevelt, October 1, 1915; Roosevelt, "A Curious Experience," 166.

25. Roosevelt, "A Curious Experience." Although moose are normally docile animals, a bull moose in rut can be extremely aggressive. The behavior that Roosevelt describes, including following and charging, is not common, but is also not outside the spectrum of male moose behavior. Thanks to Terry Bowyer, professor of biological sciences at Idaho State University, for providing this perspective on moose behavior, taken from his knowledge of the literature and from his own personal experiences with moose during field research. Given that Roosevelt killed one more moose than his permit allowed, he made a sworn statement as to the life-and-death circumstances that led to his killing of the second moose. See T. Roosevelt, *The Works of Theodore Roosevelt, Memorial Edition, Vol. 4* (New York: Charles Scribner's Sons, 1924), 604–8; Morris, *Colonel*, 437.

26. Roosevelt, "A Curious Experience," 167.

27. TRC MS Am 1541 (259), letter from Roosevelt to Kermit Roosevelt, October 1, 1915.

28. TRC MS Am 1541 (259), letter from Roosevelt to Kermit Roosevelt, October 1, 1915. Also quoted in Dalton, *Strenuous*, 462.

29. Wood, *As We Knew Him*, 395. Also quoted in Morris, *Colonel*, 437.

30. TRC MS Am 1541 (273), letter from Roosevelt to Kermit Roosevelt, March 4, 1916.

31. T. Roosevelt, "Where the Steady Trade-Winds Blow," *Scribner's Magazine* 61, no. 2 (1917): 169–88.

32. TRC MS Am 1541 (273), letter from Roosevelt to Kermit Roosevelt, March 4, 1916.

33. T. Roosevelt, "A Naturalists' Tropical Laboratory," *Scribner's Magazine* 61, no. 1 (1917): 46–64.

34. Beebe drafted a note articulating how much the Roosevelts' support had meant as he worked out of a depressing period: "You two have pulled me out of the Valley of the Shadow into sunlight again." Quoted in C. G. Gould, *The Remarkable Life of William Beebe*, (Washington: Island Press, 2004), 192.

35. "Colonel Roosevelt Joins the Staff of the 'Kansas City Star,'" *New York Tribune*, September 4, 1917; T. Roosevelt, *Roosevelt in the Kansas City Star* (Boston: Houghton Mifflin, 1921).

36. Morison et al., *Letters VIII*, 1164, letter from Roosevelt to Newton Baker, March 19, 1917.

37. Morison et al., *Letters VIII*, 1165, letter from Roosevelt to Henry Cabot Lodge, March 22, 1917. Baker's March 20 response to Roosevelt's request is reprinted in Morison et al., *Letters VIII*, 1164. Roosevelt replied again to Baker on March 23 to provide military references from his commanders in the Spanish American War, and another summary of his credentials. See Morison et al., *Letters VIII*, 1166, letter from Roosevelt to Newton Baker, March 23, 1917.

38. "Army of 100,000 For Roosevelt," *Boston Daily Globe*, March 23, 1917.

39. A transcript of Roosevelt's correspondence with Secretary of War Newton Baker

and President Wilson between February 2 and May 19, 1917, is contained in TRC fMS Am 1454.16.

40. Morison et al., *Letters VIII*, 1162–64, letter from Roosevelt to Henry Cabot Lodge, March 18, 1917.

41. R. J. Coles, "My Fight with the Devilfish," *American Museum Journal* 16, no. 4 (1916): 217–27.

42. Coles contributed additional articles to the literature on sharks and rays: R. J. Coles, "Notes on the Sharks and Rays of Cape Lookout, NC," *Proceedings of the Biological Society of Washington* 28 (1915): 89–94; R. J. Coles, "Natural History Notes on the Devilfish, *Manta birostris* (Walbaum) and *Mobula olfersi* (Müller)," *Bulletin of the American Museum of Natural of History* 35 (1916): 649–57.

43. In Roosevelt's article on his devilfish hunt (T. Roosevelt, "Harpooning Devilfish," *Scribner's Magazine* 62, no. 3 (1917): 293–05), he refers to his memory of reading William Elliott's account of devilfish hunting in "Field Sports of South Carolina." Elliott's book was published before Roosevelt was born (W. Elliott, *Carolina Sports, by Land and Water; Including Incidents of Devil-Fishing, &c.* (Charleston, SC: Burges and James, 1846). The following account of Roosevelt's hunt is gleaned from "Harpooning Devilfish," as well as from "Roosevelt to Hunt Florida Devilfish," *New York Times*, March 24, 1917; "T. R. Kills Two Devil Fish," *Washington Post*, March 27, 1917; "T. R. Just Clenched His Teeth as Devilfish Made for Him," *New York Tribune*, April 4, 1917.

44. TRP letter from Russell Coles to Roosevelt, November 18, 1916; TRP letter from Russell Coles to Roosevelt, December 12, 1916.

45. TRP letter from Russell Coles to Roosevelt, December 12, 1916; TRP letter from Russell Coles to Roosevelt, December 21, 1916; TRP letter from Russell Coles to Roosevelt, March 7, 1917; TRP letter from Russell Coles to Roosevelt, March 11, 1917.

46. TRP letter from Russell Coles to Roosevelt, March 7, 1917; TRP letter from Russell Coles to Roosevelt, March 11, 1917; TRP letter from Russell Coles to Roosevelt, March 13, 1917.

47. "T. R. Just Clenched His Teeth as Devilfish Made for Him," *New York Tribune*, April 4, 1917.

48. "T. R. Just Clenched His Teeth as Devilfish Made for Him," *New York Tribune*, April 4, 1917.

49. "Wilson, Ready, Waits upon Congress Today," *Washington Post*, April 2, 1917; "War with Germany Voted by Representatives 373 to 50," *San Francisco Chronicle*, April 6, 1917; "War Proclaimed by the President," *Boston Daily Globe*, April 7, 1917.

50. Archie's wedding took place on April 14, 1917, in Boston. For Roosevelt's letters that continued his campaign for a military appointment, see Morison et al., *Letters VIII*, 1169–70, letter from Roosevelt to Newton Baker, April 12, 1917; Morison et al., *Letters VIII*, 1170–73, letter from Roosevelt to George Chamberlain, April 12, 1917; Morison et al., *Letters VIII*, 1174–75, letter from Roosevelt to Arthur Spring Rice, April 16, 1917; Morison et al., *Letters VIII*, 1176–84, letter from Roosevelt to Newton Baker, April 23, 1917; Morison et al., *Letters VIII*, 1187–91, letter from Roosevelt to Newton Baker, May 8, 1917.

51. "200,000 Men Are Ready to Go with Roosevelt," *New York Times*, May 7, 1917; "New Rush Sets in to Join Roosevelt," *New York Times*, May 8, 1917; J. H. Bishop, *Theodore Roosevelt and His Time, Vol. II* (New York: Scribner's, 1920), 424. Latter source also cited in Morris, *Colonel*, 491.

52. Roosevelt wrote to General Pershing in the hope that he would accept Ted

and Archie (Morison et al., *Letters VIII*, 1192–93, letter from Roosevelt to John Pershing, May 20, 1917), and wrote to his old friend Arthur Lee to request that Kermit be placed with the British in Mesopotamia (Morison et al., *Letters VIII*, 1201–3, letter from Roosevelt to Arthur Lee, June 18, 1917). He was also able to "get Quentin into the flying squadron" (Morison et al., *Letters VIII*, 1199, letter from Roosevelt to Theodore Roosevelt, Jr., May 30, 1917).

53. Once Selous decided to enlist, he first went to a life insurance company for a complete physical examination, which found him in good health with his "heart in particular" in fine shape. He was 62 at the time. See Millais, *Selous*, 300.

54. Account of Selous's death and burial follows Millais, *Selous*, 344–345.

55. Quotations from T. Roosevelt, "Frederick Courteney Selous," *Outlook*, March 7, 1917.

56. Quotation in Pringle, *Theodore Roosevelt*, 601. Similar quotation in Morris, *Colonel*, 530.

57. Hagedorn, *Boys' Life*, 200; Morris, *Edith Kermit Roosevelt*, 181.

58. "Roosevelt Breaks Rib in Fall From a Horse," *New York Times*, May 28, 1915.

59. Roosevelt had discussed how many hunters thought that Selous would die next to his wagon after an epic hunt. T. Roosevelt, "Frederick Courteney Selous," *Outlook*, March 7, 1917.

60. Roosevelt, *Game Trails*, 201.

61. A thorough description of Roosevelt's health decline and ultimate demise appears in Morris, *Colonel*, 541–52. The "universal law of death" was part of Roosevelt's canon; see Roosevelt, *Strenuous Life*, 286.

62. "News of Armistice Flashed to City," *New York Times*, November 11, 1918; "Roosevelt in Hospital A Lumbago Sufferer," *New York Times*, November 12, 1918; "Col. Roosevelt Goes to Hospital Here," *New York Tribune*, November 12, 1918. Similar citations in Morris, *Colonel*, 545.

63. The account of Roosevelt's final hours follows J. E. Amos, *Theodore Roosevelt: Hero to His Valet* (New York: John Day, 1927), 154–58.

64. TRP letter from Roosevelt to William Beebe, January 1, 1919; TRP letter from Roosevelt to Russell Coles, January 1, 1919.

65. C. Barrus, ed., *The Heart of Burroughs's Journals* (Boston: Houghton Mifflin, 1928), 320.

66. J. Burroughs, "Theodore Roosevelt: His Americanism Reached into the Marrow of His Bones," *Natural History* 19, no. 1 (1919): 5–7.

67. Burroughs, "Theodore Roosevelt," 5.

68. Burroughs, "Theodore Roosevelt," 6.

69. C. Barrus, ed., *The Heart of Burroughs's Journals*, 320.

70. Depew, *My Memories of Eighty Years*, 169. See also Naylor et al., *Theodore Roosevelt: Many-Sided American*.

71. Barrus, *The Heart of Burroughs's Journals*, 321.

72. Barrus, *The Heart of Burroughs's Journals*, 321.

73. J. Street, *The Most Interesting American* (New York: Century., 1915).

74. J. H. Hammond, "Theodore Roosevelt, 'First American of Our Day," *Journal of American History* 13 (1919): 312–13.

75. J. J. Jusserand, "Personal Memories of Theodore Roosevelt," *Journal of American History* 13 (1919): 330–325.

76. Quotations in this and the previous sentence from J. E. Hedges, "The Personality and Philosophy of Theodore Roosevelt," *Journal of American History* 13 (1919): 326–34. Hedges's brief biography appears in M. C. Harrison, ed., *New York State's*

Prominent and Progressive Men, Volume II (New York: New York Tribune, 1900), 154.

77. E. Root, "Theodore Roosevelt," *The Journal of American History* 13 (1919): 299–303.

78. F. Lane, quoted in "Tributes to Roosevelt," *Journal of American History* 13 (1919): 341–50.

79. Roosevelt, *Game Trails,* 63, 237.

80. E. Root, "Theodore Roosevelt," *Journal of American History* 13 (1919): 299–303.

81. Burroughs, "Theodore Roosevelt," 6.

APPENDIX ONE

1. Examples include Putnam, *Theodore Roosevelt,* 59–60; Morris, *Rise,* 22; Morris, *Edith Kermit Roosevelt: Portrait of a First Lady,* 23; T. Lansford, *Theodore Roosevelt in Perspective* (New York: Novinka Books, 2005), 8; N. Miller, *Theodore Roosevelt: A Life* (New York: Quill, 1992), 42; Goodwin, *Bully Pulpit,* 116.

2. L. Viereck, "Roosevelt's German Days," *Success Magazine* 8 (1905): 672B–672D.

3. For a brief description of Wegener, see P. C. Merrill, *German Immigrant Artists in America: A Biographical Dictionary* (Lanham, MD: Scarecrow Press, 1997), 283.

Index